D0169633

NATIONAL GEOGRAPHIC

TRAVELER

Hawaii

NATIONAL GEOGRAPHIC

TRAVELER

Hawaii

Rita Ariyoshi

Contents

Page 1: Aloha written in
shells on Waimanalo
Beach, Oahu
Pages 2–3: Surfer on the
Banzai Pipeline on
Oahu's North Shore
Left: Walking the lava at
Kilauea Volcano,
Big Island

How to use this guide

See back flap for keys of text and map symbols

The *National Geographic Traveler* brings you the best of Hawaii in text, pictures, and maps. Divided into three main sections, the guide begins with an overview of history and culture. Following are seven island chapters with sites selected by the author for their particular interest and treated in depth. Each chapter opens with its own contents list for easy reference.

A map introduces each island, highlighting the featured sites and locating other places of interest. Walks and drives,all plotted on their own maps, suggest routes for discovering the most about an area. Features and sidebars offer detail on history, culture, or contemporary life. A More Places to Visit page generally rounds off the chapters.

The final section, Travelwise, lists essential information for the traveler—pre-trip planning, getting around, communications, money matters, emergencies, and special events—plus a selection of hotels and restaurants arranged by chapter area, shops, and entertainment possibilities.

To the best of our knowledge, information is accurate as of the press date. However, it's always advisable to call ahead.

Color coding

62

Each island is color coded for easy reference. Find the island you want on the map on the front flap, and look for the color flash at the top of the pages of the relevant chapter. Hotel and restaurant listings in **Travelwise** are also color coded to each area.

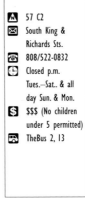

Iolani Palace

▲	57 C2
✉	South King & Richards Sts.
☎	808/522-0832
⊕	Closed p.m. Tues.–Sat.. & all day Sun. & Mon.
💲	$$$ (No children under 5 permitted)
🚌	TheBus 2, 13

Visitor information

Practical information is given in the side column next to each major site (see key to symbols on back flap). The map reference gives the page number where the site is shown on a map. Further details include the site's address, telephone number, days closed, entrance charge in a range from $ (under $4) to $$$$$ (over $25), and nearest public transportation stop. Visitor information for smaller sites is in italics and parentheses in the text.

Hotel & restaurant prices

An explanation of the price bands used in entries is given in the Hotels & restaurants section (see pp. 242–259).

TRAVELWISE

OAHU .... Color-coded island name

WAIKIKI .... Area name

🏨 **HILTON HAWAIIAN** ⎤ .... Hotel name & price range
🍴 **VILLAGE**   ⎦
$$$$

2005 KALIA RD. ⎤ .... Address, telephone, fax numbers & website
HONOLULU 96815
TEL 800/HILTONS OR
808/949-4321
FAX 808/947-7898
www.hawaiianvillage.hilton.com ⎦
It's practically a town. Three ⎤ .... Brief description of hotel
towers on 20 acres of lush
landscaping with waterfalls and
exotic wildlife. ⎦
🛏 2,545 units 🏊 3 🍴 ⎦ .... Hotel facilities & credit card details

🍴 **ORCHIDS** .... Restaurant name & price range
$$$$
HALEKULANI HOTEL ⎤ .... Address, & telephone number
2199 KALIA RD.
TEL 808/923-2311 ⎦
Hawaii Regional Cuisine
Festive seaside dining with ⎤ .... Brief description of restaurant
views of Diamond Head and
banks of orchids. Mustard-herb
crusted rack of lamb is an
excellent choice. ⎦
🍴 122 indoors, 98 outdoors ⎤ ..... Restaurant facilities & credit card details
🅿 🚫 All major cards ⎦

ISLAND MAPS

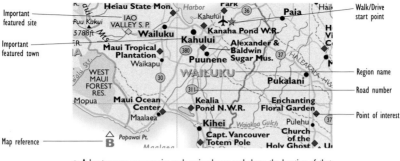

Important featured site

Important featured town

Map reference

Walk/Drive start point

Region name

Road number

Point of interest

- A locator map accompanies each regional map and shows the location of that area in Hawaii.

WALKING TOURS

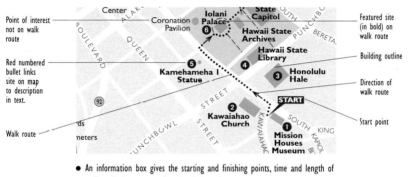

Point of interest not on walk route

Red numbered bullet links site on map to description in text.

Walk route

Featured site (in bold) on walk route

Building outline

Direction of walk route

Start point

- An information box gives the starting and finishing points, time and length of walk, and places not to be missed along the route.

DRIVING TOURS

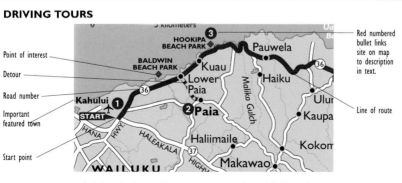

Point of interest

Detour

Road number

Important featured town

Start point

Red numbered bullet links site on map to description in text.

Line of route

- An information box provides details including starting and finishing points, places not to be missed along the route, time and length of drive, and tips on the terrain.

NATIONAL GEOGRAPHIC

TRAVELER

Hawaii

About the author

Rita Ariyoshi is the author of *Maui On My Mind* and *Hula is Life*. She served for ten years as editor of *Aloha Magazine*. Her travel articles, fiction, and memoirs have appeared in a variety of international magazines and literary journals, including *National Geographic Traveler*. She is a five-time first-place winner in the prestigious Lowell Thomas Travel Journalism Awards Competition. Her stories have been commended by the Hawaii Visitors' and Convention Bureau, the Pacific Asia Travel Association, the Hawaii Publishers' Association, and the National Catholic Press Association. She is a grand-prize winner in the annual National Steinbeck Center Short Story Competition, and recipient of the Pushcart Prize for Literature. Ariyoshi's work has been collected in anthologies and made into television productions. She lives in Honolulu with her family and travels regularly to other islands on assignment—and to visit more family.

History & culture

Male dancer at Molokai's Ka Hula Piko festival

Hawaii today

FARTHER FROM ANY LANDMASS THAN ANY PLACE ELSE ON EARTH, THE Hawaiian Islands rise as green beacons of life in the middle of "Big Blue," the vast Pacific Ocean. From the very beginning, this single factor of isolation has defined Hawaii. The distance from Honolulu to California—the closest point—is 2,397 air miles; to Tokyo, 3,847 miles; to Papeete, Tahiti, 2,741 miles.

The Hawaiian archipelago of 137 islands, islets, and atolls, which Mark Twain called the "most beautiful anchored in any ocean," is strung like uneven pearls across the Tropic of Cancer in a 1,523-mile line languidly draped from Kure at latitude 28.5° north to the island of Hawaii (generally called "the Big Island"), which gives its name to the whole group, at 19° north. The eight main Islands lie in the tropics and share the same latitude as Mexico City, Havana, and Hong Kong. Cooling trade winds breeze in from the northeast ocean about 300 days a year.

All the Islands, with the exception of the five Midway Islands, which are administered by the U.S. Navy, compose the 50th state of the United States of America. The capital of Hawaii, Honolulu, on the island of Oahu, is the only large city in the state.

More than a million people have settled in the Islands, with more than 75 percent living on Oahu. The major industry is tourism, followed by defense and agriculture.

DIFFERENT ISLES, DIFFERENT STYLES

Each island is different, not only in appearance but in personality. Oahu is schizophrenic, busy, sophisticated, and urbane, with a surprisingly rural twin personality. Maui is the dreamer. Here the arts flourish in galleries, art schools, and the forward-looking Maui Arts and Cultural Center. In small towns there are still hippie sightings. The Big Island is raw, with room to spare; it bristles with creative energy. Silver-spoon resorts sprout from obsidian lava flows. Kauai is ancient and wise and green. It has the state's only navigable river, the broad Wailua. Golf courses, hiking trails, and a Grand Canyon make this an isle for outdoor adventure. Molokai defies the times, remaining obstinately out of the mainstream, and that is precisely its charm. Lanai

right now seems to have lost its identity. When it was the world's largest pineapple plantation, it used to be called "The Pineapple Island." Since the closure of the plantation, the Island's promoters have thought up new names, such as "The Private Isle" and "The Secluded Isle," but nothing seems to stick. Niihau is privately owned and remains largely closed. Its population consists exclusively of native Hawaiians who still speak the Hawaiian language as their primary tongue. Kahoolawe, once an island of temples and ranches, was emptied of people to become a practice bombing target for U. S. military prior to World War II. In 1990 President George Bush called a cease-fire, and in 1994 the Navy surrendered jurisdiction of the island to the state.

THE ALOHA SPIRIT

Aloha. It's a word that does not translate easily, yet it defines and encompasses a race of people. In Hawaii, it's a common word, used in greeting and farewell. Taken to its roots, *alo* means "in the presence of" and *ha* means "the breath of life," with its implications of divine gift.

Egged on by well-meaning tour guides, tourists delight in drawing out the word "A-loooooo-HA." They are seldom told that aloha is not just another way of saying hello. When you say "Aloha," to someone you are acknowledging that the two of you are standing in the presence of God, and so all your words, thoughts, and deeds should be virtuous.

It is a tender word that has the power to shape a life. It is the single word that sets Hawaii apart from any place else in the world, enabling many races to come together

A young surfer achieves the ultimate thrill, riding in the tube of a great wave, at Maalaea, Maui.

in one place, and live peaceably side by side, not just in tolerance, but in mutual appreciation and celebration. Aloha says, "Come, bring your heritage, your family. Learn aloha."

The late and revered Pilahi Paki defined aloha letter by letter:

A is akahai, *kindness*
L is lokahi, *unity*
O is oluolu, *pleasantness*
H is haahaa, *humility*
A is ahonui, *patience.*

People worry about aloha. Is Hawaii losing it? Do we have enough of it? How can we make sure the aloha spirit is not overwhelmed by the waves of newcomers to the Islands? Like any love relationship, aloha takes care and commitment. It reflects the inner spirit of a person and society. To practice aloha, you must first respect yourself. It's a life-giving word.

Happily, it is very much in evidence today. It's there in the smiles that greet even the grumpiest, jet-lagged visitor, in the kindness

that treats an elderly woman stepping gingerly down from a tour bus as if she is a princess. And "Aloha aina," love of the land is an environmental cry.

The biggest festival in the state is the Aloha Festival, which takes place annually from mid-September to mid-October. Like the word itself, the statewide party ignores boundaries and overflows into a weeks-long multicultural celebration marked by parades, hula performances, luaus, and exhibitions of traditional

With the Koolau Mountains below, a hang glider rides the tradewinds over Oahu. The sheer cliffs are perfect for launching.

arts and crafts. Joyfully included in all the Hawaiiana may be marching bands from the mainland United States or an army of Japanese samurai in full regalia astride their steeds. Personified, aloha has many faces.

The aloha spirit, while carefully nurtured by the tourism industry because it works,

Orchid nurseries and gardens often welcome visitors with leis and flowers.

comes naturally to most people. It is layered over every transaction and relationship like the mist that clings to the mountains bearing life-giving water. It binds the whole diverse Hawaii into one brilliant mosaic of life.

A RAINBOW OF PEOPLE

With interracial marriages hovering around 50 percent, it becomes more and more difficult to tell not only who's who, but also who's what. Are you Hawaiian if you are Hawaiian-Filipino-Japanese? A child, upon hearing that a classmate is part Japanese and part Irish is likely to express pity—"That's all?"—then proceed proudly to proclaim his own heritage of seven ethnicities. Surveying the faces in a schoolroom, it becomes clear that a new race of Island children is emerging. Known as *hapa,* meaning "a part" or "a half," they are a bright and beautiful blend of East and West.

It is unlikely that this usually happy mixing of races would have happened if Hawaii had been, at the outset, either Caucasian or Asian, or any race but Hawaiian. It took the generosity and value system modeled by the host culture, that of the Hawaiians, with their unique spirit of aloha.

Immigrants

The first immigrants to arrive in any numbers were the Chinese who came as contract laborers in 1852. The first Japanese laborers stepped ashore in 1868 to claim their plantation contracts that paid six to nine dollars a month. By the turn of the century there were more than twice as many Japanese living in Hawaii as any other ethnic group. Because most of the immigrants were hardworking and enterprising, they left the pineapple and sugar fields as soon as the contracts were up. They founded small businesses, bought land, and sought education for their children. In their constant search for cheap labor, the plantation owners brought in workers from the Portuguese Azores and the Philippines. Later, significant immigration to Hawaii came from Korea, Samoa, and the American mainland.

Children of the land

As for the Hawaiians, their population was decimated by contact with the outside world. It is

The Aloha Festival Royal Court is commissioned at Halemaumau Crater on the Big Island.

estimated that within a hundred years of the arrival of British explorer Capt. James Cook (1728–1779) in 1778, a tragic 90 percent of the native people were dead from introduced diseases to which they had acquired no immunities, having lived in isolation for centuries. In 1892, the last full year of the Hawaiian nation (see pp. 33–34), native Hawaiians numbered 40,000. The count of pure Hawaiians today is less than one percent of the population. However, part-Hawaiians are the fastest-growing ethnic group in the Islands. No matter what their mix, most identify, culturally, with their Hawaiian heritage. There is pride in being a *keiki o ka aina*, a child of the land.

Where East meets West

In addition to the Hawaiians and part-Hawaiians, who are 23.3 percent of the population (according to the 2000 U.S. census), today's racial tapestry is woven of 41.6 percent Asians, including Japanese, Chinese, Korean, and Filipino; and 24.3 percent Caucasian, both local-born and Mainland transplants. Non-Hawaiian Pacific Islanders and African Americans comprise the remaining portion of the population.

English author Somerset Maugham (1874–1965) wrote of Hawaii in 1921: "It is a meeting place of East and West, the new rubs shoulders with the immeasurably old....All these strange people live close to each other, with different languages and different thoughts; they believe in different gods and they have different values."

Living side by side, neighbors observe each other's holidays. Kamehameha Day, Chinese New Year, Obon Season, the Fourth of July, and Christmas are celebrated with great enthusiasm by all (see p. 47).

Misunderstandings

People bring not only their colorful traditions and festivals, their faiths and foods, but their attitudes, too. It sometimes takes the *malihini* (the newly arrived), a while to settle down to "Hawaiian time," to realize he can't have it "Now!"and possibly not even tomorrow. Traffic is often the proving ground. The sensitive malihini learns to wave a thank you when a car in traffic makes room to allow him in front. Ethnic humor is pervasive and often hurtful, but in the past it

helped defuse racial confrontations and mis-
understandings. Lately, however, there is less
tolerance for it among recent arrivals, and it
has even inspired lawsuits.

Since the 1980s the population has grown
so fast that newcomers, rather than integrating
with local people, set up parallel communities,
never learning Island ways, and expecting
Islanders to "get with it." Factor in around
16,000 tourists a day in rent-a-cars, and easy-
going Island ways can be severely challenged.

Understanding through culture

Surprisingly, a movement toward Hawaiian
sovereignty finds both Hawaiians and non-
Hawaiians united in the recognition that an
injustice was done at the time of the overthrow of the Hawaiian monarchy in 1893,
and that some form of restitution must be
made. A hundred years after the coup,
President Bill Clinton issued a formal
apology for the participation of the United
States. He also signed a joint Congressional

resolution acknowledging the illegitimacy of the 1898 annexation of Hawaii.

The Hawaiian cause suffered a setback when the U.S. Supreme Court on February 23, 2000, struck down the state of Hawaii's practice of permitting only people with Hawaiian blood to vote in elections for trustees of the Office of Hawaiian Affairs (OHA). The law also stated that only native Hawaiians could serve as trustees. OHA was created by a state constitutional amendment in 1978 to help

Hikers enjoy the panoramic views from Waihee Ridge, Maui.

improve the lives of native Hawaiians using funds generated by "ceded lands," which are the 1.8 million acres of former crown lands taken by the U.S. government after annexation and later transferred to the state of Hawaii.

In 1996, Harold "Freddy" Rice, a Caucasian rancher from the Big Island, whose family has lived in Hawaii since the mid-1800s, attempt-

ed to vote in an OHA election and was denied a ballot. He sued, claiming violation of his rights under the 14th and 15th amendments to the U.S. Constitution, which guarantee equal protection of voting rights regardless of race. The case went all the way to the U.S. Supreme Court, which ruled in Rice's favor.

The full ramifications of the decision have yet to be realized. At stake is a state debt to OHA from land leases, including Honolulu International Airport. The figure could top a billion dollars. Consequently, control of OHA is a prize. In 2002 Linda Lingle, former mayor of Maui, became the first Republican governor in 40 years, and the first woman to govern Hawaii since Queen Liliuokalani. She and her running mate, Duke Aiona, pledged to lead the state into beginning restitution on the debt owed to native Hawaiians.

In spite of many assaults on its integrity, and even on its own validity in modern Hawaii, the Hawaiian culture, traditionally

Instructor

based on sharing and *lokahi,* the principle of making peace and unity, continues to be the glue holding a diverse population together.

Ironically, tourism has also made the culture commercially viable for people to earn a living being cultural practitioners. Hotels sponsor schools, create staff positions for cultural directors, hire consultants, buy native arts, stage cultural performances, and contract with instructors in various crafts such as lei making and *lauhala* (pandanus leaf) weaving.

A scuba diving lesson begins in the swimming pool of the Manele Bay Hotel, Lanai.

There are highly successful programs designed to incorporate Hawaiian values into the entire visitor industry, reminding local people of their heritage and instructing malihini employees about their responsibilities, an almost sacred responsibility as hosts in a land whose best known word, "aloha," means, among many beautiful things, "love." ■

History of the land

THE HAWAIIAN ISLANDS ARE ACTUALLY THE TOPS OF A MASSIVE OCEANIC mountain range that rises from the ocean floor to protrude above the waves. What is seen is only a fraction of what exists. Mauna Kea and Mauna Loa on the Big Island are so tall they are often crowned in snow, two giant incongruities presiding over a tropical landscape. Mauna Kea, measured from its base to its summit is, at 33,476 feet, higher than Mount Everest. However, only 13,796 feet of Mauna Kea's height are above sea level.

Wind, rain, and catastrophic prehistoric landslides have shaped Hawaii's volcanoes into dramatic peaks and valleys. The mountains are cloud catchers, drawing rain, making these islands lush and habitable. Rainwater seeps through volcanic rock into natural underground cisterns providing Hawaii with fresh water that is among the purest on the planet.

The Islands are ringed in beaches. Due to volcanic activity and coral erosion, the beach sand may come in white, gold, black, salt and pepper, red, or green olivine.

BIRTH FROM FIRE

Geologically, Hawaii is a baby. The rest of the world had settled into stable continents, the dinosaurs had come and gone, buffalo roamed the North American plains, and the ancestor cousins of Homo sapiens were foraging in the forests of the Old World. Still, Hawaii was not even a whisper upon the breath of creation.

In the Hawaiian chant of creation, the "Kumulipo," the Hawaiian Islands emerged from the dark depths of primeval night. Hawaiian legends tell of how Maui, Superman of the Hawaiian pantheon, fished up the Islands from the ocean floor. Both the chant and the legend reflect the truth.

Geologists claim that in the mid-Tertiary period, around 25 million to 40 million years ago, a rift opened in the floor of the Pacific Ocean, and fires from the molten core of the earth began spewing magma through the fissure. The fires, which are still raging, were so intense they burned unquenched in the cold perpetual night of the ocean at depths of 2,600 fathoms (15,600 feet).

Magma erupted from the fissure slowly, patiently building, pillow upon pillow, mound by mound, until the volcano was tall enough to break the surface of the waves and continue its climb skyward, becoming a new island. Great clouds of hissing steam, churning ocean, and biting fumes of sulphuric and chlorine gas announced the birth of Hawaii. According to the plate tectonics theory of geology, the islands emerged one at a time as the Pacific plate, a shifting portion of the earth's crust, moved northwest across the hot spot at the rate of 2 to 3 inches a year. Oahu is now 220 miles from its birthplace.

Over the course of 44 million years, this hot spot has cooked up the 82 volcanoes that form the backbone of the Hawaiian archipelago. And the cauldron is still bubbling. Since it began its current eruption in 1983, Kilauea Volcano has added more than 550 acres to the Big Island of Hawaii. Mauna Loa, also on the Big Island, is Hawaii's other active volcano. Mauna Kea and Hualalai on the Big Island, along with Haleakala on Maui, are classified as dormant. All others are considered extinct.

An embryonic island, Loihi (see p. 233), is forming 20 miles off the southeast coast of Hawaii—divers have seen its birth flames glowing beneath the sea. The process of volcanism is on show at Hawaii Volcanoes National Park (see pp. 170–173), where it's often possible to walk right up to a red-hot lava flow.

As new islands rise, old ones sink slowly under their own weight. The coral reefs, which form around the massive girths of middle-aged islands, become fringe reefs as the aging islands erode and succumb. Eventually, all that's left is a ring of reef, which forms its own uneven circle of islets known as an atoll. Kure in the north is a classic example of a Pacific atoll. Most main islands offer fine examples of fringe reefs, easily accessible from shore. The Big Island reefs are still in infancy.

Helicopter flight-seeing tours are a popular way to view the Islands' magnificent sea cliffs and valleys.

The Hawaiian Islands have all been formed from volcanic activity over a hot spot in the earth's crust. As the Pacific plate moves northwestward, the Islands move with it and new volcanoes form.

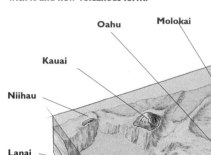

Big Island

Maui

Oahu

Molokai

Kauai

Niihau

Lanai

Kahoolawe

Movement of Pacific plate

Hawaii (the Big Island)

Ocean floor

THE LANGUAGE OF LAVA

Since volcanoes are the very bones of the Hawaiian Islands, and much of their study is conducted here, many of the terms in modern volcanology are Hawaiian. *Lava* is hot liquid rock ejected by a volcano onto the surface of the earth. *Aa* is rough, rocky lava. *Pahoehoe* is smooth ropy lava. The chemical composition of both types of flows is essentially the same, but pahoehoe is hotter.

Here are some other handy-to-know terms. Magma is lava while it is still beneath the Earth's surface. A caldera is a large, round or oval volcanic depression, while a crater is a bowl-shaped volcanic depression smaller than a caldera. A lava tube is a tunnel formed by molten lava as it travels. The outer crust cools and hardens, while lava continues to flow beneath. Afterward, the interior is often left hollow. Tephra is airborne fragments of hardened lava ejected by lava fountains and carried

by winds. The glass-like shards are also called Pele's tears. Pele's hair is cobweb-like filaments of glass, formed when volcanic gas blows through highly fluid lava.

FLORA & FAUNA

When the Hawaiian Islands emerged from the ocean, they were barren. Life came in the ocean currents and the jet streams or as gifts of migratory birds. These colonizing seeds, spores, birds, and insects evolved into an astonishing biota.

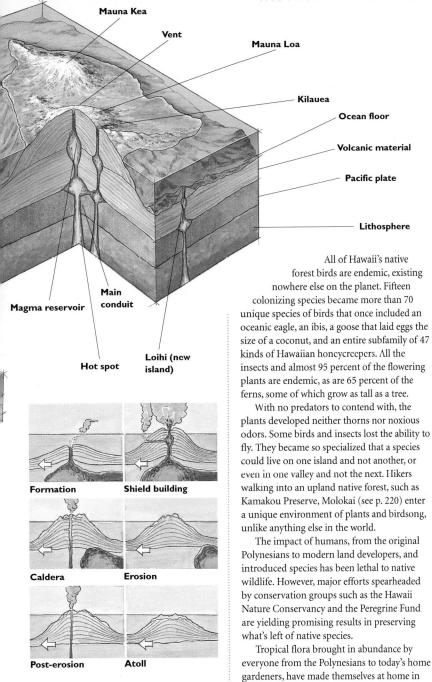

Mauna Kea

Vent

Mauna Loa

Kilauea

Ocean floor

Volcanic material

Pacific plate

Lithosphere

Magma reservoir

Main conduit

Hot spot

Loihi (new island)

Formation

Shield building

Caldera

Erosion

Post-erosion

Atoll

Shield volcanoes form over a hot spot and gradually erode as they move on. A caldera forms when the summit collapses inward.

All of Hawaii's native forest birds are endemic, existing nowhere else on the planet. Fifteen colonizing species became more than 70 unique species of birds that once included an oceanic eagle, an ibis, a goose that laid eggs the size of a coconut, and an entire subfamily of 47 kinds of Hawaiian honeycreepers. All the insects and almost 95 percent of the flowering plants are endemic, as are 65 percent of the ferns, some of which grow as tall as a tree.

With no predators to contend with, the plants developed neither thorns nor noxious odors. Some birds and insects lost the ability to fly. They became so specialized that a species could live on one island and not another, or even in one valley and not the next. Hikers walking into an upland native forest, such as Kamakou Preserve, Molokai (see p. 220) enter a unique environment of plants and birdsong, unlike anything else in the world.

The impact of humans, from the original Polynesians to modern land developers, and introduced species has been lethal to native wildlife. However, major efforts spearheaded by conservation groups such as the Hawaii Nature Conservancy and the Peregrine Fund are yielding promising results in preserving what's left of native species.

Tropical flora brought in abundance by everyone from the Polynesians to today's home gardeners, have made themselves at home in this hospitable climate. The result is a fragrant, green, and blooming Hawaii with its fiery origins still visible. ■

History of Hawaii

THE HISTORY OF HAWAII READS LIKE A GOOD NOVEL WITH HEROES, GODS, villains, kings, and queens. There are epic voyages of discovery, an idyllic isolation that is practically paradise, the rise of a star-crossed kingdom, treachery, greed, intrigue, and an overthrow with the U.S. Marines on stage. The past is still present in the culture and aspirations of *Hawaii Nei*, Hawaii today.

POLYNESIAN VOYAGES & SETTLEMENT

Eia Hawaii, he moku, he kanaka!
He kanaka Hawaii e!
He kanaka Hawaii,
He kama na Kahiki …

Behold Hawaii, an island, a people!
A nation is Hawaii!
The people of Hawaii
Are the children of Tahiti …

"Eia Hawaii" is considered by most scholars to be the oldest existing Hawaiian chant. It accounts for the origin of the people. Without a written language, the Hawaiians kept their records in a rich store of oral history composed of chants, hula, and epic stories of gods, kings, and migrations. Oral history is, of course, subject to question and becomes clouded by the loss of the specific to the poetic and by changes in language over the centuries. The prehistory of Polynesia was further blurred by the ravages a tropical climate inflicts on material objects, and a prevailing Eurocentric attitude that discounted non-Western achievements. Also, traditional radiocarbon dating of artifacts was rendered unreliable by nuclear testing done by both the United States and France in the Pacific.

Capt. James Cook, the first Westerner to find the Hawaiian Islands, asked in his log of 1778: "How shall we account for this nation spreading itself over this vast ocean?" Cook knew the rigors of ocean voyaging and he could not comprehend how a race of people in canoes fastened together with coconut fiber rope, and possessing no maps or navigational gear such as compass and sextant, could have colonized such widely separated island groups.

In 1947, Norwegian explorer Thor Heyerdahl (1914–) set out from Peru in a balsa raft, the *Kon Tiki*, to prove that the Polynesians had drifted west from the Americas in prevailing winds and currents, and that settlement of the Pacific was largely accidental. He captured the popular imagination, and believed he had solved an important question.

His answer, however, conflicted with the Hawaiians' understanding of themselves. In 1976, using oral history and sketches of early canoes, the Polynesian Voyaging Society in Hawaii built and launched a 60-foot voyaging canoe, *Hokulea*. They sailed it to Tahiti using ancient Polynesian navigational skills, guided only by the stars, wind, waves, and seabirds. They arrived to a big welcome, having proved that the oral history could be true. Their achievement launched a cultural renaissance.

In 1981, a construction crew bulldozing for a resort tennis court on the Tahitian island of Huahine discovered what has come to be called the Polynesian Pompeii. Evidence shows that around A.D. 850, a tidal wave swept across a coastal village burying it in just the right mixture of sand and silt to preserve its material culture. In it, archaeologists found the hull of an 80-foot canoe, along with artifacts connecting the site to New Zealand and the Marquesas. Further digging revealed that the village had been a thriving community of about 200 people who engaged in ship manufacture for trade. The evidence to prove the truth of the chants and hula finally existed.

Scientists now believe, from linguistic and archaeological research, that the Polynesians originated in Southeast Asia. Following the trail of a unique pottery, called Lapita, they trace the migrations to the Bismarck Archipelago between 3000 and 2000 B.C. From there, people ventured to the Solomon Islands, Vanuatu,

Man dressed in traditional ceremonial attire of nobility. Garments once made of feathers are now of velvet and plush.

Fiji, and Tonga. By 1200 B.C. they had settled in Samoa, where they spent a thousand years, becoming culturally the Polynesian people, and developing the navigational experience for the long voyages ahead of them to the Marquesas, a 1,000 miles to the east, to Tahiti, Aotearoa (New Zealand), Hawaii, and Rapa Nui (Easter Island). It is estimated that the first voyagers to reach Hawaii set sail from the Marquesas about A.D. 500. Later settlers came from Tahiti.

By the time of Western contact, these epic voyages had, for some reason, ceased, and the stories and chants were consigned to myth. A new generation of Hawaiians, taught by Mau Pialug, a traditional master navigator from Satawal, Micronesia, has revived the art of Polynesian navigation and voyagers are again crisscrossing the Pacific, retracing the ancient ocean highways. The distinctive claw-shaped sail of the Polynesian voyaging canoe is once again filled with the trade winds.

LIFE IN PRECONTACT HAWAII

It wasn't an idyll, but early life in Hawaii was mostly good. The climate was benign and predictable, the land fertile, and the sea bountiful.

The Hawaiians were very aware of the finite resources of their island environment, and became excellent stewards of nature. They gave hundreds of names to wind and rain, each highly descriptive and poetic. *Ua hanai* is the rain that nurtures the earth; *ua awa,* a cold drizzling rain. They named and classified each creature, and divided the land into pie-shaped segments called *ahupuaa.* Usually an ahupuaa stretched from a mountain summit, down through fertile valleys, and to the outer edge of the reef in the sea. This provided the families living on the land access to every elevation for the cultivation of various crops, plus fishing and gathering rights in the ocean. A freshwater stream ran through the ahupuaa with strictly regulated areas for various functions such as bathing and irrigation. No one was permitted to enter the water above the area designated for drinking water. Below the agricultural terraces, the stream was ingeniously engineered into a series of traps to catch silt so the water entered the ocean clean, thus maintaining the reefs.

Society was well organized and allowed ample time for leisure pursuits, such as sports and the arts. Politically, the larger islands of Kauai, Oahu, Maui, and Hawaii were each ruled by an *alii nui* or high chief. He divided his island into regions called *mokupuni,* each ruled by a lesser chief. The smaller islands of Lanai, Molokai, and Kahoolawe were ruled by the Maui high chief, while Niihau was assigned to Kauai. War sometimes broke out between one island and another over land or family conflicts among the *alii* (nobility).

A strict system of *kapu* or religious law governed every aspect of life from conservation practices to the status of women. A loose translation of the word kapu could be "forbidden." The "kapu" law was administered by the nobility and the *kahuna* (priests). Death was the penalty for violation of the kapu. So deeply rooted in spirituality was this system that offenders were mortified and sometimes literally died of shame before they could be apprehended and executed.

The primary gods of the ancient Hawaiian religion are Lono, Kane, Kanaloa, and Ku. Like most Polynesians, Hawaiians also believed in a Supreme Being, sometimes referred to as Io. Little is known about this god above all gods because much of the priestly knowledge was held in secret.

On a daily basis, no task was begun without prayer. Every beauty beheld, every gift received was acknowledged as coming from the gods. Communion with the divine was not just an act of worship but a way of being. Every family had an *aumakua* or guardian spirit, often represented in animal form such as a shark, lizard, owl, or turtle. More formalized aspects of religion were conducted at large temples, called *heiau.* The Tahitians introduced human sacrifice at some temples.

Education was conducted primarily by the family in the home. Gifted children were apprenticed to masters in arts such as healing, canoe building, navigation, and hula.

Family relationships were exceptionally strong and often embraced *hanai* (informally adopted) members. Rather than occupy a single thatched house, a family built as many as six houses including separate sleeping houses and eating houses for men and women. There would be a chapel, a house for beating *kapa* (tree-bark cloth) in bad weather, and a house of confinement for menstruating women.

Polynesian voyagers first reached Hawaii from the Marquesas. Later travelers came from Tahiti (broken arrow).

Fortification walls were unknown.

An annual four-month holiday called Makahiki was a time when warfare and work ceased, and taxes in the form of produce and animals were collected. After elaborate ceremonies, the temples closed and, according to Hawaiian scholar and historian David Malo (1793–1853) in his book *Hawaiian Antiquities,* there was a break even in formal religious practices. Makahiki, which began in Ikuwa, the month roughly corresponding to October, was considered to be the time of Lono, god of the harvest. Today's Aloha Festival (see p. 13) is a direct descendant of Makahiki.

CONTACT

The evening of January 20, 1778, some fishermen at Waimea, Kauai, saw two large and very strange silhouettes moving across the dark ocean, carrying lights. They hurried ashore and reported their sighting. By dawn, a large crowd of people, led by their chiefs, had gathered along the shore to see two huge ships riding at anchor. All of Waimea Valley rang with excitement. Historian Samuel M. Kamakau (1815–1876) wrote that some people were frightened. "One asked another, 'What are those branching things?' and the other answered, 'They are trees moving on the sea.'"

Captain Cook, in command of H.M.S. *Resolution* and H.M.S. *Discovery,* en route from the South Pacific, had stumbled upon the Hawaiian Islands, breaking centuries of isolation for the Hawaiian people. Life was to change forever.

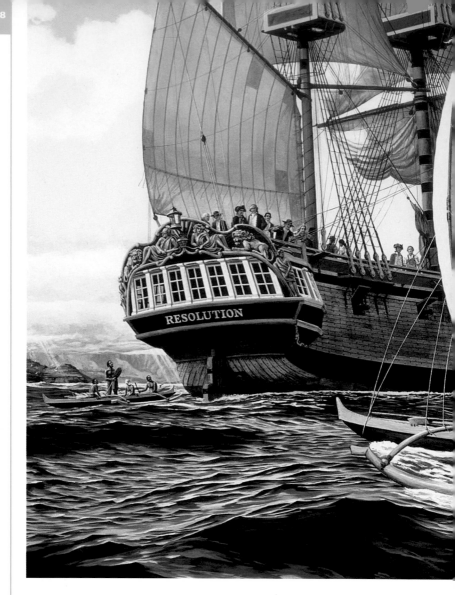

Cook put the Hawaiian Islands on his maps, naming them the Sandwich Isles after his patron, the earl of Sandwich, never bothering to consider that the people who lived there might have already named them.

During the two weeks Cook and his men spent in Hawaii, they inadvertently introduced European diseases to which the native people had no immunities. Between that first contact and 1799, some 45 foreign ships called. They brought more disease, hard liquor, tobacco,

material goods, weapons of war, and grazing animals. In less than 100 years, 90 percent of native Hawaiians are thought to have died. Their culture was eclipsed and their environment exploited by men from vast continents with no idea of stewardship of resources.

RISE OF THE KAMEHAMEHA DYNASTY

On a night in 1758 when Halley's comet streaked across the Hawaiian sky, Chiefess

Kekuiapoiwa gave birth at the sacred stones of Kohala, near Mookini Heiau, Big Island (noble women customarily gave birth on special rocks in sacred places). Because of the omen in the sky, a prophet predicted the child would become "a killer of chiefs and ruler of all the islands." Accordingly, the ruling chief ordered him killed. Loyal retainers hid the infant in Waipio Valley where he was raised in secret and schooled in the arts of warfare and statesmanship. His name was Kamehameha.

Captain James Cook, with his ships _Resolution_ and _Discovery,_ was the first Westerner to reach Hawaii, in 1778.

A brilliant strategist and courageous warrior, he was to launch a campaign of conquest that eventually united all the Islands into one nation. Kauai alone was not conquered, but voluntarily joined the union.

As was the custom of the day, the king had many wives. Keopuolani (1778–1823) was his

Sacred Wife, the one through whom the king-ship passed. But Kaahumanu (1772–1832) was his favorite wife, whom he likened to a lehua blossom. He said: "She rides the waves like a bird; she knows the heartbeat of the people."

Kamehameha proved as wise in peace as he was ferocious in war. His subjects said of him, "He is our Father. He is the taro of the land."

A bronze-and-gilded statue of King Kamehameha the Great stands in downtown Honolulu.

Upon his death in 1819, his son Liholiho (1796–1824) by Keopuolani succeeded him as Kamehameha II (R.1819–1824), with Queen Kaahumanu reigning as coregent. Kaahumanu invited the young king to dine with her pub-licly, thus violating the law against men and women eating together. Her motive may have been to improve the status of women, or to break the power of the priests. Kamehameha hesitated for days before accepting. When the people saw that divine retribution did not fall upon the pair, they rose up throughout Hawaii, destroyed their temples, and overnight became a people without a god and without the structure of religious law that had gov-erned them for centuries (see p. 149).

MISSIONARIES & WHALERS

Into this vacuum, the first party of Christian missionaries from New England unsuspectingly and fortuitously sailed. They had come at the request of a group of Hawaiian students study-ing in New England at that time. Prominent among them was Henry Opukahaia (1792–1818), a Hawaiian Christian convert and author who had wanted to accompany the mis-sion party back to his homeland, but died beforehand. Opukahaia's autobiography, *Memoir,* was a best-seller of that time.

The band of 14 men and women, headed by dedicated evangelist Hiram Bingham (1789–1869) of Bennington, Vermont, arrived in 1820 to "bring the heathens to the mansions of eternal blessedness." When Kamehameha II saw that the men had brought wives and families, he welcomed them and gave them permission to preach and build their churches. Foreigners in Hawaii at that time were mostly shrewd sandalwood traders, sailors, whalers, and rank opportunists.

The first whaling ship, the *Balena* out of New Bedford, Massachusetts, had arrived the year before. Word of Hawaii's pleasurable ports quickly spread among the captains of the Yankee Pacific fleet working the newly discovered whaling grounds off the coast of Japan. Thousands of men, who had been to sea for years at a time, were soon carousing in the streets of Honolulu and Lahaina. They said there was "no god west of the Horn," and behaved accordingly. Inevitably, their value system, which consisted of the pursuit of demon rum and willing women, clashed with the Ten Commandments brought by the mis-sionaries. The battles are legendary. Honolulu was considered a hellhole of grog shops, gambling dens, and houses of ill repute.

The first serious riot erupted in 1825 in Lahaina on Maui, when the men of the British whaler *Daniel* learned that the missionaries had succeeded in influencing Governor Hoapili of Maui to prohibit women from visiting the ships. Another English whaler actually fired its cannon at a missionary home. In response, cannon were mounted along the Lahaina waterfront, trained seaward.

Before this, King Kamehameha II had left on a state visit to England, where both he and the beautiful young Queen Kamamalu (1802–1824) died of measles. He was succeeded by his younger brother, Kamehameha III (R.1824–1854), who took the helm of a land-rich and cash-poor kingdom. On every front, his people were confronting vast changes. They were also dying at an unprecedented rate. In an attempt to modernize his government and help the common people, and also to raise revenues, he established a legislature consisting of an upper house of royalty and a lower house of representatives. In 1848, he proclaimed The Great Mahele, releasing millions of acres of land for sale for the first time. Before he died, he designated a nephew to rule as Kamehameha IV (*R.*1854–1863). He and his wife Queen Emma (1836–1885) were known for their great works of charity, including the establishment of the Queen's Medical Center. Their only child, Prince Albert, died at the age of four. The king's older brother, Lot, a bachelor, inherited the throne and was the last of the Kamehameha dynasty (*R.*1863–1872).

The missionaries have been pilloried by casual historians, and most notably by author James Michener (1907–1997) in his epic novel, *Hawaii.* Yet they did establish schools, transliterate the Hawaiian language assigning it the 12 letter alphabet still in use, import a printing press, publish the first books and newspaper in the Hawaiian language, and offer a religion whose ideal of brotherly love was completely consistent with the Hawaiians' basic philosophy of aloha (see pp. 10–14).

It has been said that the missionaries came to do good and did very well, but that is only partly true. Most of the missionaries did indeed work tirelessly as doctors, ministers, and teachers. Usually it was their children who rose to positions of power and influence, and eventually overthrew the monarchy, establishing themselves as a ruling oligarchy.

RISE OF AMERICAN BUSINESS

The Great Mahele, which was intended to help commoners own their own land, resulted instead in huge tracts going to foreigners, primarily Americans. These entrepreneurs, many of them descended from missionary families, set up the vast sugar plantations that influenced every facet of life in Hawaii for the next century.

Sugarcane, *ko,* was brought to the Islands by the early Polynesians, who planted it about their houses for its sweet taste and its use as a

natural stimulant. The first Hawaiian sugar to be commercially processed was extracted by an early Chinese immigrant on the island of Lanai. After making enough money to retire comfortably in China, he closed down and left. A few years later an English agriculturist started raising cane in Manoa Valley, Oahu. In 1826, his fields were sold to rum distillers. The

The Baldwin Home, Lahaina, Maui, shows how frugally the first Yankee missionaries lived when they came to Hawaii.

first successful plantation was established in 1835 at Koloa, Kauai (see p. 188), and by 1900, sugar was the primary industry of the Islands.

Pineapple, Hawaii's other plantation crop, was probably brought by Polynesian settlers from Tahiti. The first record of its presence is an 1813 entry in the diary of Don Francisco de Paula y Marin (1774–1837), a Spanish horticulturist and advisor to King Kamehameha I: "This day, I planted pine-apples *[sic]* and an orange tree." However, the name Dole became synonymous with pineapple. James Dole (1877–1958), fresh from Harvard, arrived in 1898. Three years later, he sowed 12 acres with 75,000 pineapples at Wahiawa, Oahu. His first crop, harvested by family and friends, produced 1,893 cans of pineapple chunks.

From the beginning, labor was a problem for the fledgling plantations. The Hawaiians, accustomed to self-sufficiency and

Immigrant plantation workers survey a bountiful pineapple harvest.

independence, had no interest in subjecting themselves to the long hours, harsh working conditions, and low pay required of workers to make a plantation profitable. Besides, there were few men left. Ninety percent of native Hawaiians died of newly introduced diseases. King Kamehameha IV stated in 1855: "The decrease of our population is a subject in comparison with which all other sink into insignificance." The shortage of labor led to an era of population politics that set the stage for Hawaii's multiracial society.

IMMIGRATION

The first indentured workers came from Fukien and Kwang-tung, China, in 1852. They had five-year contracts offering free passage, food, clothing, housing, and wages of three dollars a month. By the time the Chinese government prohibited emigration to Hawaii in 1881, due to reports of abuse, the Hawaiian kingdom had a population of 18,000 Chinese.

To further augment the labor force, planters next turned to Portugal. Between 1878 and 1887, 17 ships brought 12,000 Portuguese workers and families from Madeira and the Azores. The Portuguese became the *luna* (foremen) of the plantations. Interestingly, until recently, they were not grouped with Caucasians in census data, but enjoyed their own category; also they were accepted more warmly into the local culture than other Caucasians. Workers in smaller numbers were recruited from Scandinavia, Germany, Russia, and Puerto Rico.

Walter Murray Gibson (1822–1888), an eccentric American immigrant and a politician so influential he was known as "The Minister of Everything," addressed the Chamber of Commerce of Hawaii in 1872: "You have considered the races that are desirable, not only to supply your needs of labor, but to furnish an increase of population that will assimilate with the Hawaiian….A moderate portion of the Japanese, of the agricultural class, will not conflict with the view that I present, and if they bring their women with them, and settle permanently in the country, they may be counted upon as likely to become desirable Hawaiian subjects."

King David Kalakaua (1836–1891, see below) went off to Japan and negotiated labor procedures. Japanese workers were offered three-year contracts providing for free steerage passage, a food allowance, lodging, medical care, fuel, no taxes, rice at no more than five cents a pound, and wages of nine dollars a month for men and six dollars for women. By 1900, they were, at 40 percent of the population, the largest ethnic group in the Islands.

Always seeking fresh sources of cheap labor, the plantation owners in 1906 turned to the Philippines. The flow of labor was initially two way, with many workers returning home; nowadays, however, few do go back. In the 1970s, Filipinos were the largest immigrant group arriving in Hawaii.

Later immigration has come from Korea, Southeast Asia, and other Pacific Island groups. In all, approximately 385,000 workers from around the world were brought to Hawaii to feed the plantations. They became the rainbow of races visitors find so intriguing today.

THE PASSING OF A KINGDOM

As King Kamehameha V lay dying in 1872, he begged his childhood sweetheart Princess Bernice Pauahi Bishop (1831–1884), great-granddaughter of Kamehameha I, to accept the throne. When she declined, he left the question of succession to the legislature, as provided by the Hawaiian constitution. They elected Prince William Lunalilo (1835–1874), a grandnephew of Kamehameha I. Known as "The People's King," he reigned for a little more than a year.

Upon Lunalilo's death of a lung disease, the legislature voted for High Chief David Kalakaua to succeed him. The foreigners, who were very influential by this time, supported the election of the man they considered a scholar and gentleman. His wife, High Chiefess Kapiolani (1834–1899), was of the royal family of Kauai.

King Kalakaua's reign (1874–1891) was marked with triumph and turmoil. He breathed new life into the dispirited Hawaiians

by reviving their culture, restoring the hula to a place of prominence, and writing down many ancient chants for posterity. Hoping to secure respect in international circles for his small nation, he modeled his court on the courts of Europe. He built the beautiful Iolani Palace (see pp. 58–60), became the first reigning monarch of any country to circumnavigate the globe, and was the first to visit Washington, D.C. He negotiated the Reciprocity Treaty with the United States, which allowed Hawaiian sugar to enter that country duty free. In return, he gave the U.S. rights to use Pearl Harbor as a military base. In doing this, the king known as "the Merrie Monarch" sealed Hawaii's fate, marrying the lovely little Polynesian kingdom to the mighty Uncle Sam.

In 1887, a group of Caucasians, grown prosperous on sugar, led an armed revolt and forced the king to accept what became known as the Bayonet Constitution, which severely constricted his powers. Its key provision required an annual income of at least 600 dollars a year or ownership of at least 3,000 dollars in property to enfranchise a voter. Voters who qualified by property did not need to be citizens; this effectively eliminated most native Hawaiians, who had formed the majority of the electorate, and allowed foreigners to vote, thus shifting political power to the Caucasian minority. Four years later, the king, in poor health, journeyed to San Francisco to seek medical help, and died in that city.

He named his sister, Princess Lydia Kamakaeha Liliuokalani (1839–1917), to succeed him. A strong and brilliant woman with a deep love for her people, Queen Liliuokalani was destined to be the last Hawaiian monarch. Seven months after her ascension to the throne, she suffered the first tragedy of her reign, when her American husband John Owen Dominis (1851–1887) died, leaving her alone to face the monumental task of holding her country together.

To redress the injustices of the Bayonet Constitution and limit voting privileges to citizens, both native Hawaiians and naturalized foreigners, the queen announced she would promulgate a new constitution. This was used as an excuse by antiroyalist foreigners, primarily American, to launch a revolt. John B. Stevens, the United States minister in Hawaii, ordered the landing of Marines from the U.S.S. *Boston,* anchored in Honolulu Harbor on January 17, 1893. The insurgents, who called themselves the Committee of Safety, marched into Iolani Palace and demanded the queen's abdication.

Liliuokalani complied to avoid bloodshed, saying: "I yield my authority until such time as the Government of the United States shall, upon the facts being presented to it, undo the action of its representatives and reinstate me in the authority which I claim as the constitutional sovereign of the Hawaiian Islands."

A provisional government was imposed, headed by Sanford Dole (1844–1926). President Grover Cleveland sent an investigator, James Blount, to Honolulu. He immediately ordered American flags removed from public buildings and the withdrawal of the Marines. Acting on Blount's findings, President Cleveland ordered the restoration of the monarchy, but the revolutionaries defied him. They set up what they called "The Republic of Hawaii," continuing the voting injustices, and excluding Asians, even if born in Hawaii, from voting.

The next American President, William McKinley, signed papers annexing Hawaii in 1898, and appointing Sanford Dole as first territorial governor.

Queen Liliuokalani, after a period of imprisonment in her palace, was permitted to retire to her home, Washington Place (see p. 61), where she continued to work for the welfare of her people until her death in 1917.

In his memoirs, President Cleveland wrote: "Hawaii is ours. As I look back upon...this miserable business and as I contemplate the means used to complete the outrage, I am ashamed of the whole affair."

THE TERRITORY OF HAWAII

The year after Hawaii was incorporated as a territory of the United States under the Organic Act of 1900, the Moana Hotel was opened in Waikiki. In 1903, James Dole harvested his first pineapple crop at Wahiawa on Oahu and three years later opened a cannery in Honolulu. By 1908, sugar exports, which were at the root of the revolution, doubled, reaching 538,785 tons, even though contract labor ended under the U.S. labor laws.

Japanese laborers, protesting against poor wages and working conditions, initiated the first of Hawaii's major, and often bloody, labor strikes in 1909.

The first interisland air flight took off for Molokai from Oahu in 1918 and returned safely. The first commercial interisland flight to Maui from Oahu in 1920 took an hour and a half and cost 150 dollars.

Under the American umbrella, Hawaii contributed 9,800 men to World War I and suffered 102 fatalities. The Islands became more prosperous with the expansion of the plantations and the rise of tourism. The Depression was barely felt in Honolulu, as the major business corporations enjoyed unprecedented power and profits.

In 1920, the population of Hawaii was 256,000 people, with almost half of them living on Oahu.

WAR COMES TO HAWAII

"WAR!" screamed the headlines of the *Honolulu Star Bulletin*, in an extra edition. "OAHU BOMBED BY JAPANESE PLANES. Wave after wave of bombers streamed through the clouded morning sky from the southwest and flung their missiles on a city resting in peaceful Sabbath calm."

At first, most people, hearing the aerial artillery, thought the American military was on practice maneuvers. They could not believe that anyone would attack Hawaii—until the enemy aircraft flew low over Honolulu and the

December 7, 1941: Pearl Harbor is under attack, propelling America into the war in the Pacific.

red emblem of the rising sun was seen on the wingtips. The attack came in four waves beginning at 7:55 in the morning. Three hundred sixty Japanese aircraft, launched from carriers, devastated the U.S. Pacific Fleet anchored in Pearl Harbor, and left behind 2,323 American dead including civilian casualties. Japanese submarines sank cargo and passenger vessels and shelled Hilo, Nawiliwili, and Kahului harbors.

President Franklin D. Roosevelt immediately declared war on Japan, calling December 7, 1941 "a day that will live in infamy."

The territory was placed under martial law for the duration of the war. Schools were closed, military censorship was imposed on all outgoing messages, and a total blackout for Oahu was ordered; barbed wire was rolled out along the beaches in case of invasion.

Young Japanese Americans who naively volunteered their services to their country—thousands already belonged to the Hawaii Territorial Guard—were rejected by the military. On the American mainland, Japanese Americans were rounded up and confined to desert internment camps, a fate that did not befall German or Italian Americans. Massive incarcerations were economically and physically impossible in Hawaii, but the Japanese Americans lived under a cloud of official suspicion.

When the young *nisei* (second generation Japanese Americans) were finally admitted to military service, they were assigned to special combat units, the Army's 100th Infantry Battalion, which expanded to become the 442nd Regimental Combat Team. Nearly 3,000 were inducted in a single day on the grounds of Iolani Palace in Honolulu. They served with uncommon valor while the constitutional rights of their families were abrogated at home. The most highly decorated units of their size in American military history, their story is chronicled in the book *I Can Never Forget* by Thelma Chang.

When the nisei soldiers came home, they took advantage of the education benefits provided by the G.I. Bill of Rights. They maintained their close ties and became a formidable force in every aspect of Island life. They virtually seized control of the Democratic Party and, with the support of now powerful labor unions, instituted a political revolution that weakened the power of the Caucasian establishment. With statehood, two of their own went to Congress: Masayuki "Spark" Matsunaga as representative and Daniel K. Inouye as senator.

STATEHOOD & SOVEREIGNTY

Two things happened in the 1950s, that made Hawaii what it is today, America's sweetheart resort. One, the start of jet travel, put the Islands four and a half hours from the U.S. West Coast, and the other was statehood.

Tourism as a business had actually begun in the 1920s, when most passengers arrived aboard Matson luxury liners, the S.S *Malolo* and the *Lurline*. Air travel began in 1936, when Pan Am's *China Clipper* seaplane flew from San Francisco to Honolulu in a time of 21 hours and 33 minutes. Passengers dined on consommé and chicken fricassee served on white linen with wine and silver. After dessert, they retired to their staterooms, and the steward shined their shoes and pressed their clothes while they slept. They paid 720 dollars for their round-trip ticket—at a time when a top executive's salary was 5,000 dollars a year.

Movement toward statehood, too, had roots in an earlier time. For 50 years, beginning with the overthrow of the monarchy, various statehood petitions were placed before Congress. All were rejected due to stiff opposition from southern legislators (Hawaii had a majority nonwhite population). Finally, after a vote for statehood was held in Hawaii, and Congress passed the Hawaii State Bill, President Dwight Eisenhower added another star to the American flag on August 21, 1959.

Statehood triggered an immediate building boom as tourists began pouring into Waikiki. The Boeing 747, which began service in 1969, could economically carry hundreds of passengers, putting a Hawaii vacation-of-a-lifetime within grasp of the average person. The following year, two million tourists arrived; a decade later the numbers doubled. In the 1980s, tourism's economic meteor streaked so spectacularly across the Hawaiian sky, it obscured all else. Everyone was buying and building. The Japanese invested more than 15 billion dollars in a decade, acquiring hotels, resorts, and high-end homes.

It wasn't all good news, especially for the locals. At the opening of a luxury Maui resort, when the dignitaries were introduced they were a Japanese owner, Canadian developer, Irish general manager, and Austrian chef. Banquet wait help were primarily tanned, surf-blissed Californians. Local people found themselves no longer able to afford homes even though husband and wife might be working two to three jobs. Favorite beaches were suddenly crowded with tourists.

The whole boom fizzled in the 1990s as tourism fell during the Gulf War. The financial

Crowds gather for a rock concert at the Maui Arts and Cultural Center, Wailuku, Maui.

crisis in Asia in the late 1990s added to Hawaii's woes and plunged the economy into a recession from which it is just recovering.

Complicating the picture was—and is—Hawaii's messy land ownership situation. Only slightly more than 50 percent of the land on inhabited islands is privately owned. Forty landlords own 75 percent of this. The largest private landowner is Kamehameha Schools estate, formerly known as Bishop Estate. Princess Bernice Pauahi Bishop (see p. 33) left the vast lands of the Kamehameha family for the education of Hawaiian children; worth approximately ten billion dollars, it is one of the wealthiest foundations in the United States. Its five trustees, who earned close to a million dollars each annually, were, in the late 1990s, embroiled in a storm of controversy and scandal which none survived.

Native Hawaiians, who have little stake in the new Hawaii, being few in numbers in a democracy where the majority rules, are beginning to unite and raise their voices in protest, demanding reparation for the loss of their nation, and some form of sovereignty for the Hawaiian people. John Waihee, the state's first governor of Hawaiian ancestry, wrote in the *Honolulu Advertiser:* "The overthrow of the Hawaiian monarchy on January 17, 1893 was a hostile act against a native people who were organized as a sovereign nation and recognized by the United States of America. It was an international act of aggression conducted, if not with the tacit agreement of the U.S. government, then at least with the United States turning to look the other way."

While some people profess to want a complete break with the U.S., Ka Lahui Hawaii, the most vocal of the sovereignty groups, proposes "nation within a nation" status, similar to that enjoyed by Native Americans on the mainland. Polls show that the majority of people in Hawaii support the Hawaiians in their efforts toward self-determination, while hoping that when it comes there will still be a place for them beneath the rainbow. ∎

Arts & culture

THE POLYNESIAN ARTS ENJOYED THEIR GREATEST FLOWERING IN HAWAII. With the discovery of the Islands by the outside world, Hawaii became a cultural cross-roads of East and West. Today, it's easier to find good art, for instance on Maui, than to find chilled coconut milk. And while no visitor seeks out Hawaii for its art, it is there to be found in a great abundance of beauty and truth.

HAWAIIAN MUSIC

As I walked through the fields alone, lo!
I heard the sweet songs of many birds,
singing among the branches, for it was a
beautiful Sabbath morning. I thought of
Christians as soon as I heard these birds
tuning their joyful songs around the tree.
—Henry Opukahaia, first Hawaiian Christian

Prior to Western contact, musical expression in the Hawaiian Islands was through the chant, the *mele hula* (chanted in the rhythms of the dance) and *mele oli* (free-flowing chant). Instruments were primarily percussion, and included gourd drums, the sharkskin-covered, carved hula drum, gourd rattles, and the conch-shell horn. Various bamboo instruments include the haunting nose flute, which is played by blowing down one end with the nostril and manipulating sound holes with the fingers. Music was sacred. It celebrated the beauty and bounty of the Islands, recorded genealogy, and recounted the deeds of kings and gods. It was woven into the fabric of life.

In 1820, after 164 days at sea, the Yankee missionaries aboard the brig *Thaddeus* spotted an incredible snowcapped mountain rising above the tropical ocean. Two days later, as the ship was sailing along the Kona Coast of Hawaii toward its first anchorage, two young ministers on board, Hiram Bingham and Asa Thurston, were so overwhelmed by the soft loveliness of the evening, with the setting sun on one hand and the rising moon on the other, that they scrambled up the rigging to the top of the mast and burst into their favorite song, "Head of the Church Triumphant." The notes, reflecting utter joy, were carried on the trade winds like small seeds.

Mission journals note how pleased the Hawaiian people seemed with the new music and how they came by the hundreds to hear the hymns. The rising and descending scales were completely different from the Hawaiians' traditional system of tones and pitches, and initially caused difficulty. The resourceful Reverend Bingham established an evening singing school, where his eager pupils not only practiced Western musical scales, but learned the Bible by chanting its verses in their traditional mele rhythms. It was the birth of modern Hawaiian music, a harmony of New England hymns infused with the beautiful poetic form and ancient rhythms of Hawaii.

The singing schools spread throughout the Islands and Hawaiians were quickly composing their own songs in the new genre. The first hymnal *Na Himeni Hawaii: He Me Ori Ia Iehova, Ke Akua Mau (Hawaiian Hymns and Songs to Jehovah, the Eternal God)* was published in 1823 and contained 47 songs including the classic "Iesu Me Ka Kanaka Waiwai" ("Jesus and the Rich Man").

Missionary Lorenzo Lyons of Imiola Church, Waimea, Big Island became the dominant influence in the emerging music when he introduced gospel songs in the 1830s. These melodies were more compatible with native music, and the sincere, unpretentious sentiments more akin to their own notions of man's relationship to a god of bounty. Lyons was a gifted composer whose "Hawaii Aloha" is one of the most beloved Hawaiian songs. The other is "Aloha Oe," composed by Queen Liliuokalani.

Foreigners continued to influence music. Cowboys of Spanish and Mexican heritage (see pp. 160–161) introduced the guitar, and Hawaiians made it their own with a unique styling called *ki hoalu* (slack key). This and the

Puakeala Mann, grandmother, dancer, and chanter with Halau Hula O Maiki, performs in Waikiki.

steel guitar replaced early percussion instruments. Plantation laborers from Portugal introduced the viola, a fiddle, and their *branguiha*, which evolved into Hawaii's famous ukulele. Falsetto, a popular form of singing in the Islands, has uncertain origins, possibly in Mexican song stylings or German yodeling. In the 1930s and '40s, Hollywood discovered Hawaii and a new song form erupted. Called *hapa-haole*, it was fun, witty, and naughty, largely reflecting an outsider's impression of the culture. "Lovely Hula Hands" and "The Cockeyed Mayor of Kaunakakai" are two classics that emerged from the period.

Hawaiian music is enjoying its greatest popularity in decades with a whole new generation of gifted composers and performers taking their music everywhere from Carnegie Hall to the arenas of Asia and Europe. Among the musicians who called world attention to Hawaiian music and whose work lives after them, played daily on the airwaves of the Islands, are Gabby Pahinui and Israel Kamakawiwaole.

Because of its position, culturally and physically, midway between Asia and America, Hawaii enjoys many forms of music. Honolulu supports a symphony orchestra. There are opera and ballet seasons, and there are niches for jazz and chamber music. Country music has never really caught on, but a few places, frequented by military personnel, feature it. Top rock and pop stars drop in on their way to bigger gigs, and Broadway road musicals, Chinese opera, Indonesian gamelan, and even Irish groups come to town. You can't always get what you want when you want it, but eventually it gets to Hawaii.

ARTS & CRAFTS

The early Hawaiians were skilled artists who lived in an orderly society that allowed and encouraged the meditation and reflection necessary for art. They used the limited materials in their environment with skill and sensitivity, and at the core of all they produced—including their orally transmitted literature (see pp. 42–43)—was their deep sense of spirituality.

A wood-carver held the status of priest: Because he sculpted sacred images, he was expected to know the prayers and rituals surrounding the deity as well as the properties of each of the fine native hardwoods. Unlike other Polynesian woodwork, Hawaiian objects were not heavily carved, but relied on the grain, polish, and idiosyncrasies of an individual piece of wood for beauty. Ancient artisans carving with stone adzes created simple household goods, intimidating temple images, powerful hula drums, sleek outrigger canoes, and fine decorative pieces. Contemporary sculpted work in native woods such as koa *(Acacia koa), milo (Thespesia populnea),* and kou *(Cordia subcordata)* can be found in galleries around Hawaii today.

Featherwork was also a sacred art. Brilliant scarlet, yellow, and black feathers of native birds were woven into cloaks, capes, helmets, leis, and *kahili* (the feather standards of royalty). Sometimes they even formed images of gods. Capt. James King, a surgeon on Captain Cook's historic voyage (see pp. 27–28), wrote in his journal on January 21, 1778: "Amongst the articles which they brought to barter this day we could not help taking notice of a particular sort of cloak and cap, which, even in countries where dress is more particularly attended to, might be reckoned elegant… feathers are so closely fixed that the surface might be compared to the thickest and richest velvet, which they resemble, both as to feel and glossy appearance." People who have inherited feather capes wear them on ceremonial occasions. Feather leis are still being made, now employing a range of imported feathers.

Kapa, or tapa (cloth made from tree bark) was a women's art; the *wauke* (paper mulberry) tree yielded the best fiber. Often fragrant flowers and herbs were pounded into the material for a permanent perfume, and the sheet was then painted or stamped in decorative designs using natural dyes. Hawaiian kapa, which had the suppleness of finely woven material, was used for clothing and bed linen. Most kapa is now imported from Tonga and is almost universally decorated in bold, earth-toned, geometric patterns.

Hawaiians wove the leaves of the *hala* tree (pandanus or screw pine) into pillows, fans, sandals, toys, floor mats, and even canoe sails. The finest mats, called *makaloa*, were woven of a sedge called *ahuawa (Cyperus laevigatus).*

Hawaiian quilting, a unique form of the art, is begun by appliquéing one fabric over another.

The favored plant for making baskets and fish traps was *ieie (Freycinetia)*. Many shops today carry *lauhala* hats and bags, sometimes lined in kapa.

Personal adornment took the form of jewelry made from shells, dog teeth, whale ivory, feathers, and flora (see pp. 78–79). Both men and women tattooed their bodies.

The distinctive Hawaiian quilt, adapted from missionary needlework, has become its own art form. Families treasure these graphically strong quilts based on patterns from nature. After the overthrow of the monarchy, people made quilts after the forbidden Hawaiian flag, and hung them as bed canopies so they could at least sleep under their beloved emblem.

PAINTING

The painters who came to the Islands during the period of discovery by the Western world rendered fascinating glimpses into old Hawaii. John Webber, the official artist with Capt. James Cook, executed the first paintings of the Hawaiian Islands and Islanders after he went ashore with Cook on January 21, 1778, at Waimea, Kauai. Credit for the first recorded view of Hawaii goes to the ship's surgeon, William Ellis, a gifted amateur who sketched the shoreline of Kauai from the deck of the ship. But it is Webber's body of work, his paintings of temples, habitations, and landscapes, and his portraits of people, that provide the record, sometimes in precise detail, of life in Hawaii at the moment of contact with the outside world.

In the years following Cook's arrival, more British, American, Russian, and French ships called in Hawaii. Many had artists on board to accurately record the bays, shorelines, and landmarks, and to satisfy the curiosity of their patrons and countrymen at home, regarding these splendid "new" islands.

Louis Choris, artist aboard the Russian brig *Rurick,* did a portrait of Kamehameha the Great in 1816, three years before the king's death. It hangs in the Honolulu Academy of Arts. The great conqueror looks grandfatherly and is already wearing Western clothes, most notably a bright red vest.

These haunting portraits, by English artist Robert Dampier, of a young Kamehameha III and his star-crossed sister-lover, Princess Nahienaena, are in the Honolulu Academy of Arts.

English artist Robert Dampier, who arrived in 1825, is known for his portraits of Hawaiian royalty. His portraits of a young Kamehameha III, and his beloved sister Princess Nahienaena, in their red-and-yellow feather cloaks, are hauntingly beautiful and hang now at the Honolulu Academy of Arts (see pp. 74–75) .

The missionaries and whalers, while they kept diaries and letters, left few visual records. Edward Bailey (see p. 131) was the exception. Residing at Wailuku, Maui, he didn't begin to paint until 1865, about 28 years after he came to the Islands. His landscapes are mostly of Iao Valley, close to his home.

Hawaiian artist Joseph Nawahi left behind only six known paintings, apparently too busy to pursue his obvious talent—he served in the legislature of Hawaii from 1872 to 1892, founded a newspaper, and worked vigorously against annexation by the United States. Then in the late 19th century, the first distinctive school of Hawaii painting evolved. Known as the Volcano school, it is most widely recognized in the almost fantastic, dramatically lit interpretations of the Big Island volcanoes by Paris-born artist Jules Tavernier.

By the time the 20th century dawned, Hawaii was no longer an isolated paradise, but a multicultural corner of America in touch with contemporary art trends. Reflecting the vast changes, and the artistic climate of the times, a modernist school developed, which included locally born artists, and painters who came from elsewhere to reside in the Islands. Prominent among this group were Juliette May Fraser, Isami Doi, Madge Tennent, Reuben Tam, Mabel Alvarez, Lloyd Sexton, Keichi Kimura, Juanita Vitousek, Arman T. Manookian, Hon Chew Hee, and John Young.

The Honolulu Academy of Arts and the Bishop Museum (see pp. 70–71) have fine examples of Hawaii's distinctive genres of painting. David W. Forbes, an expert in the field, has written a lavishly illustrated book on the subject, *Encounters With Paradise*, published by the Honolulu Academy of Arts.

LITERATURE & LANGUAGE

The early Hawaiians produced a vast body of literature, passed on orally from generation to generation. Epic in scope, poetic in expression, and vibrant with drama, it explored the great themes of life: Passion, sexuality, romantic love, birth, death, ambition, jealousy, the

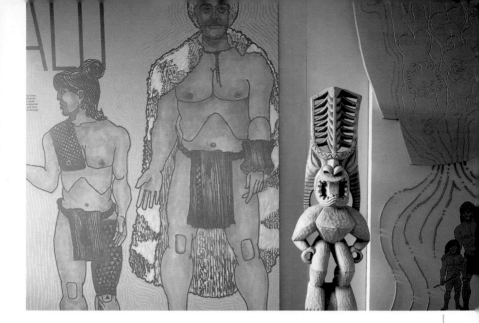

Contemporary artists interpret traditional themes in art shows at Hawaii Volcanoes National Park on the Big Island.

forces of nature, love of home, and cataclysmic battles between good and evil. It is peopled with gods, goddesses, great heroes, and villains. If it were better known, it would take its place beside the Homeric epics, the Norse sagas, the adventures of Cuchulainn, and the Ramayana.

The favorite stories are of Maui, who fished up the islands from the ocean floor; Pele, the tempestuous goddess of volcanoes (see p. 175); and Kamapuaa, the earthy pig-god and lover of Pele, whose rootings created the valleys and springs.

Hawaiian poetry is characterized by vividness of visual image and depth of thought. A poet was called *haku mele*, a weaver of song, and held an honored position in royal courts. Irish poet Padraic Colum said: "The Hawaiian poet has anticipated effects that the cultivated poets of our tradition have been striving for; he is, for instance, more esoteric than Stéphane Mallarmé and more imaginistic than Amy Lowell." He said, further: "The main thing that Hawaiian poetry has to offer an outsider is the clear and flashing images that it is in its power to produce."

The Hawaiian language is Austronesian in classification and similar to other languages of Polynesia. It was rendered into written form by the American missionaries, who based their work on that done by French Catholic priests in Tahiti, employing Latin phonetics. The softness of the language comes in its repetition, and from the fact that there are only seven consonants (h, k, l, m, n, p, w).

In modern times, the Hawaiian language fell into disuse. In fact there was a generation of Hawaiians, now elderly, who were forbidden to speak it, even though their parents were fluent; it was thought to be a handicap, perhaps even a stigma, in an American society. Today, Hawaiian is making a spirited comeback. Some private and public schools offer Hawaiian language immersion programs beginning at the preschool level, where parents are required to study with children. It is proving to be highly successful not only in forming a new generation of native speakers, but in raising Hawaiian academic performance levels in all fields.

Hawaiian and English are the official languages of the state of Hawaii. The unofficial language is pidgin, academically called Hawaiian English Dialect, which is a blend of languages that evolved on the plantations. A child, upon waking from a nap, may announce, *"All pau ne-ne,"* saying in English, Hawaiian, and Japanese, "I'm finished sleeping." Once scorned by academia, pidgin is finding its way into contemporary literature of the Islands, most successfully through the work of novelist Lois-Ann Yamanaka.

Over the years, the lure of the Pacific drew a cast of literary lions to Hawaii. In *Roughing It,* Mark Twain (1835–1910) described Kilauea Volcano: "It looked like a colossal railroad map of the State of Massachusetts done in chain lightning on a midnight sky. Imagine it—imagine a coal-black sky slivered into a tangled network of angry fire!"

Watching a group of sick people leaving for exile on Molokai, Robert Louis Stevenson (1850–1894) was inspired to portray a young girl in *The Eight Islands.* "The lepers came singly and unattended; the elder first; the girl a little after, tricked out in a red dress and with a fine red feather in her hat. In this bravery, it was the most affecting to see her move apart on the rocks and crouch in her accustomed attitude. But this time I had seen her face; it was scarce horribly affected, but had a haunting look of an unfinished wooden doll, at once expressionless and disproportioned...."

An adventure in surfing was a subject for Jack London (1876–1916): "Soon we were out in deep water where the big smokers came roaring in....One had to have his wits about him, for it was a battle in which mighty blows were struck...."

Maxine Hong Kingston (1940–) wrote in her best-seller *China Man:* "Chinese take a bit of sugar to remind them in times of bitter struggle of the sweetness of life, and Hawaiians take a few grains of salt on the tongue because it tastes like the sea, like the earth, like human sweat and tears."

ISLAND STYLE

Lifestyles in the Islands are as diverse as the people who live them, but they share certain elements in common. Most homes are so married to their gardens that the boundaries between house and garden are blurred. Furniture spills onto the lanai (veranda), while palm trees sit potted in the living room.

The home of a *kamaaina* (one who is Island born or Island rooted) is immediately identifiable, and it's hard to say how. It might be a grouping of seashells in the center of a table, old rattan furniture on the porch, shoji screens in the dining room, Hawaiian quilt pillows tossed on the sofa, a whiff of incense, a dried maile (Pacific vine) lei draped around a grandmother's portrait, or a rack of straw hats and a pile of shoes by the door.

Many of the new ultraexpensive homes—concrete, air-conditioned manses—are being built in a style locals call "developer spec." They are the antithesis of Island style, far removed from the grass houses of the Hawaiians, crafted from lava rock and tree limbs and thatched with long fragrant *pili* grass, set so unobtrusively on the beloved land as to have barely any impact.

Mission Houses Museum (see p. 62) in Honolulu represents the oldest surviving Western-style building in the Islands. The original home is a prefabricated New England saltbox, shipped around the Horn. Rooms are cramped and airless.

With the rise of the great plantations, two kinds of homes emerged. One was the small worker's house with a corrugated tin roof. Colorful and sturdy, these old wood cottages are nestled in gardens all over Hawaii, most notably in Lanai City (see p. 230). Visitors can stay in faithfully restored, modernized editions at Waimea Plantation Cottages (see p. 257) on Kauai. The other plantation homes were the spacious houses built for owners and managers. They tended to be Western style, built with local materials such as lava rock and native hardwoods. For the most part, these gracious homes remain sequestered on estates. On Kauai, the Wilcox family home at Kilohana Plantation (see p. 186) has been converted to a restaurant and gallery of shops that manages to maintain the integrity and grace of its 1930s era.

It wasn't until the early 20th century that Hawaii developed its own distinct, recognizable architectural style. Pioneered by architect Charles W. Dickey (1871–1942), it is distinguished by the high roofline borrowed from the old Hawaiian thatched house, which allows for maximum air circulation. Eaves are wide so windows can stay open, sun or rain. Appearances are inspired by other sunny climes, such as those of the Mediterranean and Southeast Asia.

This Chinese temple stands at the cultural theme park, Waipahu Plantation Village, Oahu.

Details may reflect the multiethnic culture with an antique obi running the length of a dining room table, an entryway that passes over water in the Chinese manner, art deco wood accents, or Japanese screens.

Rattan furniture, and lately bamboo, emphasize the tropical ambience. The most prized, and expensive furniture is crafted of native hardwoods, especially koa. Much of the native forest has succumbed to environmental pressures, such as domestic animals grazing on seedlings and the expansion of development, making koa pieces even more valuable. In 1793, Archibald Menzies, a naturalist aboard H.M.S. *Daedalus* on Capt. George Vancouver's Hawaii expedition, wrote of koa: "Its wood is very hard and close grained, and it takes a fine polish as may be seen by their canoes."

The Yankee missionaries were practical people, some of them good enough carpenters to build their own furniture. When Queen Kaahumanu admired a rocking chair the Reverend Hiram Bingham built for his wife, he made one for her, of koa and koaie *(Acacia koaie)*. Both chairs are at Mission Houses Museum (see p. 62). When Hawaiian and immigrant woodworkers began creating regional furniture from native woods for the monarchy, the pieces were outstanding. Some of the best may be seen at Queen Emma Summer Palace (see p. 69).

Real estate brokers traditionally hold open house for their on-the-market properties every Sunday. If you don't have Island friends, it's a good way to peek into homes. Wear shoes that will slip off easily at the door, a local custom.

FASHION

Practically the first thing most tourists do after landing in Waikiki is hit the shops and get in costume—a Halloween aloha shirt exploding in pineapples and hula maidens, with a matching muumuu (a loose-fitting, long dress) for the missus.

Fashion manufacture is a multimillion-dollar Island business, filling shop racks with T-shirts, surfer Jams, sophisticated resort ware, and aloha shirts and muumuus ranging from the tacky to the trendy.

Aloha shirts are a fashion rage, with antique shirts commanding sky-high prices.

Every man in Hawaii has his collection of aloha shirts, and most wear them daily. In fact, a man in a suit and tie is perceived as either heading for a funeral, a court appearance, or a loan office. All businesses observe the weekly "Aloha Friday," when even the stuffiest CEOs rush in, their adrenalin high and enhanced by a wicked aloha shirt.

The little Hawaiian shirt has gone international. It's everywhere. Hollywood has latched on to it: Bruce Willis and Robert Redford have been spotted in them; John Wayne wore one in *Donovan's Reef,* Elvis in *Blue Hawaii.* When Montgomery Clift got shot and fell down dead in the mud in *From Here to Eternity,* shirt fans wailed, "Oh no, he's ruined his shirt."

Vintage aloha shirts, "silkies" with coconut buttons from the 1930s and '40s, have become collectibles selling for thousands of dollars. The first Hawaiian shirt patterns were based on the geometric designs of kapa and colored with natural dyes that quickly mellowed to earth tones.

The earliest mass-produced Hawaiian shirts were made for plantation workers.

Called *palaka,* they were usually stylized check prints, worn with "sailor moku," denim trousers. In the 1920s, a local firm, Watumull's East India Store, commissioned artist Elsie Das to produce 15 floral designs. These were sent to Japan, printed on raw silk, and sewn into shirts. They sold by the boatload and were snapped up by collectors as far away as London. Designer Ellery Chun is credited by many for coining the term "aloha shirt" in an ad in the *Honolulu Advertiser* in 1935. Laser technology has enabled manufacturers to faithfully reproduce vintage shirt patterns. They are currently best-sellers.

The female counterpart to the costume is the muumuu and its glorified sister, the *holoku.* The muumuu is an everyday garment, while the holoku, with its small (or sometimes wedding-gown-long) train, goes to parties on Saturday night.

By most accounts, it was the missionaries, dismayed by the casual nudity of Hawaiian women, who quickly stitched up loose-fitting "Mother Hubbard" gowns to cover their bronze voluptuousness. This sounds suspiciously like another entertaining fable.

According to Hawaiian historians, Hawaiians had a history of sewing with *olona (Touchardia latifolia)* plant fiber and needles made from bone. They fashioned kapa into *pau* (loin skirts consisting of five layers of fabric), *malo* (loincloths for men), and *kihei*, a toga-like garment. The Russian explorer, V.M. Golovnin recorded in 1817, three years before the arrival of the missionaries, that Hawaiian women were wearing robe-like calico dresses. The fabric was no doubt acquired from early traders and valued for its novelty and coolness. Royal women draped themselves in the new silks and brocades.

The missionaries undoubtably popularized the muumuu with the establishment of sewing schools and the introduction of more varied styles based on world fashion trends. Royal attire began to follow European formal dress.

Today, the muumuu's range includes bare-backed mini dresses, tea length (just below the calf) suitable for the office, and floor length that goes anywhere. The top designer working in the field is Mamo Howell whose look is known by its strong graphic prints and innovative hem flourishes. A completely different and very popular muumuu, more feminine and old fashioned in feel, can be found in the Princess Kaiulani line. Another favorite look is the vintage reproduction print in a simple shift.

Good shoppers know that the best way to test the waters in esoteric fashion territory is to check out the most expensive lines, and then, if time permits, shop around. Department stores in Hawaii have entire sections devoted to Polynesian wear, and boutiques abound almost everywhere.

FESTIVALS

The calendar is crammed with holidays that are so colorful people often plan their vacations around them (see pp. 236–237). Many celebrations center on the Hawaiian culture and feature Hawaiian music, pageantry, crafts, hula—and always food. Anything billed as a *hoolaulea* is a pull-out-all-the-stops party. Waikiki can get so jammed during a hoolaulea that, if you were to fall, there wouldn't be

enough room to hit the ground. Rock can be blasting on one stage and steel guitar on the next. The smell of teriyaki meat perfumes the air, and hula dancers, wearing gardens in their hair, hit their gourd drums as they whirl to the beat. The biggest, splashiest of these celebrations are the Aloha Festivals, which are a reflection of the ancient Makahiki (see p. 27). They take place sequentially on each island, beginning with Oahu in September.

Hula festivals and competitions are as common as coconuts, and if there is one happening when you're here, don't miss it. People spare no expense in costuming for these beloved cultural expressions. You'll see authentic dances, both ancient and modern, performed by amateurs who devote themselves to the dance (see pp. 168–169).

Diversity of cultures simply means there's more to celebrate. Regardless of background, everyone celebrates Chinese New Year with firecrackers and ear-splitting lion dances. Then they don Japanese happi coats and fake the dancing at the Buddhist temples during Obon season, honoring ancestors. And of course, there's the Fourth of July, Christmas, and Easter. New Year's Eve is traditionally a blowout of aerial fireworks shows supplemented by all kinds of illegal home fireworks including spectacular rockets. Honolulu sounds like a war zone and the air becomes so thick with smoke that anyone with respiratory problems should stay indoors in air-conditioning.

The Hawaii International Film Festival has won worldwide recognition and manages to secure premier films, primarily from the Americas, Asia, and the Pacific. It also showcases locally produced features and documentaries. The perennial theme is "When Strangers Meet."

There's an annual jazz festival, and symphony and opera seasons. Several community theater groups thrive and harbor a surprising depth of talent.

Sports loom large on the calendar with world-class golf tournaments, marathons, triathlons, surf meets, outrigger canoe regattas, and international yacht races to name the big categories.

Many of the hotels and resorts host annual events worthy of a special visit. Often these

celebrations are an outgrowth of a hotel's Hawaiian cultural program, and are usually enthusiastically supported and participated in by the staff. The hotels also have ecologically inspired festivals such as Dolphin Days at the Hilton Waikoloa Village on the Big Island, and the Waikiki Aquarium has a full calendar of fun, eco-educational events.

Food and wine festivals come naturally in a place where almost no social intercourse happens without food. The biggest concern even on powerhouse business agendas is always refreshments—who is going to be in charge and who will bring what, or who will cater. Most of the major food events are charity benefits. Some are special promotions designed to fill hotel rooms.

For real downhome fun, always consult the local newspapers, which run regular columns announcing events. The *Honolulu Advertiser* publishes a weekly guide to entertainment and events that appears with

A student maestro conducts her classmates in a Lei Day concert at Kahala Elementary School, Oahu.

the regular Friday morning paper. You may find a fundraising luau (see p. 52) or beer-bust sponsored by a church or *hula halau* (school), a fascinating arts and crafts event, a school carnival, or even a rodeo. Visitors are always welcomed.

FOOD

Sugar is the key ingredient in Hawaii's food, not in the traditional sense of adding a cup or two in a recipe, but by virtue of the fact that it was sugar that brought to the Islands all the different immigrant groups with their pots and woks, their whisks and bamboo steamers. Living in such close proximity, in such isolation, it was natural that the food be shared.

The first colonists, the Polynesians, brought with them about 30 of their favorite

The luau centers around the *kalua* pig, here unearthed from the underground oven at Kona Village Resort. Right: Luau food

plants, among them a dozen food plants. They also brought domestic animals—dogs, chickens, and pigs. Taro (*Colocasia esculenta*) was by far their most important crop, which they grew in a vast system of irrigated agricultural terraces. The spinach-tasting leaves were steamed, and the corm was baked in an underground oven. They also pounded the corm into that purple dietary staple, poi. It is interesting to note that archaeologists excavating a site and coming upon a skeleton can tell immediately if it's a precontact site by the state of the bones—the early Hawaiians had perfect teeth, probably due to their healthy nonacidic diet.

With the arrival of whalers and traders, the Hawaiian farmers began to grow, at cooler elevations, potatoes, apples, onions, and other new crops for trade. In fact, Hawaii sent food to the forty-niners during the California gold rush (1849–1860). Parts of Maui, in particular, grew rich at this time, benefiting from the fertile soil and temperate climate (see p. 136). Unnoticed, on the back burner, fusion cuisine was being born.

As each new immigrant group added their specialties—Chinese *gao* (a New Year pudding with mochi flour and dates), Japanese sushi and teriyaki, Korean *mandoo* (savoury dumplings) and *kook su* (cucumber salad),

"It's actually a unique Hawaii concoction created by the first generation of sugar plantation cooks." Often the noodle soup was a family's first step into entrepreneurship. Matsuo explains: "They'd build a little saimin wagon. The wife would knead the noodle dough with a bamboo pole or pipe, then roll it out with a knife and ruler into strips about 12 inches

long. She'd cook the saimin over a *hibachi* (charcoal brazier). The husband would push the little wagon to a likely place and set up shop for the day."

Saimin basics are a soup base of seaweed, dried shrimp, Japanese mushrooms, and bonito shavings. The noodles have more egg than Asian noodles. "Extras" are added, usually chopped green onion, sliced *kamaboko* (pink and white pinwheel fish cake), and strips of either Chinese *char siu* pork or Spam. Often there will be wonton dumplings, bok choy (Chinese cabbage), or bean sprouts. Actually, almost anything can, and does, go in. Shiro's serves a thousand bowls a day in 60 varieties at bargain prices.

The pièce de résistance of local food is the "plate lunch," which always consists of two scoops of white rice, a scoop of macaroni salad, and an entree of anything, but usually teriyaki meat, curry stew, *tonkatsu* (breaded, fried pork), or fried fish.

Portuguese sweet bread, and Filipino adobo (meat simmered in vinegar, garlic, and shoyu), —a culinary tradition called simply "local food," or endearingly "ono grinds," emerged.

Saimin

Probably the most popular and one of the few truly local creations is saimin. Burgers, hot dogs, and pizza are left in the dust in favor of this steaming noodle soup that is a remedy for everything from the flu to the blues. Some people claim it's a rube offspring of Chinese *wonton mein*. Others claim a distinguished Japanese lineage, a ramen gone native.

The man everyone calls "Mistah Saimin," Shiro Matsuo of Shiro's Hula Hula Drive In and Saimin Haven in Pearl City, Oahu, says,

Hawaii Regional Cuisine

Tourism initially gave local food a bad reputation. Hotel cooks slathered everything in sweet-sour sauce, added pineapples, topped the congealed mass with macadamia nuts, and declared it Hawaiian. It wasn't until the late 1980s that the first stirrings of a fine regional cuisine were felt, when Peter Merriman, chef de cuisine at the Gallery Restaurant, Mauna Lani Resort on the Big Island, noticed that his kitchen help often brought their own lunch to work. Invited to try, he liked it and began to experiment. Hawaii's fusion cuisine moved to the front burner.

In 1992, it came to a full rolling boil when the top-ranked chefs working in the Islands, many of them European, got together formally to promote "Hawaii Regional Cuisine" and to publish its first cookbook as a charity benefit.

Not only have these talented chefs raised "local food" to a culinary art form, they have revolutionized the agricultural industry, contracting with farmers to grow fruit, vegetables, and herbs in the quantity, quality, and variety needed to make the cuisine commercially viable.

Pineapple, long a hallmark of Hawaiian cooking, is thought to have been brought by Polynesian settlers from Tahiti.

A centerpiece of the new cuisine is seafood, the sweet-tasting, non-oily fish found in pure tropical waters. The most common found on menus are: *ahi* (yellowfin tuna), *kajiki* (Pacific blue marlin), mahimahi (dolphinfish, not the mammal), *onaga* (red snapper), *ono* (wahoo), opah (moonfish), *opakapaka* (pink snapper), and *ulua* (jackfish).

Fruits found in abundance in the Islands include: guava (grainy pink fruit with a hint of honey taste), *lilikoi* (passion fruit), lychee, mango (far superior to mangoes from elsewhere), mountain apple (crispy and tasting like a cross between a flower and an apple), papaya, pineapple (the sweetest are the small "sugarloafs"), and star fruit (carambola).

Coffee is harvested now on most Islands, but pure Kona coffee remains the standard against which all others are measured. Read the label when purchasing coffee: Some blends contain as little as 10 percent Kona coffee.

The luau

With food and wine festivals spilled all over the calendar, the premier feast on every visitor's menu remains the luau. People lament that they've gotten too big and too commercial. Well, they were always big. And they erupt for almost any reason—a wedding, graduation, political candidacy, fundraiser, *hula uniki* (graduation) or, the most popular, the "baby luau," to celebrate a child's first birthday. A baby luau was probably the first luau, and was given by Chief Hawaii Loa who came to Hawaii from Tahiti and set the feast to honor the birth of his daughter Mahealani.

American missionary Charles S. Stewart in 1823 described his first luau, given by King Liholiho to celebrate both Kamehameha Day and his own ascension to the throne. It lasted almost three weeks. "All the natives present wore the European costume ... Tameha-maru (Queen Kamamalu) in satin and lace sustained the part of mistress of ceremonies. She personally saw that no one of the company was in any degree neglected; and extended her kindness even to those who had no claim to special civility. For instance, seeing a crowd of American seamen…she immediately gave orders to have refreshments served to them."

Traditional luau fare centers around *kalua* pig, sweet potatoes, and *laulau* cooked in the *imu* (underground oven). Laulau are bundles of ti leaves encasing taro tops, pork, and fish. Some other dishes are *lomilomi* (salmon grated with onion and tomato), raw *ophihi* (limpet) and crab, *haupia* (coconut pudding) and *kulolo* (taro pudding), and, of course, poi. Today the traditional menu is augmented with everything from fried chicken to tossed salad. ■

Oahu is Hawaii's most sophisticated and urbanized island, with the capital city, Honolulu, and its resort of Waikiki. Yet beyond the suburban fringes, it remains an island of small towns, lonesome beaches, farms, and plantations.

Oahu

Waikiki sight-seeing trolley

Oahu

OAHU IS ONE OF THE MOST AMAZING ISLANDS IN ANY OCEAN. WAY OUT IN the middle of nowhere, where no land should reasonably be expected to exist, are high-rises; universities engaged in cutting-edge research; interstate freeways that connect to no other state; more than 800,000 busy residents; and 70,000 tourists a day in bright clothes tucked into almost 36,000 hotel rooms. The visitors are ready to play, counting on their dreams of paradise to materialize, while locals engage in a nightmare struggle to make ends meet at one of the most expensive addresses in the country.

Known as "The Gathering Place," Oahu is, at 608 square miles, the third largest of the Hawaiian Islands; it measures 44 miles long and 30 miles wide with 112 miles of coastline. It has two mountain ranges: The dramatic Koolau Mountains running north–south for almost the entire length of the island, and the older, rounder Waianae Range, with the island's tallest peak,

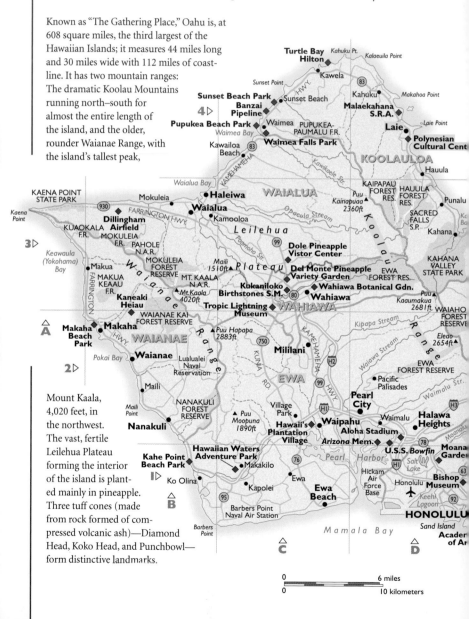

Mount Kaala, 4,020 feet, in the northwest. The vast, fertile Leilehua Plateau forming the interior of the island is planted mainly in pineapple. Three tuff cones (made from rock formed of compressed volcanic ash)—Diamond Head, Koko Head, and Punchbowl—form distinctive landmarks.

Waikiki surfing instructors can have a brand-new surfer up riding a wave in one wet lesson.

Diamond Head looms at the eastern end of Waikiki. The world-famous resort packs into its 681 acres 192 hotels and holiday condominiums, more than a thousand shops, about 500 restaurants, and more than 300 entertainment venues, all of which pump about five billion dollars into the state coffers.

Downtown Honolulu is the financial center of the Pacific. Women in flowing muumuu and men in aloha shirts flit among the steel and glass towers. At the center of the action is Bishop Street

with its banks and power structures, yet one end of the street trails off into green mountains, and the other has cruise ships bobbing at moorings.

Politically, the whole Island, plus the islets and atolls stretching 1,400 miles northwest to Kure Atoll, form the City and County of Honolulu, making this the world's longest city and the 11th largest city in the United States.

For all its frenetic activity, parts of Oahu are so wild and rugged that no road completely encircles the island. Windward Oahu is lush and green, some of it suburban, most of it dotted with farms and ranches. The North Shore is where the winter surf comes crashing ashore. Any time of year, the sunsets are magnificent.

Most of the state's cultural events, such as theater, opera, symphony, ballet, and art happen on Oahu. The top commercial tourist attractions are here, and this is where some of the most important moments in Island history unfolded. There are three national parks, 25 state parks, and 62 county parks. A hundred white-sand beaches soothe the island's sometimes harried soul. ■

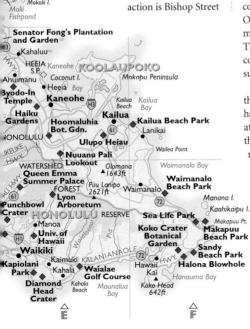

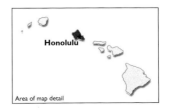

Honolulu

Area of map detail

Honolulu

Captain Cook sailed right by Oahu in the night, missing entirely the calm, deepwater harbor of Honolulu and the thatched fishing village of Kou, that would become one of the world's great cities.

Sixteen years after Captain Cook's 1778 miss, another English skipper, Capt. William Brown, aboard the H.M.S. *Jackal,* stumbled upon the bay, and renamed it Fair Haven, which coincidentally is synonymous with the name given to it by the people who lived there.

Word of Brown's wonderful bay spread quickly among the traders, and the little fishing village became a port dealing in guns, rum, furs, and sandalwood. Kamehameha I, after conquering Oahu, briefly took up residence in Honolulu in 1801, but, finding the city too loud and crowded, he and his court moved back to Kailua-Kona on the Big Island. Honolulu became the capital of the Hawaiian kingdom in 1845, when King Kamehameha III moved the seat of government from Maui.

Honolulu today is a pretty and pleasant city with the blue Pacific yawning away from its lap, and the jagged, mist-haunted cliffs of the Koolau rising behind. The rugged topography of the island places some limits on development; valley walls are so steep they defy builders. There is a conspicuous absence of billboards and aggressive signage. Art, trees, flowers, and water features are incorporated into building design. Open space is preserved in parks, conservation areas, and the Honolulu Watershed Forest Preserve, and citizen groups are vigilant in trying to protect viewplanes, shorelines, and natural areas.

The city is probably the only place in the world where East truly meets West, not just with tolerance, but with understanding and appreciation. James Michener said that a Honolulu citizen is "a man at home in either the business councils of New York or the philosophical retreats of Kyoto." ■

The Aloha Tower Marketplace, once the tallest building in the state, overlooks downtown Honolulu and the waterfront.

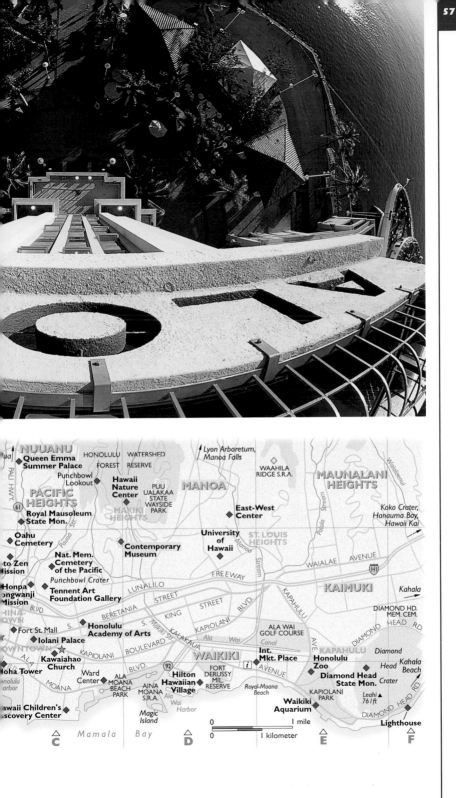

NUUANU
Queen Emma
Summer Palace
HONOLULU WATERSHED
FOREST RESERVE
Lyon Arboretum,
Manoa Falls
WAAHILA
RIDGE S.R.A.
MAUNALANI
HEIGHTS

Punchbowl
Lookout
Hawaii
Nature
Center
PUU
UALAKAA
STATE
WAYSIDE
PARK
MANOA

PACIFIC
HEIGHTS
Royal Mausoleum
State Mon.
MAKIKI
HEIGHTS
East-West
Center
Koko Crater,
Hanauma Bay,
Hawaii Kai

Oahu
Cemetery
Contemporary
Museum
University
of
Hawaii
ST. LOUIS
HEIGHTS

to Zen
Mission
Nat. Mem.
Cemetery
of the Pacific
WAIALAE   AVENUE
KAIMUKI
Kahala

Honpa
ongwanji
Mission
Punchbowl Crater
Tennent Art
Foundation Gallery
LUNALILO
STREET
STREET
KAPAHULU
DIAMOND HD.
MEM. CEM.

BLVD.
BERETANIA
KING
STREET
BLVD.
HEAD RD.

Fort St. Mall
S.
Honolulu
Academy of Arts
Ala   Wai
KAPIOLANI
ALA WAI
GOLF COURSE
DIAMOND
Diamond

Iolani Palace
BOULEVARD
WAIKIKI
Int.
Mkt. Place
KAPAHULU
Honolulu
Zoo
Head
Kahala
Beach

Kawaiahao
Church
KAPIOLANI
AVENUE
Diamond Head
State Mon.
Crater

oha Tower
Ward
Center
ALA
MOANA
BEACH
PARK
BLVD.
Hilton
Hawaiian
Village
FORT
DERUSSY
MIL.
RESERVE
Royal-Moana
Beach
KAPIOLANI
PARK
Leahi ▲
761ft

awaii Children's
scovery Center
AINA
MOANA
S.R.A.
Ala
Wai
Harbor
Waikiki
Aquarium
DIAMOND HEAD RD.
Lighthouse

Magic
Island
0   1 mile
0   1 kilometer
Mamala   Bay
C   D   E   F

Iolani Palace

IOLANI PALACE IS THE SYMBOLIC AND EMOTIONAL HEART of Hawaii. Any understanding of the cultural renaissance and political forces shaping the Islands today must begin here. Even the name, translated as "hawk of heaven," resonates with meaning. The *io* is the highest-soaring Hawaiian bird, said to fly to commune with the gods.

The cornerstone of the palace was laid December 31, 1879, on the birthday of Queen Kapiolani, wife of King Kalakaua, who commissioned the construction.

Iolani took three years to complete and cost $343,595 furnished; the nine-year restoration, completed in 1978, cost seven million dollars. The building was described in newspaper accounts of the day as "American Florentine." It is crowned with a French mansard roof, embellished with Victorian flourishes and Greek columns, but all rooted in Hawaiian cultural expression and modified for the tropical climate. It is two stories high with a basement and attic, and has wide lanais (verandas).

The approach

With skyscrapers rising around it, Iolani sits like a lovely reprimand in the midst of commerce. Four gates open into the tree-bowered grounds. The **Kauikeaouli Gate** on King Street, once used for state occasions, is the entrance used by most visitors. The coat of arms on the gate is one of eight cast in bronze at England's Royal College

Iolani Palace

- 🏔 57 C2
- ✉ S. King & Richards Sts.
- ☎ 808/522-0832
- 🕐 Closed p.m. Tues.–Sat. & all day Sun. & Mon.
- 💲 $$$ (No children under 5)
- 🚌 TheBus 2 or 13

Coronation Pavilion   Blue Room

The Throne Room at Iolani Palace has been magnificently restored. Great balls and dramas unfolded in this room.

of Arms. They contain the kingdom's motto, now the state's, *"Ua mau keia o ka aina i ka pono"* ("The life of the land is preserved in righteousness"). They were the first items removed from the palace, stripped on the very day of the 1893 overthrow of the monarchy, and like everything else that could be pried loose and carried away, they were eventually sold.

The approach to the palace is lined with royal palms. A broad staircase leads to the wide lanai and front entrance: Note the palm tree motif on top of the bright white Corinthian columns. The etched glass doors, made in San Francisco, depict a hula dancer with incongruously Caucasian features, taro

plants, and, as a nice aesthetic but irrelevant touch, Easter lilies. The ornate nickel door hardware with "no-peek" keyholes is from Germany. Windows are high and have 52,000 wooden shutters to admit and control the prevailing trade winds. During the restoration, 28,000 shutters had to be replaced primarily due to termite damage.

To your right, in a corner of the grounds, is a **fenced mound** that was once the royal tomb. In 1865, in a solemn torchlight procession, the bodies were removed to the new Royal Mausoleum in Nuuanu (see p. 68). It is believed that the bones of some chiefs still reside beneath the mound.

To your left is the copper-domed **Coronation Pavilion** built for the coronation ceremonies of King Kalakaua and Queen Kapiolani, and now used for band concerts every Friday at noon. Behind that are the **Iolani Barracks,** where tour tickets, which should be reserved ahead, are purchased. It's a good idea to arrive in time to see the dramatic

Upper Hall

Koa staircase

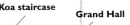

Grand Hall

Throne Room

Queen Liliuokalani succeeded her brother King David Kalakaua to the throne. She married her childhood sweetheart, John Owen Dominis, son of an American sea captain. After the 1893 coup, she campaigned vigorously to restore Hawaii's constitutional monarchy, and she continued to reign in the hearts of her people until her death in 1917. She bequeathed her wealth to Hawaiian children, through the Queen Liliuokalani Children's Trust.

20-minute film about the palace and the monarchy.

The interior

Visitors assemble on the rear lanai, where you will be asked to remove your shoes and put on bootees. After a brief talk, you are swept into the **Grand Hall,** as silent, gleaming, and lovely as a church. The glowing woods are fine native hardwoods— koa, *kamani, kou,* and ohia—augmented by cedar, black walnut, and bird's-eye maple. Chinese and English urns are tucked in carved niches, and portraits of Hawaiian royalty line the walls.

You are escorted into the **Blue Room.** From here Queen Liliuokalani could see armed U.S. Marines taking up position, and it was here she surrendered her kingdom. William Cogswell's portraits of the queen and her brother King Kalakaua grace the walls. The adjoining **Dining Room** is set for a formal dinner with French china, English sterling silver, and colored Bavarian crystal.

In the **bathroom,** the queen's copper-lined tub is 6.5 feet long, the king's 7 feet. Iolani was the first palace in the world to install flush toilets. It had the first telephone system in Honolulu and had electricity before the White House, Windsor Castle, or the Imperial Palace of Japan.

A magnificent koa staircase leads to the upper floor living quarters. The **King's Bedroom** contains a photograph of the room as it was when King Kalakaua lived in it. When the palace reopened to the public, it was almost empty of furniture, but since then, nearly half of the original furnishings have been returned. Still missing is the king's ebony-and-gold bed. A goat-footed Meissen jardiniere is one of the palace's most valuable pieces. The

adjoining **King's Office** is completely furnished and contains rare books, including one he wrote himself, *Legends and Myths of Hawaii.* A wooden table that forms the centerpiece of the **Gold Room** is the only piece of furniture that never left the palace.

Across the hall is the room that no one is ever quite prepared for, especially after the opulence of all the other rooms. **Queen Liliuokalani's Room** is austerely furnished with two cots, two chairs, and two tables. It was here the queen was imprisoned after the coup in 1893. The shutters are closed as they were ordered to be for her, so her people could not see her in the window. In the dim light, she composed the elegiac song "The Queen's Prayer," and worked on a silk quilt (on display under glass in the room). Into it, the queen stitched her beloved Hawaiian flag and the names of friends who remained loyal to her.

The **Throne Room,** with its sweep of red and gold presided over by two gilt thrones, retains all the pomp of state. A seven-foot narwhal tusk topped with a gold sphere was used as a traditional *puloulou* (tabu stick to create inviolate space around the king). Here King Kalakaua gave fabulous balls, and Queen Liliuokalani was tried for treason by the men who seized her government.

The tour ends in the basement **Gallery,** newly open to the public. Here the crown jewels of Hawaii are on view along with a collection of ancient calabashes and *kahili.* You also tour the kitchen where dinners were prepared for the many formal parties upstairs.

After Queen Liliuokalani's overthrow, Iolani Palace was used as a capitol by the ensuing governments, until the state capitol was completed in 1969 (see p. 61). ∎

State Capitol

This architectural gem, completed in 1969 across Beretania Street from Washington Place, is textured with symbolism: Columns look like palm trees, a major source of food, water, and building supplies; legislative chambers are shaped like volcanoes; and the central courtyard is open to the sky, denoting Hawaii's open society. Support pillars on the top floor are grouped in eights, representing the eight Hawaiian Islands, while other parts of the building appear in fours, to represent the four counties (Hawaii, Kauai, Oahu, Maui). The complex is surrounded by reflecting pools as the Islands are surrounded by water.

A statue of Queen Liliuokalani stands between the capitol and Iolani Palace. In front is a statue of Father Damien (see p. 213), who devoted his life to victims of Hansen's Disease (leprosy), sculpted in 1969 by Venezuelan sculptress Marisol Escobar. ∎

Distinguished by its symbolic architecture, the State Capitol stands at the gateway to downtown Honolulu.

State Capitol

🅰 Map p. 63
✉ Beretania & Richards Sts.
☎ 808/586-0178
🕐 Tours by appt.
🚌 TheBus 2

Washington Place

Queen Liliuokalani once lived in the stately, two-story Greek Revival house and, until 2002, it served as the Hawaii gubanatorial residence. Named in honor of the first U.S. President, Washington Place was built between 1842 and 1846 by Capt. John Dominis, a New England trader and the queen's father-in-law. As a private citizen, Queen Liliuokalani returned to live in the house, until her death in 1917. Currently being prepared to open as a museum, it contains many beautiful pieces of her furniture, jewelry, and other royal possessions. The most prized treasures are the queen's musical instruments. Her massive grand piano was built of koa logs that had been shipped from Kamuela, on the Big Island, to New York's Fisher Company. ∎

Washington Place

🅰 Map p. 63
✉ 320 S. Beretania St.
☎ 808/536-8040 for updates

A WALK AROUND HISTORIC HONOLULU

A walk around historic Honolulu

Be seduced by gentle trade winds breezing through flowering trees as you take your sweet Hawaiian time walking around a city that's never in a hurry.

Every year on Kamehameha Day, June 11, enormous leis festoon the statue of Hawaii's great king.

Begin at **Mission Houses Museum ❶** *(553 S. King St., tel 808/531-0481)*. The complex includes the home of the first Yankee missionaries (see pp. 30–31), and a printing press. Cross crooked little Kawaiahao Street to **Kawaiahao Church ❷** *(tel 808/522-1333)*, built of 14,000 large coral blocks cut from the reef with shark-tooth saws. Dedicated in 1842,

it was designed by Yankee missionary Rev. Hiram Bingham. Royalty worshiped here and special seating is still reserved for their descendants. Sunday services *(10:30 a.m.)* are conducted in English and Hawaiian. You can stay for breakfast for a small offering. The tomb of King Lunalilo is just inside the main church gate.

Cross King Street to **Honolulu Hale ❸**, city hall, built in 1927 by a team of architects including C.W. Dickey and Hart Wood. The courtyard, stairs, speaker's balcony, and open ceiling were modeled after the 13th-century Bargello palace in Florence, Italy. Note the ceiling frescoes. The building west of Honolulu Hale, is the **Hawaii State Library ❹**, which was a gift from philanthropist Andrew Carnegie and designed by his brother-in-law Henry D. Whitfield. When it opened in 1912, the first two books checked out were *The Government of Our Cities* by W.B. Munro, and *The Greatest Thing in the World* by Henry Drummond. Honolulu's first public library, opened in 1879, was intended to be a substitute for saloons. The library flourished, but so did the saloons. At the start, it had 130 volumes, and women were not admitted, although this ban was soon lifted.

Cross busy King Street to the gilt-robed **Kamehameha I Statue ❺**, the king who united the Hawaiian Islands into one nation. The original bronze, cast in Italy in 1883, by American sculptor Thomas B. Gould, was lost at sea, so this duplicate was made. Shortly after its arrival in Honolulu, the original statue was found in the Falkland Islands and now stands in the little town of Kapaau on the Big Island (see p. 158).

Cross King Street again to **Iolani Palace ❻** (see pp. 58–60). Stroll the shady grounds to the huge century-old banyan tree. Behind it is the ungracious **Hawaii State Archives,** worth a visit for the exhibit of vintage photographs just inside the front entrance. On the other side of the palace is **Iolani Barracks.**

Exit the palace grounds and cross to the **Queen Liliuokalani Statue,** sculpted in

1982 by Marianna Pineda. The queen's hand always holds fresh flowers, placed there daily by admirers. Proceed up the steps of the **State Capitol ❼** (see p. 61), then take the elevator to the second floor for impressive views. In front of the building is a **statue of Father Damien,** the martyr priest of Molokai (see pp. 61 and 213).

The white mansion set among big trees is **Washington Place** (see p. 61), residence of Hawaii's governor. Next door is **St. Andrew's Cathedral ❽** (tel 808/524-2822), dedicated in 1867. The Anglo-Norman building was designed in England, and much of the construction material, including the sandstone building blocks, was shipped from that country. King Kamehameha IV, and his wife Queen Emma, who supervised the building, were Anglophiles, impressed by the pomp of Church of England rituals which they encountered in London.

Across Beretania Street, down one block and fronting the Fort Street Mall, you'll find the **Cathedral of Our Lady of Peace ❾** (tel 808/536-7036). Built by French Catholic

missionaries in 1843, it houses the Islands' first pipe organ. The interior underwent a controversial remodeling a few years ago, erasing the delicate old atmosphere. Father Damien (see left) was ordained here.

Fort Street, hub of Honolulu's business district, is a pedestrian mall abounding in eclectic take-out eateries. Dine on benches and watch the parade of people. If you're lucky someone will be strumming a ukulele; if you're not, someone will try to save your soul. ∎

🚶 Also see map, p. 57 C2
▶ Mission Houses Museum
↔ 1 mile
🕐 2.5 hours
▶ Fort Street Mall

NOT TO BE MISSED
- Mission Houses Museum
- Kawaiahao Church
- Kamehameha I Statue
- Iolani Palace

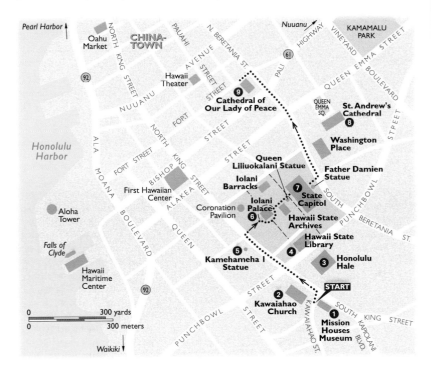

The Honolulu waterfront is a busy mix of commercial shipping, recreation, and the activities of a colorful fishing fleet.

Honolulu Harbor

FISHING BOATS, TUGS, CONTAINER SHIPS, CRUISE LINERS trace a skein of white wakes in the peacock water of this busy port. Honolulu Harbor has been sheltering boats for 12 centuries, but it was after Captain Cook put Hawaii on the world map that it became a commercial harbor. Here, fur traders swapped otter pelts from the Pacific Northwest of America for teas, spices, and silks in transit from China. When a particularly fragrant sandalwood was noticed in Hawaii's forests, a brisk trade flourished until the Islands were denuded of the wood. The whalers were next, and Honolulu became the largest whaling port in the world. Today, the wharfs handle cargo for a burgeoning, sophisticated American city.

Aloha Tower

- 57 C1
- Pier 9
- 808/566-2337
- Closed 9 p.m. Mon.–Sat., 6 p.m. Sun. Observation Deck closed 7 p.m. in summer, 6 p.m. in winter
- TheBus 19, 20, 55, 56, 57

The **Aloha Tower,** designed by architect Arthur Reynolds, was the tallest building on the island when it opened in 1926. At 184 feet high with a 40-foot flagstaff, it was the pride of the Pacific. Its seven-ton clock was the largest ever made by Howard Clark Company of Boston, and its light beamed 19 miles out to sea. The largest, most modern pier complex in the Pacific welcomed tourists arriving aboard luxury liners. On "Boat Day," when the ships docked, local residents flocked to the piers to sell leis, dive for coins, and get their mail; there was music and hula, and flowers everywhere.

The Aloha Tower today is the hub of a smart complex of shops and waterfront restaurants. It hums with activity at sunset. There's a food court catering to international tastes, a microbrewery that offers free tastings, and music and dancing around every turn. Ships still ply the waters, and the cruise liners sail away with flower-draped passengers singing "Aloha Oe." Don't miss the panoramic views from the observation deck.

Across the water at Pier 7, just behind the fully rigged sailing ship *Falls of Clyde,* is the **Hawaii Maritime Center,** which opened in 1988. A humpback whale skeleton hangs from the ceiling, and antique Hawaiian canoes dangle from the rafters. Through interactive exhibits, you can discover Hawaii's long love affair with the ocean, which was the highway of the ancients; you can even chart your own star course to faraway isles.

The ***Falls of Clyde,*** moored at the doorstep, is the world's last full-rigged four-masted sailing ship. Built in Scotland in 1898, it sailed under the Hawaiian flag and then the American. Stroll its decks and feel the ship groaning at its mooring lines in the thrall of the tides.

If it's in port, the famous ***Hokulea*** will be tied up here, too. Launched in 1976 under the auspices of the Polynesian Voyaging Society, this reproduction of an ancient voyaging canoe continues to make historic trips throughout the Pacific, retracing legendary migration routes. The most recent journey was in 1999 to Rapa Nui (Easter Island). ■

Hawaii Maritime Center
- Map p. 63
- Pier 7
- 808/536-6373
- $

The Aloha Tower beckons people at sunset to enjoy its lively shops, restaurants, and music venues.

Don Ho

Hawaii's most famous entertainer, Don Ho, is still a draw. Known as much for kissing grandmothers smack on the lips as for crooning "Tiny Bubbles," he still holds forth in Waikiki, where he has his own show at the Waikiki Beachcomber Hotel *(tel 808/922-4646)*. He also owns a restaurant, Don Ho's Island Grill (see p. 243) at Aloha Tower Marketplace. Born in 1930, Don Ho spent his boyhood in the back of his mother's famous bar, Honey's (no longer open), in Kaneohe on Oahu's Windward Side, where all the top Hawaiian entertainers of the day dropped in and jammed. The same thing is happening now at the Grill. The atmosphere is tropical tacky—bad enough to be good. They serve big, slushy drinks with umbrellas, and food such as coconut-crusted shrimp and egg rolls. You never know who will stop by with a ukulele, and a little sister or grandmother to dance. And there's always the chance the smoothie himself will appear, slide up to the mike and weave his old magic. ■

Shoppers come from all over the island for Chinatown's food. Here workers prepare duck.

A walk around Honolulu's Chinatown

A morning walk in the slightly seamy enclave of Chinatown is best, when shoppers bustle and bicker, and the produce and flowers are freshest. Chinese settlers still come from Taiwan and Hong Kong, but many businesses are now owned by Vietnamese, Laotians, Koreans, Thai, and Filipinos, resulting in a scene that is colorful and dynamic. The city has recently pumped more than 230 million dollars into improvements.

Your walk begins on the corner of King Street and Kekaulike Street with instant immersion into color and delightful chaos of a typical Asian market. The open-air **Oahu Market** ❶ is crammed with fresh fish, some still swimming in buckets, tropical flowers, local fruit, *char siu* hanging ducks, thousand-year-old eggs, and vegetables of every stripe. Cross King Street and continue left to **Yat Tung Chow Noodle Factory** ❷ *(150 N. King St.)* and watch as noodles roll out of the noodle machine amid clouds of flour, destined for city restaurants. Just a little farther on the left, you'll come to the **Viet Hoa Chinese Herb Shop** *(162 N. King St.)*. Walls of tiny drawers and rows of scary-looking jars are the backbone of a sophisticated natural pharmacopeia dating back thousands of years.

At River Street, turn right, toward the mountains, enjoying the view. Cross Hotel Street, once notorious for its fleshpots, but late-

ly gentrified with shops and galleries, and keep going until the street becomes a pedestrian mall with more shops and some of the best Asian restaurants in town. Lunch lines start at 11 a.m. At the head of the mall is a **statue of Sun Yat-Sen** ❸ (1866–1925), who was educated in Hawaii and here hatched his plans for the Chinese Revolution in 1911. On the far side of the stream is a statue honoring José Rizal (1861–1896), a hero of the Philippines.

You'll be passing the **Chinatown Cultural Plaza** ❹, with more shops and restaurants around a central courtyard. Locals flock to **Legend Seafood Restaurant** *(100 N. Beretania St., Ste. 108, tel 808/532-1868* for dim sum, the delicate dumplings of China. Sit down while waitresses wheel carts to your table stacked with bamboo steamer baskets of dim sum, stuffed perhaps with scallops and chives, spicy pork hash, or shrimp. After dining, you may want to give thanks at the little shrine on the third floor of the plaza, the **Chee Kung Tong Shrine.**

Stroll over the Kukui Street Bridge to **Izuma Taishakyo Mission Shrine ❺,** Hawaii's oldest Shinto shrine, built without a single nail in classic Japanese temple architecture. Visitors are welcome, but please remove your shoes after entering beneath the torii gate.

🅼 Also see map, p. 57 C2
► North King St. (Sea Fortune restaurant)
↔ 2.5 miles
🕒 3 hours depending on dining and browsing
► Maunakea & King Sts.

NOT TO BE MISSED
- Oahu Market
- Chinatown Cultural Plaza
- Kuan Yin Temple
- New Lin Fong Confectioners

A statue of Sun Yat-Sen stands in Chinatown. The father of the Chinese Revolution was educated in Hawaii.

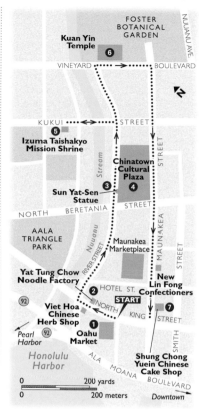

If you haven't had enough of shrines, continue up River Street to Vineyard Boulevard, cross and turn right for the incense-laden **Kuan Yin Temple ❻** with its jade-colored tile roof and flamboyant architecture. The interior sanctuary is dominated by a 10-foot statue of the Buddhist goddess of mercy.

Continue right on Vineyard Boulevard to Maunakea Street and turn right. If you have opted out of the temple, just turn right on South Kukui Street to Maunakea Street and turn right. Maunakea is lined with lei vendors weaving and stringing their fragrant wares. The **Shung Chong Yuein Chinese Cake Shop ❼** (*1027 Maunakea St.*) has bins of candied fruits such as papaya and lotus. **New Lin Fong Confectioners** (*1132 Maunakea St.*) will ambush your diet with custard pies and peanut rice squares. If you continue on down Maunakea Street you will come to King Street, where the walk began. ∎

Nuuanu Valley

CAUGHT UP IN THE URBAN RUSH OF OAHU, IT'S EASY TO
miss the stunning beauty of the island's green valleys. Nuuanu Valley,
whose name means "cool height," stretches from the edge of
Honolulu to the Koolau Mountains, and in its folds early Hawaiians
and the first foreign settlers chose to build homes.

The gates to the Royal Mausoleum bear the royal coat of arms. The motto translates as: "The life of the land is preserved in righteousness."

Royal Mausoleum
- 57 C3
- 2261 Nuuanu Ave.
- 808/587-2590
- Closed Sat.–Sun.
- TheBus 4

Today you can drive the **Pali Highway** right along the valley to a tunnel through the mountains to the **Windward Side** (see pp. 98–99). Along the way, look for "upside-down" waterfalls, cascades blown upward by strong winds barreling through the pass. At the top of the pass, a well-marked exit leads to the **Nuuanu Pali Lookout** and one of the most spectacular views in Hawaii. Below is Windward Oahu with **Kailua** and **Kaneohe Bays.** Here Kamehameha the Great defeated the defenders of Oahu, driving them over the cliffs. In the rush of wind, you can almost hear the howls.

The **Royal Mausoleum State Monument** in the lush foothills of the valley is the final resting place for all Hawaii's

monarchs but two: Kamehameha I, whose bones were buried in secret according to ancient rites, and Lunalilo, who asked to be interred at Kawaiahao Church (see p. 62). The site, which flies only the Hawaiian flag, is considered sacred. Visitors are welcome to this peaceful oasis, surrounded by royal palms, gated with the royal coat of arms, and cradling the bones of kings. If the chapel is open, stop in to see the rich koa-wood interior and ponder the course of nations.

The father of America's favorite sport, baseball, lies in nearby **Oahu Cemetery** *(2162 Nuuanu Ave.),* beneath a tombstone bearing the inscription "Alexander Joy Cartwright Jr. Born in New York City April 17, 1820. Died in Honolulu July 12, 1892." After creating the game and launching it in Hoboken, New Jersey, in 1846, Cartwright sailed to the Islands, founded Honolulu's first fire volunteer company, and served as chief. Other noted departed include Martha Root, apologist for the Bahai faith, several Isle governors, missionaries, sea skippers, sugar barons, and casualties of the attack on Pearl Harbor in 1941 (see p. 35).

Two outstanding Buddhist temples reside in Nuuanu. The brilliant white **Honpa Hongwanji Mission** *(1727 Pali Hwy.)* was built in 1819 for the 700th anniversary of the Shin Buddhist sect. The **Soto Zen Mission** *(1708 Nuuanu Ave.),* is a faithful copy of the stupa in India where Gautama Buddha first spoke about Enlightenment. ∎

Queen Emma Summer Palace

MORE A HOME THAN A PALACE, THE SUMMER PALACE'S real name is Hanaiakamalama, after a goddess who was the foster child of the moon. King Kamehameha IV, Queen Emma, and their little son Prince Albert would retreat here from the heat of the city to the cool uplands of Nuuanu. Built in 1848, and now on the National Register of Historic Places, the airy Greek Revival house, whose frame was built in Boston and shipped around the Horn, has a long Hawaiian lanai and is shaded by huge century-old trees, including a mango planted on the royal wedding day and still bearing fruit.

The beautifully restored house holds probably the finest exhibited collection of Hawaiian furniture. There are crystal chandeliers overhead and *lauhala* mats underfoot. The canoe-shaped koa-wood cradle with its wave-patterned overlay in *kou* wood was commissioned by the king in anticipation of the birth of his heir and is now a state treasure.

Among the notable palace exhibits are a well-preserved feather cape; *kahili* (feathered royal standards); the queen's fan collection, hair combs, and jewelry, including a locket with Queen Victoria's hair; and poignant gifts to the prince who didn't survive his fourth year—a ceramic child's bath from the emperor of China, and a silver christening vase from his godmother Queen Victoria.

This is a home that shows in its details the graciousness, hospitality, elegance, and desperate sadness of the monarchy era of Hawaii. ■

Queen Emma Summer Palace

⚠ 57 C3

✉ 2913 Pali Hwy. (Hawaii 61)

☎ 808/595-6291

$ $$

🚌 TheBus 4

The Queen Emma Summer Palace in Nuuanu is a remnant of the gracious age of the Hawaiian monarchy.

An authentic grass house stands in the center of Hawaiian Hall at the Bishop Museum.

Bishop Museum

IF EVER A MUSEUM LOOKED LIKE A MUSEUM THIS IS IT. THE Romanesque-style main building, built from ominous-seeming lava rock, is festooned in solemnity. Charles Reed Bishop, husband of Princess Bernice Pauahi Bishop (see p. 33), built the museum in 1892 to showcase the treasures of the Kamehameha dynasty and to "enrich and delight" the people of Hawaii. It has become the foremost museum of Polynesian culture in the world. The museum's numbers are staggering: 13 million insects, 6,481,000 zoology specimens, 442,000 botany specimens, 90,000 books, and half a million cultural objects.

Bishop Museum

- 🗺 57 B2
- ✉ 1525 Bernice St. (just off Likelike Hwy., Hawaii 63)
- ☎ 808/847-3511
- 💲 $$
- 🚌 TheBus 2

The forbidding facade is forgotten once you're inside the door and confronted with the museum's riches. The first room is the cavernous **Hawaiian Hall** with three floors of gallery exhibits around a center space as long as a football field. The skeleton of a 55-foot

sperm whale hangs overhead, and a traditional grass house from Kauai sits in honored loneliness in the middle. This is where you will encounter the gods and people of ancient Hawaii in their authenticity. Because of space constraints and the delicacy of objects, it's hard to

say exactly which treasures will be on display when you visit. The golden feather cape of Kamehameha the Great, for instance, has a projected exhibition life of only nine years—by limiting display to one month a year, it will last another century.

Other Pacific cultures are celebrated in **Polynesian Hall,** with examples of ceremonial clothing, painted masks, and vintage photographs. Upstairs, in the **Hall of Hawaiian Natural History,** follow the evolution of the Islands as they emerged from the ocean, sprang into bloom, and supported life; then follow exhibits on the epic voyages of the Polynesian mariners in the **Cooke Rotunda.** You can trace their sky maps in the **planetarium's** presentations. Children love the **Hall of Discovery,**

where the birds, bones, plants, and shells are all meant to be handled.

Castle Hall, opened in 1989, houses a series of changing displays that often venture farther afield than the Pacific. One of the most popular of these has been an interactive dinosaur exhibit.

A recent innovation is the **Back-of-the-House Tour** *(Mon.–Fri.; reservations required).* A cultural expert takes you behind the scenes at the museum, opening drawers and closets of delicate artifacts, some too fragile to exhibit. The tour changes daily, depending on the guide. Often chanting and ritual is involved in viewing the more sacred objects.

There are also daily hula performance at 1 p.m. in the Hawaiian Hall, and sharing of Hawaiian crafts such as leimaking and quilting. ■

Fierce wooden images of deities, such as Kukailimoku, the war god, displayed at the Bishop Museum, characterize Hawaiian religious art.

Honolulu neighborhoods

FINGERING INTO DEEP GREEN VALLEYS, CLIMBING impossible looking hills, and lazing along the shore, the neighborhoods of Honolulu are so distinct that when a person indicates which one they live in, you can picture what their house looks like, know which fruit trees thrive in their yard, figure which restaurants they frequent, and guess their income.

A formal Japanese garden graces the grounds of the University of Hawaii, Manoa.

KAIMUKI

A century-old working-class neighborhood of small homes with front porches, Kaimuki has the sweetest mangoes on the island. The main street, hilly Waialae Avenue, is retro 1940s revved up as an impromptu "restaurant row," with chop suey houses, saimin (noodle soup) restaurants, boomer coffee shops, authentic East Coast pizza at **Boston Pizza** (*3506 Waialae Ave., tel 808/734-1945*), and a number of good restaurants, among them **3660 On The Rise** (*3660 Waialae Ave., tel 808/737-1177*). Determined—and lucky—shoppers may find vintage aloha shirts, muumuus, or valuable Hawaiian kitsch in the many thrift shops. The 18-seat **Movie Museum** (*3566 Harding Ave., tel 808/735-8771*) screens old films such as *Blue Gardenia*. It's so right for this vintage neighborhood with its 1920s and 1930s storefronts.

KAPAHULU

Hugging the hem of Diamond Head, Kapahulu borders Waikiki. Kapahulu Avenue is another string of restaurants, mostly ethnic and inexpensive. People pack into **Kanak Attack** (*756 Palani Ave., tel 808/739-5732*), a small, hot hole-in-the-wall for industrial-strength Hawaiian food. Nearby, you can drop in for a lesson in feather lei making from master artist Aunty Mary Lou Kekuewa at her shop **Na Lima Mili Hulu Noeau** (*762 Kapahulu Ave., tel 808/732-0865*). If you didn't have any luck in Kaimuki's thrift shops, you'll definitely find vintage and reproduction aloha wear and dust collectors at **Bailey's Antiques and Aloha Shirts** (*517 Kapahulu Ave., tel 808/734-7628*). On the corner of

Kapahulu and Kihei Avenues is a small carriage-trade mall with more antique shops and fashion boutiques. Don't pass **Leonard's Bakery** *(933 Kapahulu Ave., tel 808/737-5591)* without stopping for hot *malasadas*, a Portuguese fried donut that's a local passion.

MANOA

The streets of Manoa are lined with big old houses and bigger old trees. The 300-acre **University of Hawaii campus** sits at the mouth of the cool, verdant valley. At the Visitor & Information Center you can pick up a map and find out what's going on in the way of cultural and artistic exhibits and performances not only on campus but around town. Hour-long tours of the campus are conducted Monday, Wednesday, and Friday at 2 p.m. The center's bookstore and art gallery are worth a visit. Wander through the sprawling **East-West Center,** a federally funded think tank to promote accord between the United States and the Asia-Pacific Basin. An authentic, solid teak Thai pavilion

was personally presented by King Bhumibol Adulyadej in 1967; the hand-painted Center for Korean Studies was inspired by the Yi-dynasty style of Kyongbok Palace in Seoul. Stone Chinese temple dogs stand sentinel outside **Thomas Jefferson Hall,** while behind the hall is a tranquil Japanese garden gladdened by a meandering stream filled with prize ornamental koi (carp). Along the stream are two stone lanterns, one a priceless 400-year-old traveler's lantern, and a nine-tiered stone pagoda sits near the highest waterfall. There are guided tours of the center with its murals, hangings, gardens, and sculpture.

Way in the back of Manoa Valley, at the very end of Manoa Road, opposite **Lyon Arboretum** (see pp. 80–81), is the trailhead for **Manoa Falls,** which is fed by 200 inches of rain a year. The 0.75-mile trail snakes through the thick, lush rain forest, crossing streams and ending at the plunge pool for the falls; the muddiest parts are covered in boardwalk. Be sure and stay on the trail. ■

You can enjoy splendid views of Honolulu from the many hiking trails in the mountains above the city.

University of Hawaii
- 🅰 57 D2
- ✉ University & Dole Aves.
- 🚌 TheBus 4

Visitor & Information Center
- ✉ 2465 Campus Rd.
- ☎ 808/956-7235
- 🕐 Closed Sat. p.m. & Sun.

East-West Center
- ✉ 1777 East-West Rd.
- ☎ 808/944-7111
- 🕐 Closed Sat.–Sun.

Honolulu Academy of Arts

FROM THE START, THE HONOLULU ACADEMY OF ARTS, JUST east of downtown, was mandated by its unique location, far from the art centers of the world, to become a leading art institution.

For a museum of its size, the quality of the collection is extraordinary. The **Asian galleries,** to the left of the main entrance, are especially notable, and because their treasures, such as scrolls and screens, are more perishable, they were the first to be overhauled. In the process, three new galleries were added, the **Watumull Gallery of Indian Art,** the **Christiansen Gallery of Indonesian Art,** and the **George and Nancy Ellis**

The galleries of the Honolulu Academy of Arts have been modernized to mitigate the effects of the climate on the works of art. Right: This 11th-century statue of Kuan Yin, the Buddhist goddess of mercy, is one of the most loved pieces in the Asian galleries.

It was a member of the missionary-descendant Cooke family, Mrs. Charles (Anna) Montague Cooke (1853–1934), whose vision and family generosity launched the academy. She felt it was imperative for Hawaii's children, growing up thousands of miles from the nearest art museums, to have access to fine works of art. The design was a collaboration between New York architect Bertram Goodhue, the Cooke family, and Hardie Phillip, who completed the project after Goodhue's death.

Opened in 1927 to the strains of a concert by the Royal Hawaiian Band, the building itself has come to be regarded as a Hawaiian classic, with galleries flowing into courtyards, all of it looking a little Spanish, a little Florentine. You no sooner climb the front steps and enter than you are outdoors again, as spectacular flower arrangements grace the airy stone corridors. Unfortunately, the weather has taken a toll on the collection and the academy has begun a "climate control" program to protect its many magnificent works.

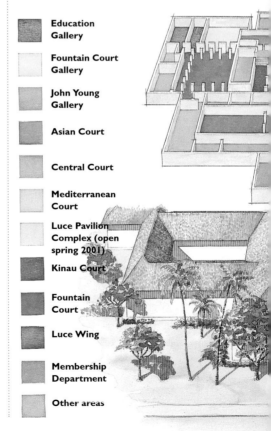

Education Gallery

Fountain Court Gallery

John Young Gallery

Asian Court

Central Court

Mediterranean Court

Luce Pavilion Complex (open spring 2001)

Kinau Court

Fountain Court

Luce Wing

Membership Department

Other areas

Gallery of Filipino Arts. Japanese works include 13th-century scrolls, a 14th-century samurai suit of armor, a seventh-century gold-and-silver basket for strewing lotus petals, and the James Michener collection of *ukiyo-e* woodblock prints. There are Indonesian masks, tribal weavings, third- and fourth-century sculptures from India, and a few examples of Philippine *santos*, wooden carvings of saints from the early Spanish settlement period.

Honolulu Academy of Arts

57 C2
900 S. Beretania St.
808/532-8700
Closed Mon.
$$. Free 1st Wed. of each month

The **Chinese painting collection** in galleries 15, 16a and 16b, boasts one of the finest Ming and Qing painting collections in America. "The Coming of Autumn" was named by James Cahill in *The Compelling Image,* his book on

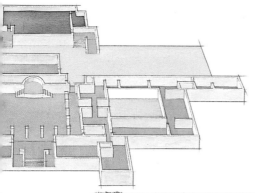

Eastern art, as the finest surviving masterpiece by the great Chinese painter, Hong Ren (1610–1663).

While the **Western collections,** to the right of the main entrance, are not as strong or deep as the Asian, there are some remarkable works, including a room of French Impressionism—including van Gogh's "Wheatfield" and Gauguin's painting of Tahiti. Also here is a group of Italian Renaissance paintings, a 14th-century French limestone Madonna and Child, a Georgia O'Keeffe landscape of Hawaii, and works by Pablo Picasso and Winslow Homer.

Hawaii and its people, as seen by the first painters to visit the Islands (see pp. 41–42), are on display in the **Hawaiian Gallery,** on the second floor of the recently completed Henry R. Luce Pavilion Complex.

A recent acquisition is **Shangri La,** the luxury Diamond Head home of heiress Doris Duke. The Islamic-styled residence, with its courtyards, tiles, and art, is exquisite. Reservations are required, usually months in advance, for this tour *(tel 866/385-3849).* ∎

The austere lines of the interior of the Contemporary Museum contrast with its classic Honolulu mansion exterior.

The Contemporary Museum

MRS. CHARLES MONTAGUE COOKE, WHO WAS BEHIND THE Honolulu Academy of Arts (see p. 74), built the home in Makiki Heights that has become the Contemporary Museum, dedicated to showcasing the best and brightest art created after 1940. The house was designed by Hart Wood in collaboration with C. W. Dickey, acknowledged as Hawaii's two greatest architects. It underwent expansions and renovations, and was finally transformed in 1988 into a modern museum.

Viola Frey sculpted this lady to lounge by the pool at the Contemporary Museum.

The building sits on 3.5 acres of lush hillside: The exquisite intimate Japanese garden of grottoes and nooks known as **Nuumealani** ("heavenly heights") was designed by a Japanese Christian minister, the Reverend K. H. Iganaki, and took 13 years to complete. Views from the terrace sweep over the city to Diamond Head. Art ambushes you at every turn throughout the manicured grounds: Two stainless steel kinetic sculptures by George Rickey play on the lawn, while Viola Frey's "Resting Woman No. 2" reclines beside the swimming pool.

The whimsy at the heart of the art at the Contemporary Museum camouflages its importance. The first thing visible upon arriving is a strange, bright red, vaguely Japanese, vaguely Moby Dick sculpture by Jedd Garet. The front door is actually a pair of bronze gates by Robert Graham, each a three-dimensional female form. You won't be sure whether you're entering an art museum or a fun house. James Seawright's "Mirror 15" hanging just inside the entry will confound you—it's a quilt of odd-angled mirrors that reflect your face in dozens of carnival variations.

The **interior galleries** are spare and spacious with sunken floors and bridges. They are devoted to rotating exhibits of the permanent collection as well as a full calendar of changing exhibitions of predominantly Hawaii artists. A separate pavilion houses a David Hockney walk-in environment inspired by the Maurice Ravel opera *L'Enfant et les Sortilèges.*

Among the artists represented are Josef Albers, Louise Nevelson, Jim Dine, Jasper Johns, Tom Wesselmann, Deborah Butterfield, Frank Stella, William Wegman, James Surls, Claes Oldenburg, and Vito Acconci.

Every third Thursday is free. The museum has an excellent café in a garden setting and a gift shop.

MORE CONTEMPORARY ART

The Contemporary Museum operates a satellite, the **Downtown Gallery,** in the new glass tower of First Hawaiian Center, corporate headquarters of First Hawaiian Bank. The ground and second floors of the ultramodern building have space for exhibiting the work of Island artists. The second-floor space is behind a glass curtain made of more than 4,000 panels of stone, glass, and aluminum designed by Jamie Carpenter.

Two prominent artists have their galleries in Chinatown (see pp. 66–67). For two decades, **Ramsay Galleries** *(1128 Smith St., tel 808/537-2787)* in the historic Tan Sing Building has shown the work of local artists, including, of course, Ramsay herself, acclaimed for her fine pen and ink work, often exhibited with a magnifying glass for you to inspect the meticulous details. Ramsay has recently added a water garden to her historic property. Pegge Hopper, known for her graphically strong illustrations of Hawaiian women, also has her own **Pegge Hopper Galleries** *(1164 Nuuanu Ave., tel 808/524-1160,*

closed Sun.–Mon.) selling originals and limited edition prints. The gallery also showcases the work of other leading Hawaii artists and has earned a reputation for carrying the latest in printmaking.

On a quiet street in Punchbowl, the **Tennent Art Foundation Gallery** *(203 Prospect St., tel 808/531 1987, open by appointment)* holds work by the late Madge Tennent, whose paintings also hang in the National Museum of Women in Washington, D.C. Tennent's heroic portrayals of Hawaiian people have exerted a great influence on contemporary artists.

Gail Bakutis, a master of the art of *raku* (a form of Japanese pottery), and 11 other artists, got together more than a decade ago and opened **Gallery at Ward Centre** *(1200 Ala Moana St., tel 808/597-8034)* in the Ward Centre shopping complex. **Native Books and Beautiful Things** *(1050 Ala Moana St., tel 808/596-8885, closed 9 p.m. & Sun. 5 p.m.)* specializes in traditional Hawaiian crafts and modern interpretations of those forms, all by local artists. ■

Arthur and Elaine Tennent pose amid his late mother's paintings.

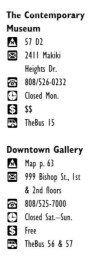

The Contemporary Museum
- 🅰 57 D2
- ✉ 2411 Makiki Heights Dr.
- ☎ 808/526-0232
- 🕐 Closed Mon.
- 💲 $$
- 🚌 TheBus 15

Downtown Gallery
- 🅰 Map p. 63
- ✉ 999 Bishop St., 1st & 2nd floors
- ☎ 808/525-7000
- 🕐 Closed Sat.–Sun.
- 💲 Free
- 🚌 TheBus 56 & 57

The lei of the land

One of the loveliest aspects of Hawaiian culture is the most fragile. The burden of seasons, the joys of life, the wonders of love are entwined in the flowers of the lei. Always given with a kiss, the lei speaks eloquently where words might fail.

Origins are uncertain, but flowers have been strung into ceremonial garlands in Asia for centuries, and from there, the custom probably moved, with the people, into Oceania. In Hawaii, it enjoys its greatest flowering.

The beauty and artistry of the lei overwhelmed early visitors, including Isabella Lucy Bird, an intrepid traveler and journalist, who met King Lunalilo in 1873, and reported: "He was almost concealed by wreaths of ohia blossoms and festoons of maile [Hawaiian vine], some almost two yards long." The other guests, she wrote, "wore two, three, four, or even six beautiful lei, besides festoons of the fragrant maile. Lei of crimson ohia lehua blossoms were universal, but beside these, there were lei of small red and white double roses, *pohas,* yellow amaranth, cane tassels, like frosted silver, the orange pandanus, and delicious gardenia, and a very few orange blossoms, and the great granadilla (passion flower)."

A lei can be made of almost anything—flowers, fruit, leaves, vine. Permanent leis are crafted from feathers, *kukui* nuts, shells, seeds, even human hair. Contemporary innovations include leis of candy and bubble gum, or the ultimate in tropical tackiness, airline-size liquor bottles. Although every lei is treasured, there is a subtle floral hierarchy: Those made of plumerias (frangipani) are the most common;

Leis for sale are artistically displayed in Chinatown, Moiliili, and at airports and shops throughout the Islands.

pansy leis are among the most expensive. Leis fashioned from flowers picked in the giver's garden are probably the most appreciated.

The lei is not above trends; the maunaloa lei and the Micronesian ginger lei, both intricately crafted floral necklaces, were popular in the late 1990s because they complemented contemporary fashion in their simple, unobtrusive appearance. A masculine favorite has been the tailored cigar-flower lei in shades of rust and orange, and also the braided ti-leaf lei, which has the advantage of being inexpensive.

The three most common lei-making techniques are traditional. The *kui* method strings flowers lengthwise with needle and thread; the *haku* approach creates a braided base of ferns or stems; and a *wili* lei entwines the flowers with fiber (purists use softened banana fiber; cheaters use dental floss).

In ancient Hawaii, a lei was worn by a farmer in the field to invoke divine blessing upon his crops. Leis were worn by nursing mothers who believed in their life-giving, life-symbolizing power. Certain leis were used in healing rites performed by the *kahuna lapaau* (medical priest), and the lei was essential for dancers of the hula.

No matter the purpose or the flower, the giving and receiving of a lei has come down through time as a beautiful gesture from one person to another. The sentiment is expressed in the song "Ka Moae":

E lei aku oe kuu aloha
I koolua nou i kahi mehemeha
Wear my love as a lei, and as your companion in lonely places. ∎

Below: President Bill Clinton on a visit to Hawaii received the traditional lei greeting.
Right: Extravagant leis drape pau rider and her horse, ready for a parade.
Bottom: Vanda orchids are strung into a double lei.

Couples come
from all over the
world to be wed
in Hawaii's
beautiful gardens.

Lyon Arboretum
- 55 E1
- 3860 Manoa Rd.
- 808/988-0456
- Closed all holidays
- TheBus 5

**Foster Botanical
Garden**
- Map p. 67
- 50 N. Vineyard Blvd.
- 808/522-7065
- $$
- TheBus 4

Moanalua Gardens
- 54 D1

Gardens of Oahu

THE FLORAL HERITAGE OF HAWAII IS ABUNDANT AND
unique: 90 percent of native species grow no place else on Earth (see
pp. 22–23). The first Polynesian settlers brought with them about 30
plants to add to the garden, and later immigrants from Europe, Asia,
and the Americas brought their favorite clippings and seeds. It is
estimated that about 800 exotic species have become fully naturalized
in the Islands: What we now think of as a Hawaiian garden is actual-
ly, like the people, a composite of many strains. There are more than
5,000 hybrids of hibiscus, the state flower. As for orchids, more than
700 species exist in Hawaii, as well as thousands of hybrids.

Nestled deep in the verdant folds of
Manoa Valley (see p. 73), the **Lyon
Arboretum** is a well-planned,
124-acre garden that manages to
look unplanned. Its experiments in
hybridization, especially of hibis-
cus, calathea, rhododendron, and

ginger, have introduced 148 hybrids
to the world. You can trek through
a valley of ferns, a natural rain
forest, an herb garden, and beneath
towering trees, while lily ponds,
benches, and pavilions offer quiet
places for contemplation. One of

Rain falling on a lobster claw heliconia, a popular garden ornamental

1352 Pineapple Pl.
808/833-1944
Closed 5:30 p.m. in winter, 7 p.m. in summer
TheBus 12

Koko Crater Botanical Garden
55 F1
400 Kealahou St.
808/522-7060
TheBus 58, Kealahou St.

Hoomaluhia Botanical Garden
55 E2
45-680 Luluku Rd., Kaneohe
808/233-7323
TheBus 55 or 56

Wahiawa Botanical Garden
54 C3
1396 California Ave., Wahiawa
808/621-7321
TheBus 52 from Ala Moana Shopping Center

the more intriguing areas is the Beatrice H. Krauss Ethnobotanical Garden of useful Hawaiian plants. The arboretum's gift shop carries books, local crafts, and jams and jellies made from the fruits and herbs of the garden.

More than a century old and originally planted by the royal physician, Dr. Hillebrand, **Foster Botanical Garden** blooms on the border of downtown Honolulu. Approximately 4,000 tropical species have found a home in this 20-acre urban oasis of ferns and tall trees. The Prehistoric Glen, which has earned national recognition, contains some of the oldest plant forms on Earth, some left over from the dinosaur age, all organized and displayed in chronological order. There's also an excellent orchid collection and amazing bromeliads.

West of downtown Honolulu are **Moanalua Gardens.** This private garden open to the public, as well as the valley behind it, is steeped in history. The pretty cottage under the trees with a taro patch in front was built in 1853–54 for Lot, who became Kamehameha V. When ancient petroglyphs were discovered in the valley, the state, after a long costly battle with activists, had to reroute a major freeway, with the result that the 16-mile H-3, originally estimated at 70 million dollars, came in at 1.25 billion dollars.

Koko Crater Botanical Garden lies within the basin of an extinct volcano on the southeastern shore of Oahu (see p. 96). The garden is a testing ground for Xeriscape gardening, a system aimed to conserve precious water resources along this arid coast. Its important collections include climbing cactuses, aloes, sansevierias, euphorbias, and palms. A self-guided walk will take an hour and a half. Bring drinking water.

On the Windward Side near Kaneohe (see p. 101), **Hoomaluhia Botanical Garden** is 400 acres of serenity with a 32-acre lake. Labeled plants—many of them endangered—representing the world's tropical latitudes, are grouped by area of origin. There are good hiking trails, and it's a rewarding place for bird-watching. Camping is allowed by permit.

Wahiawa Botanical Garden, is set in 27 acres of high-elevation tropical rain forest in the middle of Wahiawa, central Oahu. It has a notable fern collection, a Hawaiian garden, an aroid (plants of the arum family) garden, and 60 exceptional trees from around the world. It is the venerable old trees that give this garden its character. Bring mosquito repellent. ■

Hawaii Nature Center & hikes

Hawaii Nature Center
- 57 D3
- 2131 Makiki Heights Dr.
- 808/955-0100
- TheBus 15

SURROUNDED BY A 2,000-ACRE PRESERVE, THE HAWAII Nature Center is a nonprofit environmental education organization, offering a variety of nature-centered activities and hikes to the general public. Most are easily accomplished by children, and hands-on exhibits at the center encourage young people to learn about the plants and animals in their surroundings. The center operates another facility on Maui (see p. 132).

Hikers walk through the leafy bowers of the Makiki Valley Loop Trail.

The easy **Makiki Valley Loop Trail,** 2.7 miles long, begins at the bridge behind the environmental education center, and should take two hours. Stop at the center to acquaint yourself with the history of the Makiki Valley and what to look for on the trail.

The first thing you'll see are reconstructed taro patches where different varieties of the Hawaiian staple are being propagated. The trail stretches out along a row of Norfolk and Cook Island pines. If you pause and listen you may hear the clear song of the *shama* thrush, a large black bird native to Malaysia and now resident in Hawaii.

You'll spot trees with distinctive silver leaves: These are *kukui,* whose nuts contain an oil used as lamp oil and which makes an excellent furniture polish. When polished, the nuts are worn in leis. Other trees you'll pass are avocado (free samples August through October), the lemon-colored guava with its juicy pink flesh, mountain apple (in fruit July, August, and November), mahogany, and the beautiful koa, a native hardwood tree used for fine furniture, art objects, and even outrigger canoes.

Along the way you'll smell yellow ginger, eucalyptus, and allspice. Birds you may spot are the spotted dove, mynah, house sparrow, the bright green *amakihi,* the warbling bulbul, and the small, green Japanese white-eye. The trail will cross streams five times and reach a 760-foot elevation. Sometimes through the lush tropical vegetation, you'll get a fine view of Honolulu. ∎

See by seaplane

Pat Magie and his wife, Debbie, operate Island Seaplane Service from the old sea runways in Keehi Lagoon.

THE SEA RUNWAYS OF THE PAN AM CHINA CLIPPERS HAVE been reopened in Keehi Lagoon, and a new seaplane flight-seeing company, Island Seaplane Service, Inc., offers airborne tours of Oahu. Island Seaplane has two aircraft: A Cessna 206 that can accommodate the pilot and four passengers, and a six-passenger DeHavilland Beaver. Book either a half-hour or one-hour narrated flight. Complimentary van service gets you to and from your hotel.

Taking off from water is thrilling, like being in a speedboat revving up to full horsepower and then finding yourself suddenly airborne. On the half-hour flight, you fly over downtown Honolulu and Waikiki at 300 to 400 feet—perfect for aerial photography. You'll peer into Diamond Head Crater, see the mansions along Kahala Beach, and head out toward Koko Head, Hanauma Bay, the spouting Blow Hole, and along Sandy Beach with its white-haired surf. Around the mountains, the beauty of the Windward Side bursts upon the senses, and you'll see green palisades, offshore islands, and beautiful Kaneohe Bay before heading back to home port.

The hour flight follows the same route, but continues to the valley where parts of *Jurassic Park, Godzilla,* and *Mighty Joe Young* were shot. You'll get a view of the Polynesian Cultural Center and the surf beaches of the North Shore, then you'll power in over the air path used by the Japanese bombers in the infamous attack on Pearl Harbor. In calm water, you may be able to see the rusting hulk of the U.S.S. *Arizona* beneath the waves.

Landing on Keehi Lagoon is exhilarating, with the plane hovering for the right moment, the right ripple of sea, before you feel the warm breath of the ocean as the plane glides to its pier. ∎

Island Seaplane Service, Inc.

🅰 54 D1
✉ 85 Lagoon Dr.
☎ 808/836-6273
$ $$$$$

From the pink Royal Hawaiian Hotel and other hotels, the views go all the way to Diamond Head.

Waikiki

Waikiki. The name is magic: It conjures images of moon-drenched surf, Diamond Head, hula maidens, bronze beachboys, and ukulele music. Early Hawaiians gave it this name, which means "spouting water," because of its rushing streams and gushing springs.

AN OLD RETREAT

Ancient chants sing of the best surfing spots, including a *kapu* (forbidden) break reserved for chiefs and chiefesses, who rode naked on 18-foot wooden boards. Since surfing was considered a religious activity, temples to the sport once stood all along the beach. The site of the principal one, Papaenaena at the foot of Diamond Head, overlooked the popular surf-ing spot now called First Break. To signal that the surf was up, the priest flew a kite.

In 1804 Kamehameha the Great, having conquered all Islands except Kauai, assembled an army of 7,000 warriors on Waikiki Beach to assault this last bastion. The sea bristled with his armada of 27 well-armed schooners, a 20-cannon gunboat, and 500 war canoes. However, the invasion was never launched, owing to a plague that afflicted the ranks.

The ruler of all the Islands had a villa in Waikiki. Here he married his sacred wife, High Chiefess Keopuolani, from Maui. No other Waikiki wedding has equaled it in importance.

The first written accounts of Waikiki came from Capt. George Vancouver and his crew in 1792. On board was naturalist Archibald Menzies, who described Waikiki as "one of those interesting landscapes which the eyes of a meditative mind could long contemplate with new felt pleasure." In his time, it was a land of taro farms and fishponds with thatched homes scattered in the verdure.

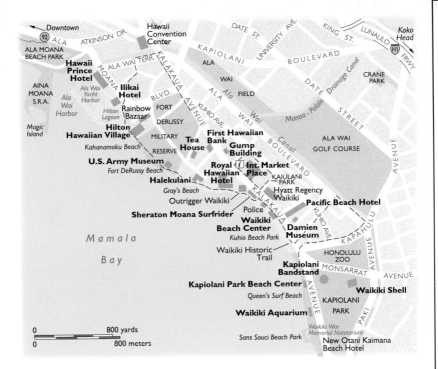

To set an example of industry for his people, King Kamehameha personally worked in the taro patches, as did his royal sons.

In 1863, Charles de Varigny, a Frenchman who became prime minister of the Hawaiian kingdom, wrote of visiting the site (near the present Royal Hawaiian Hotel), which was in ruins and "covered with periwinkle." He also wrote: "Waikiki is today a charming little village where the people of Honolulu like occasionally to spend several weeks at a time for the pleasure of sea bathing."

BIRTH OF A RESORT

About this time the first road made its way around the duck ponds and taro patches from Honolulu to Waikiki. The first public transportation followed—a mule-drawn bus. In 1863, King Kamehameha IV offered to sell a strip of land running from downtown Honolulu to Diamond Head to Eliza Sinclair, a rancher's widow from New Zealand, for $10,000. She turned him down because it wasn't good grazing ground and bought the island of Niihau (see p. 232) instead. That

same year, the first Waikiki cottages were opened as guest bungalows and named "Sans Souci." Author Robert Louis Stevenson came to stay and wrote: "If anyone desires such old-fashioned things as lovely scenery, quite pure air, clear sea water, good food, and heavenly sunset hung out before his eyes over the Pacific and the distant hills of Waianae, I recommend him cordially to the 'Sans Souci.'"

All those attributes still describe Waikiki, except "old-fashioned." The 500-acre resort, a mere 2 miles long and half a mile wide, is the epicenter of a 12-billion-dollar tourism industry. A wall of hotels rises behind the people-packed sands and the waters are dotted with swimmers, surfers, canoes, sailboats, water-bikes, rafts—in fact, anything that floats, and some that don't, such as sight-seeing submarines. Yet in spite of the crowds, the hustle, the tacky souvenirs, and alien bongo drums, that old magic asserts itself, and people who haven't been on terms of endearment for years hold hands and stroll through moonlit surf. Waikiki may be high and brash, but it isn't fake, and it's definitely fun. ∎

Tourists
accompanied by
experienced
paddlers surf the
Waikiki rollers.

The beaches

WAIKIKI IS ACTUALLY A STRING OF BEACHES, ONE FLOWING
into the other in a long line of golden sand with Diamond Head
rising to the east in a perpetual Kodak moment. Each has its own
character and, like all beaches in Hawaii, is open to the public.

Waikiki

⬛ 55 E1

**Visitor
information**

✉ Hawaii Visitors &
Convention Bureau,
Royal Hawaiian
Shopping Center,
2201 Kalakaua Ave.,
Suite 401A

☎ 808/923-1811

🕐 Closed Sat. & Sun.

Beginning in the west,
**Kahanamoku Beach and
Lagoon** is calm enough for babies.
From a pier at one end, people are
water-taxied out to sight-seeing
submarines and catamaran cruises.
    Fort DeRussy Beach, a 20-
acre property owned by the U.S.
government, is bordered in green
lawns and big shade trees with
picnic tables beneath.
    Gray's Beach, in front of the
Halekulani Hotel, is often inundated by tides, but the swimming is

grand because of the cool freshwater
springs feeding the ocean. The beach
was named for Mrs. LaVancha Gray,
who operated a boardinghouse
where the hotel is now. In ancient
times, it was a favorite place to beach
canoes, and *kahuna* (masters,
priests) practiced their healing
arts here. People still come to
these waters for healings.
    The best swimming is at **Royal
Moana Beach** in front of the
Royal Hawaiian, Outrigger Waikiki,
and Moana hotels. The Outrigger

operates a comprehensive beach activity center where you can sign up for a surprisingly inexpensive outrigger canoe ride, surfing the foamy rollers sweeping in past Diamond Head. Or you can learn to surf—the beachboys guarantee, tongue in cheek, to have even grandmothers standing on their boards, riding the waves like a hot-dogger, in one lesson.

The **Waikiki Beach Center,** across from the Hyatt Regency Waikiki, has food concessions, canoe rentals, a bathhouse, benches, and chairs. Locals come to play cards and "talk story." At adjacent **Kuhio Beach Park,** a long wall extends into the ocean: It's a great place to watch surfers, body-boarders, and the tangerine sunsets. The water behind the wave berm looks deceptively safe, but non-swimmers have drowned by falling into unseen holes beneath the waves. Another danger here is the bacteria count, which can be high because the water is both still and much used.

Queen's Surf on the other side of the pier is a favorite body-boarding spot. The grassy lawn and coconut palms make it popular with picnicking families. Check newspapers or your concierge desk for dates for Sunset on the Beach, a night of free movies and inexpensive food kiosks from some of the best Waikiki restaurants.

Right: Rental surfboards are stacked along Waikiki Beach. First-timers can sign up for lessons.

Kapiolani Park Beach Center has rest rooms, dressing rooms, and refreshments. The surfing area there is known as Public's. **Sans Souci Beach** in front of the War Memorial Natatorium (see p. 94) is another good, calm swimming area. ∎

The Duke

It was Duke Paoa Kahanamoku (1890–1968) who brought the Hawaiian-born sport of surfing to California, Australia, and New Zealand. As a young man his swims were timed and the results sent to the Amateur Athletic Union in New York. They shot back, "Unacceptable. No one swims this fast." In 1912, he won a gold and a silver swimming medal from the Summer Olympics in Sweden. He caught Hollywood's eye and was cast in 30 films. In 1990, the centennial of his birth, a bronze statue of the Hawaiian who won the hearts of the world was unveiled in Waikiki, at Kuhio Beach near the spot where he was said to have ridden a 30-foot wave for a mile. ∎

Waikiki's hotels

HOTELS ALONG "LIFE'S GREATEST BEACH" ARE MORE THAN just places to flop at the end of a day of sun, fun, and sight-seeing: Many are attractions in themselves.

A swimmer floats above the glass mosaic petals of the 30-foot orchid at the bottom of the Halekulani Hotel's swimming pool.

If you ride the glass elevator at the **Hawaii Prince Hotel,** you'll get a wonderful view of the Koolau Mountains, the Ala Wai Canal where outrigger canoes practice for races, and the Hawaii Convention Center. The **Ilikai Hotel** also has a good glass-elevator ride and, from the second-floor pool deck, a view of the Ala Wai boat harbor.

The **Hilton Hawaiian Village** is bigger than many small towns. When full, its 3,400 rooms, plus a staff of 2,000, could give the hotel complex a population of 9,600 people. The Rainbow Shopping Bazaar incorporates a Thai temple, a Japanese pagoda, an authentic Japanese farmhouse, and two granite lions guarding a Chinese moon gate. The world's tallest mosaic mural splashes up the side of a 30-story tower in rainbow colors. There's a penguin pond, a flamingo lawn, homes for endangered Hawaiian birds, and every Friday evening a free Hawaiian show and fireworks. The Bishop Museum (see p. 70) has a branch at the hotel with exhibits on early Waikiki.

The **Halekulani** is easily the beach's most elegant hotel. Its prized mosaic blooms on the bottom of the swimming pool: The 30-foot orchid is composed of 1.25 million glass tiles. In 1925 author Earl Derr Biggers plotted his Charlie Chan mystery, *House Without A Key,* while staying in a cottage next to the hotel. The new "House Without a Key" is the hotel bar, a great place to watch the sunset. Now you have the added pleasure of Hawaiian music and Kanoe Miller, one of Hawaii's prettiest dancers, who weaves a hula

Opposite: The Rainbow Tower mosaic at the Hilton Hawaiian Village, Waikiki, often competes with real rainbows.

magic Biggers would have loved.

Looking like a movie set, the **Royal Hawaiian Hotel** opened in 1927 at a black-tie dinner costing an exorbitant 10 dollars a plate. The "Pink Palace of the Pacific" was designed by a New York firm, Warren and Wetmore. Its lush landscaping was planned around surviving coconut palms from King Kamehameha the Great's royal retreat, by landscape architect R.T. Stevens. The gardens, and the palms, are still one of the hotel's main attractions.

You can't miss the **Sheraton Moana Surfrider.** The Victorian "first lady of Waikiki," the oldest hotel resides among the high-rises like a big white wedding cake. The beaux arts building, which is now on the National Register of Historic Places, was designed by Oliver P. Traphagen and opened in 1901. For 40 years, the famous Hawaii Calls radio show was broadcast from under the huge banyan tree (planted in 1885) beside the hotel's old-fashioned veranda, where high tea is served in the afternoon and ladies delicately cool themselves with sandalwood fans. Robert Louis Stevenson wrote poems beneath the tree, and told stories to Princess Kaiulani. Stop in at the Historical Room to see memorabilia and photographs of old Waikiki.

A thousand fish swim in the lobby of the twin-tower **Pacific Beach Hotel.** A huge 280,000-gallon aquarium rises two stories with two restaurants, Oceanarium and Neptune, wrapping around it, and one on the top lip called Shogun. ∎

Waikiki off the beach

THE U.S. ARMY MUSEUM AT FORT DERUSSY HAS A - collection from the darker side of the human psyche, beginning with weaponry of ancient Hawaii, through the American Revolution, the Spanish-American War, and both World Wars, to Korea and Vietnam. The museum is housed in Battery Randolf, one of six coastal defenses built on Oahu between 1908 and 1915. On its ocean side, the concrete walls are 22 feet thick; when the military attempted to demolish the massive structure in 1969, Battery Randolf broke the wrecking ball. Not to be defeated, the Army outfitted it and opened it as a museum on the 35th anniversary of America's entry into World War II, December 7, 1976.

In Waikiki luxury boutiques and tacky souvenir stalls offer shoppers a full range of wares.

U.S. Army Museum
- ⓜ Map p. 85
- ✉ Kalia & Saratoga Rds.
- ☎ 808/438-2821
- ⊕ Closed Mon.
- 🚌 TheBus 8, 19, 54

Tea House of the Urasenke Foundation
- ⓜ Map p. 85
- ✉ 245 Saratoga Rd.
- ☎ 808/923-3059
- 💲 $
- 🚌 TheBus 8, 19, 54

The **Tea House of the Urasenke Foundation,** right across the street from the U.S. Army Museum, seeks to promote international understanding through the Zen of tea. The authentic teahouse was designed by grand tea master Soshitsu Sen of the Urasenke Foundation in Kyoto, Japan, and was a gift to the Japanese Chamber of Commerce in Hawaii in 1952.

On Wednesday and Friday mornings, you may partake of the ancient Japanese tea ceremony (it's a good idea to make a reservation). While you sit on the floor in a tearoom, ladies in kimonos will serve you foamy *matcha,* the chartreuse tea made from the tops of 400-year-old tea bushes. In his book, *Chado, The Japanese Way of Tea,* Soshitsu Sen wrote: "In the practice of tea,

a sanctuary is created where one can take solace in the tranquillity of the spirit."

Stop in at **First Hawaiian Bank** *(2181 Kalakaua Ave., tel 808/943-4670; closed 4 p.m. Mon.–Thurs., 6 p.m. Fri.; closed Sat.–Sun.)* to see the six massive murals in the lobby by Jean Charlot (1898–1979). Charlot, whose work is represented in the Uffizi Gallery in Florence, Italy, the British Museum, London, and the Metropolitan Museum of Art and the Museum of Modern Art in New York, depicted the peopling of Hawaii and the evolution of the culture.

One of Waikiki's architectural gems is the 1929 **Gump Building** *(2200 Kalakaua Ave.)* built in Hawaiian colonial style with its blue tile roof. Once the premier store of Hawaii, it now houses a T-shirt shop and a McDonald's.

You won't be able to miss the **International Market Place** *(2330 Kalakaua Ave., tel 808/923-9871 closed at 11 p.m.).* In the face of beautification and upscaling all around it, this hodgepodge acre or so of shops, pushcarts, psychics, wood-carvers, candlemakers, and juice squeezers remains resolutely, defiantly tacky. Looking for dashboard hula maidens, obscene

ashtrays, cheap eats, or Micky Mouse towels? This is your one-stop mini-mall. At night, the sidewalk fronting the market is a magnet for street musicians and others, such as bongo drummers, mimes, and doomsday prophets.

Next to the Honolulu Police substation *(2405 Kalakaua Ave.)*, you'll see four big rocks known as the **Stones of Kapaemahu.** According to tradition, the stones, each weighing thousands of pounds, were quarried in Kaimuki and brought to Waikiki sometime before the 16th century to honor four healing priests from Tahiti who, it is said, transferred their healing powers to the stones before departing for home. The ceremonies lasted for a "full moon," wrote historian George S. Kanahele in his book *Waikiki 100 B.C. to 1900 A.D.* It's a good thing the police station wasn't there then, because, Kanahele noted, "A sacrifice was offered of a virtuous young chiefess whose body was placed beneath one of the stones."

A **statue of Princess Kaiulani,** last heir to the Hawaiian throne, who died at the age of 23, stands in **Kaiulani Park** *(Kaiulani & Kuhio Aves.).* The 7-foot bronze sculpture is by Jan Gordon Fisher.

The small but fascinating **Damien Museum** honors the self-sacrificing Belgian priest, Joseph Damien de Veuster, known around the world as Father Damien (see p. 213). Ask to see the 20-minute video documentary; it's low-budget, but well done and emotionally powerful.

New bronze surfboard-shaped history markers have been placed throughout Waikiki to mark significant sites (see p. 116).

Separating Waikiki from the rest of Honolulu, the 25-block **Ala Wai Canal** was built between 1921 and 1924 to channel rainwater from the mountains into the ocean and dry out the marshes of Waikiki, setting the stage for the resort you see today. If you stroll beside the canal in late afternoon, you'll usually see rainbows over the mountains, and outrigger canoe paddlers training for races. Watch out for joggers and Rollerbladers lost in their headset music. ■

In addition to the many regular Polynesian revues, festivals and special events brighten the Waikiki night.

Damien Museum

- Map p. 85
- 130 Ohua Ave.
- 808/923-2602
- Closed 3 p.m. Mon.–Fri., closed Sat.–Sun.
- TheBus 3 & 5

The outrigger canoe

The outrigger canoe is as central to Hawaii's identity as the philosophy of aloha (see pp. 10–14), and it is as common around the Islands as the coconut palm. Some anthropologists suggest that when the Polynesians set out on their epic voyages of exploration (see pp. 24–26) across the Pacific, those people who were large and had fat to spare had the best chance of surviving. So by natural selection, the Polynesians evolved into a race of generously proportioned people.

On Hawaii, they found hardwood trees with girths of 20 feet across, large enough to yield an entire canoe hull from a single trunk. With these, the Hawaiians perfected their shipbuilding techniques, using stone, shell, and wood tools to fashion the craft, braided coconut husk ropes for lashing, and woven plant fiber for sails. In the process, they created what is possibly the most versatile, seaworthy rough-water vessel ever to sail any sea.

The distinct outrigger or arm of the canoe is an ancient design that stabilizes the vessel in the Pacific's notorious swells. It is said that the early Hawaiians trained the branches of young *hau* trees to grow in the curved shape of the outrigger booms (the pieces that hold the small outrigger to the main body of the canoe). For long voyages, a second hull was added and a deck lashed between the two. The romantic upward thrust of the prow of these voyaging canoes, once assumed to be ornamental, was discovered to be essential to "plow" the swells—the sleek vessels were, in fact, conspicuous in their lack of decoration.

Building an outrigger canoe took more than skill. Historian David Malo wrote in 1836, "The building of a canoe was an affair of religion." Tommy Holmes, in his authoritative book *The Hawaiian Canoe*, lists 26 canoe deities. The *kahuna kalai waa* (master canoe builder) was as adept at ritual as he was at carving. The consecration ceremony and feast for the completion of a canoe was called *lolo ana ka waa i ka halau,* meaning "imparting brains to the canoe," so it would be "rooted in the sea" and "tear apart the billows of the ocean." Each canoe was said to have a destiny.

The outrigger canoes plying the tourist trade on Waikiki Beach today differ very little from the canoes seen by Captain Cook on his voyage of discovery in 1778. At Kealakekua Bay (see p. 150) on the Big Island, two of Cook's officers estimated that between 2,500 and 3,500 outrigger canoes came out to greet his ships, the *Resolution* and the *Discovery.* When Kamehameha the Great assembled his armada of war canoes on the shore of Oahu, they stretched more than 5 miles solid, from Waikiki to Waialae. Historian and author Abraham Fornander wrote in his *History of the Polynesian People* that an ancient Big Island king, setting out to conquer Maui, assembled a fleet of outrigger canoes so numerous they "covered the ocean from Hawaii to Maui and the people used them as a road to cross over on." That would be an almost unbelievable 30 miles of ocean.

Canoe paddling has always been a popular Hawaiian sport, and with the arrival of Western culture, the races were formalized into regattas. The first recorded outrigger regatta was held in honor of the first birthday of Crown Prince Albert, son of King Kamehameha IV, on May 20, 1859. Two of Hawaii's top racing clubs today, the Outrigger Canoe Club and Hui Nalu, were founded in 1908.

During June and July, canoe races take place almost every weekend somewhere in the state; usually they are listed in the local newspaper. The biggest is the race from Molokai to Oahu, a 40-mile haul through the treacherous Kaiwi Channel. Competition is fierce and race finishes are spectacular—paddlers and canoes, are drenched in kisses and draped in leis.

Outriggers are launched daily along Waikiki Beach as veteran paddlers take visitors to sea in canoes. It's a wild ride down the white crests with sea foam spraying like wings and Diamond Head in the background. ■

Top: Paddlers compete in a Maui outrigger canoe regatta.
Bottom: A paddling team carries its canoe into the waves for a race at Kaanapali, Maui.

Kapiolani Park & Diamond Head

HAWAII'S FIRST PUBLIC PARK, WAS DEDICATED ON Kamehameha Day 1877, and named by King Kalakaua for his beloved wife Queen Kapiolani. The 200-acre sweep of lawns and trees is backed by Diamond Head. In its earliest days, women swathed in yards of satin, and draped in leis, feathers, and hats would parade their flower-adorned horses through the park. *Pau* riders are still a colorful part of every Hawaiian parade. Kapiolani Park once hosted horse races, polo games, and auto races. Today's activities include archery, softball, basketball, tennis, martial arts, and family picnics. In December, the annual Honolulu Marathon finishes here.

The **Honolulu Zoo** anchors one end of the park. There are bigger and better zoos elsewhere, but this one is pretty, and where else can you photograph monkeys with Diamond Head in the background or watch an endangered nene (the goose that is the state bird) waddle about? On Wednesday evenings in summer, the zoo offers "The Wildest Show in Town," a free musical entertainment; check local newspapers for particulars. On Wednesdays, Saturdays, and Sundays, look for the **Zoo Fence Art Mart;** many acclaimed local artists got their start hanging on the zoo fence. Much of the work is affordable and certainly makes a better souvenir than some of the Hawaiian vulgarities made in Taiwan and the Philippines.

The Honolulu Symphony and visiting talent perform in the park at the **Waikiki Shell,** and people bring their beach mats and picnic suppers to be serenaded under the stars. The park's other entertainment stage, the **Kapiolani Bandstand,** has been completely rebuilt with more outdoor seating and new landscaping that includes streams and a reflecting pond. It is the site of Sunday afternoon hula shows or concerts by the Royal Hawaiian Band.

The **Waikiki Aquarium,** the nation's third oldest, is oceanside in the park, and built on a coral reef. Opened in 1910, and recently renovated, the excellent facility harbors more than 300 species of Hawaiian and Pacific marine life, including giant hundred-pound clams, chambered nautilus (the only ones bred in captivity), sea horses, and sharks. There's also a special habitat for the endangered Hawaiian monk seal, a touch-me tide pool, a small theater with continuously screened short films, and many interactive educational exhibits with a focus on the status of coral reefs.

The nearby **Waikiki War Memorial Natatorium,** built in 1927 has occasioned fierce battles between those who want to tear down the decaying monument and those determined to save it. The swimming pool, the largest saltwater pool in the country and once a training pool for champions, is falling apart and infested with eels.

DIAMOND HEAD HIKE

You can climb to the 760-foot summit of **Diamond Head** and enjoy panoramic views of Waikiki in one direction and clear out to

Views from the summit of Diamond Head stretch over Kapiolani Park and Waikiki to the Waianae Mountains.

Honolulu Zoo

🗺 Map p. 85
✉ 151 Kapahulu Ave.
☎ 808/971-7171
💲 $$
🚌 TheBus 2, 8, 19, 20, 47

Koko Head in the other, with the Diamond Head Lighthouse, brightest light in the Pacific, at your feet. The trailhead is inside the crater, which you enter by walking or driving through a tunnel—the entrance is well marked on Diamond Head Road. In October 1999, a thousand youth attending the Millennium Young People's Congress planted 900 native Hawaiian plants in a new Peace Garden not far from the park entrance.

Trail signs will tell you the 1.4-mile hike will take an hour, but you can easily do it in half an hour, even with a child in tow. Popular information is that there are 99 steps to the top: That's true of one flight, but there are three more. Be sure to bring drinking water,

and a flashlight for navigating a dark tunnel. Diamond Head was a military installation in World War II and is headquarters for the island's civil defense. Sirens are tested at 11:45 a.m. the first Tuesday of every month. There is a dollar fee for the hike.

Diamond Head was first called Leahi, meaning "place of fire," by Hawaiians, because Pele, goddess of fire and volcanoes, (see p. 175) once sojourned here. However, British sailors in 1825 saw calcite crystals glittering in the sun and thought they had found enough diamonds to marry all the girls in England. The name stuck, and was oddly prophetic because the real estate at the base of the volcanic tuff cone is more precious than crown jewels. ∎

Waikiki Aquarium

🗺 Map p. 85
✉ 2777 Kalakaua Ave.
☎ 808/923-9741
💲 $$
🚌 TheBus 19 or 20

Diamond Head National Natural Landmark

🗺 57 E1
✉ Montserrat & 18th Aves.
🚌 TheBus 58

Hanauma Bay, a natural aquarium, was formed when the seaward wall of a volcanic crater collapsed.

East Honolulu

KAHALA, HONOLULU'S MOST PRESTIGIOUS RESIDENTIAL neighborhood, basks along the beach on the eastern side of Diamond Head. Kahala Avenue dead-ends at the Kahala Mandarin Oriental, Hawaii hotel. Built in 1959, this luxury enclave is the choice of visiting heads of state. Anyone, with or without tiara, can enjoy the gardens and the free porpoise shows *(11 a.m., 2 p.m., & 4 p.m.)* in the hotel's lagoon. Adjacent to the hotel is the exclusive Waialae Golf Course, where many top televised championship tournaments are played.

Hawaii Kai, built around a series of lagoons and canals emptying into Maunalua Bay, is a bedroom community of 30,000 people. The sheltered bay is a mecca for jet skiing and parasailing. (You can also rent snorkel gear for Hanauma Bay.)

Six thousand years ago, when a wall of Koko Head Crater fell away, the ocean rushed in and formed a natural aquarium in the crater. A reef stretches across the mouth of Hanauma Bay, separating the shallow interior from deep ocean. In **Hanauma Bay Nature Preserve,** thousands of brightly

hued tropical reef fish swim elegantly about in this marine sanctuary. Although it is an ideal place for novice snorkelers to discover underwater worlds, do not be deceived by the bay's beauty, as people have been swept from the lava ledges on the sides by sea surges. Also remember that coral is a living organism, so treat it tenderly. Elvis Presley preened around the bay in *Blue Hawaii.*

A new **visitor center** with interactive, child-friendly exhibits and a 7-minute film educates people about the fragile preserve.

The drive along the lava-lined Halona Coast at the edge of Koko Head on **Kalanianaole Highway** is dramatic, with views, on a clear day, of Molokai and

Lanai, and, when atmospheric conditions are right, of Maui. The **Halona Blowhole,** a lava tube (see p. 22) seen from the scenic pullout, is invaded by high surf, which it spits out in salty plumes that may go 50 feet in the air. Be content to watch from the lookout, as people have slipped into the hole and only one lived to talk about it. In season *(Nov.–April)* you can see humpback whales cavorting offshore (see pp. 126–127). To your right, in beautiful little Halona Cove, green sea turtles ride the wave surge.

The long golden beach to your left is **Sandy Beach,** the island's most dangerous beach due to rip currents and a pounding shore break. Note that the swimmers and body-boarders are all young and local, and even they are not immune to the broken necks and backs Sandy inflicts. On weekends, teenagers congregate around their cars to watch the wave warriors—and the bikinis.

Environmentalists have waged fierce, and so far successful, battles to preserve this wild stretch of Oahu coastline from various development schemes. ∎

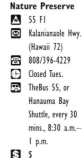

Snorkelers examine a slate pencil sea urchin.

Kahala Mandarin Oriental, Hawaii
- 55 E1
- 5000 Kahala Ave.
- 808/739-8888
- TheBus 22

Hanauma Bay Nature Preserve
- 55 F1
- Kalanianaole Hwy. (Hawaii 72)
- 808/396-4229
- Closed Tues.
- TheBus 55, or Hanauma Bay Shuttle, every 30 mins., 8:30 a.m.– 1 p.m.
- $

The Windward Side

The magnificent natural beauty of Windward Oahu never sneaks up on you, but bursts upon your senses, whether you see it from the Nuuanu Pali Lookout (see p. 68) with the Koolau Mountains rising in jagged green ramparts all around, or from Makapuu Point where suddenly the world opens up into a glorious opulence of sea and sky, mountains and islands. Wind blows about your body filling your lungs with some of the cleanest air on the planet, sweeping in from thousands of miles of open ocean.

Geographically, the Windward Side runs from Makapuu Point to Kahuku Point. Makapuu is a black lava thumb protruding into a teal-and-cerulean sea, lashed by white-crested waves. A white lighthouse stands at its tip. Legends claim that a lava tunnel, its entrance now beneath the water, once ran from Makapuu to Molokai, and that people walked through it from island to island. In Waimanalo there is a hill called Puu O Molokai, named, it is said, for the Molokai people who settled there. Hike to the lighthouse for spectacular views.

The two offshore islands are Manana, an off-limits bird sanctuary commonly called Rabbit Island because it was once a rabbit ranch, and the smaller Kaohikaipu Island. In the blue hazy distance, the turtle-like land formation lying on the horizon is Mokapu Peninsula, home to the Kaneohe Marine Corps Base Hawaii. The rugged volcanic peak is 1,643-foot Olomana, in whose shadow Queen Liliuokalani wrote her love song "Aloha Oe." Hang gliders can often be seen drifting in the thermal currents.

A hang glider enjoys a bird's-eye view of Sea Life Park and all of Windward Oahu.

Makapuu Beach is practically a pilgrimage spot for bodysurfers, but it can be dangerous for the novice, especially in winter when the waves break close to shore.

Sea Life Park *(41–402 Kalanianaole Hwy., tel 808/259-7933, closed 5 p.m. daily)* sits between the mountains and the sea. This is the only place in the world you'll see a wholfin—love child of a whale and dolphin who met on the job. A 300,000-gallon aquarium incorporates a real reef populated by sharks, rays, and the same colorful tropical fish you'd see yards away in the open ocean if you wanted to get wet. The **Pacific Whaling Museum,** included in the park's entrance fee, has a large assemblage of memorabilia from Hawaii's colorful whaling era and an outstanding scrimshaw (see p. 126) collection. Look for the ivory dollhouse miniatures and the castle-like ivory birdcage.

Oahu's longest strand of sand, **Waimanalo Beach,** almost 4 miles, curls around a bay and is backed by the magnificent Koolau Mountains that run the length of this side of the island. If you swim here, be careful, as the beach is frequented by young toughs who can break into a car and disappear in seconds. The former sugar plantation town of **Waimanalo** is "downtown" for the local banana, corn, organic greens, and flower farmers. If you're staying in a condo, be sure and pick up some sweet white corn from the roadside stands. Waimanalo's two most famous sons are the late slack-key guitar virtuoso Gabby Pahinui (1921–1980) and champion sumo wrestler Chad Rowan, known to the world as Akebono, the first non-Japanese *sumotori* to earn the exalted rank of *yokozuna,* grand champion.

It's hard to believe this rural area shares the same island with Waikiki and Honolulu. ∎

Kailua

Kailua Beach Park
55 F2
Kawailoa & Alala Rds.
TheBus 56 or 57 to Kailua, then 70

Naish Hawaii
55 E2
155-A Hamakua Dr.
808/262-6068
TheBus 56 or 57

Windsurfing champion, Robby Naish

THE TOWN OF KAILUA IS ONLY A 15-MINUTE DRIVE FROM downtown Honolulu (double the time in rush hour), but crossing through the tunnel from town to the Windward Side is like crossing a frontier from routine into freedom. Although most of Kailua's wage earners work in Honolulu, this is more than a bedroom community.

Everything revolves around the 2-mile strand of sand, **Kailua Beach,** a family beach with lots of room and few tourists. Hobie Cats with colorful sails whip across the bay in the gusty trade winds; windsurfers, looking like big plastic butterflies, skim the waves; and from the dunes of **Kailua Beach Park,** kayakers set out for the

offshore islands. Rentals and water sports lessons are available in town; windsurfing champion Robby Naish has his own school **(Naish Hawaii).** President Bill Clinton lunched at Buzz's Steak House *(413 Kawailoa Rd., tel 808/261-4661),* the rickety little restaurant with the tree growing out of the porch; a plaque marks the table.

Nearby **Lanikai Beach** packs a lot of scenery into a 1-mile strand. The shore is lined with million-dollar houses, and the horizon dotted with offshore islands. Swimming is safe in sheltered waters, but protective seawalls are causing serious erosion of this little gem.

South of Kailua town, behind the YMCA *(1200 Kailua Rd.),* stands a well-preserved ancient *heiau* (temple) called **Ulupo.** The name means "night inspiration," and it is said that Menehune (Hawaii's little people, see p. 187) built it in a night of a full moon. It may well predate the Hawaiians. Note the skilled workmanship in the 30-foot high flat-topped pyramid. The temple stands at the edge of **Kawai Nui Marsh,** the largest freshwater marsh in the Islands. Millennia ago it was a vast open lagoon. Those who settled here used it as a *loko wai* (inland stream-fed fishpond). Still a major fish nursery, it is home to four rare species of waterbirds: the Hawaiian coot *(alae keo keo),* the gallinule *(alae ula),* the Hawaiian duck *(koloa maoli),* and the long-legged Hawaiian stilt *(aeo).* ■

Kaneohe

Boats rendezvous at the sandbar, Kaneohe Bay.

THE TOWN IS LARGELY A BEDROOM COMMUNITY WHERE residents' homes creep as close to beautiful Kaneohe Bay as their finances permit. On calm days the blue waters of the bay mirror the grandeur of the surrounding mountains. The island that opened the ridiculously popular television series *Gilligan's Island* is, in reality, Mokuoloe, better known as Coconut Island, home to the University of Hawaii's Institute of Marine Biology. Anyone actually marooned there is close enough to town to order take-out Chinese food. The other distinctive island in the bay is Mokolii, which everyone insists on calling Chinaman's Hat. When you see it, you'll know why.

Kaneohe Bay harbors three of the last five ancient fishponds remaining on Oahu. A fourth is in nearby Kahana Bay, and the fifth at Pearl Harbor. These aquaculture facilities (see p. 214), amazingly advanced for their time, once numbered almost a hundred and circled the island. The biggest and best preserved is at **Heeia State Park.** The 5,000-feet-long wall once enclosed an 88-acre fish nursery.

The area that is now **Kualoa Regional Park** was once so sacred that passing canoes lowered their sails in salute. From this beach, the *Hokulea* (see p. 65), a reproduction Polynesian voyaging canoe, sets out on its historic voyages of rediscovery. Sleek outrigger canoes are still beached on Kualoa's shores. At low tide you can walk on a shallow reef out to Chinaman's Hat. Wear a hat for the sun, and shoes for the sharp coral, and check the tide table in the newspaper so you won't be cut off by inrushing currents on the way back. There's a sandy cove on the ocean side of the islet, but swimming is dangerous. Views of the bay and mountains from the island are spectacular. ■

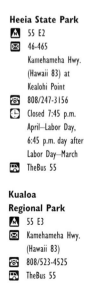

Heeia State Park
- 55 E2
- 46-465 Kamehameha Hwy. (Hawaii 83) at Kealohi Point
- 808/247-3156
- Closed 7:45 p.m. April–Labor Day, 6:45 p.m. day after Labor Day–March
- TheBus 55

Kualoa Regional Park
- 55 E3
- Kamehameha Hwy. (Hawaii 83)
- 808/523-4525
- TheBus 55

Koolau

THE SHEER, GREEN PALISADES OF THE KOOLAU MOUNTAINS dominate the Windward Side, shortening its days by hiding the setting sun, catching clouds, and making the land bloom. It was thought that rain and wind had sculpted the cliffs, but the latest sonar imaging has revealed a different story. In prehistoric times, half the island of Oahu fell into the ocean, and the cliffs were formed and gouged by the landslide. The resultant tidal wave covered the island of Lanai. Commuters on the Pali Highway (Route 61), Likelike (Route 63), and new H-3 Freeway are treated to mist-haunted vistas every morning.

At the foot of the mountains at Haiku, a vermilion temple sits beside a lake. The enormous bronze bell echoes against the Koolau ramparts, and there is not a more peaceful place on the island than the **Byodo-In.** The faithful copy of a temple of the same name at Uji, Japan, is surrounded by meditative gardens and little bridges. Ten thousand prize golden koi (carp) swim in its ponds, and peacocks strut about like runway models.

In the shadow of the great Koolau, several gardens have sprung up in this lush environment.

been in *Jurassic Park, Godzilla,* and *Mighty Joe Young.* The Morgan family, owners of the ranch, have branched out from cows to tourists, and have come up with a mix of activity packages including hiking, horseback riding, kayaking, jet skiing, snorkeling, sailing, handgun shooting, or just beaching it on their private island on the far side of ancient Molii fishpond.

Kahana Valley State Park is just around the bend, fronting Kahana Bay. The **Huilua Fishpond** here has been designated a National Historic Landmark. A hiking trail follows beside Kahana stream into the forested valley. If you hike, obey all warning signs and let someone know when you are setting out and when to expect you back. Some valley trails, such as those in Sacred Falls State Park, have been closed due to tragic accidents. The valleys slice into the deepest part of the mountains, and therefore are subject to rock slides and flash flooding. Enjoy Kahana from a picnic table in the coconut grove, or on the shady beach. ■

If you go to **Hoomaluhia Botanical Garden** (see p. 81) in the morning, when the fish are sleeping and the water is still, the lake perfectly reflects one of the best views of those spired mountains. Free guided nature hikes are held on Saturday and Sunday. **Senator Fong's Plantation and Garden** offers tram tours of Senator Hiram Fong's estate. Or, if you'd like to lunch in the company of the mountains, the **Haleiwa Joe** restaurant *(46-336 Haiku Rd., Kaneohe, tel 808/247-6671)* sits over a tropical garden right in the heart of the mountain's embrace.

A working cattle spread, **Kualoa Ranch & Activity Club,** is situated in Kaaawa, a valley deeply etched into the Koolau. You may recognize it—it's

Horseback riders from Kualoa Ranch pause in Kaaawa Valley. Left: People come to the Byodo-In Temple for the beauty of the setting and to gaze on the huge golden Buddha.

Kualoa Ranch & Activity Club
⚐ 55 E3
✉ 49-560 Kamehameha Hwy., Kaaawa
☎ 808/237-7321
🕐 Closed 3 p.m. daily
💲 $$$$$
🚌 TheBus 55

Kahana Valley State Park
⚐ 54 D3
✉ 52-222 Kamehameha Hwy. (Hawaii 83), Kahana
🚌 TheBus 55

The Polynesian
Cultural Center & Laie

IN ANCIENT TIMES LAIE WAS A *PUUHONUA* (PLACE OF refuge), where a person who trespassed against another was given the chance to earn forgiveness. Mormon missionaries settled here in 1883, and King David Kalakaua came for the dedication of the Mormon chapel. In 1919, the first Mormon temple outside continental United States was dedicated at the site. Built of pulverized coral and volcanic stone, it overlooks formal gardens and a pool. The church has been the cornerstone of the Hawaii Campus of Brigham Young University, attracting students from all over the Pacific.

In 1963, the church founded the **Polynesian Cultural Center** as a visitor attraction to give students an opportunity to live out the brotherhood embodied in both the Mormon faith and Polynesian tradition, and to earn their tuition by sharing their various cultures with the public. The center brought elders from the home islands to teach the history and culture of the region, and to oversee a way of life

Polynesian Cultural Center

- 54 D4
- 55-370 Kamehameha Hwy.
- 808/293-3333 or 800/367-7060
- Closed Sun. & 9 p.m. Mon.–Sat.
- $$$$$
- TheBus 55 or PCC coaches from Waikiki

consistent with the students' Polynesian backgrounds. The formula has really worked, and now the center is the largest paid visitor attraction in Hawaii.

From the minute you clear the box office, you are in the colorful world of Oceania. Enthusiastic students in native garb greet and direct you to where the action is— shows, films, craft demonstrations. Everything is arranged in villages around a series of lagoons.

The **Fijian Village** is the easiest to spot because of the high thatched roof of the chief's house. Here you can learn ropemaking, lei weaving with dried material, or watch a fashion show of traditional styles in unusual fabrics. Follow the drums to the **Tahitian Village** and learn the *tamure,* the Tahitian version of the hula.

Somehow the **Samoan Village** seems to be the most fun. Handsome young men climb 40-foot palm trees, start fires, and crack open coconuts to share the milk and "spoon" soft coconut meat. They do it all with such warmth and humor that visitors are infected with their enthusiasm. If you see people walking around with *lauhala* woven hats and visors stuck with jaunty flowers, the wearers probably wove them here.

Altogether there are seven villages each offering different crafts, dances, and music. In the regularly scheduled, highly photogenic "Pageant of the Long Canoes," the music and dances of all Islands are showcased on canoe stages that travel the lagoons.

In the evening, you have your choice of a luau, or an extensive buffet. No alcoholic beverages are ever served at the center. After dinner, everyone moves to the open theater for a dramatic 90-minute musical production complete with "erupting volcanoes" and lighted

Above: A fire dancer jokes with his audience before beginning his daring performance at the Polynesian Cultural Center.

Above right: At the Samoan Village you can watch a man climb to the treetops to harvest coconuts.

fountains of water. The young people who make up the cast are enthusiastic, and the timing and pace are professional down to the last drumbeat. The center also has an IMAX theater and a marketplace. You can travel about the 42-acre complex on foot or by canoe. You'll want to spend hours here—it's an expedition all by itself.

Laie town is a quiet, mostly Mormon community. Drive toward the ocean on Anemoku Street then to the end of Naupaka Street to see a natural lava sea arch and a bird sanctuary on a nearby islet. Just beyond Laie, **Malaekahana State Recreation Area** (*Kamehameha Hwy. at Kalanai Point, tel 808/293-1736, closes 7 p.m.*) is a good swimming beach with a shady picnic area and scenic views. ∎

The North Shore

The North Shore of Oahu is as much a state of mind as a geographic location. Some North Shore beaches are ragged coves framed in lava promontories. Others are long sweeps of sand scoured by wind. Sunsets sear the soul, cattle graze in oceanfront meadows, houses bravely face the sea only feet from its foam. The ocean is the center of life, whether it's gentle and rolling ashore in whispers or whipped to storm fury. Winter is surf season and sometimes the monster waves roll in at 30 feet. In summer the same beaches can look like lakes. It conjures images of youth, beach, laid-back lifestyle, sand, salt, sunblock, small towns, and big surf.

The quiet end of the North Shore is Mokuleia and sleepy Waialua town. The only reason to head this way is to hop a hang glider (*Mr. Bill's Glider Rides, Dillingham Airfield, Hawaii 930, Mokuleia, 5 miles past Waialua High School, tel 808/677-3404, closed 5:30 p.m. daily, $$$$*) or to pick up the trailhead for a 2-mile, three-hour trek around Kaena Point, an area that's so rugged it defies roadbuilders. (To get to the trailhead, just drive to the end of Hawaii 930.) People talk about a circle-island tour of Oahu, but the truth is, you can't circle Oahu because of Kaena. Many temple ruins sleep in the brush.

The celebrated beaches of the North Shore begin at Haleiwa town (see p. 111) and stretch to the Turtle Bay Hilton. The hotel dining room, which is on a promontory jutting into

With an arsenal of boards behind him, a surfer appraises the waves at Banzai Pipeline, Oahu.

Champion surfer Liam McNamara braves the face of a monster wave. The sport was invented by the ancient Hawaiians.

the high surf, is an excellent place to see daredevil wave jockeys up close. At Sunset Beach the surf is so powerful it scoops out whole sections of the 2-mile beach. At sunset, the waves are backlit and surfers riding the wild white crests are silhouetted against a blazing sky. Notorious Banzai Pipeline is famous for its "tube" waves caused by a shallow reef just offshore that forces waves to rise dramatically. Snorkelers head for the large protected tide pools at **Pupukea Beach Park** (59–727 Kamehameha Hwy.); in winter, these pools are often inundated by surf. Waimea Bay in winter sounds like a war zone. Jumbo rollers come boiling in and their roar, echoing against the walls of the bay, sounds like cannon fire. At such times, spectators gather on the cliffs above Waimea Bay as at a gladiator match to watch the wave warriors in their wild rides down the thundering liquid mountains. At the first weather forecaster's warning of jumbo surf, mothers rush home to lock up their sons' boards, to make sure they aren't among the daring surfers enjoying the ultimate thrill of a North Shore wave at its full height.

Extreme caution is urged, even walking these beaches in winter: Rogue waves have swept many a stroller out to sea, often with tragic results. From a safe place, watching a champion surfer ride down the face of one of these mighty walls of water is thrilling. You see him paddle furiously into the top of the foamy crest, stand up, then slide down the concave wave, speeding sideways as he drops, often being swallowed by the tube, then streaking out the other side, on the ride of his life. ■

Surfing

At least a thousand years ago, Hawaiians mastered the sport of surfing, which they called *hee nalu*. An ancient *pohuehue* (surf-coaxing chant) collected by historian Abraham Fornander (1812–1887) pleads:

*Ku mai! Ku mai! Ka nalu nui mai
Kahiki mai,
Alo poi pu! Ku mai ka pohuehue,
Hu! Kaikoo loa.*

Arise, arise, the great waves from Kahiki,
The powerful curling waves.
Arise from the chant.
Well up, long raging surf.

Many great love stories in Hawaii's vast literary heritage begin with or revolve around surfing. One tells of a handsome, duplicitous chief of Kauai, who complicated his life when he fell in love with a goddess he first saw surfing at Puhele near Hana, Maui. In another, a *moo* (lizard) goddess, while surfing, lured an unsuspecting royal surfer to her own board and carried him away to Kaena Point, Oahu. Yet another surfer abduction took place when a chief of Oahu kidnapped Kelea, a beautiful Maui chiefess, while she was riding the waves.

In 1778, Lt. James King, aboard Captain Cook's H.M.S. *Resolution,* described his amazement at first seeing the sport of surfing: "The boldness and address, with which we saw them perform these difficult and dangerous maneuvers, was altogether astonishing and is scarce to be credited."

John Papa Ii (1800–1870), a leading citizen of the Hawaiian kingdom and an associate justice of its supreme court, reported in *Fragments of Hawaiian History* his delight at entering Lahaina harbor, Maui, and seeing boys "surfing on the north side of Pelekane, with banana trunks for surf boards."

Jack London took a leaf from the ancient tales and wrote a short story of surfer love, "The Kanaka Surf." In his 1908 book *The Cruise of the Snark,* he described actually learning to surf: "Soon we were out in deep waters where the big smokers came roaring in….When a breaker curled over my head, for a swift instant I could see the light of day through its emerald body; then down would go my head, and I would clutch the board with all my strength. Then would come the blow, and to the onlooker on shore I would be blotted out. In reality, the board and I have passed through the crest and emerged in the respite of the other side."

James Michener must have read these stories. In his novel *Hawaii,* he wrote: "She was a tall girl with sun-shot black hair streaming behind her in the wind….As she stood naked on the board her handsome breasts and long firm legs seemed carved of brown marble, yet she was agile, too, for with exquisite skill she moved her knees and adjusted her shoulders so that her skimming board leaped faster than the others, while she rode it with a more secure grace."

The father of modern surfing was Duke Paoa Kahanamoku (see p. 87). The athlete attracted great attention for the sport, which had almost died in the wake of Western culture, when he rode his 114-pound koa board in the long rollers sweeping in past Diamond Head in Waikiki surf.

Professional surfing matches started in California but the sport received the biggest boost in 1965, when Honolulu businessman Kimo Wilder McVay, working with the Duke and surfer Fred Hemmings, created the Duke Kahanamoku Surfing Classic and got CBS to film the meet for the world's first network broadcast of a surfing contest. The top 24 surfers in the world came to Hawaii to compete and surf with the Duke. The Classic was held at Sunset Beach, and it was Jeff Hakman of Sunset Beach who won the competition. It helped make surfing a respectable sport, not quite on a par with golf and tennis, but definitely elevated above its onetime hippie trappings. Today the ancient sport of hee nalu is televised internationally, and lures people around the world into its "endless-summer" lifestyle. ∎

Surfer Liam McNamara wears a helmet camera to capture the inside of a wave.

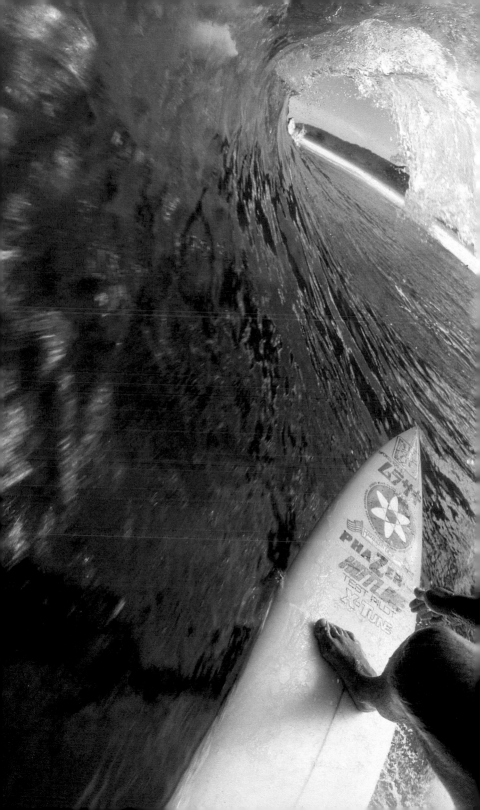

Waimea

Waimea Falls Park

🅰 54 C4

✉ 59-864
Kamehameha Hwy.

☎ 808/638-8511

💲 $$$$

🚌 TheBus 52 or park
shuttle from Waikiki

WHEN THE VALLEYS OF OAHU PASSED FROM ONE KING TO another, only Waimea was reserved for the *kahuna* (priests). It was a major religious center of the ancient Hawaiian civilization. Two temples guard the entrance to the valley; one, Puu o Mahuka Heiau, is a state monument and a National Historic Landmark.

Turn off Kamehameha Highway onto Pupukea Road as it winds up the 250-foot bluff. The 5-acre temple has sweeping views of the entire North Shore, and the glorious panorama was sometimes the last thing the sacrificial victims saw. Two seamen, perhaps three, from Capt. George Vancouver's ship H.M.S. *Daedelus* were offered on the altar in May 1792, after being captured drawing fresh water from the mouth of the Waimea River. In 1819, a year before the arrival of the first Christian missionaries, all the *kii* (god images) in the valley were destroyed by order of King Kamehameha II. The power of the priests was broken (see p. 30).

The sacred site is now open as **Waimea Falls Park.** Nature paths meander along a stream and past ancient lava walls and platforms, a prayer tower, and thatched temple buildings. Narrated tram tours introduce you to a few of the myriad plants, and explain the valley's history. The park claims 6,000 varieties of plants, many rare and endangered.

Bananas are also a specialty. There were once 50 known forms of the Hawaiian banana, but the count today is down to 30, 25 of which grow in Waimea. You can watch *hula kahiko,* the oldest form of the dance (see p. 168), participate in Hawaiian sports and crafts, and learn about traditional herbal medicines. At the head of the park, a 55-foot waterfall cascades into an icy plunge pool, into which professional divers do swans from the top.

To further explore Waimea, you can rent a mountain bike for the hills or a kayak for the streams. There is a restaurant and picnic grounds. The park often schedules nighttime nature walks when the moon is full. The biggest festival is the Makahiki held every October, marked with hula competitions, traditional sports events, and pageantry. ∎

**Kahuna lapaau,
a practitioner
of traditional
Hawaiian
medicine**

Haleiwa & central Oahu

THERE'S NOW A FAST BYPASS AROUND THE FUNKY LITTLE
surfer town of Haleiwa, but if you take it you'll miss driving over an
art deco bridge for the world's most famous shaved ice (snow cones).
It comes in flavors such as coconut, *li hing mui* (salty and sweet red
Chinese spice mixture), and lychee.

The best place to queue up for
shave ice is **Matsumoto's** *(66-087
Kamehameha Hwy., tel 808/637-
4827, closed 6 p.m.).* You'll also miss
some of the best active-wear and
boutique shopping on the Island,
several interesting art galleries
featuring well-priced work of fine
local artists, and the free **North
Shore Surf and Cultural
Museum** *(North Shore Marketplace, 66-250 Kamehameha Hwy.,
tel 808/637 8888, closed when the
surf is up).* Though not state-of-
the-art, it's crammed with unusual
ephemera such as beach blanket
movie posters starring Sandra Dee
and Frankie Avalon. You can trace
the evolution of the surfboard from
the early wooden boards to today's
sleek fiberglass speed demons.

Return to Honolulu through
the pineapple fields of the central
Leilehua Plateau. First stop is **Dole
Pineapple Visitor Center** for
fresh juice, fruit, and ice cream. You
can get lost in one of the world's
largest mazes and win a prize if you
get out in par time. The Pineapple
Express train will take you on a
tour of the plantation. Just down
the road, at the intersection of
Hawaii 80 and 99, you can pull out
for the small but interesting **Del
Monte Pineapple Variety
Garden** *(no telephone).* No
booths, no souvenirs, just all kinds
of pineapple, even pink.

At the intersection of Kameha-
meha Highway and Whitmore
Avenue, you'll see a sign for the
**Kukaniloko Birthstones State
Monument.** In the middle of the

pineapple fields, in a grove of eucalyptus and coconut trees is a group
of stones where early Hawaiian
royalty came to give birth (see p.
29). Some historians speculate the
site may also have served as an
astronomy center, and there are
interesting petroglyphs in the rocks.
This is probably the most sacred of
the ancient sites on Oahu.

Children enjoy
the local treat
in Haleiwa—
shaved ice.

The U.S. Army's Schofield
Barracks in Wahiawa is worth a
stop if you enjoy military curiosi-
ties. In the base's **Tropic
Lightning Museum** *(tel
808/655-0438, closed 4 p.m.
Tues.–Sat., closed Sun.–Mon.)* is a
reproduction of a section of the
notorious Cu Chi Tunnels. During
the Vietnam War, the tunnel network was used to secretly move
large numbers of Viet Cong into
and out of South Vietnam. ■

**Dole Pineapple
Visitor Center**

🅰 54 C3
✉ 64-1550
    Kamehameha Hwy.
☎ 808/621-8408
💲 Maze: $. Train: $$
🚌 TheBus 52

The Waianae Coast

Heading for the Waianae Coast doesn't look very promising as the H-1 Freeway zips past crowded suburbs and malls, but there are a few interesting stops on the way. One is Pearl Harbor (see pp. 113–115), and another is the former sugar town, Waipahu.

To remember plantation days, **Hawaii's Plantation Village** *(94–695 Waipahu St., Waipahu, tel 808/677-0110, closed 3 p.m. Mon.–Sat., closed Sun.)* has created a 3-acre hamlet of replicated ethnic dwellings representing the eight major groups that immigrated to the Islands as sugar workers (see pp. 32–33). Plantation owners kept ethnic groups segregated, so cultural links to the old country remained strong.

From the freeway you can see the rusting **Aloha Stadium** *(99–500 Salt Lake Blvd., tel 808/486-9300)*, where the National Football League all-stars come for the Pro Bowl every winter. On Wednesday, Saturday, and Sunday the parking lot is awash in merchandise for a huge **flea market** *(closed 3 p.m.)*. It's the cheapest place to buy souvenirs, an extra piece of luggage, T-shirts, and casual clothes.

As you reach Kahe Point, Oahu changes character: It's like landing on an outer island—laid-back, local, and unspoiled by sophistication. The beaches that punctuate the 6 miles of sunny shoreline are the best

on the island, but in winter, the surf can be treacherous and extreme caution should be exercised. The beauty of this region is compromised by its tough-guy reputation, so don't linger after sundown.

Surf meets happen at **Makaha Beach.** The most famous is the annual Buffalo's Longboard Contest, organized by legendary waterman Buffalo Kaulana to revive old-time bigboard surfing (see pp. 108–109).

At **Makua Beach,** commercial operators run dolphin encounters. In summer when these coastal waters are normally calm, the playful mammals frequent the pretty bay.

The last beach before rugged Kaena Point is a long treeless swath of sand baking in the sun. Popularly called **Yokohama Bay** because so many immigrant Japanese laborers fished here during the plantation era, it is popular with young people who come for the surf and "scene." The real name is Keawaula ("red harbor"), because great schools of shrimp once congregated here in such numbers that the water appeared to turn red. ■

Pearl Harbor

PEARL HARBOR, BRISTLING WITH MILITARY HARDWARE, was once known as Wai Momi, "pearl waters," because of its abundant oyster beds. As soon as Hawaii was annexed to the United States in 1898, Pearl Harbor became a staging area for ships heading to Guam and the Philippines during the Spanish-American War.

Pearl Harbor
🔺 54 CI

The war that seared Pearl Harbor into the American consciousness, however, was World War II. For America, it began on a sunny Sunday morning, December 7, 1941, when, in a daring air raid, the forces of imperial Japan devastated the American fleet in the harbor and killed 2,300 people. It happened so quickly and with such surprise that the U.S.S. *Arizona* went down with 1,102 men, who are still entombed in the metal hull today. They are honored by the lyrical white concrete **Arizona Memorial** erected above the sunken ship.

Designed by Honolulu architect Alfred Preis, the monument was made possible in large measure by the late Elvis Presley who gave a benefit concert for the *Arizona* in 1961. It draws almost 1.4 million visitors a year, so it's advisable to arrive early and immediately secure a number for the launch ride to the memorial. Lines have been known to last three hours.

Before you board the launch, you will be ushered into a theater for a dramatic documentary of the infamous attack. It is poignant to see the sweet Sunday innocence of Hawaii suddenly shattered; most Islanders, at first, didn't realize it was a real attack, as they assumed the military were playing war games.

The Visitor Center has a museum of battle photographs and navy paraphernalia, a gift shop with a good selection of books on the attack, and a snack shop.

There are tour companies offering boat rides to the *Arizona*, but only designated USN boats can dock at the memorial.

Across the parking lot from the Visitor Center, the **U.S.S. *Bowfin* Submarine Museum and Park** is a tribute to the vital role of the submarine in warfare and national security. You can study

Opposite: Fishermen fold away their nets on the Waianae Coast. Below: The U.S.S. *Missouri*, where Japan surrendered in World War II, is in Pearl Harbor.

Throngs of people come every day by Navy launch to pay their respects at the *Arizona* memorial, Pearl Harbor.

U.S.S. Arizona Memorial

✉ 1 Arizona Memorial Dr.

☎ 808/422-0561

🚌 TheBus 20 or Arizona Memorial Shuttle from Waikiki

wartime posters with their jaunty victory slogans, examine the innards of a Poseidon missile, and see a Japanese one-man kamikaze suicide sub. You can even board the U.S.S. *Bowfin* and poke around a real submarine responsible for 44 enemy sinkings in the war.

New developments at Pearl Harbor include a bridge to Ford Island and the pier on "Battleship Row" for the **U.S.S. *Missouri*.** The 58,000-ton battleship, launched in 1944, provided fire-power in the battles of Iwo Jima and Okinawa, and it saw action in the Korean War and the Gulf War of 1991. In June 1998, "Mighty Mo" was greeted by thousands of Islanders as it was towed into its final berth at Pearl Harbor to begin a new life as a museum ship. The

event that has enshrined Mighty Mo in history occurred in Tokyo Bay, September 2, 1945. Three years, eight months and 25 days after the attack on Pearl Harbor, Gen. Douglas MacArthur received the unconditional surrender of Japan on the *Missouri*'s deck. A plaque marks the spot, and from there you can look up and see, 1,000 feet away, the *Arizona* Memorial. The two ships bookend America's part in World War II.

As soon as you step aboard the shuttle trolley that takes you from the Visitor Center to the Mighty Mo, you step back into the 1940s. Music and news bulletins of the era are played, and guides and greeters are dressed in period uniforms.

When you get to the ship, you can wander about on your own or

sign up for a guided tour. The tour begins on the main deck with its 16-inch guns, then circles the ship before going into a mini-theater for a brief film of the ship's history. At the rear of the ship, you'll learn about the Tomahawk Missile System that was employed so effectively during the Gulf War. From the top deck, the views of Pearl Harbor, the *Arizona* Memorial, and the island of Oahu are breathtaking. ■

Above: John Harvey, a volunteer guide, poses before a mural of the U.S.S. *Arizona*.

Below: Names of crew members killed during the Japanese attack are engraved in marble.

U.S.S. Bowfin
✉ 11 Arizona Memorial Dr.
☎ 808/423-1341
$ $$

Battleship Missouri Memorial
✉ Pier 5
☎ 808/423-2263
$ $$$

More places to visit on Oahu

HAWAIIAN WATERS ADVENTURE PARK

Why anyone would want to go to a fake beach and a wave pool when the island is ringed with the real thing is a mystery. Faux sands aside, this 14-million-dollar water-themed amusement park entices with such novelties as two seven-story free-fall water slides, a children's lily pad walk, a fake river with a current for floating in an inner tube, and water-toboggan slides.
▲ 54 C1 ✉ 400 Farrington Hwy., Kapolei ☎ 808/945-3928 🕐 Closed 4:30 p.m. Mon.–Fri., 5 p.m. Sat.–Sun. 💲 $$$$$ 🚍 TheBus 51

HAWAII CHILDREN'S DISCOVERY CENTER

Don't go there with an agenda. Let your children's curiosity lead you through a pint-size village where they can shop, bank, and pump gas; through a digestive system; aboard an

Swimmers in magenta rubber tubes enjoy the fake surf at the Hawaiian Waters Adventure Park.

airplane; and inside a kaleidoscope. They can play house in a Japanese teahouse and dress up in kimono.
▲ 57 C1 ✉ 111 Ohe St., Honolulu ☎ 808/524-5437 🕐 Closed 1 p.m. Tues.–Fri., 3 p.m. Sat.–Sun.; closed Mon. 💲 $$ 🚍 TheBus 19, 20, 47

NATIONAL MEMORIAL CEMETERY OF THE PACIFIC

The cemetery and the Honolulu Memorial are cradled in an extinct volcanic crater known as Punchbowl because of its shape. Its ancient Hawaiian name is oddly prophetic: Puowaina, "hill of sacrifice." Among the first to be buried there were 776 casualties from the 1941 attack on Pearl Harbor. One of the last to be interred was Ellison Onizuka, the Hawaiian astronaut who died in the 1986 *Challenger* explosion. The Honolulu Memorial honors those who fought in the Pacific in World War II, the Korean War, and the Vietnam War. You can see one of the best views of Honolulu from the overlook on Memorial Walk.
▲ 57 C2 ✉ 2177 Puowaina Dr. ☎ 808/532-3720 🕐 Closed 5:30 p.m. Oct.–Feb., 6:30 p.m. March–Sept. 🚍 TheBus 15

OLD PALI ROAD

Ten minutes from the financial district of downtown Honolulu, you can do a 2-mile drive-in rain forest tour. Take the Pali Highway (Hawaii 61) to the stoplight at Nuuanu Pali Road and turn right. You will immediately be enveloped in a jungle where it rains 300 inches a year. Great trees form a leafy canopy, while fragrant wild ginger blossoms bloom beside the road. The road rejoins the Pali Highway where you can continue to Kailua, return to Honolulu, or proceed to the Nuuanu Pali Lookout (see p. 68).

WAIKIKI HISTORIC TRAIL

Waikiki's colorful past, when kings and queens called it home, comes alive when narrated by local guides who tell their tales with whimsy and passion. Together you will follow the newly laid Waikiki Historic Trail, marked with bronze surfboards highlighting great events. You'll hear how Princess Kaiulania's pet peacocks screamed so loudly upon her death that they awakened people miles away; and you can almost peek in on Queen Liliuokalania's lavish little dinners.
▲ Map p. 85 ✉ Royal Hawaiian Shopping Center, center stage, 2201 Kalakaua Ave. ☎ Native Hawaiian Hospitality Assoc., tel 808/841-6442 🕐 Tours 9 a.m. Mon.–Sat. ■

Maui was formed by two distinct volcanoes, and East and West Maui are almost like two separate islands. Miles of sandy beaches ring the shores, with well-planned, well-spaced resorts adding luster to the natural beauty.

Maui

A Lahaina T-shirt says it all.

Maui

EVERYTHING ABOUT MAUI IS YOUNG—ITS ATTITUDE, ITS ORIENTATION, AND even its actual age. Haleakala, the massive dormant volcano that dominates the island, rose from the ocean only a million years ago. Its older sister, Mauna Kahalawai, broke the surface of the waves two million years ago. The lava flows from these mid-ocean giants were so profuse, they connected with other submarine volcanoes that later became the separate islands of Lanai, Molokai, and Kahoolawe. In early times, they were all one landmass, which scientists refer to as Maui Nui, or Big Maui. The islands still maintain their ties, as all are governed as Maui County.

The island of Maui is the second largest in the Hawaiian chain with a land area of 727 square miles, measuring 48 miles long and 26 miles across at its widest. The shoreline runs a linear 120 miles with 81 accessible beaches, whose sands may be white, gold, black, salt and pepper, green, or garnet, due to ancient volcanic activity. That amounts to more swimmable beaches than any other island—and more color.

Beaches dominate the lifestyle of not only the two million visitors who arrive every year, but the 117,644 residents, who plan their calendars around outrigger canoe regattas, fishing seasons, and family picnics at favorite strands of sand. Many people come to Maui and experience what they can only call rebirth. Scratch the surface of a restaurant waiter in Kihei and you may find a former lawyer who now rides a bicycle to work after surfing all day, and who lives on granola and smoothies.

Artists are drawn to Maui for the beautiful natural canvas, for the ready art market provided by well-heeled tourists, and for the less tangible spirit of the island, a creative energy born of its youth.

The island is blessed with diversity and consists of tropical lowlands, rain forest, cloud forest, and high mountains. Because of the height of the mountains, Maui has areas with something approximating a temperate zone climate, suitable for ranching and farming a variety of crops. The island has the dubious distinction of bearing the coldest temperature ever recorded in Hawaii, 11°F in 1961 on the summit of Haleakala.

Less than 25 percent of Maui is inhabited or developed. Resorts are primarily limited to particular, and rather choice, parts of the island: Kaanapali and Kapalua in West Maui,

the Kihei-Wailea-Makena sun corridor in East Maui, and little Hana, all by itself on the far side of Haleakala. The Hotel Hana-Maui, the island's first resort, opened in 1961.

The island is named for the demigod Maui, Superman of the Hawaiian pantheon. The capital of the united Hawaiian kingdom was Lahaina, until it was moved to Honolulu in

1845. Kamehameha the Great married a Maui girl, Kaahumanu, and appointed her coregent of the kingdom on his deathbed.

Maui's history is rich and colorful with a cast of Hawaiian royalty, Yankee whalemen, missionaries, immigrant plantation workers, hippies, New Agers, surf rats, and ordinary people living their lives in an extraordinarily beautiful part of the planet. ■

Children stand on the seawall of the Lahaina waterfront, before the bow of the *Carthaginian,* a museum ship.

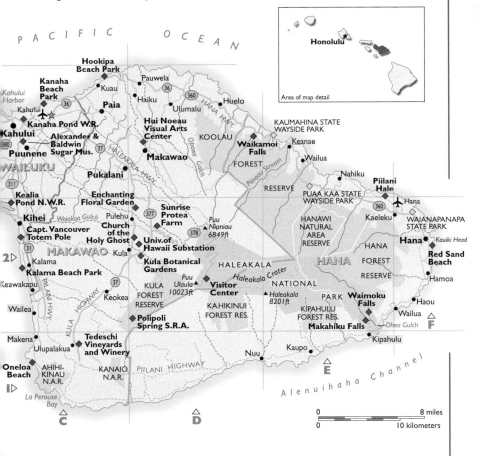

PACIFIC OCEAN

Hookipa Beach Park
Pauwela
Kanaha Beach Park
Kuau
Kahului Harbor
Haiku
Paia
Ulumalu
Huelo
Kahului
HANA HWY.
36
360
Kanaha Pond W.R.
KAUMAHINA STATE WAYSIDE PARK
Alexander & Baldwin Sugar Mus.
Hui Noeau Visual Arts Center
KOOLAU
Waikamoi Falls
Keanae
Puunene
380
37
Makawao
FOREST
Wailua
WAIKU
WAILUKU
HALEAKALA HWY.
Opana Gulch
Piinau Stream
Nahiku
311
Pukalani
RESERVE
Piilani Hale
Kealia Pond N.W.R.
Enchanting Floral Garden
Pulehu
Sunrise Protea Farm
PUAA KAA STATE WAYSIDE PARK
360
Hana
Kihei
Waiakoa Gulch
377
Puu Nianiau 6849ft
Kaeleku
WAIANAPANAPA STATE PARK
Capt. Vancouver Totem Pole
Church of the Holy Ghost
378
HANAWI NATURAL AREA RESERVE
HANA
Hana
Kauiki Head
31
Univ.of Hawaii Substation
MAKAWAO
Kula
Kula Botanical Gardens
HALEAKALA
HANA
FOREST
Red Sand Beach
2
Kalama
Puu Ulaula 10023ft
Haleakala Crater
Visitor Center
RESERVE
Hamoa
Kalama Beach Park
37
KULA FOREST RESERVE
Keokea
Haleakala 8201ft
NATIONAL
Waimoku Falls
Keawakapu
Wailea
KAHIKINUI FOREST RES.
KIPAHULU FOREST RES.
PARK
Haou
Polipoli Spring S.R.A.
Makahiku Falls
Wailua
Oheo Gulch
F
Makena
Tedeschi Vineyards and Winery
Kipahulu
Ulupalakua
Kaupo
Oneloa Beach
AHIHI-KINAU N.A.R.
KANAIO N.A.R.
PIILANI HIGHWAY
Nuu
E
La Perouse Bay
Alenuihaha Channel

0   8 miles
0   10 kilometers

C   D

Area of map detail

Honolulu

The promontory of Kahakuloa is part of the range known as the **West Maui Mountains.**

West Maui

The green slopes of the mountains roll down to the sea, and rainbows crown the misty peaks. The highest is Puu Kukui, "the hill of light," once regarded as the juncture between Heaven and Earth. The great gods Kane and Kanaloa pierced the earth with their spears and created Manowai, a lake said to hold the last waters from the Great Deluge. Its lip, from which many waterfalls flow, was called Omaka, "the beginning." Mauna Eke is where the Hawaiians who survived the flood landed their canoe as the waters receded.

Parts of the West Maui Mountains are so wild they have never been explored, yet they are within 10 miles of hotels and holiday condominiums. The shoreline is scalloped in pristine bays and beaches with names that resound like a chant borne on the wind— Honokowai, Honokeana, Honokahua, Honolua, Honokohau, and Hononana. Honolua and neighboring Mokuleia bays are home to so many jewel-toned tropical reef fish they have been declared a Hawaii State Marine Conservation district, where snorkelers and divers visit their coral canyons.

The town of Lahaina, the resorts of Kaanapali and Kapalua, and a string of little hamlets between them, sit basking on lovely beaches, sheltered by the magnificent hills.

Much of the land is set aside in vast nature preserves, laced with hiking trails. The 9,000-acre Puu Kukui Nature Preserve in Memory of Colin C. Cameron (see p. 129), managed by the Nature Conservancy of Hawaii, is the largest private preserve in the state and shelters a biologically diverse ecosystem containing hundreds of flora that exist nowhere else on earth. Even the part of West Maui that is developed is green. There are five championship golf courses (see pp. 228–229) at two resorts, Kaanapali and Kapalua, and 9,000 acres of pineapple plantation.

There are still functioning *ahupuaa* in this district, a holdover system of land stewardship in which the land was divided into pie-shaped wedges running from the tops of the mountains to the sea (see p. 26).

A long line of Maui kings and queens, and later the scions of the Kamehameha dynasty, made their homes in West Maui. ■

The western coast

THE KAHEKILI HIGHWAY (HAWAII 340) CONNECTS THE remote areas of the West Maui Mountains with the resorts of Kapalua and Kaanapali on one end, and the city of Kahului on the other. Driving this narrow, twisting shoreline route is a white-knuckle experience in places, but the scenery is spectacular. It's a 20-mile road that will take you two hours to drive. Sometimes you'll be crawling around cliffs that plunge down to the sea only inches from your car window. Parts of the coast look as haunted and forsaken as Ireland, while other parts are lush and green.

Leaving the resorts of Kaanapali and Kapalua behind, the road winds around the wonderful litany of bays. If it's winter you may see some mighty waves rolling in: **Mokuleia Bay** is known to surfers as "Slaughterhouse." If it's summer, the snorkeling will be pristine.

Nakalele Point looks like a hunk of alien turf that was flung in fury from some other galaxy. Completely at odds with its lush surroundings, this weird lava landscape is seemingly tormented and twisted into eerie shapes. It hisses and moans as the ocean worms its way under the lava and erupts into geysers, one of which sprays 50 feet in the air when the surf is up. Some people call it Hobbitland, and claim it is at its best when the sun is hidden and rain comes misting in from the ocean.

Look for the U.S. Coast Guard lighthouse, which is really more like a toy light stick than a fully fledged lighthouse (*18 miles W of Lahaina*). Walk down for half a mile toward the shore, keeping to the right side of the beacon, to reach the lava formations. You will hear the geyser rumbling before you see it; be careful of surging surf and incoming tides.

At **Kahakuloa** ("the tall lord"), a huge promontory 636 feet high rises dramatically from the sea, offering refuge to great seabirds: the frigatebird, shearwater, and *koae kea* (white-tailed tropicbird). The pretty little village of Kahakuloa nestled beside it is just the kind of place that makes you want to kiss your job goodbye and settle down in paradise. ■

Blowholes, ocean water spouting through lava tubes, are common at Nakalele Point.

Lahaina

PICTURE A TRIM, TIDY NEW ENGLAND COASTAL TOWN: white picket fences, widow's walks, grey clapboard houses. Move it to the middle of the Pacific Ocean. Add rainbows, high green mountains, palm trees, and the biggest Buddha outside Asia. Now give it a history that reads like a novel, and a cast of characters: kings, queens, a young star-crossed princess, stern Bible-thumping missionaries, scoundrels, and sailors. Now you've just about got Lahaina.

Lahaina

🗺 118 A3

Visitor information

✉ Lahaina Courthouse,
648 Wharf St.

☎ 808/667-9193

On October 1, 1819, the *Balena* out of New Bedford, Massachusetts, was the first American whaling ship to call in Hawaii (see p. 30). The port was Lahaina, a thriving coastal village and capital of the Hawaiian nation. The 2,400 residents were primarily engaged in fishing, farming, and foresting for the lucrative sandalwood trade with China. King Kamehameha II sat on the throne,

with his stepmother, Queen Kaahumanu ruling beside him.

It was a year of great portent. King Kamehameha the Great had been buried. The ancient *kapu* (taboo) system was overthrown by the people, leaving them without their traditional system of religious law. The first party of American missionaries had set sail from Massachusetts to arrive in Hawaii

The waterfront of the old whaling port of Lahaina is dominated by the Pioneer Inn and the brig, *Carthaginian*.

Right: Fishing charters can be arranged along the Lahaina waterfront.

the following year, and reach Maui in 1823. Lahaina basked in the eye of a storm.

Between the 1820s and the 1860s, the Lahaina Roadstead became the principal anchorage of the Yankee Pacific whaling fleet, and the town took on a distinctly New England flavor. The peak year was 1846 when 429 whalers called, and the harbor was described as a forest of masts. Up to 1,500 sailors at a time rampaged in the streets of the small town, in search of grog and women, proclaiming that there was "no god west of the Horn." Among them was Herman Melville, gathering material for his novels *Moby Dick, Typee,* and *Billy Budd.*

Hoapili, governor of Maui, influenced by the missionaries, passed laws shutting down the grog shops and forbidding everything, from spitting in the street to women boarding the ships. The riots that ensued are legendary, with whaler cannon firing on the town, targeting the home of the spoilsport the Reverend William Richards. The missionary the Reverend Lorrin Andrews wrote, "'The devil is busily engaged at Lahaina."

In the midst of the conflict, the missionaries transliterated the Hawaiian language (see p. 31) and taught an eager populace *palapala* (writing); built Lahainaluna, the first high school west of the Rocky Mountains; imported the first printing press to the Islands; published the first newspaper; held singing classes; and translated the Bible into Hawaiian. The Hawaiians, a deeply spiritual people, bereft of their old religion, flocked to the new faith. In a decade, the Hawaiians became literate and Christian.

Lahaina today is a salty survivor. Approximately 55 acres have been set aside as historic districts with several sites designated as National Historical Landmarks. In place of ships' chandlers and grog shops serving demon rum, the weathered wooden buildings loitering along **Front Street** and its byways now house boutiques, along with more than 40 art galleries offering the works of both local artists and masters such as Dalí, Chagall, and Miró, and restaurants showcasing Hawaii's seafood and regional cuisine. The art market is so successful the galleries host a weekly "Friday is Art Night in Lahaina," featuring hors d'oeuvres, wine, music, and art demonstrations.

Where whaling ships once lay at anchor, an armada of pleasure boats now waits to take you snorkeling, diving, whale-watching, on a sunset dinner cruise, or on a picnic sail to other islands.

Lahaina might be called the Williamsburg of Hawaii, except that it is a living, vital town. The whalemen are long gone but, ironically, the whales are still around (see pp. 126–127). ∎

A walk through Lahaina's history

Walk through history, following in the footsteps of whalers, missionaries, and royalty. But be distracted, too, by ice cream parlors, enticing shops, and restaurant decks over the water.

Art festivals often take place beneath the broad shade of the historic banyan tree, Lahaina.

Begin at the **Baldwin Home ❶** *(696 Front St., tel 808/661-3262)*, where you can pick up a free historical map of the town. The original four rooms, built in 1834, have walls 24 inches thick to minimize the heat outside and the high times in the streets. Note the old medical instruments and flag quilt. Next door is the **Masters' Reading Room,** built in 1836 to elevate the spirits of seamen with something other than grog. You can pick up a free walking map here at the Lahaina Restoration Foundation *(120 Dickenson St., tel 808/661-3262)*.

Cross Front Street and head toward the harbor on Market Street. At the edge of the seawall, there's a fine view of the waterfront. For a panorama of the picturesque old town with the majestic green West Maui Mountains rising behind, stroll out on the breakwater and look back. Lahaina appears to be a town from

another, sleepier era. Right on the waterfront, the **Pioneer Inn** *(658 Wharf St., tel 808/661-3636)*, built in 1902, is still a salty saloon. The tidy white building next door is the 1859 **Lahaina Courthouse ❷** *(649 Wharf St., tel 808/661-3636)*. It now has an art gallery and gift shop inside. Upstairs, there's an exhibit of old photographs and artifacts from early Lahaina. You may pick up maps and brochures at the Visitor Information desk. Behind the courthouse, stroll beneath the immense boughs of what is reputed to be the largest **banyan tree** in the United States, shading almost an acre. You might be surprised by a crafts fair here.

Turn toward the mountains on Canal Street; walk to Front Street, and turn right. The softball field, **Maluuluolele Park ❸**, was once the most important site on Maui. Intrigued by stories of a "lost island," volunteers began excavation in 1993. They found confirmation of a 1-acre island and its 17-acre lake. The island was home and burial site for Maui royalty. In the 1880s, Princess Pauahi, the great granddaughter of Kamehameha I, had the royal bodies moved to nearby Wainee Cemetery, and in the early 20th century, with a disregard of Hawaiian culture that wouldn't be tolerated today, the lake was filled in.

Turn left on Shaw Street and left again on Wainee Street for **Wainee Cemetery ④** (*535 Wainee St., tel 808/661-4349*), which contains headstones for Keopuolani, sacred wife of Kamehameha I, and Princess Nahienaena who, according to ancient royal tradition, fell in love with her brother Kamehameha III and bore his child, who lived only hours. Nahienaena died at age 21 in 1836.

Continue on Wainee Street, passing the **Hongwanji Mission** (*551 Wainee St., tel 808/661-0640*), a Buddhist temple built in 1927. On the corner of Prison and Wainee Streets is the old jail. **Hale Paahao ⑤** ("stuck-in-irons house") was built by convict labor in 1852. After visiting, keep walking on

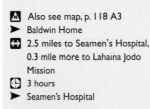

- 🅼 Also see map, p. 118 A3
- ▶ Baldwin Home
- 🔄 2.5 miles to Seamen's Hospital, 0.3 mile more to Lahaina Jodo Mission
- ⏱ 3 hours
- ▶ Seamen's Hospital

NOT TO BE MISSED
- Baldwin Home
- Pioneer Inn
- The banyan tree

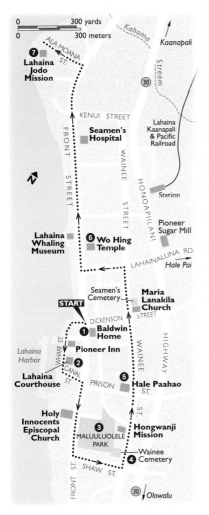

Wainee Street two blocks to Dickenson Street. Adjacent to the **Maria Lanakila Church** is the **Seamen's Cemetery.** A cousin of Herman Melville is buried here, as well as a shipmate who died, according to the marker, "of a disreputable disease." At Lahainaluna Road, turn left two blocks and you'll be back on Front Street. Turn right and find the exotic **Wo Hing Temple ⑥** (*858 Front St., tel 808/661-5553, closed 4 p.m. daily*), built in 1912 by the Chee Kung Tong, a fraternal society dating from the 17th century. The adjacent cookhouse shows a 15-minute film about Hawaii made by Thomas Edison.

Continue along Front Street to the 1833 **Seamen's Hospital** (*1024 Front St.*). You can end your walk here, or push on another ten minutes, turning down Ala Moana to see the largest Buddha outside Asia at the **Lahaina Jodo Mission ⑦,** sitting outdoors with a pagoda beside him and the mountains behind. ■

Whales

On the first page of his epic whaling novel *Moby-Dick*, Herman Melville wrote: "Whenever it is damp, drizzly November in my soul ... then I account it high time to get to sea as soon as I can." Whales must feel the same November of the soul, for in that month more than 1,500 humpbacks begin arriving in Hawaiian waters from their Arctic feeding grounds. They come for the same reasons most visitors do—rest, recreation, and romance. They also give birth to their two-ton babies in the warm tropical seas, after which they stay until April while the young whales gain 200 pounds a day. Then they begin the long swim north again.

The humpbacks can be seen from every island, leaping, splashing, blowing great geysers of ocean into the air. At 60 feet long and weighing over 100,000 pounds, they create quite a commotion in the ocean.

Whales come in two families: the *Odontoceti,* the toothed whales, and the *Mysticeti,* which are toothless. The latter name refers to the whales' strange mustache-like feeding mechanism, the baleen. Made of a substance similar to fingernails, it is remarkably efficient and traps as much as two tons of plankton, shrimp, small fish, and swarms of krill in a single feeding. Humpbacks belong to the *mysticeti,* which include the largest animals on earth.

Like other mammals, the humpback whale breathes air and nurses its young. Humpbacks are distinguished by their great knobby heads and enormous, individually marked flukes, which they wave in the air. But most of all, humpbacks are known for their music. Beneath the ocean, great choirs sing. Swimmers are sometimes enraptured by the strange, haunting, very melodic cries, moans, and crescendos. In the morning, when the air is very still, and the whales are close to shore, people on land claim to hear the song. While singing, the whales hang suspended, motionless, and carry on for hours. Whaling museums and aquariums in the Islands often have recordings of the divas of the deep.

Every winter the whales compose a new song, which they all sing. Throughout the season it changes slowly but dramatically. The song is more complex than that of a bird and may have eight or ten themes to it. The whole process seems an indication of the mammal's great and legendary intelligence.

Humpbacks are the third most endangered species of whale, with only 7,000 to 8,000 individuals left in the world. Strictly enforced federal and state laws forbid boats from approaching closer than 300 feet. The whales,

Scrimshaw

Between whales, life aboard a whaler was boring. To pass the time, whalemen took to carving, etching, and whittling the bones, teeth, and baleen of their prey. In the process, they created what many regard as the only nonaboriginal American folk art—scrimshaw. Predictably, the most common subjects the sailors chose were women and the sea. It is estimated that half the pieces were pornographic and were later destroyed. In contrast, more noble themes, such as religion and patriotism were also favorites.

Often the men made practical items such as nautical gear, belt buckles, and combs. For sweethearts back home they crafted hairpins, clothes pins, pie crimpers, and corset stays.

When the Endangered Species Act of 1973 put whale ivory off limits, scrimshanders turned to fossilized walrus, wooly mammoth bone, and plastic imitations.

Due to its year-round selling season, Maui is the largest scrimshaw market in the world, surpassing its two closest rivals, Alaska, and Cape Cod, Massachusetts. ∎

however, are a law unto themselves, and often thrill whale-watchers by swimming quite close to the boats. Great numbers congregate in the sheltered waters of the Auau Channel between Maui and Molokai. Maui claims the largest whale-watching fleet, with nearly every commercial boat in the harbors of Lahaina and Maalaea pressed into service in the season.

Hawaiian waters host substantial populations of other cetaceans including dolphins—actually a variety of toothed whales. Other *Odontoceti* found in Hawaii are false killer whales, melon-headed whales, beaked whales, pilot whales, and even the great sperm whale. Black pilot whales are the most numerous;

A humpback whale breaching in the waters off Hawaii. These endangered creatures are a magnet for whale-watchers.

they travel in pods of 20 to 40 and are most common off the Kona Coast of the Big Island and in the Alenuihaha Channel between the Big Island and Maui. While the sperm whale is plentiful, it is rarely seen because it frequents deep waters far from land.

Before Western contact, the Hawaiians, although they were lords of the sea and great fishermen, never hunted the whale. Any that washed up on shore were deemed the property of the king. ■

Kaanapali

Kaanapali
🗺 118 A3

Visitor information
✉ Kaanapali Beach
Resort Association,
2530 Kekaa Dr.
☎ 808/661-3271
🕐 Closed Sat.–Sun.

WHEN AMERICAN FACTORS DESIGNED THE WORLD'S FIRST master-planned resort in the 1950s, they already knew the best location—Kaanapali, the favorite holiday retreat of Hawaiian royalty. They would come to the perfect 3-mile beach to surf the long rollers and race their swift outrigger canoes in the channel between Maui and Lanai. On what is now the Royal Kaanapali Golf Course, they'd play *ulu maika,* a form of lawn bowling. Come evening, there'd be luaus along the beach, with succulent pigs lifted ceremoniously from the underground ovens. The beat of the *pahu* drums would call the dancers to begin telling the old stories in chant, gesture, and step.

A refurbished sugarcane train makes the run between Lahaina and the resort at Kaanapali Beach.

Lahaina Kaanapali & Pacific Railroad
✉ Lahaina Station;
Kaanapali Station;
Puukolii Station
☎ 808/661-0080
💲 $$$

They always remembered the tales of Kekaa, the towering black lava promontory at the end of the beach. It was said that at sundown, a hole opened on the horizon, and through it, souls could leap into the next world. King Kahekili (1713–1794) would leap from the point into the sea to encourage his troops in feats of courage. When the capital of the kingdom moved to Honolulu, Kaanapali, like Sleeping Beauty, began a long slumber.

In 1849, Hawaiian scholar David Malo began experimenting with raising sugar. It proved to be an excellent crop. A narrow-gauge railroad was laid running from the Pioneer Mill in Lahaina through the new sugar plantation to a ship landing constructed at what was once a sacred site, Kekaa Point.

Kaanapali today is a 1,200-acre resort with six hotels, five holiday condominiums, two 18-hole championship golf courses, 40 tennis courts, a tennis stadium, 20-plus restaurants, and more than 75 shops.

The skeleton of a 40-foot sperm whale welcomes you to **Whaler's Village** *(2435 Kaanapali Pkwy.),* a shopping complex at the resort. Up on the second floor the **Whale Museum** *(tel 808/661-5992)* has a fascinating collection of memorabilia recalling Maui's 19th-century whaling heyday. Videos and self-guided audio tours tell you all about the nasty business of hunting the world's largest living mammal. There are weapons, ship models, a life-size diorama of the miserable living quarters aboard ship, and some intriguing diaries and letters written by the sailors.

The old sugarcane train, the **Lahaina Kaanapali & Pacific Railroad,** is still running the 6 miles into Lahaina, but sacred Kekaa, now popularly called Black Rock, is no longer on the route. However, each evening, a diver leaps from the pinnacle into the sea, as King Kahekili once did, and for a moment, the spirit of old Hawaii does, indeed, seem to pass through the portals of sunset. ∎

Kapalua

SITUATED AMID A 23,000-ACRE WORKING PINEAPPLE PLAN-
tation, Kapalua is fringed by five exceptional bays, all open to the
public. In 1992, Maui Land & Pineapple, the parent company of
Kapalua, dedicated 8,661 acres of native forest to the Nature
Conservancy of Hawaii, creating Puu Kukui Nature Preserve in
Memory of Colin C. Cameron (conservationist and former ML& P
president). This is home to three native bird species; five very rare
snail species; 20 rare native plants, 18 of them endemic and unique to
West Maui; fragrant species of sandalwood; rare violets; and the
world's only *Lobelia gloria montis,* a white-and-purple blossom.

A second preserve of 70 acres has
been set aside for **The Gorilla
Foundation** and, by about 2005,
funds permitting, should be home
to primates including Koko, the
famous female gorilla who has
learned to communicate with
humans using sign language.

In 1996 Kapalua, after conform-
ing to stringent environmental
requirements, became the first
resort in the world to be certified by
the environmental watchdog group
Audubon International.

The **Kapalua Nature Society**
publishes a journal about Maui's
natural history. The society also
organizes hikes into preserves, to
the 75-year-old Maunalei
Arboretum, and tours of the
pineapple plantation *(Kapalua
Activities Desk, tel 808/669-8088).*

Kapalua has two luxury hotels, a
number of holiday home and condominium rentals mixed in with
residential communities, three
championship golf courses (see p.
228), 20 tennis courts, 16 restaurants, and more than 20 shops.

Several notable events take place
at the resort. Acclaimed artists
gather over Easter weekend and
conduct free classes for the public.
The Kapalua Wine & Food
Symposium in July has been
attracting leading chefs for more
than two decades. The most ambi-
tious event, and the one most in
keeping with the resort's character,
is the annual September Earth
Maui Summit, a week-long celebration of nature with a spectrum of
ecological seminars, activities,
hikes, and exhibits. ■

**A kayaker at
Napili Bay heads
to sea on a calm,
clear day.**

Kapalua
🅜 118 A4

**Kapalua Nature
Society**
✉ 800 Kapalua Dr.
☎ 808/669-5622

Visitors learn to weave baskets and hats from hala tree fronds at Maui Tropical Plantation.

Central Maui

Kula-o-ka-Mao-Mao, "the land of mirages," is what Hawaiians called the broad central isthmus between the verdant West Maui Mountains and the massive flanks of Haleakala. Shimmering with heat, teased by almost constant winds, this land belongs neither to East Maui nor West, yet it is the heart of the island, where locals live and tourists land.

The airport was originally built by the U.S. Navy during World War II, to supply the Pacific armada. The military also developed a beach which is now **Kanaha Beach Park** (*Hawaii 380, 1 mile N of Kahului International Airport*), a protected shallow-water shoreline that is the best beach on this part of the island. Windsurfers like Kanaha for the steady, strong onshore trade winds.

Nearby, directly in the flight path of silver birds with their noisy jet engines, endangered Hawaiian birds, such as the *koloa* and Hawaiian stilt, have set up housekeeping in and around former royal fishponds, playing host to annual migrations of Alaskan birds. Actually, the birds were here first. In 1971, the area was declared a National Natural History Landmark, and is known as **Kanaha Pond Wildlife Refuge** (*2 miles W of jct. of Hana Hwy. and Haleakala Hwy. Extension, tel 808/984-8100*).

In spite of the glut of commerce around the airport, much of the central plain is carpeted in pineapple fields and acres of emerald sugarcane waving their silver tassels in the breezes. Workers wear colorful protective gear when laboring in the fields.

You can visit a working plantation at the touristy **Maui Tropical Plantation** (*1670 Honoapiilani Hwy., tel 800/451-6805*). Admission is free, but they charge for a tram tour. There's a restaurant, gift shop, and attractive garden and ponds.

The **Alexander & Baldwin Sugar Museum** (*Puunene Ave. & Hansen Rd., Puunene, tel 808/871-8058, closed Sun.*) chronicles the heyday of King Cane in photographs and artifacts. Located in the former residence of the manager of the state's largest sugar company, it is next to a working sugar mill with all its clatter and wonderful molasses smell. ■

Kahului & Wailuku

THE CONTRASTING TOWNS OF KAHULUI AND WAILUKU
are 3 miles apart. Kahului was built in the 1950s by the plantation
company Alexander and Baldwin, to provide housing for workers.
Ships carry away sugar and pineapple, and return laden with the latest gizmos and fashions. Kahului has the impressive **Maui Arts &
Cultural Center** (see p. 144), but otherwise its landmarks are pedestrian—three shopping malls, plus chain stores and discounters.

All these new arrivals have hurt
little old **Wailuku.** Much of Main
Street is shuttered as small businesses have caved in. In spite of
economics, however, the charming
streets are anything but depressed.
They still invite walking, and there
are antique shops, home furnishings stores, and odd little galleries.

Wailuku is the perfect setting for
Kaahumanu Church *(103 S.
High St., tel 808/244-5189, closed
Mon.–Fri.).* Built in 1837 on the site
of a former grass chapel and an
adobe church, it is named for the
favorite wife of Kamehameha I,
who precipitated the overthrow of
the old religion, paving the way for
Christianity (see p. 30).

Caroline and Edward Bailey,
missionaries turned sugar growers,
lived happily for 45 years in what is
now **Bailey House Museum.**
Built in 1833, and added on for
years, the house still feels like someone's cozy home, with the porches,
angled staircase, comfortable old
furniture, dolls, books, and bed
quilts. There are also fascinating
precontact artifacts including an
unusual replicated temple image—
the Bishop Museum in Honolulu
(see pp. 70–71) collected the original. One room is devoted to
Edward Bailey's oil paintings of
Maui done between 1866 and 1896
(see p. 42). They make you long to
have seen Maui in the old days. ■

Kaahumanu
Church, Wailuku,
named for Queen
Kaahumanu

Kahului
🅰 119 C3

Wailuku
🅰 118 B3

Visitor information
✉ Maui Visitors
Bureau, 1727 Wili
Pa Loop, Wailuku
96793
☎ 808/244-3530 or
800/525-MAUI
🕐 Closed Sat.–Sun.

**Bailey House
Museum**
✉ 2375-A Main St.,
Wailuku
☎ 808/244-3326
🕐 Closed Sun.
💲 $$

Iao Valley

THE VALLEY OF THE KINGS, IAO, IS NAMED FOR THE GOD above all gods, the Supreme Light. In ancient days, the Hawaiians carried their royal dead into the valley for secret ceremonial burial. A natural altar, now known as Iao Needle, rises 1,200 feet from the stream at its base. As recently as 1959, old rituals were reenacted during an Aloha Week pageant when, on a clear night, a pathway of bamboo torches blazed all the way to the tip of the Needle. A chanter walked to the top and called out almost forgotten prayers across the dark and deep valley.

The Chinese pavilion at Kepaniwai Heritage Garden

Iao Valley State Park

🅰 118 B3

✉ Hawaii 32, Iao Valley Rd.

☎ 808/984-8109

Hawaii Nature Center

🅰 118 B3

✉ 875 Iao Valley Rd.

☎ 808/244-6500

💲 $$

Opposite: A bridge across a stream affords excellent views of Iao Valley and its famous Needle.

One of the bloodiest battles in Hawaiian history took place here in 1790, when the army of King Kamehameha I thundered across the plain in pursuit of Kalanikupule, defender of Maui and son of his archenemy King Kahekili. With a terrible new weapon—cannon salvaged from a defeated American ship, the *Eleanora*—Kamehameha took a terrible toll on the Maui forces. So many were killed that their bodies choked the Wailuku River, which ran red with their blood. The cannon was forever called Waha-ula, "the red mouth," and the battle was Kepaniwai, meaning "the damming of the waters."

Kepaniwai Heritage Garden (*Hawaii 32, 2 miles from Wailuku*), named for the battle, is a cool and peaceful sanctuary. Designed by local architect Richard Tongg, it contains homes and gardens representative of the major ethnic groups that settled Maui. Among them are a New England saltbox, a Japanese teahouse, a Chinese pagoda, and the proverbial "little grass shack." It's quite photogenic and a good place to have a picnic.

Just up the road, farther into Iao Valley, is a sign pointing out a natural profile of President John F. Kennedy, etched into the mountainside. Such profiles often require a generous imagination, but this one is startling.

Iao Valley State Park is a 6.2-acre park within the 4,000 acres of the valley. You can take in the most breathtaking vistas on an easy 0.3-mile loop trail that crosses the stream. From the bridge you can see the green Needle. Other trails go deeper into the valley, but they enter private land and are posted.

To learn more about the natural history of this significant valley, stop in at the **Hawaii Nature Center.** This Maui branch of the Oahu-based environmental education group (see p. 82) has more than 30 hands-on exhibits in the Interactive Science Arcade plus dioramas, games, and a solarium with stunning views of the valley. On weekends they offer guided hikes into Iao. ∎

Windsurfers line up for a race from Wailea to Molokini islet.

East Maui

Haleakala, the world's largest dormant volcano, dominates the eastern end of Maui. At 10,023 feet, it towers a mile higher than any other Maui mountain. Arrayed at its feet on the sunny southwest shore is a series of resort areas—the hodgepodge of Kihei, manicured Wailea, and secluded Makena—that die away into dry lava-strewn wilderness surrendering to the sea. Rain is rare, which is obvious when you look at the parched scrub beyond the reach of resort sprinklers. It's an ideal holiday climate.

From this leeward shore, you can see Lanai, Kahoolawe, Molokini, and West Maui, which appears to be a separate island from here.

Day-trip boats beat a path to Molokini, a moonsliver of an islet whose volcanic crater has slipped beneath the waves creating a natural aquarium where colorful reef fish swim with pelagic species from the open ocean—and with the snorkelers who arrive on the excursion boats. Molokini is a Marine Conservation District so the fish are plentiful.

The shore road (South Kihei Road) is lined with condominiums, strip malls, inexpensive restaurants, relaxing mai tai spots for a tropical drink while watching the sunset, activity centers, and farmers' markets. Accommodations range from luxe to "cheap and cheerful." Don't be surprised to see the flag of Canada flying from many a pole. This is snowbird

country: Beleaguered Northerners come here to sit out the winter in their time-shares.

Beyond the resorts, Oneloa Beach spreads out in golden splendor. The water is exceptionally clear, here and at La Perouse Bay, because of the absence of any development. Both have been incorporated into the Makena-La Perouse Bay State Park. Nudists still tiptoe into the little cove on the other side of Puu Olai promontory; if they get caught they can face jail as nudity is illegal.

Around a corner to the northeast, Maui remains rugged and remote, but becomes lush and green, beribboned with waterfalls, veiled in mists. Hana lies pinioned on a lonely road both picturesque and precarious. This is the most genuinely Hawaiian part of the island, gentle in spirit, unpretentious, and happy to be pretty much left alone. ■

Kihei, Wailea, & Makena

This is a wonderful area for budget travellers, and it happens to be one of the finest coasts of the state. Don't be put off by the dike of condos. Once you're in one, the views are glorious, with more isles sitting on the horizon and Haleakala rising in the back.

The beach at **Kihei** runs for 6 miles and is easily accessed in a string of beach parks. **Kalama Beach Park** *(Kihei Rd., 4 miles S of Kihei village)* is 36 acres of shady lawn and coconut palms. It's a great place to picnic, and you can pick up famous barbecued ribs and Maui potato chips at **Azeka's** *(1280 S. Kihei Rd., tel 808/879-0611)*.

Just across from the Maui Lu Resort *(575 S. Kihei Rd., tel 808/879-5881)* is a totem pole. Brought from British Columbia by a former manager of the resort, Gordon Gibson, it was placed to commemorate the Hawaiian voyages of Capt. George Vancouver.

Endangered Hawaiian stilts, coots, and ducks, as well as sanderlings and Pacific golden plover congregate at 700-acre **Kealia Pond National Wildlife Reserve.** A boardwalk through the ponds begins near Milepost 2 on Piilani Highway.

At the **Maui Ocean Center** you walk in a clear tunnel through a 600,000-gallon aquarium while tiger sharks cruise past, eyeball to eyeball. This new 5-acre facility is about the world beneath the waves, and features tanks and ponds with some very strange creatures.

The jumble of Kihei stops abruptly where the meticulously tended lawns and gardens of **Wailea** begin. Even though billions of dollars built the 1,500-acre resort and its three championship golf courses (see pp. 228–229), there are some moderately priced accommodations amid the conspicuous luxury. All the beaches are

public, as they are throughout Hawaii. You can walk the shore on a paved nature path for one and a half miles from the **Kea Lani Hotel** *(4100 Wailea Alanui, tel 808/875-4100)* to the

A "tunnel beneath the sea" is the most popular aspect of the Maui Ocean Center.

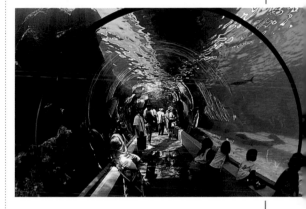

Renaissance Wailea Beach Resort *(3550 Wailea Alanui, tel 808/879-4900)*. Many of the Hawaiian shoreline plants are labeled. It's amusing to take time to explore the fantastic superhotel **Grand Wailea Resort and Spa** *(3850 Wailea Alanui, tel 808/875-1234)*. Their Spa Grande is bigger than all other Maui spas combined. There's a river pool with a swim-up bar in a swim-in cave, waterfalls, water slides, a water elevator, a fake beach, gardens, sculptures, and lily ponds.

Beyond Wailea is the resort of **Makena,** a quiet, dignified retreat before the island goes wild again. At Makena Landing, cowboys mounted on Percherons once drove cattle from the Upcountry ranches into the sea (see pp. 160–161). ∎

Kealia Pond National Wildlife Reserve
- 🅰 119 C2
- ✉ Jct. of Piilani Hwy. (Hawaii 31) & Mokulele Hwy. (Hawaii 350)
- ☎ 808/875-1582

Maui Ocean Center
- 🅰 118 B2
- ✉ 192 Maalaea Rd., Maalaea
- ☎ 808/270-7000
- 💲 $$$$

Upcountry

TAKE MONTANA, MOVE IT TO MAUI, CROWN IT WITH A crater that looks like the face of the moon, and you have Upcountry, one of Hawaii's biggest surprises. Girdling the mid-slopes of 10,023-foot Haleakala Volcano, the area—also known as Kula—is blessed with a temperate-zone climate, making it ideal for agriculture and ranching. During the whaling era, Hawaiian farmers switched from traditional crops of taro and sweet potato to feed the crews on Irish potatoes, corn, wheat, apples, peaches, plums, and pears. During the California gold rush, they shipped the same fare to the forty-niners and grew so prosperous the area was called Nu Kaliponi, New California. Kula cotton clothed the Union Army during the American Civil War.

Today's food crops range from big plump strawberries to the famous Maui onion, so sweet it can be eaten like an apple. The bumper crops, however, are flowers, from roses to the exotic protea, huge and other-worldly, looking more like a bloom of the moon than anything an earthly garden could grow. Many of the flower farms welcome visitors and will ship bouquets home for you. **Sunrise Protea Farm** *(416A Haleakala Crater Rd., tel 808/876-0200)* has rows of various protea from king to mink, growing just feet from picnic tables and a snack shop.

The **University of Hawaii Maui Agricultural Substation** *(209 Mauna Place, off Copp Rd., tel 808/878-1213, closed Fri.–Sun.)* pioneered the protea as a cash crop

and offers free walking maps of their 34-acre garden. Thirty varieties of protea grow at the quirky **Enchanting Floral Garden** where Kazuo and Kazuko Taketa planted 1,500 species of flora in 8 charming acres. You can also see the world's only white pineapple. After strolling the gardens, you'll be offered a fruit cup of whatever is in season—orange, star fruit, banana, papaya, guava. **Kula Botanical Gardens** is primarily 5 acres of orchids, bromeliads and trees, including koa, king of the Hawaiian forest. They also grow 11 acres of fat, fragrant, and fluffy Monterey pines for Christmas trees.

Upcountry's biggest surprise is the grape. On the sprawling **Ulupalakua Ranch,** a former Napa Valley vintner, Emil Tedeschi, experimented with 140 different grapes to find what grew best in Maui's rich volcanic soil. He's now producing respected white, red, and sparkling wines, one of which was served at Ronald Reagan's 1985 inauguration as President of the United States. **Tedeschi Vineyards and Winery** *(end of Hawaii 37, tel 808/878-6058)* offers a tour, and has a shop and tasting room.

Left: The shadow of a chameleon appears on a heliconia leaf.

Enchanting Floral Garden
🅐 119 D2
✉ Hawaii 37 at the Milepost 10, Kula
☎ 808/878-2531
💲 $

Kula Botanical Gardens
🅐 119 D2
✉ Hawaii 377, uphill from jct. with Hawaii 37
☎ 808/878-1715
💲 $

Stitched into the patchwork quilt of farms and ranches are country towns with old mom-and-pop stores, trendy boutiques and galleries—and more surprises. In **Kula,** the white octagonal **Church of the Holy Ghost** is like an exquisite Fabergé egg. Designed and built in 1897 by Father James Beissel, it cradles a magnificent baroque-style altar, crafted in Germany and shipped around the Horn; and also a reproduction of the crown of Queen Isabella of Portugal, which the Portuguese royal family sent for the new church as a gift to their former subjects on Maui. Members of the parish bake and sell traditional Portuguese sweet bread as a fundraiser every other Monday *(tel 808/878-1091 to reserve a loaf).*

Makawao is a town in transition. Once known as Macho-wow, it used to be the domain of the Marlboro man: Stores sold feed, saddles, and ammunition. Now they dispense fashion, books, art, crystals, and quality gifts. But the old **Komodo Store and Bakery** *(3674 Baldwin Ave., tel 808/572-7261, closed Wed. & Sun.)* is still, after 60 years, selling its yummy cream puffs. The biggest event locally is the Fourth of July Rodeo.

The **Hui Noeau Visual Arts Center,** on the edge of town, has been a magnet drawing an international colony of artists to Maui. Headquartered in a gracious estate, Kaluanui, the center serves as a prestigious gallery and school, and has a gift shop selling reasonably priced local arts and crafts. ■

Neil Waldow tends his giant blossoms at his Kula Vista Protea Farm.

Church of the Holy Ghost
🅰 119 D2
✉ Hawaii 37 and Lower Kula Rd., Kula
☎ 808/878-1091

Hui Noeau Visual Arts Center
🅰 119 D3
✉ 2841 Baldwin Ave., Makawao
☎ 808/572-6560

Haleakala National Park

HALEAKALA MEANS "HOUSE OF THE SUN." LOOKING ACROSS the crater from the summit lip at dawn, the sun appears to rise from inside the caldera to ignite the world into daylight. According to legend, Maui, Superman of Hawaiian myth, climbed to the top of Haleakala and lassoed the sun to force it to move more slowly across the Hawaiian sky. La, the mighty sun, as a compromise agreed to slow his pace for half the year, granting people longer summer days.

Haleakala National Park

🏕 119 D2

☎ 808/572-4400;
808/871-5054
(recorded weather
forecast)

🕐 Daily nature talks,
hourly 9:30 a.m–
11:30 a.m. from
Park Headquarters
(1 mile from
entrance)
Summit Visitor
Center (11 miles
from entrance)

💲 $

The summit has always been sacred. Hawaiians came to the land above the clouds to quarry stone for adze heads and to worship their gods. The Specter of the Brocken, a natural phenomenon of the volcano that allows a person to see his own shadow in a halo of rainbow-hued mist, they called *aka-ku-anue-nue*—the seeing of one's own soul.

The summit area of Haleakala was declared a part of Hawaii Volcanoes National Park in 1916 and acquired full status of its own as a national park in 1961. In 1969, the ecologically fragile lower slopes at Kipahulu (see p. 143) were added to the park. The crater dimensions are awesome: 21 miles in circumference, 3,000 feet deep. Thousand-foot cin-

der cones that once spewed lava, lie napping in its lap. The volcano last erupted in 1790. Looking into its silent depths, Mark Twain wrote: "I felt like the last Man, neglected of the judgment and left pinnacled in mid-heaven, a forgotten relic of a vanished world."

Some of the life-forms you'll encounter in the park are among the rarest on Earth. The nene, the Hawaiian goose, was rescued from the brink of extinction. Even though it's still endangered, you will probably see some in the park, maybe even with goslings in tow. Once plentiful, they are being bred in captivity and successfully returned to the wild. The strangely beautiful *ahinahina*, or silversword, is an evolutionary descendant of the sunflower. For up to 20 years it sits like a spiked silver crown and then throws out hundreds of blooms on a stalk up to 9 feet tall. On close examination, the individual blossoms resemble their sunflower ancestor. The easiest place to see the silversword is the enclosure at the **Kalahaku Overlook.** At the **Leleiwi Overlook,** just beyond Milepost 17, there's a good lunar-like view of craters and shale. Around sunset, if the clouds are low, you may experience the Specter of the Brocken. The **Puu Ulaula Overlook,** near the visitor center is the most popular stop, especially at sunrise, because the panorama is so broad. Be careful when stepping out of your car. Not only will it be cold, but at 10,023 feet the altitude could make you dizzy. If you experience drowsiness or headache, have someone drive you to a lower elevation.

For a more intimate experience of the park, there are 36 miles of hiking trails in the crater, although rangers warn that only those in excellent physical condition should attempt them. Allow twice as long

to come back out as it takes to go in. An easy solution is the quarter-mile **Hosmer Grove nature walk** that doesn't go into the crater, but will introduce you to the unique ecology of the park. There are two campgrounds, and three cabins in the crater: The latter are awarded on a lottery basis. **Pony Express Tours** *(tel 808/667-2200)* offers horseback rides to the floor of the caldera.

The place that's off limits is one you can't help seeing—the domed white buildings called Science City,

sitting on the crater lip. They do spacey things here like bounce laser beams off prisms placed on the moon by American astronauts.

Getting to the park is a good part of the fun. The entrance is at the 7,000-foot elevation of **Haleakala Highway,** encompassing legs of Routes 37, 377, and 378, and is an amazing drive. Climbing from sea level to 10,000 feet in only 40 miles is like driving from Mexico to Alaska in two hours. Palm trees give way to pine and eucalyptus, and all finally shrink into the lava desolation above tree line. Summit temperatures average 35° to 77°F in summer, 26° to 75°F in winter. Most people make the trip in predawn darkness and sightsee on the way down. Wear layers of clothing. ∎

From the lookout, the lunaresque crater of Haleakala spreads to the horizon.

Right: The sun rises behind a rare silversword growing at Haleakala National Park.

HANA DRIVE

Hana drive

The scenic but twisty Hana Highway is only a slight compromise with the impregnability of Hana, whose people maintain a good-natured but determined standoff with modern Hawaii.

Along the road you will drive 53 miles across 56 mostly one-lane bridges and around 617 turns. It's slow going, so it's good to remember that the purpose of this road is the journey itself. You will be traveling beside waterfalls, through rain forest, and along rugged lava coastline. You will find paradise on a road that promises to be "Hell on wheels."

The road begins as Route 36 at **Kahului Airport ❶** heads innocently, flatly through sugarcane fields, then passes the sandy sweep of **Baldwin Beach Park.**

The first—and last—town of consequence is **Paia ❷,** last gas till Hana. This former plantation town went psychedelic in the sixties and has never quite gotten over it. Windsurfers congregate here because it's only 2 miles to **Hookipa ❸,** a pilgrimage site for the sport.

At Milepost 16, the twists, turns, and bridges begin. The name of each bridge and stream is announced with a sign, and the names have lovely meanings, such as Kolea, "happiness that comes on the wind," and Makapipi, "desire for blessings."

Just beyond Mile 16, Route 36 becomes Route 360 and the mileposts begin again at zero. Between the tiny towns of Huelo and Kailua, you can probably pick up roadside guava, mountain apple, banana, and mango. The trees with the colorfully streaked bark are rainbow eucalyptus.

In 2 miles you will pass three waterfalls **Waikamoi, Puohokamoa,** and **Haipuaene ❹.** There's a 30-minute nature walk at Waikamoi and the picnic tables have grand views; but bring mosquito repellent. You can revisit *Jurassic Park* at **Garden of Eden Arboretum and Botanical Garden** *(Mile 10, tel 808/572-9899, closes 3 p.m. daily).* Scenes from the dinosaur saga were shot here.

At Mile 11, **Puohokamoa Falls** plunge 30 feet into a good, icy swimming pool. Just past Mile 12 you can find rest rooms at **Kaumahina State Wayside Park ❺.**

The size of the plants attests to the region's fecundity and rainfall—about 300 inches a year. Coastline views are breathtaking.

The **Keanae Arboretum ❻,** free and open 24 hours, is *makai* (toward the sea) and less than half a mile beyond Mile 16. You'll find Hawaiian ethnobotanical gardens, and you can picnic and swim in the pools.

To see Hawaii's traditional food crop, taro, growing in all its emerald glory, turn makai at Mile 17 and drive down to **Keanae Peninsula** where the *kalo loi* (flooded fields)

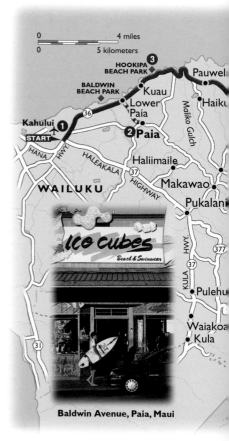

Baldwin Avenue, Paia, Maui

are more than 500 years old. The road dead-ends at the ocean where waves tear savagely at the lava shore.

If you don't want to take time to drive down to Keanae, keep going a few feet, just past Mile 17, for an **overlook 7** and a splendid photo opportunity. You're now halfway to Hana. One of the roadside fruit and snack stands will be open and selling ice cream or freshly baked banana bread.

Between Wailua and **Puaa Kaa State Wayside Park** at Mile 22, you'll pass **Waikani Falls**. Gurgling streams and ponds make this a good picnic spot.

Next stop is **Waianapanapa State Park 8** (Mile 51, tel 808/984-8109). Lava shoreline at its most dramatic is on show in black craggy cliffs, sea stacks, arches, lava

caves and tubes, and a gleaming black-sand beach. Campsites and cabins are available by permit. The roads winds down into **Hana** town **9**. ∎

▲	Also see map, p. 119 C3
▶	Kahului Airport
⬌	53 miles
⏱	3 hours
▶	Hana town

NOT TO BE MISSED
- Paia town
- Hookipa Beach
- Keanae overlook
- Waianapanapa State Park

On the road to Hana

Rounding a headland on the drive to Hana

Hana-Kipahulu

THERE'S SOMETHING ABOUT THE AIR OF HANA THAT induces a peace bordering on euphoria. Some people claim the thick lush vegetation results in more oxygen. Others know it's the spirit of the place itself. You can drive in and out of Hana town in less than five minutes. There's a hotel on one side of the street, cows on the other, plus a couple of glorious old churches and a few stores. The minute you arrive in this small town hugging the bay, you recognize this as one of the world's special places, safe and friendly.

Kahanu Gardens
🖾 119 E3
✉ Ulaina Rd., Mile Marker 31
☎ 808/248/8912
🕐 Closed Sat. & Sun.
💲 $$

Hana Cultural Center
🖾 119 F2
✉ Uakea & Hana Rds.
☎ 808/248-8622
🕐 Closed Sun.
💲 $

Kipahulu Ranger Station
🖾 119 E1
☎ 808/248-7375

Hana is dominated by two forces, the 3,000-acre **Hana Ranch,** and the upscale **Hotel Hana-Maui** *(Hana Hwy., tel 808/248-8211),* the first resort built outside of Waikiki. Guests have included Walt Disney, Clark Gable, and the von Trapp family. On top of **Lyons Hill,** a lava stone cross was erected in 1960 in memory of Texas millionaire Paul Fagan who brought the first tourists to town. It's a 3-mile hike through open cow pasture to the hilltop for panoramic views of Hana. It's especially nice at sunset.

The promontory at the right end of the bay, **Kauiki Head,** looms large in history and legend. When Noenoe Ua Kea O Hana, daughter of the great Maui, fell in love with Kauiki, an adopted son of the Menehune (see p. 187), her enraged father changed the unsuitable lover into the hill, and Noenoe into the beautiful, white, misty rain of Hana. Many fierce battles,

primarily between Hana and Big Island chiefs, were waged on and around Kauiki Head. It was also the birthplace of Queen Kaahumanu.

At the base of Kauiki, on the right side is Kaihalulu, usually called **Red Sand Beach** because its sands, eroded from the surrounding cinder cone, are the color of garnets. The sea, foaming in at the mouth of the cove, is teal and cream. Inspired by the beauty and seclusion, people who ordinarily might not do such a thing, shed their suits and swim stark naked, despite its being illegal. Kaihalulu is at the end of the parking lot for the Hotel Hana-Maui's Sea Ranch Cottages, then left across a field, following a worn footpath along a cliff. The trail is hazardous but mercifully short, about 15 minutes.

Hana's other favorite beach is **Hamoa.** Salt-and-pepper sands line a 1,000-foot shoreline at the base of 30-foot sea cliffs.

Kaahumanu

Born in a cave at Kauiki Head in 1772 during a time of war, Kaahumanu lived her life in a period of great turmoil and seized the reins of power of the Hawaiian kingdom. When she was ten, a prophet told her she would be loved by a chief and become the wife of a king. At 17, she married Kamehameha the Great and was

always the favorite of his 21 wives. Capt. George Vancouver called her "the most beautiful woman in the South Seas." She was also brilliant. Upon Kamehameha's death in 1819, Queen Kaahumanu, in a single act called *Ai Noa,* "free eating," toppled the ancient system of religious law (see p. 30). She died just before dawn June 15, 1832. ■

Opposite: Take a guided hike to spectacular Waimoku Falls from the Kipahulu Ranger Station.

Piilani Hale, the largest *heiau* (temple) in Hawaii, and a national historic landmark, broods over the Hana coast just north of town. Its walls are 60 to 90 feet high. The temple is maintained by direct descendants of its builder, King Piilani (late 14th–early 15th century). It is said to emanate such force that pilots approaching nearby Hana Airport refuse to fly over it. Hawaiian ceremonies are still held here. The temple stands within **Kahanu Gardens,** 126 acres of tropical flora and lava coastline, with an extravagant background of green mountains.

You can explore the history and culture of the area at **Hana Cultural Center** in an 1871 former police station. There are some exceptional Hawaiian quilts, *kapa* (tree-bark cloth), a century-old *olona* fishing net, historical photographs, and a collection of moving portraits of Hana's people by the late Leslie Eade.

KIPAHULU

About 10 miles south of Hana, Haleakala National Park spills down the mountainside to Kipahulu. The dense rain forest has yet to be properly explored, yet trails have been laid to some of the most beautiful segments. The best known is **Oheo Gulch.** If you want to sound like a dumb tourist, call it Seven Sacred Pools. There are about two dozen pools spilling into each other as they descend to the ocean. Swimming is grand. Hawaii 31 crosses over Oheo Stream, with waterfalls on both sides of the road. You can hike the **Pipiwai Trail** a half mile to **Makahiku Falls** overlook. Continue 1.5 miles through a thick bamboo forest to reach 400-foot **Waimoku Falls.** Check on weather conditions at the ranger station before setting out. ∎

More places to visit on Maui

ART SCHOOL AT KAPALUA

Spend a few hours painting, decorating, and firing pottery, learning yoga or ballet, improving camera skills, or any number of other creative activities. Ceramic painting is always in session; check to see what else is going on during your stay. Sessions are geared to all skill levels in this nonprofit center. The setting is a light, airy 1920s studio that was once part of a pineapple cannery at Kapalua Resort.

⚑ 118 A4   ✉ 800 Office Rd.   ☎ 808/665-0007   ⏺ Closed 4 p.m. Mon.–Fri., 1 p.m. Sat.   💲 $$

HALEKII-PIHANA HEIAU STATE MONUMENT

These twin temples just outside Wailuku were once significant religious and governmental sites. Little remains of Pihana Heiau, which was a *luakini*, a place of human sacrifice. After his bloody victory in Iao Valley in 1790 (see p. 132), Kamehameha I offered a sacrifice here. Halekii was a royal compound with what were probably thatched guesthouses for noble attendees at the rites; lava foundations are still standing. There is a commanding view of central Maui and the Wailuku Plain from this 10-acre park. Take Waiehu Beach Road (Hawaii 350) to Kuhio Place, turn inland, to Hea Place, go left to the end.

⚑ 118 B3   ⏺ Closed 7 p.m. daily

KAHAKULOA VALLEY

Kahakuloa in West Maui is one of the last functioning *ahupuaa* (a segment of land, allocated under Hawaii's ancient system of land tenure, see p. 26). It is private property, but you can go there with Ekahi Tours, which is run by Kahakuloa residents. You hike into the forest, beside streams, and along the walls of the *kalo loi* (flooded taro fields). Lunch is taken on the lanai of a Hawaiian home, where you listen to stories. You'll learn how the old system still works. It could be a model for an ecologically sound community today. It's an easy hike, and the seven and a half hours spent here will fly by.

⚑ 118 B4   ☎ Ekahi Tours 808/877-9775   💲 $$$$

MAUI ARTS & CULTURAL CENTER

The 27-million-dollar Maui Arts and Cultural Center, which opened in Kahului (see p. 131) in 1994, demonstrates Maui's commitment to the arts. More than 11 million dollars was donated by island residents. Entertainers have included Ziggy Marley and Tony Bennett, the Moscow Ballet and hula groups. It's also a showcase theater for local artists, and theater and dance companies. Aside from two performing arts theaters, there's a visual arts gallery. Check to see what's happening during your stay.

⚑ 119 C3   ✉ 1 Cameron Way, Kahului   ☎ 808/242-2787

PALAPALA HOOMAU CONGREGATIONAL CHURCH

Famed American aviator Charles Lindbergh (1902–1974) fell in love with Kipahulu (see p. 143). He spent the last seasons of his life here with his wife Ann Morrow Lindbergh. When he was dying, he planned all the details of his funeral, insisting he wanted to be buried barefoot in a rough-hewn eucalyptus coffin at the little country church built in 1857. The inscription on Lucky Lindy's simple granite headstone is from Psalm 139: "If I take the wings of morning and dwell in the uttermost parts of the sea...." Up to 500 people a day make the pilgrimage to his quiet resting place.

⚑ 119 E1   ✉ Route 31, 1 mile S of Oheo Gulch

POLIPOLI SPRING STATE RECREATION AREA

Pine trees, a sequoia forest, nippy weather—overnight the grass becomes white with frost. At 6,200 feet, Polipoli is set amid the vast fog belt of the Kula Forest Reserve. An extensive trail system meanders through the park. The 5-mile **Polipoli Loop** through eucalyptus, plum, pine, and redwood trees should take three hours. Dress warmly, in layers.

To get there, take Kekaulike Avenue (Hawaii 377) from Kula, turn uphill on Waipoli Road to the end. Camping and cabin available from the Division of State Parks (*54 High St., Wailuku, tel 808/984-8109*).

⚑ 119 D2 ∎

The island that gave its name to the whole archipelago is like a microcontinent, with balmy coasts, snowcapped mountains, desert, lush rain forest, huge cattle ranches, acres of spectacular flowers, and active Kilauea Volcano.

Hawaii: the Big Island

Kilauea Volcano, Hawaii Volcanoes National Park

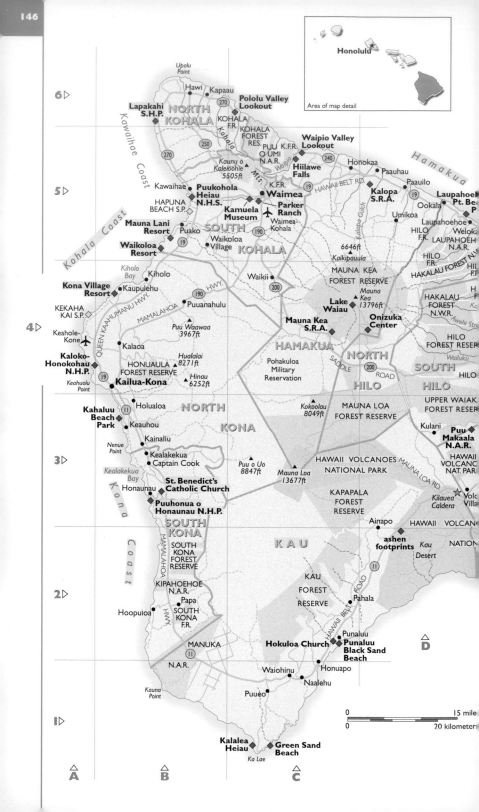

Honolulu

Area of map detail

6▷

Upolu
Point

Hawi Kapaau

Pololu Valley
Lookout

270

Lapakahi
S.H.P.

NORTH
KOHALA

KOHALA
F.R.

KOHALA
FOREST
RES.

250

PUU
O UMI
N.A.R.

K.F.R.

Waipio Valley
Lookout

240

5▷

Kawaihae

Puukohola
Heiau
N.H.S.

HAPUNA
BEACH S.P.

19

Hiilawe
Falls

Honokaa

Paauhau

HAWAII BELT RD.

Paauilo

Waimea

Kalopa
S.R.A.

19

Laupahoe
Pt. Be
P

Kaunu o
Kaleioohie
5505ft

K.F.R.

Mauna Lani
Resort

Puako

Parker
Ranch

Kamuela
Museum

Waimea-
Kohala

Ookala

Umikoa

Laupahoehoe

Welok

SOUTH

190

HILO
F.R.

LAUPAHOEH
N.A.R.

Waikoloa
Resort

19

Waikoloa
Village

KOHALA

6646ft
Kaikipauula

HILO
F.R.

HILO
F.R.

HAKALAU FOREST N.
F.

4▷

Kona Village
Resort

Kiholo
Bay

Kiholo

Kaupulehu

Waikii

MAUNA KEA
FOREST RESERVE

HAKALAU
FOREST
N.W.R.

H

KEKAHA
KAI S.P.

190
HWY.

Puuanahulu

200

Mauna
Kea
13796ft

Lake
Waiau

Keahole-
Kone

MAMALAHOA

Puu Waawaa
3967ft

Mauna Kea
S.R.A.

Onizuka
Center

Awehi Str

Kaloa

HAMAKUA

HILO
FOREST RESER

Kaloko-
Honokohau
N.H.P.

HONUAULA
FOREST RESERVE

Hualalai
8271ft

Hinau
6252ft

Wailuku

Keahuolu
Point

19

Kailua-Kona

NORTH
HILO

200
ROAD

SOUTH
HILO

HILO

3▷

Holualoa

Kahaluu
Beach
Park

Keauhou

NORTH

Kokoolau
8049ft

MAUNA LOA
FOREST RESERVE

UPPER WAIAK
FOREST RESER

Kainaliu

KONA

Kulani

Puu
Makaala
N.A.R.

Nenue
Point

Kealakekua

Captain Cook

Puu o Uo
8847ft

HAWAII VOLCANOES

HAWAII
VOLCANO
NAT. PAR

Kealakekua
Bay

St. Benedict's
Catholic Church

Mauna Loa
13677ft

NATIONAL PARK

Honaunau

Puuhonua o
Honaunau N.H.P.

KAPAPALA
FOREST
RESERVE

Kilauea
Caldera

Volc
Villa

SOUTH
KONA

SOUTH
KONA
FOREST
RESERVE

Ainapo

HAWAII VOLCAN

ashen
footprints

Kau
Desert

NATION

2▷

KIPAHOEHOE
N.A.R.

Hoopuloa

Papa

SOUTH
KONA
F.R.

KAU
FOREST
RESERVE

Pahala

MANUKA

11

N.A.R.

Waiohinu

Honuapo

Hokuloa Church

Punaluu

Punaluu
Black Sand
Beach

Naalehu

Puueo

1▷

Kauna
Point

Kalalea
Heiau

Ka Lae

Green Sand
Beach

0   15 mile

0   20 kilometer

△
D

△
A

△
B

△
C

Hawaii: the Big Island

THE BIG ISLAND, AS HAWAII IS GENERALLY CALLED, IS SO BIG THAT ALL THE other Hawaiian Islands could be tacked onto one half and leave the other half to spare. The island is twice the size of Delaware and three times the size of Rhode Island. Five enormous volcanoes, Mauna Loa, Mauna Kea, Kilauea, Hualalai, and Kohala, created its bulky 4,028 square miles. Kilauea, the world's most active volcano, is making the Big Isle bigger by the day. There are 266 miles of coastline: You can go to a different beach park every day for a month. Some days you'll go home with purest white sand clinging to your bathing suit, some days jet black, and some days even glistening green olivine.

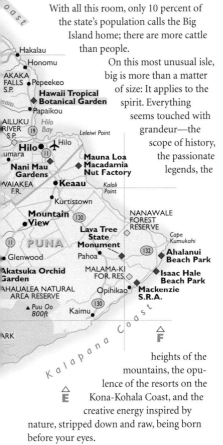

With all this room, only 10 percent of the state's population calls the Big Island home; there are more cattle than people.

On this most unusual isle, big is more than a matter of size: It applies to the spirit. Everything seems touched with grandeur—the scope of history, the passionate legends, the

Gourmet Kona Coffee is sold up and down the Kona Coast.

heights of the mountains, the opulence of the resorts on the Kona-Kohala Coast, and the creative energy inspired by nature, stripped down and raw, being born before your eyes.

The Big Island is the cradle of the Hawaiian kingdom. Kamehameha the Great was born on the Kohala Coast, and from these shores he launched his campaign of conquest and unification. Remnants of history are everywhere, with temples crowning hills, village ruins tucked into valleys, and archaeolog-

ical sites smack in the middle of golf courses.

The skies above Hawaii are so consistently clear, and clean of pollution, that scientists from all over the world come to study the universe from powerful telescopes atop Mauna Kea. Technology, however, seems to be left to the techies on the mountaintop. Down below, the towns of the Big Island are rural with a kind of creaky charm. Behind the weathered, often unpromising storefronts are surprisingly sophisticated galleries and delightful restaurants, where your meal naturally climaxes with locally grown Kona, the world's standard for good coffee. In fact, Hawaii's regional cuisine first emerged on this island amid a natural bounty of land and sea.

It is pure pleasure to drive around the Big Island, making your own finds, but don't bite off more than you can chew in a day. ∎

Outrigger canoes race off Kailua-Kona.

Kona Coast

The districts of North and South Kona form the sunny 60-mile leeward shore of the Big Island, encompassing resorts, villages, farms, commercial centers, and wide open spaces. Here the sun seems brighter, intensifying colors. Flowers are so vivid they are almost harsh, the sea seems deeper and bluer than elsewhere, the lava is inky and iridescent, and the sunsets, ignited by volcanic particles, are positively fluorescent in tangerines, golds, magentas, and flashes of brilliant emerald just as the sun sizzles into the sea.

People come to Kona to catch the biggest marlin, or to run the Ironman World Triathlon, consisting of a 2.4-mile open ocean swim, a 112-mile bicycle race, plus a 26-mile run. They end up being absorbed so seamlessly into the balmy climate, the immensity, and the unhurried pace that they barely make an impression as they race across the strange landscape.

Predictably, the flat coastal lowlands are sprinkled with hotels, condominiums, and retirement villas. The hills above wear a lei of small towns that are fun to poke around in: Holualoa, Kainaliu, Kealakekua, Captain Cook, and Honaunau. Higher than that is the forest. Macadamia nuts grow in North Kona, while South Kona excels in coffee.

Weary of war, and sick of eight years of city life in Honolulu, Kamehameha the Great, with

his family and court, retired to Kailua. With three ships and accompanied by a fleet of outrigger canoes, they set sail for Kailua on August 12, 1812. Upon landing, the king built a residential compound for his royal relatives, and a temple to Lono, god of harvests.

Lt. Otto von Kotzebue, captain of the Russian trader *Rurick,* wrote in 1816 of his first encounter with the king: "I now stood at the side of the celebrated Tamaahmaah, who…inspired me with the greatest confidence by his unreserved and friendly behavior. He conducted me to his straw palace…he prefers this simple dwelling, not to forsake the customs of his country…as he only wishes to increase the happiness and not the wants of his subjects." The warrior king died in Kailua seven years later, May 8, 1819, aged 60. ■

Kailua-Kona

PARTLY FISHING VILLAGE, PARTLY PARTY TOWN, AND—
lately—mostly shopping mecca with its new shopping malls and discounters on the fringes of town, Kailua-Kona maintains a castaway
charm. Its main street, Alii Drive, follows a 2-mile stretch of waterfront that claims a major chunk of history.

Ahuena Heiau juts into Kailua
Bay like a sentinel of another age.
The temple has now been restored.
The most critical event in Hawaiian
history occurred at this site when
Kamehameha II, defying the *kapu*
(law) against men and women
dining together, sat down to eat
with his mother and stepmother.
According to eyewitness accounts,
the king seated himself and "began
to eat with a fury of appetite that
showed he was doing violence to
himself…. The whole assembly was
struck with horror … but no harm
to the king ensuing, they at length
cried out with one voice, 'The kapu
is broken!'" Word spread like wild-
fire, triggering minor insurrections
and violence that left the old
temples in ruins and the *kii* (god
effigies) toppled and burned.

One year later in 1820, the brig
Thaddeus sailed into Kailua Bay.
Mrs. Thomas Holman, wife of the
physician in the party, described
Ahuena Heiau: "It was sure enough
in ruins, and such a scene of
devastation, I never before beheld.
There appeared to me to have been
stone enough among the ruins of
the temple to build a city."

In 1836, the missionaries built
Mokuaikaua, the first church in
Hawaii. Its 112-foot white steeple
dominates the little town. Across
the street, **Hulihee Palace** sits
between the church and temple, as
if still caught between old and new
ways. Built in 1838, it hosted a
succession of Hawaiian guests and
was eventually purchased by King
Kalakaua. After his death in 1891, it

was sold and fell into ruin. In 1927,
it was turned over to the Daughters
of Hawaii, a group concerned with
preserving Hawaii's cultural legacy.
They faithfully restored it and
opened the palace as a museum. It
has many of the original furnishings, including a koa-wood bed
whose beautifully carved posts
came from Kamehameha's grass

palace. The furniture indicates the
size of the noble residents. Kamehameha I was probably close to 7 feet
tall. Hawaiian music and hula
events are held at the palace the last
Sunday of the month at 4 p.m.

A simple thatched chapel marks
the site of the first Catholic Church
in Kona, St. Michael's. Built in
1840, it sits beside its more modern
incarnation *(75-5769 Alii Dr., tel
808/326-7771).* ■

**Men hold *kahili*,
the feather
standards of
royalty, before
Hulihee Palace,
Kailua-Kona.**

Ahuena Heiau
✉ On grounds of King
Kamehameha Kona
Beach Hotel, 75-
5660 Palani Rd.
☎ 808/329-2911

**Mokuaikaua
Church**
✉ 75-5713 Alii Dr.
☎ 808/329-5179

Hulihee Palace
✉ 75-5718 Alii Dr.
☎ 808/329-1877
💲 $$

Keauhou & south

Below: Interior
of St. Benedict's
Catholic Church,
known as "the
painted church."
Opposite: A
swimmer jumps
from a boat at
Kealakekua Bay.

ONCE IT LEAVES KAILUA, ALII DRIVE BECOMES A MEAN-dering country road. About 4.5 miles from town you come to Kahaluu Beach Park, a fascinating place to snorkel, made special by its black-sand bottom against which the myriad jewel-hued reef fish look like Vegas dancers. On the north end of the bay, tiny, white St. Peter's Catholic Church, its blue tin roof framed by sea and palms, makes a perfect photo. The diminutive chapel, which was built in 1839 on the site of an old *heiau* (temple), always has fresh flowers on the altar.

Places. The nonprofit society conducts walking tours of Kailua, Kealakekua Bay, and Keauhou. You can also tour the **D. Uchida Coffee Farm,** founded in 1925, another site on the National Register of Historic Places.

Kealakekua Bay is where Captain Cook met his demise at age 49, February 14, 1779. To expedite the return of a stolen rowboat, he attempted to kidnap a Kona chief as hostage. A fight ensued and Cook was killed. David Samwell, assistant surgeon aboard Cook's flagship, H.M.S. *Resolution,* reported the death at the water's edge: "He endeavored to scramble on the rock when a fellow gave him a blow to the head with a large club and he was seen alive no more." Heavily outnumbered, the British retreated to their ships. A 27-foot white obelisk on the far north shore of the bay marks the spot where he fell. The Hawaiians took his body and accorded it the mortuary rites of a great chief. Fifty years after his death, American missionaries, perhaps wary of British influence in the isles, began to publish a cautionary tale about how Cook was deified by the Hawaiians as the god Lono, his collaboration incurring the wrath of Jehovah. Cook's deification came to be accepted as fact, although there is no evidence, either in journals of the time or in Hawaiian oral history. The bay is

**Kona Historical
Society**
🏛 146 B3
✉ 81-6551 Mamalahoa
Hwy. (Hawaii 11),
Kealakekua
☎ 808/323-2005
🕐 Closed weekends
💲 $

Kealakekua Bay
🏛 146 B3

**St. Benedict's
Catholic Church**
🏛 146 B3
✉ 84-5140 Painted
Church Rd.,
Honaunau
☎ 808/328-2227

On the grounds of the **Keauhou Beach Resort** *(78-6740 Alii Dr., tel 808/322-3441)* there is a sacred bathing pool once reserved for royalty. Beside it, in lush tropical gardens, is a reproduction of the beach cottage used in the 1800s by King David Kalakaua as his private retreat. Down by the shoreline are petroglyphs, an ancient house site, and a swimming cove once the exclusive prerogative of nobility.

A very worthwhile stop is the **Kona Historical Society** in Kealakekua, which has a small museum with Hawaiian artifacts, and memorabilia and photographs from the early days of ranching and coffee plantations. It's housed in the old stone Greenwell Store, built in 1875 and now on the State and National Registers of Historic

reached via Napoopoo Road, *makai* south of Captain Cook town about 4 miles.

Kealakekua today is a state marine life preserve. The crystal-clear water runs from teal to jade. Most people come by boat for the snorkeling, and hoping to see sea turtles and dolphins. The ruins of **Hikiau Heiau** mark the approach to the bay. On New Year's Day, 1779, Cook conducted the first Christian service in the Islands when, with the permission of the chief, he conducted a burial rite atop the temple platform for his valet, William Watman.

St. Benedict's Catholic Church, "the painted church," once stood along the shore near Kealakekua, but was moved to its present location around the turn of the 20th century. Behind the white latticework and beneath the Gothic Revival steeple is a grand cathedral in miniature. Between 1899 and 1904, a Belgian priest, Father John Berchmans Velghe created a masterpiece, which is now on the State and National Registers of Historic Places. He created depth and size in his church by painting a trompe l'oeil version of the cathedral of Burgos, Spain, behind the altar. The ceiling represents the Hawaiian sky; the church pillars sprout palm trees, whose branches growing toward the altar are green while those growing away are dry brown. Biblical scenes glow on the walls, illustrating Scripture for the faithful who had not learned to read. On the second Sunday of the month, Mass is in Hawaiian and everyone is invited to breakfast afterward.

The small towns you pass through in this region are worth exploring for their art galleries, boutiques, and restaurants (see pp. 250–252). Many of the coffee farms welcome visitors, and there is a great variety of roadside stands. ■

Fierce kii, god images, guard the sanctuary of Puuhonua O Honaunau, an ancient refuge.

Puuhonua O Honaunau National Historical Park

FOR LONGER THAN ANYONE CAN REMEMBER, PUUHONUA O Honaunau was a sacred site, a place of refuge. To the Hawaiians of old there was no more powerful word than *kapu,* meaning the laws based on spirituality, environmental stewardship, and civil order. Punishment for violation of kapu was severe, often death. Justice, however, was tempered with mercy: On every island there were *puuhonua* (places of refuge). If a lawbreaker or defeated warrior could reach one of these sacred sanctuaries ahead of his pursuers, he was put through atonement and purification ceremonies by the resident priests. When he left the puuhonua, no one could harm him under penalty of breaking a kapu themselves. The puuhonua were also refuges for the elderly, conscientious objectors, women, and children during times of war.

Puuhonua O Honaunau National Historical Park

🅰 146 B3
✉ Park entrance on Hawaii 160, 3.5 miles from jct. with Hawaii 11.
☎ 808/328-2288
💲 $$

When Puuhonua O Honaunau's great stone walls were built around 1550, it was already old. One legend credits a Chief Ehu Kamalino with its founding in 1200. A temple, its name lost to time, lay in the middle of the 12-acre enclosure. Next to it, tradition maintains, another temple was built, Alealea Heiau. In 1650, Ka Iki Alealea ("the little Alealea") was built at the north corner of the

Great Wall. Now reconstructed and known as Hale o Keawe, it once held the remains of 23 high chiefs, whose bones conferred even greater protection on the refuge.

At the visitor desk, pick up a self-guided tour leaflet. Numbered coconuts at the sites correlate with the map. As you walk beside a tile mural, you'll hear taped histories and stories of the puuhonua woven

in with the "Kumulipo," the Hawaiian creation chant.

In the park are thatched homes and work areas. Local canoe builders, wood-carvers, and other traditional craftspeople are often working here. Note the canoes, probably the only ones in existence made in the old way from koa with coconut fiber lashings.

You can walk around to the far side of the bay, to the enclosed Hale o Keawe and its fierce *kii* (god effigies). You can only imagine how this refuge must have looked to the fugitive, heart pounding, running for his life, his enemies crashing through the brush behind him, the gods before him, as with one last superhuman effort he reaches safety.

The temple is at the northern apex of the Great Wall which runs for 1,000 feet, stands 10 feet high, and is 17 feet thick, all constructed without mortar and ingeniously held together by friction. The wall is reflected in the fishpond, an ancient aquaculture facility to supply royal tables. If you enjoy photography, there is not a more dramatic place to frame a sunset.

On the first weekend in July, a three-day Establishment Day cultural festival is held with great pageantry, a *hukilau* (community net fishing), crafts, music, and hula. There are no food facilities at the park, but there is a picnic area. ■

Below: Dancers perform the *hula kahiko*, using *iliili*, stone implements.

Canalboats transport guests to their rooms at the Hilton Waikoloa Village.

Kohala

Massive and vital, a more powerful landscape than Kohala cannot be imagined. Along the dry sunny coast from Waikoloa to Upolu Point, luxury resorts have been hacked out of old lava flows. More than two billion dollars have been very carefully bestowed to make this black desert bloom. The Hilton Waikoloa Village, built in 1988, is an attraction in itself. You can tour it by yacht or mini-bullet train, both of which stop in the main lobby. A network of canals, lagoons, and swimming pools splash across 62 ocean-front acres. You can even sign up to swim with dolphins in their own private lagoon.

The **Mauna Kea** (see p. 250), doyenne of the luxe-on-lava hotels, has so much fine art scattered about the property that books have been published about it. Morning tours take in the splendid collection of Hawaiian quilts, Asian treasures, old temple toys used to keep children quiet, and contemporary masterpieces.

The sweep of lava coast is so immense that each resort is a green enclave, tucked around a gleaming white-sand beach, unencumbered by neighbors. Queen Kaahumanu Highway (Hawaii 19) knifes across the eerie landscape, with lava stretching away on both sides.

Away from the tropical shore, the temperature drops a degree a minute and the land becomes green as it rises—tentatively at first, spotted with remnants of the desert: cactus

and plumes of ocher grass—until at Waimea, the mighty volcanic hills and Kohala Mountains are robed in forests and grasslands, thick and plush as an Aubusson carpet. Ranches, including the famous Parker Ranch, spread across the land where rainbows are as common as cows. In fact they sometimes hang in veils of color; the rain comes so lightly that when it falls through sunlit air, it swirls with the glitter of fine snow. True snow crowns Mauna Kea, towering over everything.

In Kohala, history is your constant companion. Kamehameha the Great was born here; the temples are among the oldest in the Islands; golfers play amid sacred rocks and prehistoric petroglyphs; and restaurants serve fish raised in ponds built for kings. ■

Kohala Coast

SELDOM ARE HISTORY LESSONS SO BEAUTIFULLY PRESENTED as those on the Kohala Coast. The easiest petroglyph viewing, in the most pleasant setting, is from a boardwalk across a 15-acre site at **Kona Village Resort** *(Queen Kaahumanu Hwy., tel 808/325-5555)*. Some images date back 900 years; experts surmise they may have been concerned with seafaring rituals, myths, and royal genealogy. The resort is built around the beach and ponds of an old fishing village and resembles one today. Guest accommodations are thatched-roof bungalows. Of particular note is the panoramic wallpaper in the Hale Moana dining room. "Les Sauvages de la Mer Pacifique," by French artist Joseph Dufour, depicts scenes from Captain Cook's voyages. Printed in 1804, it is the first of this decorative art genre.

You can find more easily accessible petroglyphs (see p. 158) at the **Waikoloa Resort.** You walk the old **King's Trail** *(free guided tours Mon.–Fri. at 10:30 a.m., Sat.–Sun. 8:30 a.m., from King's Shops, tel 808/886-8811),* an ancient shoreline footpath along Anaehoomalu Bay. Around the bay are many prehistoric house and temple remnants in a parklike setting.

At **Mauna Lani Resort,** informative signs guide you through 15 acres of restored fishponds (see p. 214) and 27 acres of archaeological preserve. The **Kalahuipuaa Fishponds** have been faithfully restored and the ancient aquaculture facility is again providing a steady supply of seafood. The highlights will take 30 minutes.

From the resort parking lot, you can take a 1.4-mile hike northward on the well-signed **Malama Trail** to a collection of more than 3,000 petroglyphs at **Puako.** Go early morning or late afternoon, wear

Hapuna Beach is one of the best swimming beaches on the island of Hawaii. Mauna Kea rises behind it.

Visitor information

Big Island Visitors Bureau

 146 B5

✉ King's Shops, Waikoloa Resort, 250 Waikoloa Beach Dr.

☎ 808/886-1655

🕐 Closed Sat.–Sun.

Mauna Lani Bay Hotel

📍 146 B5

✉ 68-1050 Mauna Lani Point Dr.

☎ 808/885-6622

A corner of temple Mookini Heiau, still cared for by the Mookini family

Hapuna Beach
- 146 B5
- Queen Kaahumanu Hwy. (Hawaii 19), 12 miles N of Waikoloa
- 808/974-6200

Puukohola Heiau National Historic Site
- 146 B5
- Hawaii 270, 1 mile S of Kawaihae
- 808/882-7218

sturdy shoes, and bring water. The little community of Puako runs along a ribbon of white sand; its crowning glory is **Hokuloa Church** *(Puako Beach Dr., tel 808/ 883-8295)* built in 1859 by the Reverend Lorenzo Lyons, a missionary who founded 13 other churches. Well-liked by his parishioners, he composed the beloved Hawaiian hymn "Hawaii Aloha," which has become an unofficial anthem. Emotionally powerful, the song concludes almost every gathering of import, as all hold hands and lift their voices in gratitude for this place, Hawaii.

E Hawaii e kuu one hanau e
Kuu home kulaiwi nei
Oli no au i na pono lani e
E Hawaii, aloha e.
Hui: E hauoli na opio o Hawaii nei.
Oli e! Oli e!
Mai na aheahemakani e pa mai nei,
Mau ke aloha, no Hawaii.

O Hawaii, O sands of my birth,
My native home,
I rejoice in the blessings of heaven.
O Hawaii, my love.
Chorus: Happy the young of Hawaii today.
Rejoice! Rejoice!
Gentle breezes blow toward me now,
Forever I will love Hawaii.

The best public beach on this coast is **Hapuna,** a half-mile stretch of flat, white sand embraced by lava outcroppings. It gets only 10 inches of rain a year so sunshine is almost guaranteed. On the north end of the beach, if you walk across the lawn of the luxe **Hapuna Prince Hotel,** you'll come to a tiny cove, excellent for snorkeling and visiting with sea turtles. The pool deck restaurant, Beach Bar, of the Prince usually has live music.

North of Hapuna are the ruins of the massive **Puukohola Heiau.** Kamehameha the Great was having little luck in his campaign of Hawaiian unification until Kapoukahi, a powerful prophet from Kauai, told him that if he built a great temple to his war god

Kukailimoku, he would be unstoppable. In the hot summer of 1790 he began construction of the temple. Attempts to halt the project were launched by rival chiefs, but Kamehameha prevailed and fulfilled the prophecy. Even in ruins, the temple is impressive, 224 feet long by 100 feet wide, built of unmortared stones hand carried from Pulolu Valley, 14 miles away.

On a hill below is **Mailekini Heiau,** an older temple dedicated, ironically, to peace. Submerged over time in the offshore waters is Hale o Kapuni Heiau, a temple to the shark gods.

For a look at how non-gods and non-kings lived in old Hawaii, visit **Lapakahi State Historical Park.** It's hot with not much shade, so an early morning visit is best *(park opens 8 a.m.).* Well-marked paths with good explanatory signs guide you through the detailed remains of this fishing village that thrived from the 14th to the 19th century. Some thatched buildings have been reconstructed, and you'll see many of the small things that are big indicators of a

way of life: fishing shrines, nets, and implements, saltmaking pans, a family temple, poi (taro) pounders, a lampstand for burning kukui nuts. On an overlook where fishermen gathered to watch for signs of arriving schools is a stone *konane* board, a game similar to checkers.

One of the secrets of Lapakahi is the snorkeling just offshore of the coral beach. Park attendants don't mind people swimming, but they discourage lounging about in bathing suits.

The stones on which Chiefess Kekuiapoiwa gave birth to the baby who would become Kamehameha the Great (see p. 29) are now known as **Kamehameha Akahi Aina Hanau,** and lie a few yards from **Mookini Heiau** where the baby was taken to be blessed before being spirited away (the ruling chief had ordered his death). According to oral historians and the Mookini family, who have been its custodians for eight centuries, the original heiau was built in A.D. 480 and was rededicated as a *luaki-ni,* temple of human sacrifice, in the 13th century by High Priest

Hawaiian pageantry marks the 200th anniversary of the establishment of Puukohola Heiau, built by Kamehameha the Great.

Lapakahi State Historical Park

🄰 146 B6

✉ Akoni Pule Hwy. (Hawaii 270), 12 miles N of Kawaihae

☎ 808/882-6207

Mookini Luakini Heiau & Kamehameha Akahi Aina Hanau

🄰 146 B6

✉ Akoni Pule Hwy. (Hawaii 270) at Milepost 20

Petroglyphs

Although most petroglyphs cannot be deciphered today, they continue to intrigue.

The picture writings on rocks which the Hawaiians called *kaha kii,* are found in thousands of places on all islands. Some images are obvious—dogs, people, canoe paddles. Others are obscure: concentric circles, geometric shapes, lines that might be charts. There are even images of men with wings. The meanings are a mystery. Some petroglyphs may mark a person's passing by; others are thought to be diagrams used by astronomy

schools for navigators or to have religious significance.

Many are from prehistoric times, but those depicting horses, were obviously made after the horse was introduced in 1803. Earliest human representations are stick figures, with the unique triangular-shaped torso coming later.

Some of the best petroglyphs are on the Kona-Kohala Coast, at Puako, Waikoloa, and at the Kona Village Resort (see p. 155). ■

Kauamoo Mookini from Tahiti. The stone walls run 267 feet long and 135 feet wide and are, on the perimeter, 35 feet high. Inner walls define altars, ceremonial stones, and the *mu* (body catcher), a sacrificial stone. The 3.2-acre park was the first site in Hawaii to be placed on the National Register of Historic Places.

A **statue of King Kamehameha** stands on Akoni Pule Highway (Hawaii 270) in the little town of **Kapaau,** in front of the courthouse (now a senior citizen center, where they dispense friendly advice and pamphlets to tourists). The statue is the original of the one in Honolulu (see p. 62). When it was lost at sea off the Falkland Islands, a new statue was

commissioned. A few weeks after it arrived in Honolulu, in 1883, the nine-ton original turned up, salvaged from a Falkland dump. King Kalakaua bought it for $850 and shipped it to Kapaau, near the king's birthplace. The statue lacks the grandeur of its clone because it is given a fresh coat of house paint once a year, in preparation for Kamehameha Day, June 11.

Akoni Pule Highway ends at the **Pololu Valley Lookout** where the rugged land defies civilization. You will see a long blue-green parade of cliffs that is the beginning of the lush, wild Hamakua Coast (see p. 163). It's a 20-minute hike down a switchback trail to the beautiful valley rimmed in black sand dunes. ■

Waimea

WAIMEA IS DEFINITELY CATTLE COUNTRY, BUT IT'S BEEN discovered by escapist glitterati who, even though they don jeans and cowboy hats, exude a tattletale bit of sparkle. High and cool at 2,700 feet above sea level, the town is embraced by the verdant Kohala Mountains. Dominated by the 225,000 acres of Parker Ranch, and other smaller ranches of the area, Waimea, sometimes called Kamuela, is now known for its gourmet restaurants (see pp. 252–253) and sophisticated country stores (see pp. 260–261).

Parker Ranch was founded by seaman John Palmer Parker of Newton, Massachusetts, who first arrived in Hawaii in 1809, at age 19. Hired by Kamehameha to round up the wild cattle on the island, he married the king's granddaughter Kipikane. His small land grant, plus her own 640 acres, and the best of the wild cattle, formed the core of what grew into the largest privately owned cattle ranch in the United States, producing 10 million pounds of beef a year.

The **Parker Ranch Visitor Center'**s museum has photos of early cowboy life, old family Bibles, saddles and ranch gear, Hawaiian quilts, and memorabilia dedicated to Duke Kahanamoku (see p. 87). A 15-minute video gets you right at home on the Hawaiian range.

A dual ticket *(sold until 3 p.m.)* entitles you to the museum plus entry to the ranch's two historical homes. **Mana,** the original home, built in 1847, is made entirely of warm, rich koa. Imagine yourself curling up with a good book in the snug embrace of wood.

Puuopelu, the newer ranch house, built in 1862 by John Parker II, has a deceptively modest exterior opening to a surprise of chandeliers and a stunning collection of art, including works by Corot, Utrillo, Boudin, Degas, Bonnard, and Renoir. Wander from room to room among Ming and Chien Lung vases, Louis XVI china, and carvings of jade, amethyst, and lapis lazuli. At the visitor center you may arrange horseback riding lessons, or take a wagon ride through the ranch. ■

Parker Ranch cowboys head out for the day's duties.

Parker Ranch Visitor Center
🅰 146 C5
✉ Parker Ranch Shopping Center, Mamalahoa Hwy. (Hawaii 19), Waimea
☎ 808/885-7655
💲 $$ (museum)

Hawaiian cowboys

The Hawaiian cowboy has been celebrated in song, portrayed in lively hulas, and woven into the colorful legends of the Islands. He was riding, roping, and branding decades before Texas or any other western state had even one cowboy.

Hawaiians didn't see a cow until the British captain George Vancouver brought the first ashore in 1792. Although he had never tasted a T-bone, Kamehameha recognized a good food source and turned the cattle loose in the verdant valleys of the Islands. He placed them under royal protection for ten years so they could multiply. They enjoyed a population explosion. The first horses arrived from Mexico in 1803, also as gifts to the king. They, too, enjoyed royal favor and made themselves equally at home. Twelve to 14 hands high, the wild *kanaka* mustang, descendant of the mounts of the conquistadores, weighed up to 900 pounds.

To control this unbridled bounty, the king sent to California for Mexican *vaqueros* in 1832. The first *paniolo*, as they were called because the word *"espanole"* was not harmonious with the Hawaiian language, were Kossuth, Louzeida, and Ramon. Dressed in their brilliant ponchos, sashes, bandannas, fringed leather leggings, boots, jangling spurs, and sombreros, they were instant heroes. The Hawaiians were so eager to learn equestrian skills that they would lash themselves to the backs of unbroken horses until they had mastered both the technique and the animal. Many men were killed or maimed in the process, but aspirant cowboys persisted and became experts.

In 1908, encouraged by visiting rodeo champion Angus McPhee, a group of paniolo headed for the big time—Frontier Day Rodeo in Cheyenne, Wyoming. Wearing their best aloha shirts and floppy leather hats with bands of fresh flowers, and riding borrowed mounts, they were a curiosity. When the dust cleared, Ikua Purdy of Hawaii was the new world's champion steer roper, accomplishing the feat in 56 seconds flat. Archie Kaaua was second, and Jack Low, also of Hawaii, was sixth.

Paniolo have been bringing home the trophies ever since. In 1999, Ikua Purdy was inducted into the National Rodeo Cowboy Hall of Fame in Oklahoma.

The working life was not so glamorous. Cattle drives were timed for nights of the full moon because the heat of the tropical sun exacted such a great weight loss from the animals. The cattle moaned mournfully as they moved down the mountains and across the lava flatlands to the shore. The shipping operation would begin with the first light of day. Mounted on well-trained, sturdy Percherons, the men would drive the cattle, one by one, into the surf. Some animals would be fighting mad, others in a state of panic. Once beyond the breakers, each had to be lashed to the side of a shore boat, usually a former whaleboat. With five or six animals tied to the sides, the boats would make their way out to an inter-island barge, where each animal would be hauled aboard by a sling. In addition to the obvious dangers in such work, the paniolo had to be on the alert for sharks. More than once, schools of tiger sharks caused havoc. The last sea roundups were in the 1950s.

Through it all, the paniolo developed his own distinctive style of saddle, wore hats intricately woven from pandanus leaves, and decorated them with bands of flowers, shells, and feathers. He sang his own songs and came up with his own jargon.

Today's paniolo, though enshrined in legend, is still supplying 80 percent of the beef in Island markets. Some days he may ride a "Japanese quarter horse" (Suzuki motorscooter), but for roundups, he's back in the saddle, calling out as his forefathers did, over the thundering hooves and bawling cattle, *"Hah pipi,"* (Hey, cow!) and *"Ai lepo!"* (Eat dirt!). On Saturday mornings, driving the country roads of Waimea, you may come across a roundup or branding operation, when Parker Ranch paniolo freelance their services to the smaller ranches. ∎

Hawaiian cowboys were riding and roping before the American West was won. They hone their skills at Island rodeos.

The Hamakua Coast, with its black-sand beach, as seen from the Waipio Valley Lookout.

East Hawaii

Considering that you can get grandstand seats at the act of creation in Hawaii Volcanoes National Park, go snow skiing, and pick wild orchids by the side of the road, there is not much standard tourism on this huge hunk of the Big Island, stretching from the Hamakua Coast in the north to Ka Lae, the southernmost tip of the United States. There are a few forgettable hotels, a couple of fine lodges, and some good bed and breakfasts.

The rain can come in such torrents around lush Hilo, that looking out the window you'd think you were in a submarine; in the Kau Desert it comes not at all.

The ultratech eyes of the observatories atop Mauna Kea are focused on the far reaches of the universe, while in the deep coastal valleys, men knee-deep in the mud of the ancient *kalo loi* (flooded taro fields) focus on pulling enough corms to feed their families.

Flower farms quilt the greenery in bright and delicate colors—anthurium, heliconia, ginger that perfumes the air, and orchids everywhere. When they are at the height of bloom, wild bamboo orchids are so profuse they flower like fields of cotton, and creep across lawns to battle home owners for the turf. Without weed whackers, the latter would lose. And when the African tulip trees are flowering, the hills blaze red as running lava.

Sugar was, until recently, the main agricultural crop, but after a reign of more than a century, King Cane fell to foreign competition. To combat the economic depression left in its wake, farmers are trying new crops, growing vegetables on order for the chefs of the Kona-Kohala Coast, while more and more acreage is being planted in macadamia trees. The buttery nut has given rise to a whole new industry—candy. Cacao trees have also been planted to meet the need for chocolate.

Towns, with the exception of Hilo, are small, weatherbeaten, tin-roofed, and picturesque—an artist's delight. Hilo claims all the above adjectives, except that it's big.

If you don't see this wildly contrasting side of the Big Island, dominated by massive volcanoes, you will miss one of the most unusual landscapes on Earth. ■

Waipio & Hamakua

THE CLIFFS OF THE HAMAKUA COAST RISE IN GLOWING greens from the sea, mist haunted and streaming with waterfalls. So many men from Scotland settled here to "boss" the sugar plantations, it was once called "the Scottish Coast." The Highlanders must have felt right at home in the wild gloom with shafts of brilliant sunlight lancing the hills.

Seven magnificent amphitheater valleys are carved into the Hamakua Coast; **Waipio** is the largest and the only one with a road. And it's a road you don't want to tackle in a car, even in a four-wheel-drive—an almost perpendicular, mile-long 7 to the floor of the valley. You can hike it in 30 minutes, or take a shuttle and tour from the **Waipio Valley Lookout**.

Many people are content just to look at the long cobalt rollers washing up on the black-sand beach below and the fields of green taro, grown by the few inhabitants of the area, that stretch into the wild back of the valley. The clear flowing streams that water the taro are fed by the twin cascades of **Hiilawe Falls** plunging 1,300 feet, Hawaii's highest free-falling waterfall.

A long succession of Hawaiian chiefs ruled from Waipio, beginning with Pili in the early 14th century and ending with Umialiloa, who moved the court to Kona in 1600. Kamehameha the Great spent time here during his youth.

Honokaa is the only town of note in the rural district, worth a stop if you like to poke around small galleries and shops. ■

Waipio Valley Lookout
⚞ 146 C5

Honokaa
⚞ 146 C5

A taro farmer in Waipio shows off his produce.

Taro

In old Hawaii, at least 300 kinds of taro, the Hawaiian staff of life, were cultivated. Its leaves taste similar to spinach. The corm is baked or boiled like a potato, or—more likely—pounded for poi, the bland, clean-tasting purple paste served in big bowls on local tables or in thimbles at tourist luaus. Doctors ship poi around the world to patients with severe ulcers and to newborns who can't tolerate either mother's milk or formula.

Taro is the very symbol of Hawaiian culture, regarded as a brother of mankind. According to legend, when the first-born infant son of Papa and Wakea, the mother and father of the human race, died, his parents buried him. From his body a new plant, taro, sprang up from the earth to nurture all the siblings who were to come.

Nowadays poi is added to pancakes, muffins, and breads, turning them lavender and sweet. ■

Hilo

LIKE A FAVORITE AGED AUNT, HILO SEEMS KINDLY YET tenacious, and it smells faintly of flowers as you pass. Most of its buildings are a century old, but rouged in optimistic paint. The more you know Hilo the better you like it.

Liliuokalani Gardens spreads along the Hilo waterfront where tsunami have roared ashore.

Hilo

🗺 147 E4

Visitor information

✉ Hawaii Visitors & Convention Bureau, 250 Keawe St.

☎ 808/961-5797

🕐 Closed Sat.–Sun.

Residents claim the rain, for which the town has a reputation, falls mainly in the night; statistics put the rainy days (or nights) at 278 a year. On the bright side, you should see the gardens—lush botanical gardens, opulent front yards, acres of orchid and anthurium farms, yellow ginger and wild bamboo orchids blooming by the wayside.

A walking map of Hilo can be obtained from the Hawaii Visitors and Convention Bureau and from Lyman House. Many of the colorful buildings are on the National Register of Historic Places.

At the **Lyman Museum and Mission House** you'll see the oldest wood-frame house on the island, built of koa planks in 1839.

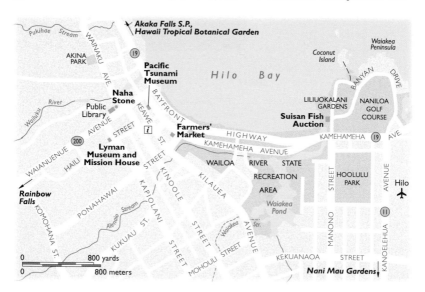

Furnishings that belonged to missionaries David and Sarah Lyman provide a window into life almost two centuries ago.

This contrasts with the **Earth Heritage Gallery** in the museum next door, with its astronomy and geology exhibits: Rock hounds will love it. The **Island Heritage Gallery** features reproductions of homes from the island's diverse cultures, including a grass house.

The **Naha Stone** in front of the public library *(300 Waianuenue Ave.)* is Hawaii's Excalibur. Similar to the story of King Arthur and the famous sword, it was said that whoever could move this stone would be king of all the Hawaiian Islands. When he was a lad of 14, Kamehameha the Great moved the 2.5-ton rock, then went on to fulfill the prophecy.

To get a real feel for Hilo, go where local folks go: the **Farmers' Market** *(Kamehameha Ave. & Mamo St., Wed. & Sat. mornings)* and the **Suisan Fish Auction** *(85 Lihiwai St., closed Sun.).* And you'd better get there early for the good stuff. The fishing boats have

been out during the night, and bring in their catch at sunrise ready for sale. The fish auction bell clangs at 7 a.m., and the bidding starts early for the beautiful pink *opakapaka* (pink snapper), the silver *mahimahi* (dolphin fish), and the big round moonfish. At the farmers' market you can buy luscious Waimea strawberries, homemade lychee-pepper jelly, and woven *lauhala* bags lined with genuine *kapa* (tree-bark cloth).

The 30-acre **Liliuokalani Gardens** *(Banyan Dr.),* named after the Islands' last queen, is the largest formal Japanese garden east of the East. Stroll beneath a crimson torii gate, over a moon bridge, and past a tea pagoda. You can cross the footbridge to Coconut Island and look back at the Hilo waterfront backed by mighty mountains.

Rainbow Falls *(Wailuku River State Park, Waianuenue Ave., just past the fork to Kaumana Dr.)* are not spectacular unless you see them in early morning or late afternoon when rainbows gather about the cascade as it tumbles into its 100-foot diameter plunge pool. ∎

Hilo is a big little town resting complacently in the neighborhood of active volcanoes.

Lyman Museum & Mission House

✉ 276 Haili St., Hilo
☎ 808/935-5021
🕐 Closed Sun.
💲 $$

Around Hilo

FOR A REGION WHERE TOURISTS SELDOM LINGER, THE Hilo area offers some outstanding attractions, aside from Hawaii Volcanoes National Park (see pp. 170–77).

You can see two glorious waterfalls at **Akaka Falls State Park** *(Hawaii 220, 3.5 miles W of Honomu).* In a half hour you can walk the easy loop trail connecting 420-foot Akaka Falls with the smaller Kahuna Falls. Along the way you'll see blue, red, and pink ginger, banks of wild impatiens, orchids, and tunnels of jungle vegetation. Akaka Falls are among the prettiest in the state, and really easily accessible.

Along the **Pepeekeo Scenic Drive,** a 4-mile detour off Hawaii Belt Road 19 *(4 miles N of Hilo),* you'll pass dramatic lava coastline, surf-drenched coves, streams gushing with waterfalls, and lush stands of jungle. At Onomea Bay is **Hawaii Tropical Botanical Garden,** a sprawling bouquet of tropical flora, complete with lily lake, ginger jungle, banyan canyon, waterfalls, and orchid garden. Everything is labeled.

Nani Mau Gardens *(reached off Hawaii 11, 3 miles S of Hilo Airport)* is a little more commercial. They've got restaurants, a gift shop, and tram tours. But there's some serious botany going on here, with 2,000 varieties of flora. The orchid collection is outstanding, and there's a botanical museum, Japanese garden, and hibiscus collection.

Farther along Hawaii 11, you can walk for free around the **Akatsuka Orchid Garden,** and see one of the largest orchid collections in the state. If Hilo is having one of its rainy days, this nursery has covered walkways. ■

Left: A jade vine thrives in the moist climate.

Hawaii Tropical Botanical Garden
- 147 E4
- ✉ Pepeekeo Scenic Dr.
- ☎ 808/964-5233
- $ $$$

Nani Mau Gardens
- 147 E4
- ✉ 421 Makalika St.
- ☎ 808/959-3500
- $ $$

Tsunami

Tsunamis are ocean waves triggered by a major disturbance of the ocean floor caused by earthquakes, volcanoes, or landslides. Only a few feet high when they begin, they can travel thousands of miles undetected in open ocean at typical speeds of 600 miles per hour. As they approach shore, they may slow down and steepen to heights of 100 feet. Since the early 1800s, when records began to be kept, about 50 tsunamis have been reported in the Hawaiian Islands.

An Alaskan earthquake in 1946 sent tsunamis south to Hawaii. On the morning of April 1, they sped ashore at Hilo at 57 feet high, destroyed half the town, and killed 96 people along the coast. Hilo rebuilt itself after the devastation, only to have another tsunami, this one from off the coast of Chile, slam the city in 1960, taking 61 lives. This time, the town retreated, moving inland, and created parkland along the shore. The tsunamis also devastated Waipio Valley and Laupahoehoe.

Visit the **Pacific Tsunami Museum** in Hilo's historic First Hawaiian Bank Building to see fascinating exhibits and videos. On display is a quilt made by students from Laupahoehoe in memory of children and teachers who lost their lives in the 1946 tsunami. ∎

Akaka Falls State Park has an easy nature trail through jungle.

Akatsuka Orchid Garden
 147 E3
✉ Hawaii 11, just after Milepost 22
☎ 808/967-8234

Pacific Tsunami Museum
✉ 130 Kamehameha Ave.
☎ 808/935-0926
🕐 Closed Sun.
💲 $$

Hula

Hula is Hawaii's history book. Without a written language, Hawaiians incorporated their values, tales of gods and kings, epic romances, accounts of great events, and their genealogies from one generation to the next in the chants and dances of hula. In the old days, a dancer could not change a single step or movement under pain of death, for to change the dance was to change history.

Dressed for the *hula kahiko* (ancient hula), a dancer chants his song.

Although the dance is the most famous cultural expression of the Islands, its importance is often underestimated and its message misunderstood. Missionaries were shocked at its sensuality. C.S. Stewart wrote in his journal of 1823: "The dull and monotonous sounds of the native drum and calabash, the wild notes of their songs ... and the pulsations, on the ground, of the tread of thousands in the dance ... fell on the heart with a saddening power, for we had been compelled ... to associate with them unrivaled licentiousness and abominations which must forever remain untold." Hollywood loved the hula but treated it as a sort of Polynesian go-go dance.

Hula has evolved so drastically from its ancient religious origins that today the dance is divided into two distinct categories. *Hula kahiko* is the oldest form; its energy is primal. The costume is a skirt of grass, ti leaf, or cotton imprinted to look like *kapa* (tree-bark cloth), worn with a simple, loose top. Leis woven of flowers, vines, and ferns are worn about the head and shoulders, and often the wrists and ankles. It is danced to the driving beat of drums, gourd rattles, bamboo sticks, and nose flutes.

Hula auana evolved after Western contact and the introduction of Western musical instruments. In this form, guitars and ukuleles join the ancient instruments. The dancers smile more and use very specific hand gestures to illustrate the message of the dance, which may often be hidden in symbols, the most common being a flower to symbolize a person. Costuming is often rather elegant, reflecting the clothes of the monarchy era, which were modeled on the courts of Europe. Leis and flowers are lavishly worn with slender *holoku* (Hawaiian gown with train).

An aspiring dancer does not "take lessons." Rather, he or she joins a *halau,* a group presided over by a *kumu hula* (master teacher). Close bonds of loyalty are formed among the dancers as they study not only the words, music, and movements, but also the language and all facets of Hawaiian culture.

Hula still holds an honored place in the hearts of the people, and is part of the official and daily life of Hawaii. It attends every party and opens the state legislature. Even the palatial megaresorts have found that without the hula, their guests simply don't think they're in Hawaii.

A full calendar of hula festivals and competitions throughout the Islands keeps dancers on their toes. Visitors will find hula everywhere—luaus, dinner shows, shopping malls, and cocktail terraces.

The late Maiki Aiu, founder of Halau Hula O Maiki, and the woman considered to be "the mother of the Hawaiian renaissance," summed it up concisely: "Hula is life." ■

Top right: Arrayed in ferns, the dancers, in their gestures, symbolize love. Bottom right: Three generations of hula are shown by the dancer, drummer, and student.

Hawaii Volcanoes National Park

KILAUEA (4,078 FEET), THE WORLD'S ONLY DRIVE-UP - volcano, is the red-hot heart of Hawaii Volcanoes National Park. It also happens to be the world's most active volcano, having erupted continuously since January 3, 1983, when it came to life in a trembling of the earth and a 40-foot fountain of fire.

Hawaii Volcanoes National Park
- 146 C3
- Hawaii Belt Rd. (Hawaii 11) 29 miles from Hilo
- 808/985-6000 (information on visitor center, Jaggar Museum, park activities, and recordings of latest eruption updates)
- $$$ (7-day pass)

Opposite: The Puu Oo vent of Kilauea Volcano in an eruptive phase. Helicopter tours are breathtaking.

The 377-square-mile park was founded in 1916 to protect, and make accessible to the public, the amazing natural wonders of Kilauea and its simmering neighbor, Mauna Loa volcano. It was the first national park in Hawaii, and originally included Haleakala, on Maui (see pp. 138–39). In 1982, the park was named a World Heritage Site by UNESCO. It encompasses the summit calderas of both Kilauea and Mauna Loa (currently quiet on the surface) and sections of the Kalapana Coast.

The composition of lava here is such that the eruptions are usually not as explosive as they are in other parts of the world, although history indicates they have that potential. In 1790 and 1924 there were nasty explosions. Ashen footprints imbedded beside the **Mauna Iki Trail** are all that's left of 100 warriors of Chief Keoua, who were killed by the 1790 eruption as they marched to do battle with Kamehameha. Still the "good volcano" image persists so that when Kilauea erupts, instead of heading for the nearest escape route, people pack a picnic and head for the park to see the most spectacular fireworks show on Earth. Saturday night crowds can number in the thousands when Kilauea is really pumping.

Park rangers are heroic in their efforts to help people see the eruption safely, often marking new walking trails several times a day as lava flows change course. One scientist said, "It's like playing with a jigsaw puzzle with moving parts."

The volcano is most awesome at night when the fires rage against the darkened sky. Sometimes lava flows in blazing cascades down the side of the mountain and into the sea, creating great billows of steam for miles along the seething coast.

Since it began its current eruptive phase, Kilauea has added more than 500 acres to the Big Island. As lava flows into the sea, it quickly cools and hardens, building up in the shallows along the coast. It has also covered 16,000 lowland acres in as much as 80 feet of lava, destroying rain forest, towns, subdivisions, a 700-year-old temple, a park visitor center, and famous Kaimu Black Sand Beach.

The most recent activity centers on Puu Oo, a cinder-and-spatter cone. Although it is in a remote area of the park, the red-hot lava is often visible miles from its source, as it makes its way to the sea. Sometimes you can see it from your car window.

Volcanoes are notoriously unpredictable, and it is entirely possible that on the day of your visit, all the lava will be moving through underground chambers. Even if you don't see red, Hawaii Volcanoes National Park is still an awesome experience. It has 150 miles of some of the most unusual

who have disobeyed signs and directives have been fried, steamed, and boiled by the volcano. Infants, pregnant women, and people with health problems, particularly heart and lung, should avoid the park.

Lodging can be found within the park, just outside at Volcano Village, or in Hilo.

VOLCANO SITES

Every visit to the park should begin at the **Kilauea Visitor Center,** the only surviving center (lava consumed the other), where the day's activities are posted, such as guided nature walks and ranger talks, along with the latest eruption information. If you're planning on taking an overnight backcountry trip, this is the place to register, so rangers know where you are in the event of an emergency.

Every hour on the hour, a 25-minute film on the park and the volcanoes' most impressive eruptions is aired in the center's theater *(last screening at 4 p.m.).* There are also exhibits of volcanology, Hawaiian culture, and park wildlife and flora. Maps and books are available for purchase.

The **Thomas A. Jaggar Museum** is a playground of seismometers, computers, videos, and hands-on displays. A million-dollar Vax 11-750 computer, linked to the scientific headquarters next door at **Hawaiian Volcano Observatory** *(closed to the public),* gives instant printouts of every earthquake on the island, and there are several hundred microquakes a day. A bank of seismographic drums, looking like a network of electrocardiographs, actually records the pulse of the volcano, registering any movement of the earth. Next to the real thing is a small seismograph set up to record "people tremors." When you hop, jump, or leap, the instrument records the shock to

Students examine the interactive volcano exhibits at the Thomas A. Jaggar Museum.

Kilauea Visitor Center

🏕 173 C2
✉ Just inside park entrance
☎ 808/985-6000

hiking trails in the world, each revealing different facets of this utterly fascinating terrain, and a glimpse of the mighty forces that shaped our planet. Features range from a 15-minute stroll through an old lava tube to a four-day trek to the top of Mauna Loa. There are also 50 miles of paved roads in the park, although some may be blocked by lava flows. Many of the plants and birds in the park are rare and endangered. In the middle of lava flows are *kipuka,* areas unmolested by the flows and left as pristine islands of life in the bleak, black desert. Some are quite large and offer refuge to endemic species of flora and fauna.

It can be extremely hazardous to stray from marked trails or enter closed areas of the park. People

the floor as if it were a shock to the volcano's heart.

Screens show videotapes of past eruptions: fountains of fire, churning rivers and lakes of lava. A display case with a ragged, singed safety suit is dramatic testimony to the dedication of the park's volcanologists. The suit was worn by a scientist who fell kneedeep into lava at 2,000°F, and lived to tell about it. Sharing space with the technology are huge murals depicting the intriguing legends of Pele, the goddess of volcanoes. Painted by Hawaiian artist and historian Herb Kawainui Kane, the murals portray how the Hawaiians personified their emotional response to their awesome environment.

The museum is named for Professor Thomas A. Jaggar (1871–1953) who founded the observatory in 1912. He worked tirelessly to have the area declared a national park.

Volcano House, the only hotel in the park is perched right on the edge of Kilauea caldera. When there is summit activity, you can dine in its restaurant and watch the show; otherwise watch the continuous-run video in the bar. The lobby fireplace is always burning, and there are people who claim to have seen the face of Pele in the flames. The original Volcano House was built in 1846. After several reconstructions, it was built in its current form in 1941. Comments in the guest book are fascinating.

At the **Volcano Art Center** (*tel 808/967-8222, closed 5 p.m. daily*) more than 200 artisans exhibit their creative work, much of it centering on the volcano and its energy. *Lauhala*-weaving virtuoso Glenn Okuma sits on the center's porch almost every day, fashioning his acclaimed baskets. You'll also find paintings, jewelry, bronzeware, ceramic, textiles, and photography. There are new shows monthly at this nonprofit arts center housed in another Volcano House building dating from 1877. ■

Artists claim the volcano's creative energy is an inspiration. Many exhibit at the Volcano Art Center.

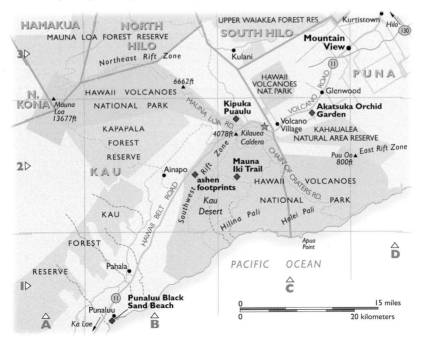

Crater Rim drive

Crater Rim Drive, the road encircling Kilauea's oval summit caldera, 2.5 miles across and 300 feet deep, is the main attraction of the park. On the drive you will pass through lush rain forests with tree ferns, and see raw, steaming craters and vast areas of devastation. Along the road are well-marked trails and overlooks to encourage you to get out of your car periodically and explore this strange landscape.

Leaving the **Kilauea Visitor Center,** go right to begin the loop road. You'll immediately pass **Volcano House** and the **Volcano Art Center** ❶ (see p. 173). If you wish, you can rent a self-guided audiotour of Crater Rim Drive for a nominal fee at the art center.

Next is a sign for **Sulphur Banks** ❷. Follow your nose to a steamy, smelly area where the rocks are mustard color from sulfur carried by volcanic fumes. From the fenced steam vents across the road you can get a good look at the steam vaporized from the groundwater that seeps into lava crevices.

The first big lookout point is **Kilauea Overlook** ❸, with a view onto the crater's crackling, steaming floor. The **Hawaiian Volcano Observatory** and **Jaggar Museum** (see pp. 172–73) are just beyond, and from there, too, you can gaze into the crater. In the opposite direction, massive Mauna Loa looms in the west. This area was sacred to the ancient Hawaiians. Impressive fields of lava mark the **Southwest Rift Zone,** scene of a 1971 eruption.

At **Halemaumau Crater** ❹, you can park and walk to this steamiest, most odorous area of the caldera. On some days the fumes are so toxic the area is closed. Halemaumau last erupted in 1974 but is obviously just napping. In one of the most dramatic moments in Hawaiian history, High Chiefess Kapiolani, a devout convert to Christianity, climbed down onto a ledge in Halemaumau while it was erupting in 1824. She stood just above the lava lake and defied Pele by eating *ohelo* berries (sacred to the goddess), then threw rocks into the pit, shouting, "Jehovah is my God."

Keanakakoi, next crater on the route, spewed 200-foot fountains of fire in the air and poured out the lava that first interrupted the Chain of Craters Road.

A good place to get out and walk is **Devastation Trail** ❺, a half-mile,

15-minute, family-friendly stroll through hell. In 1959, lava fountains of 1,900-feet gushed into the air, spilling ash and pumice, wiping out an ohia forest and leaving white tree skeletons standing in black cinders. Life has begun to proliferate again along the boardwalk, however, so that the name of the trail may have to be changed as it looks less and less devastated.

The next stop is a walk of a completely different nature. The **Thurston Lava Tube** ❻ is an easy 20-minute loop that descends quickly into a forest of tree ferns. Native birds have begun to nest in the area. With luck, you may see the scarlet *iiwi* or the chartreuse *amakihi*. You will cross a bridge over a small chasm and enter an electrically lit tunnel that once ran red with magma from the bowels of the Earth. It is 450 feet long and in places as high as 20 feet, all of it eerie and awesome. Ferns drape themselves over the entrance and exit.

Last stop on the drive is **Kilauea Iki Overlook** ❼. The 1959 eruption that shaped so many of the park's features filled this crater with a lava lake, as fire fountains shot into the air. One of the park's most popular hiking trails ventures into this nuclear-looking wasteland. ■

🅰 Also see map, p. 146 D3
▶ Kilauea Visitor Center
↔ 11 miles
🕐 1 hour
▶ Kilauea Visitor Center

NOT TO BE MISSED
- Volcano Art Center
- Jaggar Museum
- Devastation Trail
- Thurston Lava Tube
- Kilauea Iki Overlook

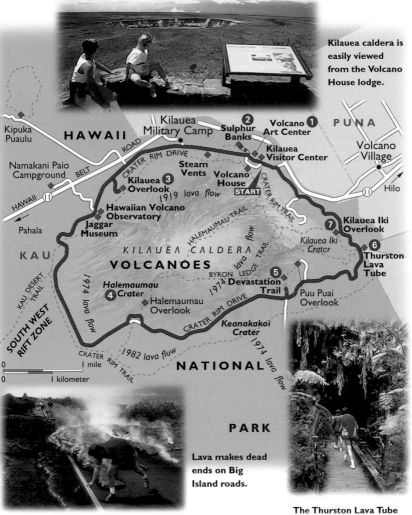

Kilauea caldera is
easily viewed
from the Volcano
House lodge.

Lava makes dead
ends on Big
Island roads.

The Thurston Lava Tube

Pele

The goddess of fire and volcanoes came to Hawaii by canoe from a land in the far reaches of the ocean. From Niihau, she traveled southward through the Islands, looking for the perfect place of fire in which to dwell. She settled finally in Halemaumau Crater of Kilauea Volcano, where she dwells to this day.

She appears as a beautiful woman dressed in red, or an old crone hitching a ride on a country road. If you pass her by, the sages say, your car will develop trouble. If you pick her up, she will sit quietly in the back seat; when you turn around, she will vanish.

Pele's love affairs, rivalries, and jealousies are the raw material of Hawaii's literature. Her presence is everywhere: In the obsidian stretches of hardened lava, the fiery rivers of lava flowing to the sea, the steam rising from fissures and cracks, the warm-water ponds, and in the trembling of the earth. ■

Kilauea trails & birdlife

THE CHARACTER OF HAWAII VOLCANOES NATIONAL PARK
is best discovered on foot. More than 150 miles of trails explore the
various environments of the park, and even if there were no active
lava flow, the terrain is unique. Walking around, you'll encounter
some of the rarest flora and fauna on the planet. You'll need sunscreen, a hat, sturdy walking shoes, and drinking water.

The most unusual trail you'll ever
walk is **Kilauea Iki.** It will take
four hours to walk the 6.5-mile
round-trip from the Thurston Lava
Tube (see p. 174) parking lot. The
trail descends 400 feet through rain
forest to the crater floor. You'll see
the scarlet blossoms of the ohia
lehua and the cranberry-like ohelo

**A bird-watcher is
out early on the
Sandalwood Trail.**

berry. Then, as you set out across
the crater floor, you'll follow the
rock cairns into what looks like a
nuclear accident scene. Walking on
the brittle, hardened lava is like
walking on potato chips, while
beneath your feet, the ground is
toasty warm, steam vents hiss, and
their clouds drift. The graceful
white bird you'll see overhead is the
koae kea, an endemic seabird that
nests in nooks of the crater wall; it
carries squid dinner 7 miles from
its oceanic hunting grounds to
its nestlings.

The **Sandalwood Trail** is a
good bet for bird-watchers. It's an
easy trail, less than a mile, and
would take 15 minutes to do, if you
weren't lingering to look at birds.
The trailhead is right across from
Kilauea Visitor Center parking lot.
The first birds you'll encounter will
probably be mynahs quarreling in
the grass at the entry. In just a few
steps, you cross a profound biologi-
cal divide and find yourself
enveloped in rain forest. It feels
holy. Ferns tower 20 feet overhead
forming a lacy canopy, and dew
sparkles like crystal in the scarlet
pompoms of the ohia lehua blossoms. All around, if you stop, is the
sweet song of birds, unnoticed in
the parking lot only feet away.

The brilliant red *apapane* is the
endemic bird most likely to be
spotted. It has a distinctive whirring
of wings as it flies and has about 50
melodious songs. The best strategy
for sighting Hawaiian birds is to
stake out the flowers they feed on,

the bright yellow *mamane,* the creamy bouquets of the giant koa tree, and the red ohia lehua.

The trail winds through the forest, in the cool shadow of the crater wall, into rocky crevices, and out to panoramic views across the crater. The *elepaio* frequents the koa trees. In days gone by, canoemakers seeking suitable trees for their vessels would watch the elepaio carefully. If it landed on a koa tree and began to probe for insects, the tree was deemed unacceptable.

Some other native birds commonly found in the park are *pueo,* the Hawaiian owl; *io,* the Hawaiian hawk; the crimson *iiwi;* and *omao,* a Hawaiian thrush. The coastal area of the park has populations of *noio,* the black noddy; *akekeke,* a ruddy turnstone; *kolea,* the Pacific golden plover; and *kioea,* the bristle-thighed curlew. The nene (Hawaiian goose, see p. 139) struts around the park like an owner doing inventory. Watch the nene from the dining room of the **Volcano Golf and Country Club** *(35 Pii Mauna Dr., tel 808/967-8228),* where they gather on the greens.

Aside from native species of birds, the park has populations of introduced mynah, melodious laughing thrush, Japanese white-eye, northern cardinal, nutmeg mannikin, common barn-owl, California quail, chukar, francolin, and Kalij pheasant.

To really experience the park on its own terms, you can hike around the Crater Rim rather than drive (see pp. 174–175). Allow an entire day to walk the 11.6-mile **Crater Rim Trail.** Start in the early morning from the trailhead in front of Volcano House and walk counterclockwise to get the hot, treeless Kau Desert area out of the way before the midday heat. If you want to hike a part of the trail you won't see from the road, pick up the portion that crosses Chain of Craters Road and walk west to Keanakakoi Crater. Along the way you'll see eerie tree molds, natural black lava sculptures created when flowing hot lava engulfs a tree and hardens around it while the tree burns inside. The small crater often has rainbows around it. Allow an hour's round-trip back to the road. ∎

The *iiwi (Vestiaria coccinea)* sips nectar from the ohia lehua blossom.

Mauna Loa & Mauna Kea

MAUNA LOA, AT 13,679 FEET, IS SECOND TO MAUNA KEA AS the highest peak in the Pacific, but it is the most massive mountain anywhere on Earth. One hundred times the size of extinct volcano Mount Rainier in Washington State, it's so big California's entire Sierra Nevada mountain range could fit inside it. The name means "long mountain"—the summit caldera, Mokuaweoweo, is 3 miles long and 600 feet deep.

Onizuka Center for International Astronomy

🅰 146 D4

✉ Summit Rd., at the 9,600-foot marker

☎ 808/961-2180

The summit caldera of Mauna Loa, an enormous shield volcano

Mauna Loa was born three million years ago, 18,000 feet beneath the ocean. Too young to be sculpted by erosion, its shape is a perfect shield. Having erupted 37 times since 1832, it is classified as active; the last eruption in 1984 threatened Hilo, but stopped in time.

The hike to the top is a tough four-day round-trip, and you must be equipped for winter mountaineering. Driving up to the 6,662-foot elevation on **Mauna Loa Road** (*from Hawaii 11*) gives you a grand experience of the mountain.

One mile up the road is **Kipuka Puaulu,** commonly called Bird Park. About 400 years ago, an eruption from the northeast rift zone of Mauna Loa covered vast areas of 2,000-year-old forest. The erratic flow left *kipuka,* islands of untouched forest in the sea of lava, and Kipuka Puaulu is a vestige of this ancient environment. Allow at least an hour to appreciate the 1.2-mile loop trail through the kipuka. Listen to the arias sung by cardinal,

iiwi, apapane, amakihi, and *elepaio,* then stroll beneath giant koa trees, ohia lehua, and *mamane.*

Stands of koa line Mauna Loa road as you continue upward. Watch out for the exotically plumed Kalij pheasant; it has crowned itself king of the road, and is disdainful of traffic. A native of Nepal, the bird was imported in 1962 and is completely at home here.

To really enjoy this drive, pull over occasionally and experience the quiet. Overhead the *io,* once the symbol of Hawaiian royalty, may be surfing wind waves above the trees. At the end of the road, where the arduous trail to the summit begins, there are picnic tables.

MAUNA KEA

Driving the 55-mile Saddle Road, Hawaii 200, between Hilo and the Kohala Coast, you cross a high valley with Earth's most massive mountain on one side of the road and its highest on the other. Mauna Kea, at 32,796 feet if you add the

13,796 feet above sea level to 19,000 down to its base on the ocean floor, is higher than Everest. Its name means "white mountain," as its peak is usually mantled in snow.

Pele's rival, Poliahu, the snow goddess, dwells in the high air of the mountain and weeps crystal tears for lovers who never stay.

Mauna Kea hasn't erupted for 3,500 years. During the Ice Age, 15,000 years ago, a glacier locked the heights in ice, leaving a layer of permafrost that exists today. It feeds Lake Waiau, the third highest lake in the United States, at 13,020 feet.

Skiing for the experienced enthusiast is available usually in February and March, but snow can fall anytime at that altitude. Contact **Ski Guides Hawaii** *(tel 808/885-4188, $$$$$)* for a guided tour including equipment.

Astronomers from eleven nations have set up their extremely powerful telescopes, including the world's largest, the Keck Telescope, on top of the mountain to study the far reaches of the universe. The Keck is eight stories high with a lens diameter of 33 feet. Proximity to the Equator and pollution-free skies make this the premier star-gazing location. It's an awesome sight, even to the naked eye.

The road to the top of Mauna Kea begins at Milepost 28 on the Saddle Road. You can easily drive the steep 6 miles to the **Onizuka**

Center for International Astronomy *(tel 808/961-2180, no children under 16 years, no pregnant women)*, but only a four-wheel-drive vehicle can attempt the summit. Free summit tours, in your own vehicle, leave the center Saturdays and Sundays at 1 p.m. You'll be able to walk around inside one of the observatories. Star-gazing is offered nightly from 6 to 10 p.m. The center has a powerful telescope and Big Island skies are among the clearest in the world.

The Onizuka Center is named for Big Island astronaut, Ellison Onizuka, killed in the *Challenger* space shuttle in 1986. Memorial exhibits, plus items of Mauna Kea's geology, form the bulk of the display. ■

High-altitude skiing atop Mauna Kea, beside an observatory

Puna

RECENT LAVA FLOWS HERE HAVE OBLITERATED FAVORITE beaches and entire towns. Yet all around the devastation life persists in lush greenery. Puna draws risk takers, edgier elements, and those comfortable with notions of doomsday. They settle among old-timers and never quite blend in, but put their mark on the district.

Orchid growers consider the soil and climate around Hilo to be ideal growing conditions.

Mauna Loa Macadamia Nut Factory

🅐 147 E4

✉ End of Macadamia Nut Rd. off Hawaii 11

☎ 808/966-8618

The town of **Pahoa** has never gotten over the 1960s. Third-generation flower children, raised around the peace symbol and confirmed in tie-dyed regalia, can be spotted along the old wooden sidewalks and in the rickety stores reborn as New Age boutiques, funky second-hand emporiums, and health food stores. The 1917 **Akebono Theater** enjoys a crowded calendar of rock and reggae concerts. The town's weekend outdoor market draws an interesting crowd of bead traders and farmers.

Visitors are welcome at the **Mauna Loa Macadamia Nut Factory,** featuring one of the district's chief crops. You approach through 3 miles of orchards. At the factory, you can watch the gourmet nut get cracked, sorted, cooked, and

processed into snacks, cookies, candy, and ice cream. Samples? Of course, and there's also a gift shop.

A whole stand of ohia forest got cooked in 1790 when a molten river of red-hot lava surged across the land. When it cooled, the trees had become eerie black sculptures. At **Lava Tree State Monument** (*Hawaii 132, 2.7 miles SE of Pahoa*), pleasant paths wander among 17 acres of these tree molds. The ohia forest has now regenerated, so the park is shady and cool.

The volcano has created several thermal ponds in Puna, where you can simmer in Earth's own bath. The most accessible is a 60-foot seaside pool at **Ahalanui Beach Park** (*look for a chain-link fence and what looks like a private house on Hawaii 137, 1 mile N of Pahoa-Pohoiki Rd.*); be aware that the bacteria count in this warm, popular pond can sometimes be high enough to cause illness. Two more thermal pools, near **Isaac Hale Beach Park** (*end of Pahoa-Pohoiki Rd.*), are smaller and unimproved, but that is their charm.

Cape Kumukahi (*end of Hawaii 132*), the easternmost tip of Hawaii, has led a charmed life. The spectacular 1960 volcanic outburst that destroyed the town of Kapoho shot geysers of fire into the air from a 2,600-foot-wide eruption. The lava stopped within 6 feet of the base of the lighthouse (really an unattractive light tower), and politely went around it. ■

Kau

FOR TOURISTS, THE MOST FAMOUS THING ABOUT THE Kau district is Ka Lae, the southernmost tip of the United States. For locals, it's the ugly Kau orange with the sweetest taste of any orange. Ka Lae, also known as South Point, is for people given to extremities: It's the end of Hawaii, the end of America. The next stop is Tahiti.

Ka Lae is also believed by scholars to be the first landfall of the first Polynesians (see pp. 24–26), probably around A.D. 500. Here in the fierce winds are the ruins of an ancient temple, **Kalalea Heiau.** Winds are so strong that they support a thriving wind farm along the road. Mooring holes for securing canoes are perfect circles carved into the lava rocks. A fishing village once flourished here, and thousands of bone hooks have been found in the mixed green-and-black sand. Platforms for launching boats dot the high cliffs. Daring tourists jump from there, probably unaware of the notorious currents often lurking below.

Papakolea, popularly called **Green Sand Beach,** is 3 miles east. It's about an hour's hike (or a 2.5-mile trip by four-wheel-drive) into the wind to an unprotected beach with dangerous surf. The big draw is the emerald green olivine "sand." Olivine is the first mineral to crystalize as basaltic lava cools. The semiprecious crystal is also found in Iceland and on the moon.

Two quiet towns east of Ka Lae are Naalehu and Waiohinu. There are some small, very agreeable restaurants at **Naalehu** (see p. 254). The island's famous Punaluu Portuguese sweet bread is made here at **Punaluu Bake Shop** (Mark Twain Sq., Hawaii 11, tel 808/929-7343, closed 5 p.m.). Stop by for free samples flavored with guava or taro.

Waiohinu's claim to fame is Mark Twain Square (Hawaii 11, tel 808/929-7550), a charming pit stop.

The famous author planted monkeypod trees here in 1866—surviving offshoots offer shade. All around the luxuriant garden are quotes from Mark Twain, who rode in on horseback and liked it enough to stay awhile.

Farther east at **Punaluu,** the beautiful **Punaluu Black Sand Beach** (Hawaii 11, 5 miles W of Pahala) is lined with coconut palms and lapped by turquoise surf. You couldn't find a more picturesque spot to swim. On a hill overlooking the ocean, historic **Hokuloa Church,** rebuilt in 1957, is a memorial to Henry Opukahaia (see p. 30), the young Hawaiian Christian who had been studying in New England and who was most instrumental in persuading missionaries to come to Hawaii. ■

Ka Lae, also known as South Point, is the southernmost tip of land in the United States.

Ka Lae
🗺 146 C1
✉ End of South Point Rd. off Hawaii 11

More places to visit on Hawaii: the Big Island

KALOPA STATE RECREATION AREA

This little known park, up in the northeast, is one of the loveliest on the island. A hundred acres of ohia forest can be explored at the cool, 2,000-foot elevation. Some of the giant trees are three to five centuries old. This is one of the last and most accessible vestiges of native rain forest left. There's a 4-acre arboretum for native species. In 1979, a stand of koa trees were planted as part of an effort to save the species, which had been dying out. The trees were so at home among their kin in the native forest that some grew from seed to 8 feet in the first year. Many are now more than 75 feet high. An easy 0.7-mile nature trail loops through the rain forest. Many of the rare trees and plants beside the path are labeled. Additional trails go into the forest reserve, and there's also a horseback trail.

Telescopes of the Keck I and Keck II observatories atop Mauna Kea are trained on space.

146 D5 End of Kalopa Rd., 3 miles inland from Hawaii 19. 5 miles southeast of Honokaa 808/974-6200

KAMUELA MUSEUM

This small, eclectic museum at Waiaka, just west of Waimea, has collected and displayed its artifacts with no apparent order or criteria.

You'll find sombreros, surfboards, feathered fans from Japan, *kahili* (Hawaiian feather standards of royalty), a Viet Cong flag, stone poi (taro) pounders, an antique brass diving helmet, and much more. You can't help but smile, and stay longer: The stuff is fascinating.

146 C5 Hawaii 19 & Hawaii 250, Waimea 808/885-4724 $$

KECK OBSERVATORY CENTER

The first celestial photograph taken with the partially completed Keck Telescope atop Mauna Kea was of Galaxy NGC 1232, about 65 million light years from Earth. A model of the world's largest telescope is on view here along with a video on the observatory's exploration of the universe. The actual telescope is eight stories high and weighs 270 tons. Most people don't make it to the top of Mauna Kea, so this is an intriguing, educational substitute, right in Waimea town.

146 C5 65-1120 Mamalahoa Hwy., Waimea 808/885-7887 Closed Sat.–Sun.

LAUPAHOEHOE POINT BEACH PARK

It is said that one day Poliahu the snow goddess came down from the heights of Mauna Kea to go *holua* sledding (sliding on leaves down a mountain slope) at Laupahoehoe. She was joined by Pele, goddess of volcanoes. The two got into a tiff when Pele caused an eruption that drove Poliahu back to the summit. Poliahu carried the day by sending freezing winds and snow over the lava forcing it to enter the ocean and form Laupahoehoe Point on the Big Island's east coast, 25 miles north of Hilo. The beach park is reached along Hawaii 19.

On April Fool's Day, 1946, a tsunami (see p. 167), which devastated Hilo, swept across the Laupahoehoe Point, killing 32 people, most of them schoolchildren. A memorial stands where the school once did. A teacher who survived had her story published in *Reader's Digest,* March 1959. The surf at this point is spectacular as it assaults the craggy black lava shoreline.

146 D5 ■

Kauai is everyone's dream of a South Sea island. Its mountains are Bali Hai peaks where spectacular waterfalls cascade and rainbows leap over jagged ridges. And nowhere is there a building higher than a palm tree.

Kauai

**Brightly painted gourds are
souvenirs of Kauai.**

Kauai

OLDEST OF THE EIGHT MAJOR HAWAIIAN ISLANDS, KAUAI WAS CREATED BY one massive volcano, which became extinct six million years ago. Nature has had a lot of time to sculpt this island into a great beauty, etching majestic sea cliffs along the Na Pali Coast, carving a grand canyon into the heart of the island, and blessing the interior with tremendous rains while leaving the coast in sunshine. Forty-three white-sand beaches lie like a lei around the island, more per mile of coastline than any other isle.

The island is 33 miles long by 25 miles wide, with a total land area of 533 square miles. It is the only Hawaiian isle flowing with navigable rivers. Much of it may look familiar. Because of its extraordinary and diverse natural beauty, Hollywood has cast Kauai in more than 50 feature films and full-length television productions. That lyric waterfall in the opening sequence of *Jurassic Park* is Kauai's; in *South Pacific* Mitzi Gaynor "washed that man right out of her hair," at Lumahai Beach; King Kong went rampaging in Honopu Valley, coincidentally scaring the wits out of a honeymoon couple who had been camping there; and Elvis swayed beneath the swaying palm trees of the Coconut Coast in *Blue Hawaii* (see p. 192).

Three times in the past century, Kauai has been ravaged by hurricanes, the most recent being Hurricane Iniki in 1992 (see p. 188). Steven Spielberg, who happened to be on the island at that time shooting his dinosaur blockbuster, mobilized his camera crew and got some authentic storm footage for the film. After the monster storm, the island bounced back with admirable spirit.

Courage has always been Kauai's guiding light. When the forces of Kamehameha the Great swept across the other Islands, conquering all in their path, Kauai alone remained stubbornly independent. Each time the warrior king planned an invasion of Kauai, fate intervened. Eventually, when it was good and ready, Kauai voluntarily joined the fledgling kingdom.

Even developers have had to tiptoe lightly across this landscape. Although Kauai hosted Hawaii's very first visitor when Captain Cook stepped ashore in 1778, residents later took a look at the tourism gravy train on other Islands and said, "No way." Well, at least, "Not that way." They passed a law that no building

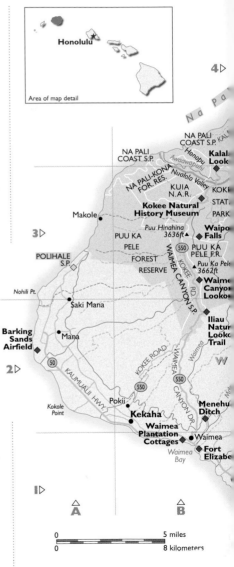

Area of map detail

Honolulu

can stand higher than a coconut palm, and so what you see when you look at this island, is a hundred grades of green. Ninety-seven percent of the island remains rural and cast into vast nature preserves. Man has not so much imposed himself on this place as insinuated himself, sometimes a bit truculently, into its embrace.

Kauai may well have been the first island to be settled, perhaps as early as A.D. 500, and by some estimates even a few centuries before that. The first wave of colonists came from the Marquesas; later groups sailed from Tahiti. This is the home of the Menehune, the legendary little people (see p. 187).

Known as the Garden Isle, Kauai does, indeed, abound in botanical gardens. Homes are overwhelmed by the flowers around them. If it's Christmas, you'll see poinsettias as high as a house. ■

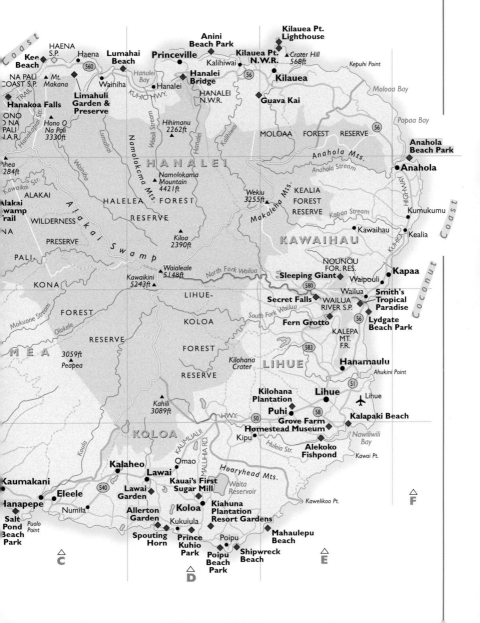

Lihue

THE COUNTY SEAT OF KAUAI IS ONE OF THOSE SMALL towns that got big without a lot of planning. Lihue is a confusion of multistreet intersections and small malls, but it's where visits to the island start because the airport is here. Most people get out as fast as they can, heading for the resorts—which is a mistake, because in and around Lihue are some gems.

Lihue

⚑ 185 E2

Visitor information

✉ Kauai Visitors
Bureau, 433 Rice St.

☎ 808/245-3971

If you want to understand Kauai, its people, and culture, you ought to make at least a brief stop at the **Kauai Museum.** It looks like a library, because that's what it was until 1970, but it has a remarkable collection of ancient Hawaiian artifacts. The museum is also noted for its fine Hawaiian quilts, one of

Mrs. Hamura serves her world-famous saimin, the ubiquitous Island snack.

Kauai Museum

✉ 4428 Rice St.

☎ 808/245-6931

🕐 Closed Sun.

💲 $

which is fashioned into *holoku* (a Hawaiian gown with train). There are large calabashes of native wood, *kahili* (the feather standards of royalty), and even a hand-carved canoe. You'll see vintage photographs of old Kauai through the eyes of a Japanese immigrant, and a bird's-eye helicopter video of the legendary beauty of the island as it is today.

History that doesn't feel like history can be found 2.5 miles away in Puhi, at **Kilohana Plantation.**

Designed for missionary-descended sugar baron Gaylord Wilcox and his wife Ethel by Honolulu architect Frank Stewart Potter, Kilohana was completed in 1935, and the grand house quickly became the social center of the island. It still is, although now they let anybody in. You can lounge around the living room with its period furniture and artifacts, or you can dine in a fine restaurant (see pp. 254–255). All the other rooms—even some of the nine bathrooms—are shops crammed with arts, crafts, and gifts. A century-old coach pulled by a Clydesdale will take you on a narrated tour of the estate, where sugar is now more a tourist attraction than a cash crop.

Another legacy of the Wilcox family is **Grove Farm Homestead Museum.** George, the bachelor son of missionaries Abner and Lucy Wilcox (see p. 197), established Grove Farm Plantation in 1864. He put in irrigation, built up a profitable sugar business and lived there until he died, a millionaire and still a bachelor at 94, in 1933. Tours guide you not only through the gracious koa-walled rooms, but also through a typical day on the plantation, which seems to have been very charming as long as you weren't working hard in the fields.

Lihue's port is the spectacular harbor of Nawiliwili, embraced by brooding mountains. Adjacent to the harbor is **Kalapaki Beach.** Its white sands front a megaresort, the

An inter-island cruise ship calls at Nawiliwili Harbor.

Kauai Marriott, claiming the biggest swimming pool in the state, which tends to keep Kalapaki Beach relatively uncrowded.

On Hulemalu Road, above the picturesque harbor, is a lookout for one of the aquaculture wonders of ancient Hawaii, the **Alekoko Fishpond.** The walls of this rare inland fishpond run 900 feet long and stand 5 feet above water with another 13 to 30 feet below water. The 39-acre facility for raising mullet is sometimes called the Menehune Fishpond because it was said to have been built in a single night by the little people (see below). According to legend, they passed rocks man to man from what is now Niumalu Beach Park, a distance of 25 miles. The actual origins of the pond are unknown, but it was here when the Tahitians arrived. You can't go down to see it close up because it's private property, but the view of the huge pond, backed by the Hoaryhead Mountains, is painted in an Impressionist's palette, soft and infused with light. ∎

**Kilohana
Plantation**

 185 E2

✉ 3-2087 Kaumualii Hwy. (Hawaii 50)

☎ 808/245-5608

🕐 Closed 9:30 p.m. Mon.–Sat.; shops closed 5 p.m. Sun., restaurant closed 8 p.m.

**Grove Farm
Homestead**

 185 E1

✉ 4050 Nawiliwili Rd. (Hawaii 58)

☎ 808/245-3202

🕐 Closed Tues. & Fri.–Sun. Tours 10 a.m. and 1 p.m., must be arranged a week in advance

💲 $

The Menehune

The leprechaun-like little people of Hawaii are credited with great feats of engineering and construction, and blamed for every mischief. Even today, "The Menehunes must have done it" is an explanation for something missing or broken.

In their homeland, Tahitian commoners were called Manahune. It is thought that this name was applied to the people the Tahitians met on Kauai when they first arrived, said to have numbered more than half a million people. Legend says they left Kauai on a floating island to curb intermarriage with the newer Hawaiians. Stone relics on Necker and Nihoa—remote, small islands to the north—indicate a group of people sojourned there.

Intriguingly, in an 1800s census, 65 people in Wainiha Valley listed their ethnicity as "Menehune." ∎

Koloa

THE LITTLE SUGAR TOWN OF KOLOA SITS BENEATH spreading banyan and monkeypod trees where Maluhia Road joins Poipu Road. Long before it was a plantation town, Koloa was a thriving Hawaiian settlement, whose inhabitants probably grew sugar for their own sweets (the name means "long sugarcane"). With the decline of the sugar industry, Koloa went to seed. In 1983 the town was purchased by a developer, who gave it the face-lift it needed.

Koloa
🅰 185 DI

**Yamamoto Store
(Crazy Shirts)**
✉ 5356 Koloa Rd.
☎ 808/742-7161

Spouting Horn
🅰 185 DI

Take a look at the colorful old wooden storefronts that now house boutiques and restaurants. Each has a story. The Ashida Soda Works Building was once a poi factory. The 1900 **Yamamoto Store,** which may be Kauai's most photographed building, was once the

Koloa Hotel catering to traveling salesmen, and is now home to Crazy Shirts, a T-shirt retailer. Pick up a Koloa Heritage Trail map at most shops, or call the Poipu Beach Resort Foundation *(tel 808/742-7444).*

You approach Koloa beneath eucalyptus trees on **Tree Tunnel Road,** a.k.a. Maluhia Road. The tattered smokestack of Kauai's first sugar mill lies in the brush at the entrance to town. On the road's right side stands what looks like a war memorial, but it's a tribute to the plantation laborers who came to Koloa from around the globe.

Along the lava shoreline, southwest of Koloa is Kukuiula Bay and **Spouting Horn,** a lava tube that spits salty surf as high as 50 feet. At sunset the geyser becomes incandescent with the colors of the rainbow. You may encounter some unexpected fellow sunbathers on the coast—sometimes rare Hawaiian monk seals haul themselves up on the sand only yards from beach blankets. ∎

Restored buildings of the plantation era characterize Koloa town, gateway to the Poipu resorts.

Iniki

Hurricane Iniki slammed into Kauai the afternoon of September 11, 1992. The name means "fierce piercing wind;" it was that and more. Winds were clocked at 227 miles per hour before the wind meters broke. When the next day dawned, it broke the hearts of all Hawaii. Kauai, the green and

beautiful isle, did not have a leaf left on a tree, and barely a branch; 70 percent of the homes were destroyed or damaged.

Today the island is lush and emerald again, though you can still see a few remnants of the savage storm along the Poipu and Coconut Coasts. ∎

The Poipu Coast

POIPU BEGAN LIFE AS A MAJOR RESORT IN 1962, WHEN THE
beach home of sugar planter Valdemar Knudsen was demolished to
make way for the first hotel.

The plantation manager's home
and garden have become the centerpiece of **Kiahuna Plantation**
(see p. 255), a holiday condominium. The garden grows more than
3,000 kinds of tropical flowers
and has a noteworthy cactus
collection. At the front desk, they'll
give you a map.

Poipu is actually several beaches,
beginning with Poipu itself. Next is
Waiohai Beach. On a point of land

Shipwreck Beach from the sands
to the east. A dawn walk along the
dunes, cliffs, and nature trails on
the western end of the beach is
exhilarating. Some people like to
bicycle beyond Shipwreck to
unspoiled Mahaulepu Beach, a
2-mile stretch of golden sand.
Lithified dunes contain fossils,
and there are also petroglyphs (see
p. 158), as this was the most settled
area of Poipu in ancient times.

**Kiahuna
Plantation Resort
Gardens**
🅰 185 D1
✉ 2253 Poipu Rd.
☎ 808/742-6411

Prince Kuhio Park
🅰 185 D1
✉ Lawai Rd.

there's an old temple, Kiahuna
Heiau, dedicated to the 2 shark
gods. Snorkeling in the lee of the
point will acquaint you with many-
hued tropical fish, and the offshore
surfing site is very popular. Poipu
Beach Park, next in line, is much
frequented by families because of
its sheltered waters. Body-boarders
and bodysurfers favor Brennecke
Beach; be careful of a strong rip
current. Makawehi Point separates

Prince Kuhio Park com-
memorates Prince Jonah Kuhio
Kalanianaole, a tireless worker for
the rights of native Hawaiians, who
was born on the coast at Kukuiula,
March 26, 1871. The foundation of
the royal home and its fishpond are
incorporated into the park. The
prince's birthday is a state holiday,
celebrated on Kauai with island-
wide cultural events, canoe races,
and a ball (see p. 236). ■

**Horseback riding
is one of the
many activities
enjoyed by
visitors to Kauai's
sunny southern
shore.**

National Tropical Botanical Garden

Lawai Garden

🗺 185 D1

✉ Visitor Center, Lawai Rd., across from Spouting Horn parking lot

☎ 808/742-2623

🕐 Guided tours by reservation only, 9 a.m., 10 a.m., 1 p.m., 2 p.m. Mon.–Sat. (Free for children under 5)

💲 $$$$$

The exotic bird of paradise is a common plant on Kauai.

Limahuli Garden & Preserve

🗺 185 C4

✉ Kuhio Hwy., Haena

☎ 808/826-1053

🕐 Closed Mon. & Sat. Guided tours by reservation.

💲 $$ ($$$ for guided tours)

THE U.S. CONGRESS GAVE A GREEN THUMBS-UP TO Hawaii's unique biota in 1964 when it chartered the National Tropical Botanical Garden. Of its five facilities, four are in Hawaii. The fifth is the 9-acre Kampung Garden in Florida.

LAWAI GARDEN

With 186 acres on Kauai's south shore, Lawai Garden is the most extensive facility. The national garden's headquarters are here. The Lawai Herbarium contains 26,000 specimens of tropical plants. The 8,000-volume research library holds an impressive collection of publications on tropical flora and more than one thousand botanical prints.

The focus here is on rare and endangered Hawaiian species and economically important tropical plants. More than two-thirds of Earth's known plant species are found in the tropics, and many are disappearing faster than they can be collected or studied for medicinal and other purposes.

With more than 200 species, the garden has the largest collection of Hawaiian plants in the world. Some 90 percent of the flowering plants in Hawaii are endemic, a far greater percentage than anywhere else on Earth. More than half are considered extinct in the wild, threatened, or endangered. In the 200 years since contact with the outside world, approximately 6,000 new species have been introduced to the environment, and the native plants are overwhelmed. Lawai has significant collections of palms and erythrinas, and the world's largest collection of breadfruit.

Adjoining Lawai Garden is the oceanfront **Allerton Garden**. The 100-acre estate was originally planted in the 1870s by Queen Emma. Gardening gave a measure of peace to the queen, who had lost both her husband, King Kamehameha IV, and their only child, Prince Albert. Emma was an educated, well-traveled woman who had been received by Queen Victoria at Windsor Castle and by President Andrew Johnson at the White House in Washington, D.C. In rough clothes with a hat, veil, and gloves, the queen worked beside her gardeners. She planted *lauae* fern, ginger, heliconia, rose apple, bamboo, pandanus, haole lehua, pikake (*Jasminum sambac*), and spider lily. She added trees— tamarind, thornless *kiawe*, the almond-like *kamani*, and mango. If you look up, you'll see magenta bougainvillea cascading from the cliffs above the queen's cottage.

Emma's garden was expanded during the 30-year proprietorship of Robert and John Allerton. Today it is an enchantment of sculpture pools, fountains, and flowers, set amid pathways, beside a stream, and along the sea.

LIMAHULI GARDEN & PRESERVE

The other national facility on Kauai is Limahuli Garden and Preserve at Haena. This magnificent 17-acre site is notched into towering mountains near the end of the road on the North Shore. Its beauty is almost a distraction to the garden's impor-

tance. Within Limahuli are two vital ecosystems: the lowland rain forest and the lower mixed mesophytic (moderately moist) forest. Together, these two systems are the natural habitat of over 70 percent of Kauai's and 59 percent of Hawaii's endangered plant species. The valley receives an annual rainfall of 80 to more than 200 inches. Adjacent to the garden are approximately 990 acres of preserve. Limahuli Stream is home to the last five species of Hawaiian freshwater fish.

The garden was begun in the 1960s when missionary descendant Juliet Rice Wichman set out to create a garden that would be a living museum of Hawaiian flora.

In ancient times, Limahuli was a prime agricultural area, and ruins of terraces and house sites are scattered throughout the beautiful valley. ■

Limahuli Garden is tucked into the ramparts that form the beginning of the Na Pali Coast.

Mail a coconut home. The U.S. Post Office accepts these nutty nuts with the addresses painted on them.

COCONUT POSTCARDS
HAND PAINTED only $14.99
INCLUDES 1ST CLASS POSTAGE
DELIVERED IN 3 DAYS
ANYWHERE IN THE U.S.A.

Anahola Beach Park
 185 F3
✉ Anahola Rd., makai (oceanside) of Kuhio Hwy. (Route 56)

Below: The King of Rock and Roll appears in this promotional poster for his film, *Blue Hawaii*.

Coconut Coast

THIS BREEZY STRETCH OF COASTLINE ON THE EAST OF THE island has become the most popular part of Kauai—and it has the traffic to prove it. Kapaa and its neighbors, Kealia, Waipouli, and Wailua, have become one long oceanfront community linked by hotels, holiday condominiums, restaurants, shops, mini-malls, Kuhio Highway, and a line of beaches. Towering over everything are the hundreds of coconut palms that give the area its name, and its charm.

Kauai royalty once ruled from the Coconut Coast. The island's last queen, Deborah Kapule, favorite wife of King Kaumualii, lived here. In the 1800s, a German immigrant planted one of the largest stands of coconut palms in the Islands. The site later became the Coco Palms Hotel, still mourned after its destruction by Hurricane Iniki. The trees have nicely recovered, however; you'll pass right by them driving along Kaumualii Highway, just past Wailua. Walking among them could be dangerous: Those nuts come down like cannonballs in the wind.

Cove after sandy cove scallops the shoreline, while the Anahola and Makaleha Mountains stage a dramatic backdrop for the towns. The mountain that gives Kauai its verdure, 5,180-foot **Waialeale,** lies behind Kapaa like a great rain magnet, sucking the clouds away from the coast, leaving it dry and

sunny. Waialeale, whose summit is almost always swathed in clouds, receives 40 feet of rain a year, making it the world's wettest place. Helicopter tours (see p. 264) drop into the green crater streaming with waterfalls.

Near Milepost 7 on Kuhio Highway, you'll see a sign pointing toward the Coconut Coast's other famous mountain, Nounou, and its natural formation commonly known as **Sleeping Giant.** He's stretched out flat, face up, with his head in Wailua and his feet in Kapaa.

The safest swimming beach on this often tempestuous coast is **Anahola Beach Park.** If you're lucky, you may find a glass fishing float from the Japanese fleet. The currents must be just right, for they often wash up here.

Note: A new bypass skips the worst of the area's traffic at Kapaa, but then you miss the town's shops and restaurants. ■

Elvis

The King of Rock and Roll, Elvis Presley, came to the Coconut Coast in 1961 to film *Blue Hawaii*. Some of the Kauai landmarks seen in the film include the Coco Palms Hotel, Lydgate Park, Lihue Airport, the Wailua River, Anahola, and Opaekaa Falls. The King returned to Kauai in 1966 to shoot *Paradise Hawaiian Style*, later retitled and remarketed as *Girls! Girls! Girls!*. ■

Up the Wailua River

A family sets out to paddle up the Wailua River.

THIS 12-MILE-LONG RIVER WAS ONCE KNOWN AS WAILUA Nui Hoano ("great sacred Wailua"), and had nine temples lining its green banks.

To explore its many fingers, rent a kayak in **Kapaa** (see p. 264), and pick up a picnic lunch at nearby Safeway *(4-831 Kuhio Hwy., tel 808/822-2461).* Before you launch from the boat ramp at **Wailua River State Park,** take a look at the temple ruins and birthing stones at the park.

Paddle up the river, toward the mountains, keeping to the right to avoid the strongest currents and the tourist barges heading for **Fern Grotto.** After an hour, take the left fork to the grotto, a huge amphitheater cave lipped in ferns. Pull up on the muddy bank past the docks, and a few minutes' walk takes you to the grotto, where weddings happen every day.

Back at the fork in the river, take the right branch. In a few minutes you'll be gliding beneath cliffs, as you head into the jungle. Great

banyans dangle giant philodendron vines, and the dense foliage overhead forms a canopy. Pull out along the riverbank for lunch.

The farther inland you paddle, the shallower the water gets. When you come to a small island, you can tie your kayak to a tree and hike to 100-foot-high **Secret Falls.** The kayak company will provide a trail map. It's only a mile, but it takes an hour each way through the tangled forest. Hidden in the jungle are the falls, with their milky jade plunge pool. Like all Hawaiian mountain pools, this has the potential danger of falling rocks and boulders.

Back at the river, turn your kayak around to glide, with the current, back downstream. On the way, explore little fingers of water going into the habitat of rare Hawaiian birds, where you'll hear songs heard no place else in the world. ■

Wailua River State Park
- 185 E2
- Kuhio Hwy. (Hawaii 56) & Kuamoo Rd. (Hawaii 580)

Kilauea & Princeville

Kilauea
⚑ 185 E4

Kong Lung Store
✉ Kilauea Rd., Kilauea
☎ 808/828-1822

Princeville Resort Hotel
⚑ 185 D4
✉ 5520 Ka Haku Rd., Princeville

LITTLE KILAUEA, A FORMER SUGAR PLANTATION TOWN, is the gateway to Kauai's North Shore. Here, life proceeds at a leisurely pace and the scenery is magnificent.

Two lava-built churches here are worth a peek: **St. Sylvester's Catholic Church** *(tel 808/828-2818)* has murals by Island artist Jean Charlot, and **Christ Memorial Episcopal Church** *(tel 808/826-4510)* has 11 stained-glass windows from England.

Kilauea, however, is better known for its commerce than its prayers. For many years, Mr. Lung Wah Chee (1850–1931) operated a

The Princeville Resort Hotel, overlooking Hanalei Bay, enjoys views of mountains, waterfalls, and the sea.

plantation general store in Kilauea. In 1902 he moved to the present site of the **Kong Lung Store.** In 1940, his landlord built him the unique lava store, which served as post office, general store, barbershop, and butcher. Everything was sold, from axes to opium (legal at that time). Now, even Honoluluans fly over to shop among the art, home furnishings, designer Hawaiian-wear, and thousand-

dollar shell necklaces, all with an emphasis on local artisans. The Kong Lung shaved ice (snow cone) stand appeared in the movie *Six Days, Seven Nights,* which starred Harrison Ford.

The nearby **Princeville Resort** is Kauai's largest resort. Scattered across its 1,000 acres, are golf courses, holiday condominiums, residences, restaurants, and shops. One of the most stunning views in Hawaii is from the **Princeville Resort Hotel.** You walk into the sumptuous lobby and look out the glass wall at Hanalei Bay and the jagged massifs of Namolokama streaming with waterfalls, and at Mount Makana, which was cast as Bali Hai in *South Pacific.* The same view can be captured from the hotel's terrace and Café Hanalei.

The resort is named for Prince Albert Edward Kauikeaouli, who visited the area with his parents, King Kamehameha IV and Queen Emma, when it was a plantation owned by Hawaii's foreign minister, Scottish-born Robert Crichton Wyllie (1798–1865). The 13-year-old daughter of the plantation manager wrote of a royal birthday party given May 20, 1861: "The celebration consisted of a parade of 200 Hawaiian men and women on horseback dressed alike, the men in red and white shirts and blue pants, and the women in red and yellow pau and maile leis.... In the evening the large bonfires were lighted in the low lands, and on the hill tops, making a fine display and discharging bombs which resembled cannonading." ∎

Kilauea Point National Wildlife Refuge

KA LAE O KILAUEA IS THE ANCIENT NAME OF THIS WAVE-lashed bastion of land at the northernmost tip of Kauai. The Hawaiians of old, who knew intimately every reef and shoal of their shores, once gathered at such geographically prominent places for nightwatch parties to tend the *kukui ahi,* the fires that guided fishermen home.

Kilauea Point Lighthouse is the high-tech end of a noble tradition. The 52-foot-high white tower on a 216-foot cliff dominates the 200-acre refuge. It was dedicated at sundown May 1, 1913, preceded by a day-long luau and shark shoot. To lure the sharks within shooting range, a dead cow would be lowered into the offshore waters. The lighthouse has the world's largest clamshell lens, which can shine 90 miles out to sea. In 1927, aviators attempting the first trans-Pacific flight from California to Hawaii suffered instrument failure, and would have flown past Hawaii into oblivion had they not seen Kilauea's beam. They were able to readjust, and landed safely on Oahu after more than 25 hours in the air. The lighthouse is enjoying retirement as a national historical landmark in the midst of a wildlife sanctuary.

Among the birds you'll see are the great frigatebird with its 8-foot wingspan, the red-footed booby, and the nene, Hawaii's state bird. Good signage helps you identify them. In the coves on either side of the point, you may spot the rare Hawaiian green sea turtle, and whales and porpoises often make an offshore appearance. The small islet at the base of the cliff, **Mokuaeae,** is a sunning spot for

monk seals; Mokuaeae means "fragment frothing in the rising tide," and it's easy to see why.

One-hour guided hikes *(included in adm. fee)* go to the 568-foot Crater Hill for grand views of the refuge and lighthouse. ■

Kilauea Point National Wildlife Refuge

🗺 185 E4

✉ Kilauea Rd. to the end at Kilauea Point

☎ 808/828-1413

💲 $

Hikers look down on Kilauea Point Lighthouse and the National Wildlife Refuge.

Hanalei

FOR MORE THAN A THOUSAND YEARS, PEOPLE HAVE farmed at Hanalei. Looking down from the Hanalei Valley Lookout (just past Princeville Shopping Center, on the right), you'll see the Hanalei River flowing through brilliant emerald green *kalo loi* (flooded taro fields). Brooding mist-shrouded mountains weep with waterfalls. Interpretive signs tell you about the Hanalei National Wildlife Refuge. It's not open to the public, but often you can see gallinule, coot, spindly legged stilt, and endangered Koloa duck in the kalo loi.

Unique boutiques make shopping an adventure in the Hanalei region.

The district of Hanalei (meaning "crescent bay") is actually three valleys—Hanalei, Waioli ("singing waters"), and Waipa ("touched waters"). Three villages, Hanalei, Wainiha, and Haena, are lost in the greenery.

One reason the area has remained so pastoral is the rusty one-lane **Hanalei Bridge,** too narrow for tour buses. Made in New York, this national historic landmark was installed in 1912.

If you see buffalo grazing, don't be surprised. The Hanalei Buffalo Ranch has 200 head of American bison, some of which end up as buffalo burgers on local menus.

HANALEI TOWN
The **Ching Young Village** mini-mall *(5-5190 Kuhio Hwy., tel 808/826-7222)* on the east end

of town was founded by Ching Young and his wife Man Sing, who arrived from Chungshan, China in 1896. They raised eight children here and eventually bought a rice mill and general store. Man Sing continued to operate the store after her husband's death, and was so generous in giving food to the poor and needy that, at one point, she had to sell her jewelry to pay her debts. Her descendants now run the center with its shops and healthy restaurants.

On the way out of town, you can't miss the graceful **Waioli Huiia Church** *(Kuhio Hwy., tel 808/826-6253)*. Built in 1912, its green shingles blend perfectly into the landscape, and its stained-glass windows shine like the waterfalls. Behind it is the 1836 **Waioli Mission House Museum**

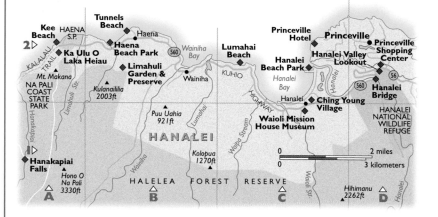

(*Kuhio Hwy., tel 808/245-3202*), home of Yankee missionaries Abner and Lucy Wilcox. Lucy gave birth to eight sons in the main bedroom. The wooden house, designed by the Reverend William Alexander from Kentucky, has a southern generosity to it. With its wraparound lanai (veranda), it is comfortably furnished and still feels like a home. An eight-dollar clock, installed in 1866, is still keeping perfect time.

BEACHES

The first of these incredibly beautiful beaches is **Hanalei Beach Park** (*Weke Rd., between Aku & Pilikoa Rds.*). Sheer volcanic palisades rise 4,000 feet behind golden sands, and yachts anchor in the lee. The bay, calm as a lake in summer, reflects the mountains. The swimming is excellent, too.

The most famous strand of sand in the district is **Lumahai Beach** (*Kuhio Hwy., at Milepost 33*). You can pull over to the side of the road for a good photograph of the beach that starred in *South Pacific*. There's a steep trail down, just east of the lookout. White surf crashes on high black boulders, creating streaming waterfalls. Riptides and a strong undertow are extremely treacherous, so swimming on all but the calmest summer days is not recommended.

Less famous but equally beautiful is **Tunnels Beach** (*Kuhio Hwy., at Milepost 8*). Also known as Makua, it has a lacy coral reef that invites snorkelers. The name Tunnels was bestowed by surfers who come for the famous tubular waves in winter.

A lava tube cave known as **Maniniholo Dry Cave** is directly across from **Haena Beach Park,** another extremely dangerous swimming beach. The cave runs several hundred yards under the lava cliff. A mile down the road, are two more caves, **Waikapalae** and **Waikanaloa.** It is said that Pele, the volcano goddess, dug here hoping to find a home, and instead struck water, so she moved on. The caves and beaches are all part of **Haena State Park** (*W end of Hawaii 560*). Right at the end of the road is **Kee Beach,** also part of the park's more than 230 acres of scenic wildland, and the start of the Kalalau Trail (see p. 198). Kee is the prettiest swimming beach in the park. The sandy-bottomed lagoon is fringed in lacy coral. Swimming on the reef can be dangerous in times of high surf. **Limahuli Garden and Preserve** (see pp. 190–191) is nearby.

Just above the west end of Kee Beach, a path leads to **Ka Ulu O Laka Heiau,** an ancient hula temple. To train themselves in chant, dancers would pit their voices against the surging seas below. Hula dancers from all over Hawaii still visit this shrine in the place where Pele fell in love with Lohiau, a handsome chief of Kauai. She was drawn to Haena by the sound of the hula *pahu* (drum). ■

Before descending into Hanalei Valley, stop at the lookout to see the broad sweep of river, mountains, and taro fields.

Na Pali Coast

TOWERING GREEN CLIFFS RISE 2,000 FEET OUT OF A turbulent sea. Their fluted ramparts follow that part of Kauai's northern shore called the Na Pali Coast, stretching 15 miles from Kee west to Polihale (see p. 201). The names of the valleys roll from the tongue like a sacred litany: Hanakapiai, Hoolulu, Waiahuakua, Hanakoa, Kalalau, Honopu, Awaawapuhi, Nualolo Koahole, and Milolii. Rainbows crown them, and waterfalls feed them. They are deep and green and so remote it is like entering a time warp and seeing the land before it was peopled and priced. The coast has ocean-filled caves with waterfall curtains, sea arches, and five sandy beaches. There is no way to see this remote and magnificent wilderness except by air or boat, or on foot (see p. 264). It is much too rugged for a road.

In **Na Pali Coast State Park** *(808/274-3444; 8 miles west of Hanalei at end of Hawaii 560),* the ancient **Kalalau Trail** winds along the *pali* (cliffs) 11 miles from Kee Beach to Kalalau Valley. The trail traverses lofty sea cliffs and lush amphitheater valleys. It dips and drops, gets slippery with fallen guava and rivulets of rain, and all the time rewards you with impres-

sive turrets, pleats, and peaks. In the first half mile you'll have splendid, almost aerial views of Kee and its lacy reef. Looking ahead, you'll get a preview of the long line of fluted cliffs arrayed in sunshine. Sometimes the surf is so powerful the ground trembles beneath your feet, even hundreds of feet above the sea.

The 2-mile, two-hour hike to **Hanakapiai,** the first of the valleys, is a popular day-hike and an overnight stop for backpackers. Once there, you can take a further 2-mile hike into the valley to spectacular Hanakapiai Falls. The trail at first seems easy but becomes progressively more difficult.

From Hanakapiai Beach, the trail climbs 800 feet. The strenuous 4 miles to **Hanakoa** will take almost three hours and traverse two hanging valleys—valleys where streams have not yet carved a way to the ocean. A third of a mile into Hanakoa is a 2,000-foot waterfall. Pushing on, it's another 5 miles to the trail end at Kalalau. Beyond that, Na Pali resists even a footpath.

Jack London (1876–1916) wrote a poignant story, "Koolau The Leper," about a Waimea cowboy afflicted with leprosy, who led a band of fellow sufferers into the Na Pali wilderness to escape shipment

Left: Hikers explore the Kalalau Trail in Na Pali Coast State Park.

to a remote spot on Molokai, where all those afflicted with the diseaase were sent (see p. 212).

These remote valleys were once inhabited. Agricultural terraces and *auwai* (irrigation ditches) suggest that Kalalau was the most culti-vated valley in old Hawaii. Hawaiians lived here until 1919 when the last were lured away by the dubious comforts of towns. Artifacts carbon-dated back to A.D. 800 show strong cultural links to the Marquesas Islands.

In the 1960s archaeologists exploring Nualolo Valley unearthed a treasure trove of surprisingly well preserved bows, arrows, fishhooks, poi pounders, adzes, tattoo needles, and fine examples of cord and *kapa* (tree-bark cloth). They cataloged more than 4,000 specimens.

Na Pali abounds with tales of kings, gods, and the little people—the Menehune (see p. 187). And there are more recently born legends. Honopu became the Valley of the Lost Tribe in the 1920s, when an archaeologist found skulls which he declared were not Hawaiian. Speculation as to their origins ranged from Menehune to one of the lost tribes of Israel. The skulls were subse-quently proven to be Hawaiian, but the legend persisted.

Na Pali inspires awe, whether you see it from a helicopter, soaring above the windlashed pali; from the sea, plunging into its caves and beneath its waterfalls in a Zodiak, or more sedately in a motor launch; or from the ground itself, walking its old and mysterious paths. ■

Above: Boat tours afford glimpses of the Na Pali Coast valleys and beaches, which are inaccessible any other way.

West Kauai

YOU CAN TAKE DAYS TO EXPLORE THE HISTORY, TOWNS, and natural wonders on the driest, sunniest side of Kauai.

The old car with new paint fits right into Hanapepe, with its vintage buildings enjoying new life as galleries and boutiques.

About 10 miles west of Lihue is sleepy **Lawai,** at the intersection of Hawaii 53 and Hawaii 50. Down in a little hollow is the **Old Hawaiian Trading Company,** looking suspiciously like a tourist trap. It has its share of plastic hula skirts and chicken-feet purses, but tucked among the kitsch you'll find an exceptional collection of treasured Niihau shell necklaces at good prices (see p. 232).

You can't miss **Hanapepe.** It's where you see wild bougainvillea blooming madly on a mountain above one of Kauai's most colorful towns. Beneath the flowers are old wooden storefronts, dogs sleeping in the dusty road, some mom-and-pop stores, plus the requisite boutiques and a dozen or so galleries. One gallery worth a peek, even for nonshoppers, is **Kauai Fine Arts** (3848 Hanapepe Rd., tel 808/335-3778). They have a

fascinating inventory of antique maps, original engravings from the voyages of Captain Cook to Hawaii, and rare 19th-century ships' logs. Friday nights from 6 p.m. to 9 p.m., the galleries host an Art Walk. Look for the little **Taro Ko shop** (tel 808/335-5586) at the east end of Hanapepe Road. When they sell out of their famous taro chips, they just close for the day.

Hawaiian Salt Ponds (Hawaii 543) by the ocean at Hanapepe, reflect age-old salt-gathering practices. People say a luau isn't a luau without Hanapepe salt. The same families have been working the basins for hundreds of years.

They were there when the Russians established a fort down the coast on the east bank of the Waimea River in 1816. Built by Dr. Georg Anton Scheffer, and named for the wife of Czar Alexander I, **Fort Elizabeth** (Hawaii 53, near

Milepost 22) was the most prominent of several Russian forts established in Hanalei and Honolulu. The fort was completed by the Hawaiian army, who occupied it until 1864, when the guns were removed. Nature has done its work on the 17-acre site, and walls once 30 feet thick are mere rubble.

On the opposite bank of the river, a cement slab in the mud marks the spot said to be the first footfall of Europeans on Hawaiian soil when Captain Cook anchored in Waimea Bay, January 20, 1778. A statue of the British explorer stands among palm trees on a medial strip in **Waimea** town.

At **Waimea Plantation Cottages,** actual plantation houses have been moved from all over the island, restored, decorated with period furniture, and rented to vacationers (see p. 257). On the east side of the little resort is an old section of Waimea town where families still occupy distinctive plantation homes.

Just outside Waimea, **Kiki a Ola,** popularly called the Menehune Ditch *(Menehune Rd., 1.5 miles from intersection with Hawaii 50),* is an unimpressive 2-foot stone wall, but it's all that's left of an aqueduct that once ran 5 miles up the Waimea River. It was an amazing engineering achievement attributed (like so much else) to the Menehune.

Polihale State Park is where civilization yields to the fortress of Na Pali. To get there, follow Kaumualii Highway (Hawaii 50) to the end, then follow signs through sugarcane fields for 5 miles on dirt roads. The beach actually begins 15 miles away in Kekaha, wraps around the Mana Coastal Plain, and stretches out, blazing white, to the state park at the northwestern end of the beach. And these sands bark: The tiny grains are perforated with small cavities causing them to emit sounds when rubbed together by motion.

Polihale is as wide as three football fields and backed by dunes up to 100 feet high. The Na Pali cliffs tower on the western end. The safest place to swim is an inlet called **Queen's Pond.** In winter and spring, however, high surf can sweep over the entire beach, including the pond. Extreme caution is called for at this beautiful but very remote beach. ■

A monument to Capt. James Cook, who discovered Hawaii for the Western world in 1778, stands in the middle of Waimea town.

Did the Spanish get here first?

Two centuries before Cook's voyages, Spanish galleons were sailing the 8,000-mile route from Mexico to the Philippines, carrying gold and silver one way, and silks, spices, and porcelain the other. Several Spanish navigational charts, secret in their day, do show islands at the latitude of Hawaii. In 1743, a Manila galleon carrying such a map was captured by the English. Cook carried a copy of that chart. French explorer Jean François de Galaup La Perouse, who sailed to Hawaii in 1786, wrote: "In the charts might be written: Sandwich Islands, surveyed in 1778 by Captain Cook, who named them, but anciently discovered by the Spanish navigators." Hawaiian accounts support the theory. King Kamehameha II and others told the Reverend William Ellis about white-skinned foreigners who had landed eight generations earlier at Kealakekua Bay, and immediately knelt in prayer. On Kauai, Cook's men discovered "many iron utensils," including a broken sword blade, convincing them the Spaniards were first. ■

Waimea Plantation Cottages

🏨 184 B1

✉ 9400 Kaumualii Hwy. (Hawaii 50)

☎ 808/338-1625

Polihale State Park

🏨 184 A3

Waimea Canyon

Helicopter tours are the easy way to explore the Grand Canyon of the Pacific.

IT MUST HAVE BEEN QUITE AN EARTHQUAKE, BECAUSE IT almost split Kauai in two. Sometime in the Hawaiian dawn, long before sails appeared on any horizon, before even the Menehune, the earth convulsed and opened, and all the mountain streams which previously had their own paths, now flowed into one river, the Waimea. As the swollen river swept to the sea, age after age, it carved the cleft in the earth into a magnificent canyon unlike any other in the Pacific.

Waimea Canyon has a continental grandeur to it, a visual scope associated with larger landscapes. You think of Arizona with its buttes, crags, and palette of earthen colors. It invites comparisons to America's Grand Canyon, and is called the "Grand Canyon of the Pacific."

It's smaller, of course, 14 miles long and 3,567 feet deep, but the eye cannot see to its limits. It is the domain of wild goats and mouflon sheep, which you can see on precarious perches. Wild pigs inhabit the valley forests. From the rim of the canyon at Puu Ka Pele, the fire goddess leapt from Kauai to find a home on another island.

You can see Waimea Canyon by car from the lookouts, via hiking

tributary canyons adding dimension. You will be impressed with the overwhelming quiet, as if all sound has fallen into the jaws of the gorge. You can see the silver ribbon of river below, and you may see 800-foot Waipoo Falls to the left, but you won't hear them. Graceful *koae kea* (white-tailed tropicbirds) soar silently in the drafts of the canyon.

You get another good view at **Puu Hinahina Lookout** *(between Miles 13 and 14).*

From **Kokee State Park** (see pp. 204–205) several hiking trails explore the canyon. The canyon drive continues another 2 miles past the park to the cool and glorious **Kalalau Lookout,** 4,120 feet above the floor of this broad Na Pali Coast valley. No matter how many times you visit this site, it is never the same. It changes every moment as clouds sail in and out of the valley, and sunlight and shadows steal across the awesome green cliffs. It has the quality of light associated with Ireland, where brooding greenery is suddenly shot through with glowing sunlight. ■

Hiking trails descend into the bottom of Waimea Canyon.

trails, on horseback, or from a helicopter (see p. 264).

From Kaumualii Highway (Hawaii 50) at Waimea, turn inland on **Waimea Canyon Drive** (Hawaii 550) and begin the 20-mile climb that skirts the canyon rim. At 6 miles the drive joins Kokee Road, which comes up from Kekaha. You can get your first taste of Waimea by walking the 0.3-mile **Iliau Nature Lookout Trail** *(between Mileposts 8 and 9),* giving you your first breathtaking vista of canyon walls and waterfalls. Along the way, rare plants are identified in signs, including the *iliau,* a spectacular green relative of Maui's silversword (see p. 139). At **Waimea Canyon Lookout** *(between Miles 10 and 11),* the natural masterpiece of the canyon unfolds, with three

Kokee

IN THE COOL UPLANDS OF KAUAI, HIGH IN THE CLOUD forest above Waimea Canyon, lies a land strange to the tropics. The air is nippy, maybe in the 50s or 60s. No coconut palms here, but eucalyptus, fir, and redwood.

Kokee State Park is 4,354 acres of forest, meadows, streams full of trout, and hiking trails. From here you can look down at the Na Pali Coast, peer into Waimea Canyon, and explore the foggy, foggy dew of

the Alakai Swamp, wettest place in the world.

For a crash course in the legends, history, birds, and plants that you'll encounter at Kokee, your first stop is the **Kokee Natural History Museum.** It includes photographs, hiking maps, books, exhibits of flora, the head of a wild boar, and a mounted six-pound rainbow trout, the Kokee record. You can also get trail maps, and information on weather and trail conditions, at park headquarters. Staff at the Kokee Lodge *(tel 808/335-6061)* right next to the museum are helpful. There is a restaurant there *(closed 3:30 p.m.),* and cabins for rent (see p. 257).

The first wildlife you'll meet, probably in the parking lot, are the *moa.* Though they look like common barnyard chickens, they are rare red jungle fowl, the last descendants of the poultry brought to Hawaii as domestic stock by early Polynesian settlers.

Kokee and the surrounding forest and swamp are the last stand for some of the rarest birds in the world, such as the *nuku-puu,* a rare honeycreeper; and the *puaiohi,* a thrush that ornithologists hope can be saved from extinction through captive breeding programs. Another rare bird, the *kauai oo,* has not been seen for some time and is now believed to be extinct. Other fauna are so prolific that the park has hunting seasons for wild boar, goats, black-tail deer, and game birds.

WALKS IN THE PARK

If you want to hike in the park, be sure to check weather conditions at headquarters and on the bulletin board of the museum. Bring plenty of drinking water and rain gear, and, most important of all, stay on established trails.

The easiest trail is the **Nature Walk** that begins behind the museum and makes a 0.1-mile loop through the rain forest. Plants along the way are identified.

The **Canyon Trail** runs 4.8 miles, skirting the rim of Waimea Canyon, passing through distressed koa forest that has been devastated by hurricanes, and then dipping down to Waipoo Falls with its pool fringed by ginger plants. Parts of the trail are strenuous and scary but the views are awesome. Allow four hours to complete the route.

Left: Alakai Swamp, wettest place on earth

Kokee State Park

⛰ 184 B3

✉ Hawaii 550. Headquarters at park entrance

☎ 808/335-8405 (Kauai Division of State Parks)

Kokee Natural History Museum

☎ 808/335-9975

The **Alakai Swamp Trail** traverses fascinating terrain. Alakai is the soggy bottom of a huge caldera, 13 miles in diameter and 4,000 feet above sea level. Parts of it have never been explored. Thigh-high mud used to be the norm on this 7-mile hike, but a new board-walk across the swamp makes things easier. Alakai is the source of all the rivers on Kauai. Deep in the bog, trees take on a bonsai look because of the extreme dampness, growing only a foot tall, while ferns and violets tower overhead. Mosses are green, brown, orange, and even white. If the clouds clear, you may be treated to a view into Wainiha Valley, as big as Waimea, but much less accessible. All along, you will be cheered by birdsong, a harmonious singing in rarest notes.

Queen Emma, intrigued by the descriptions of Alakai, in 1871 mounted an expedition into the wilderness. The rather large royal party of about one hundred people started out on horseback, but the trail became so impenetrable the animals had to be left behind. Tree fern logs were dropped over the mud for the queen, who insisted on pausing for chants and hula along the way. This slowed things down, so that the party was forced to spend the night, soaked and chilled, in the swamp. The queen kept singing, cheering her companions.

The annual **Eo E Emalani I Alakai Festival,** which is held every October at Kokee State Park, celebrates Queen Emma's journey with drama and music perfor-mances, and hula displays. ■

Kalalau Valley, often crowned in rainbows, is visible from the lookout at Kokee State Park.

More places to visit on Kauai

ANINI BEACH PARK

The big attraction here is the 2-mile-long fringing reef that runs as wide as 1,600 feet out into the ocean. Between the reef and the golden sands of the shore there is a perfect turquoise lagoon, more typical of Tahiti than Hawaii, which is too young to have formed many lagoons. People come to Anini for swimming, windsurfing, snorkeling, diving, and fishing. You'll often see fishermen using the old Hawaiian throw-net technique. Poised on rock or reef, or in shallow water, they'll stand motionless, net carefully pleated under their arms, watching for fish. At the right moment, in movements as graceful as a dancer's, they whip out the net, watch it arc over the water like a cloud, then quickly haul it in with their catch. On summer Sunday afternoons, polo matches are often held on the broad lawns of the park.

🅰 185 D4 ✉ From Kuhio Hwy. (Hawaii 58) take Kalihiwai Rd., then turn left on Anini Beach Rd.

BARKING SANDS AIRFIELD & PACIFIC MISSILE RANGE

Highly sophisticated computers and electronics monitor the depths of the Pacific and the skyways above it from this military installation. The beach is a continuation of the long strand that began at the base of the Na Pali cliffs at Polihale (see p. 201). It is popular for shoreline fishing and surfing. The forbidden island of Niihau (see p. 232) can be clearly seen from the shore. If you want to visit the airfield, you need only check in at the security desk at the entrance.

🅰 184 A2 ✉ Kaumualii Hwy. at Milepost 30 ☎ 808/335-4111

GUAVA KAI

Pink, gritty guava juice is a local favorite. You can tour Guava Kai, a commercial guava orchard near Kilauea (see p. 194), and see how the yellow-skinned, pink-fleshed fruit is grown. Guava has more vitamin C than an orange, and is also a good source of calcium. After you have walked among the trees, you'll be rewarded with a glass of the chilled juice. You can buy jams and jellies in the gift shop.

🅰 185 E4 ✉ End of Kuawa Rd., Kilauea ☎ 808/828-6121

HAWAII MOVIE TOURS

This famous innovative five-hour tour takes you to locations where Hollywood filmed major motion pictures on Kauai. On the way to each site, you'll see clips from the film on large video screens in the van, complete with surround sound. Among the sites you'll view are locations from *Jurassic Park, Blue Hawaii, South Pacific,* and that of the TV series *Gilligan's Island.* You can swing on a rope over a river as Harrison Ford did in *Raiders of the Lost Ark.* A picnic lunch is provided at beautiful Anini Beach County Park (see above). The company now has additional tours so you can choose by the films you want to see.

✉ 4-885 Kuhio Hwy., Kapaa ☎ 808/ 822-1192 🕐 Tour 9 a.m.–2 p.m. 💲 $$$$$

ST. CATHERINE'S CATHOLIC CHURCH

Inside this very modern house of worship at Kealia, on the Coconut Coast, are murals by three of Hawaii's most acclaimed artists, Jean Charlot (1898–1979), Juliette May Fraser (1887–1983), and Tseng Yu-ho (1923–). Miraculously, the murals were not damaged by Hurricane Iniki (see p. 188).

🅰 185 F3 ✉ 5021-A Kawaihau Rd., Kapaa ☎ 808/822-7900

SMITH'S TROPICAL PARADISE

The many cultures of Kauai are celebrated in this well-maintained 30-acre garden at Kapaa on the Coconut Coast. You'll find a curved, red Japanese bridge over a stream, a thatched Hawaiian house with a taro patch, a lily pond, and riots of tropical flowers. In the evening, the Smith family, who own the garden, stage a spectacular luau and show, reflecting the multiethnic theme. It features a Chinese Lion Dance with fireworks. The stage is set over a lagoon, so the effects are magnified.

🅰 185 E2 ✉ 174 Wailua Rd., Kapaa ☎ 808/822-4111 🕐 Luau: Mon., Wed., & Fri. evenings 💲 $ ■

Undeveloped and over-
looked, this small island
has some big attractions,
including the tallest sea cliffs in
the world, the longest waterfall
in Hawaii, and one of the state's
largest white-sand beaches.

Molokai

**A statue of Father Damien
draped in leis**

Molokai

THE ANCIENT NAME OF THE ISLAND IS MOLOKAI PULE OO (MOLOKAI OF the Powerful Prayer). It is the heart of Hawaii, not only geographically, but in the infinitely larger matters of the spirit. A mere 22 miles across the Kaiwi Channel from Honolulu, Molokai is wild, unspoiled, and very Hawaiian.

Fifth largest of the Hawaiian Islands, Molokai is a mere 38 miles from end to end and 10 miles wide. A fringe of ancient fishponds scallops the shoreline. The highest mountain is Mauna Kamakou at 4,970 feet.

Because of its small size, and its strategic position in the center of the Island chain, Molokai would have been a plum in the many interisland wars of old. Its saver was the reputation of its *kahuna* (priests), who practiced a fearsome sorcery. The island's largest temple, Iliiliopae, whose altars ran red with human blood, was notorious throughout Hawaii. A grove of *kukui* trees, still regarded as sacred, marks the burial site of Lanikaula, the most powerful of the kahuna.

Molokai's internationally famous man of prayer was Father Damien, the Belgian Roman Catholic priest who devoted his life to the victims of Hansen's Disease (leprosy), living exiled on Makanalua Peninsula, now Kalaupapa National Historical Park. To reach it, you fly in by small plane, hike down a sheer palisade, or take the Molokai Mule Ride.

Many people believe the hula (see pp. 168–169) was born on Molokai, and the island's biggest festival, Ka Hula Piko, celebrates the assertion every May. Hula groups come from around the state for a day of music, dance, arts, and eating.

Molokai isn't for everyone. If you want nightclubs, gourmet dining, cute boutiques, or even the morning paper, you'll be disappointed. In fact, there's a famous Molokai T-shirt you can buy in Kaunakakai, the only town of size, that reads "Molokai Night Life." It's just a black shirt, which is all you need in the way of resort fashion. As for cuisine: Fresh seafood and vegetables from local farms will have to do. Instead of excitement you get serenity, plus recklessly lovely scenery, small towns, big

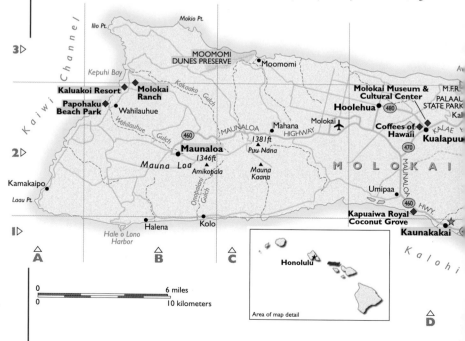

beaches, and a feeling of incredible freedom.

The first Westerner to set foot on the island was Capt. George Dixon, who landed uneventfully in 1786. Kamehameha the Great's arrival in 1795 was another matter. The warrior chief beached his war canoes at Pakuhiwa and tucked this small island into his kingdom. The missionaries arrived 1832 and estimated the population to be about 6,000, which is not much under its present count of 7,000.

Molokai entered the 20th century as a quiet island of ranches and pineapple fields. When Del Monte closed its plantation in 1982, the island sank into an economic depression from which it has yet to recover.

If recovery means development, many islanders prefer their poverty, relying on the gifts of land and sea for subsistence, supplemented by various forms of welfare. Activists are outspoken in their defense of the environment and their right to live a traditional culture-based, nature-centered way of life in one of the last places in Hawaii where this is possible.

Despite its problems, Molokai prides itself on being "The Friendly Isle." The majority of people are native Hawaiian, and the spirit of aloha is the governing principle. ∎

Jonathan Sosher, owner of the Big Wind Kite Factory in Maunaloa, shows off one of his creations.

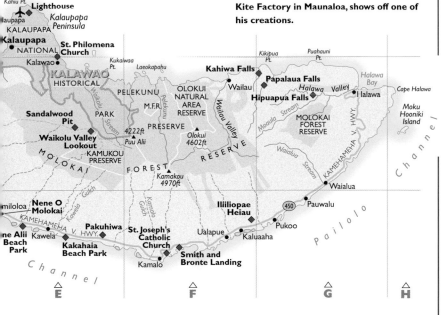

Kaunakakai may
be one of Hawaii's
smallest towns,
but residents still
put on an Aloha
Week Parade in
full regalia.

Central Molokai

MOLOKAI'S ACTION CENTER IS KAUNAKAKAI, IN THE
middle of the south coast. The main street, Ala Malama, is three
blocks long, its old wooden storefronts making the place look like a
movie set from a vintage Western.

Kaunakakai
🗺 208 D1

Visitor information
✉ Molokai Visitors
Bureau, 28 Kamoi
St. Ste. 700,
Kaunakakai
☎ 808/553-3876
🕐 Closed Sat. & Sun.

**Kapuaiwa Royal
Coconut Grove**
🗺 208 D2
✉ Maunaloa Hwy.
(Hawaii 460), 2
miles W of
Kaunakakai

If you want to laugh, visit the
Molokai Fish and Dive Shop
*(Ala Malama, tel 808-553-5926,
closed Sun. p.m.)* and read the
T-shirts. In late afternoon trucks pull
up in front of the post office *(Ala
Malama)* selling just caught fish,
shrimp raised in local ponds, and
homemade *laulau* (ti-leaf-wrapped
packets of steamed fish, pork, and
taro greens). If you walk out to the
end of the big stone jetty and look
back toward land, you'll have a wonderful view of the island, from the
golden sand beach to the mountains
with gauzy clouds about their heads.

Around 11 at night, people
hurry to the back door of
Kanemitsu Bakery *(Ala
Malama, tel 808-553-5855, closed
Tues.)*, knock, and whisper the
variety they want of famous
Molokai sweet bread—pineapple,

coconut, taro, cheddar—hot and
fragrant from the oven. Condo
renters have the adventure of shopping for all other groceries at the
legendery **Misaki's Grocery and
Dry Goods** *(Ala Malama, tel
808/530-5505)*—including fresh fish,
and taro greens and bananas from
just down the road.

Molokai's only traffic jam of
note happens on Sunday morning
when all seven Hawaiian churches
along **Church Row** let out about
the same time, around 11 a.m.
Visitors are always welcome, and
attending services in one of these
small chapels is an experience in
aloha. The singing in Hawaiian is
wonderful. The Catholic church,
St. Sophia *(Ala Malama, tel
808/553-5220)*, is under a blazing
orange tulip tree.

Across from the row of tidy

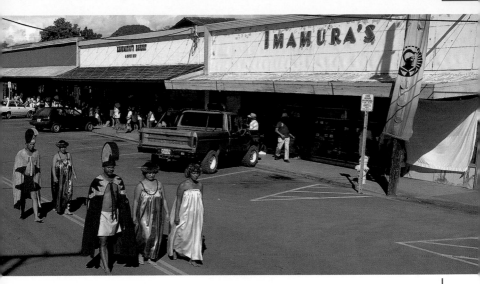

churches, by the seaside, you'll see a thousand towering coconut trees planted on 10 acres in 1863 by Chief Kapuaiwa, who was soon to be crowned as Kamehameha V. **Kapuaiwa Royal Coconut Grove** is a beautiful place to watch the sunset, but walking among the trees, especially in a breeze, could cost you your life: Those coconuts are heavy when they come crashing down from their lofty heights. The adjacent beach is a popular spot with families, and children are usually paddling and splashing about in the shallow waters. In the evening, outrigger canoes are launched from here as paddlers head out to practice their skills for the highly contested canoe races.

North of Kaunakakai, **Coffees of Hawaii** is growing coffee on former pineapple land. You can tour the plantation. The Plantation Store sells the full-bodied, low-acidic coffee, grown, harvested, roasted, and packaged on the estate. They offer free samples and there's an espresso bar (not free). The gift shop carries a good selection of local products and gifts crafted by more than 30 artisans.

The **Molokai Museum & Cultural Center** is housed in Hawaii's smallest sugar mill. Built in 1878, it displays old photos of plantation life and early Molokai, and has been fully restored to working order. It is on the National Register of Historic Places. Festivals and a schedule of crafts classes take place in the adjoining sugar museum. It is a very peaceful and picturesque site.

Two miles farther along, at **Palaau State Park,** you'll find an interesting, even intimidating rock nestled in the cool upland forest, easily reached by a short trail. In ancient times, barren women slept beneath the 6-foot Phallic Rock and reportedly had no infertility problems later. The rock's name is Ka Ule O Nanahoa, and its shape is not entirely natural (ancient stoneworkers skillfully enhanced it). The 234-acre park also has an arboretum and a commanding view of **Kalaupapa Peninsula** (see p. 217). The trailhead down the cliff is here, and you'll often see mule riders negotiating the sheer route. ∎

Coffees of Hawaii
- 208 D2
- Hawaii 480, Kualapuu, near junction with Hawaii 470
- 808/567-9023
- Tours 9:30 a.m. & 11:30 a.m. Mon.–Fri.
- $$

Molokai Museum & Cultural Center
- 208 D2
- Hawaii 470, just after Ironwood Hills Golf Course sign
- 808/567-6436
- Closed 2 p.m. & Sun.
- $

Palaau State Park
- 208 D2
- Hawaii 470, 3 miles N of Kualapuu
- 808/567-6923

Mule riders brave the hairpin turns of the trail down the face of a cliff to Kalaupapa.

Kalaupapa National Historical Park

A BLACK LAVA SHORELINE OF TEMPESTUOUS SURF AND riptides surrounds the park on three sides. On the fourth is a sheer palisade, 2,000 to 3,000 feet high. It is a magnificent natural prison.

Kalaupapa National Historical Park
🅰 209 E3

Father Damien Tours
✉ P.O. Box 1, Kalaupapa, HI 96742
☎ 808/567-6171 Fax 808/567-6171
💲 $$$$$

Molokai Mule Ride
✉ 100 Ka Lae Hwy. (Hawaii 470)
☎ 808/567-6088 or 800/567-7550
💲 $$$$$

The Hawaiian people had lived isolated from other cultures for so long that they had no resistance to European and Asian illnesses, from the common cold to leprosy. The first authenticated case of Hansen's Disease (leprosy) appeared in the Islands in 1840. By 1868, it had cut such a swath through the population that King Kamehameha V, in desperation, decreed a policy of isolation for those infected, and established the remote peninsula of Kalaupapa on Molokai as the place of confinement.

Government officials imagined that the people, who were normally so self-reliant, would farm and provide for themselves. Instead, Kalaupapa became a wild and hostile social environment, for the exiles had nothing to lose;

their watchword was "Prepare for Molokai as for the grave." They lived in caves, under rocks, and in trees; a fortunate few had huts made of rubbish. They fought over the meager rations sent over from Honolulu.

Although a cure was found for Hansen's Disease in 1946, about 60 former patients chose to live out their lives at Kalaupapa. You may visit the colony on an organized tour, run by a resident.

The **Molokai Mule Ride** will take you on an all-day adventure, riding on a well-trained mule down the cliff trail from "topside" at Palaau to Kalaupapa. In 2.9 miles, this vertiginous route descends 1,600 feet to sea level with 26 hairpin turns, each numbered so you can chart your progress. You can also tell how close you're getting by the volume of the roaring surf. At Kalaupapa, in addition to hauntingly beautiful scenery, including small offshore islands and the tallest sea cliffs in the world, you will see Father Damien's little **St. Philomena Church,** his grave, a well-done museum, the volcanic crater that formed the peninsula, and a memorial to Mother Marianne, a Franciscan nun from Utica, New York, who arrived at the colony in 1888, five months before Father Damien's death. She continued his work and died at Kalaupapa in 1918 at the age of 81. The cause for her sainthood is being championed by her Franciscan order. ∎

Father Damien

A 33-year-old Belgian Roman Catholic priest, Joseph de Veuster, who became known as Father Damien, stepped ashore at Kalaupapa leper colony on May 10, 1873. He immediately besieged the Board of Health, the crown, and the church with requests for building supplies, medicine, food and clothing. He refused to sleep indoors until every patient had decent shelter. Instead he curled up under a *hala* (pandanus) tree beside tiny St. Philomena Church. With the help of the patients, he built cottages, roads, a wharf, and an orphanage for infected children. He started farms and laid the pipes for a water system that is in use today. He dressed wounds, built coffins, and almost daily buried the dead, 6,000 of them in his time. St. Philomena Church became a place of celebration. The church was strewn with leis and fragrant flowers, and though leprosy attacks the vocal chords, he assembled choirs. At times it took two people to play the organ so that there would be ten fingers to make the music.

Damien was diagnosed with leprosy in 1885 and died in 1889. He was buried beneath the hala tree where he had started his mission. In 1936, amid great lamentations, his body was exhumed and returned to Belgium. On June 4, 1995, Pope John Paul II beatified the priest, and the bones of his right hand were given to a delegation of Kalaupapa patients. They were reinterred beneath the hala tree with full state honors at a Mass and luau (Catholic veneration of relics is consistent with Hawaiian belief in the spiritual power of bones). ∎

Father Damien's right hand is buried beside his church at Kalaupapa. The rest of his body is in his native Belgium.

East End drive

Kamehameha V Highway (Hawaii 450) skirts the southeastern and eastern shores of Molokai, with mountains on one side and the ocean on the other, ending at one of the most beautiful valleys in the world, Halawa. When setting out from Kaunakakai have a full tank of gas, drinking water, and food.

The 60 or so fishponds that scallop the shoreline are among the best preserved in Hawaii, although most are in disrepair. On the outskirts of town, you'll see your first one, **Kalokoeli ❶.** It's just past the Molokai Shores Condominium on the oceanside of Aahi Place.

Beyond Milepost 4, at what appears to be two barn-like houses, Hawaii's state bird, the endangered nene, is being raised for release into the wild. The nonprofit **Nene O Molokai ❷** *(tel 808/553-5992, by appointment only),* offers free one-hour tours.

The Kawela area you'll be passing through was the scene of a fierce battle in 1786 for control of Molokai. **Kakahaia Beach Park** *(6 miles from Kaunakakai)* is a national wildlife refuge, and a good place to bird-watch.

The tiny white church with the high white steeple, just past Mile 10, is **St. Joseph's Catholic Church ❸,** built in 1876 by Father Damien (see p. 213). The Damien statue in front of the church always wears a lei of fresh flowers.

About a mile farther, a Hawaii Visitors Bureau sign marks **Smith and Bronte Landing.** In 1927, the first civilian flight from California to Honolulu ended upside down here in a *kiawe* tree. Ernest Smith and

Emory Bronte emerged shaken but unhurt. The story is interesting but the site's a shrug.

To see a fishpond that's in working order, stop at **Ualapue ❹,** just after Mile 13, where mullet are being raised.

Father Damien in 1874 built **Our Lady of Seven Sorrows Catholic Church** at Kaluaaha. You'll see its red roof standing out against the lush green background on the *mauka* (upland) side of the road.

Fishponds

Before Christopher Columbus set sail for America, Hawaiians had perfected an aquaculture system that is being examined and restored today. Typically, stone walls were built into the sea in a semicircle from one point of land to another. An ingenious system of gates and grates allowed for circulation of fresh seawater, and the capture of fish on incoming tides. Fish would be raised and fattened in the ponds for a steady supply of seafood. ∎

The oldest and largest *heiau* (temple) on the island, and the second largest in the state, is 13th-century **Iliiliopae ⑤,** now on the National Register of Historic Places. Pick up a five-minute trail between Miles 15 and 16.

At Pukoo, just before Mile 16, is the **Neighborhood Store ⑥** *(tel 808/558-8498),* last chance for water and food. The roughest and most spectacular part of the drive is in front of you.

The road twists around blind bends, clinging to cliff faces and dipping down to lonely bays such as Honouli Maloo and Honouli Wai. Between the two, the road hugs a huge boulder called **Pohakuloa ⑦.**

In the last few miles before **Halawa ⑧,** the road climbs inland through the grasslands and hills of **Puu O Hoku Ranch.** When it comes to the sea again, it makes a hairpin turn, and below you will be the dark sands, the stream, and the waterfalls of **Halawa Valley** (see pp. 216–217). The view from the pullout near Mile 26 is breathtaking.

You can drive down to the valley to **Halewa Beach Park,** which has rest rooms. If you wade across the stream, which should be attempted only in summer, there's a nice swimming beach. When the bay is turbulent, beware of the currents and riptides.

A guided hike to the 250-foot **Moaula Falls** can be arranged. ■

🅼 Also see map, p. 208 D1
► Kaunakakai
↔ 27 miles one way
🕐 90 minutes one way, but allow all day for the round-trip
► Halawa Valley (one way)

NOT TO BE MISSED
- Nene O Molokai
- St. Joseph's Catholic Church
- Ualapue Fishpond
- Iliiliopae Heiau
- Halawa Valley

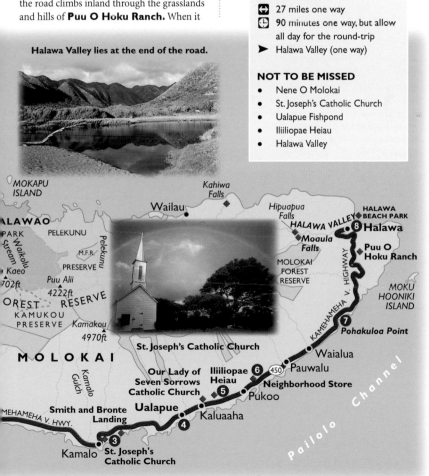

Halawa Valley lies at the end of the road.

St. Joseph's Catholic Church

Halawa Valley & the North Shore

MOLOKAI LOOKS SOMETHING LIKE A FISH, LONG AND slender, the North Shore its spine and Kalaupapa Peninsula its dorsal fin. Along the coast from Kalaupapa to Halawa emerald green sea cliffs rise from an ocean the colors of peacock's feathers. The ramparts tower to almost 4,000 feet, their peaks crowned in mists. Waterfalls by the hundreds tumble in spectacular columns from their heights. Teased by the trade winds, they live up to the Hawaiian word for waterfall, *wailele* (leaping water), as they leap and dance, splash on ledges, and soar upward in breeze-tossed veils. The record holder is Kahiwa, "the sacred one," at 1,750 feet. Their names sing like their waters: Puukaoku, Oloupena, Haloku, Hipuapua, and Papalaua.

Halawa Valley is the first and most accessible of the magnificent North Shore valleys.

The nearly vertical forests support some of the rarest plants on Earth. To save them, dedicated botanists drop from helicopters and rappel down cliffs, thousands of feet above the roaring surf. They have built a fence around the last survivor of a species of *loulu* palm (*Pritchardia munroi*) to protect it from goats. In the absence of pollinators, which are probably extinct, the scientists themselves pollinate the creamy flowers of a succulent-stemmed *Brighamia rockii*. Fewer than 200 survive in the wild, although they are now being propagated at the National Tropical Botanical Garden on Kauai (see pp. 190–191).

Halawa was one of the earliest Polynesian settlements in Hawaii.

For more than a thousand years, people farmed here. They built 18 temples to their gods. All that changed April 1, 1946, when a 45-foot wave came roaring in across the valley, destroying major sections of the ancient *kalo loi* (flooded taro fields). Another tsunami inundated the valley in 1957, finishing off the taro. Most people abandoned the valley. Only recently, a new generation has started reviving agriculture and resettling Halawa, the only one of these spectacular valleys accessible by road (see p. 215).

Wailau ("many waters") is the largest valley. There is no way in but from the ocean. This was no problem for the ancient Hawaiians, who used the ocean as their highway. Fishermen and taro farmers settled the valley, dwelling between green walls that rise to 4,970 feet. Silver ribbons of waterfalls coursing down the mountain walls fed a skein of streams coursing to the sea. The last of the people left for work and a more comfortable life in town, and the public school closed in 1920. The taro still grows untended, and there are mango, banana, guava, papaya, and avocado trees for the plucking.

Pelekunu Valley is so narrow and its walls so high that the sun's rays find it only four or five hours in a day. It rains almost half the time. In the old days, fishermen had to travel to Kalaupapa and Moomomi to find enough sunshine to dry their fish. The lyrical sounding name means "moldy smell." It's so lovely to look at, intrepid people of the 20th century periodically carved little niches for themselves and lived for periods in the glorious gloom. John H. Wilson, the engineer who built a road over Oahu's precarious Nuuanu Pali (see p. 68) and for whom Oahu's Wilson Tunnel is named, lived here with his

wife Jennie, who was born in Pelekunu. Author Audrey Sutherlin swam from Halawa to Pelekunu towing a raft with construction materials for a home, then wrote about life on the North Shore in *Paddling My Own Canoe*.

The waters of Waikolu bring life to **Kalaupapa Peninsula.** It was this stream that Father Damien (see p. 213) tapped to build his irrigation system for crops to feed the leper colony. An irrigation tunnel also carries water to the arid west end of the island (see p. 222).

No roads invade this wilderness of water and cliffs. Kamehameha V Highway gets as far as Halawa and is thwarted by the terrain. The only ways to see the North Shore are by boat or, if your interisland plane flies along the coast, from the air. ■

Kayakers paddle along the sheer green palisades with their misty waterfalls.

Molokai with native guides

Experiencing the island with islanders is a unique feature of Molokai. Most of these guides are experts in fields such as Hawaiian culture, fishing, hunting, diving, or hiking; often they have access to special places on private lands. Most guides will customize their activities to suit visitors' schedules, abilities, and interests. The trips are special because of the people who conduct them. They offer an intimate, personal perspective on Molokai.

Pelipo Solatorio *(tel 808/553-9803, $$$$$)*, as a landowner in Halawa Valley, has access to the valley's trails (see p. 216). His tour starts in his own backyard, amid photographs of family and vintage Halawa scenes. Born and raised in the valley, Pelipo knows the trails well and all the stories that go with them. He takes you to ruins of early civilizations, through the rain forest, naming the plants. He guides you nimbly across streambeds, and all the way to Moaula Falls. There he tells the tale of the *moo*, the lizard deity who lives in the pond beneath the falls. He floats a ti leaf on the plunge pool: If it sinks, the moo is waiting to snatch a victim to her watery lair; if the leaf floats, it's safe to swim. The trail is challenging, but men in their 80s and young children have handled it and enjoyed it.

Walter Naki *(Ma a Molokai Action Adventures, tel 808/558-8184, $$$$$)* has been a teacher of marine studies, youth counselor, member of the Army National Guard, decathlon champion, and fitness teacher. He quit his job to share his adventures with visitors, and he enjoys taking people hiking. Walter is also a hunting guide for deer, wild boar, and goats—hunting can be done with rifle or bow and arrow. He can skin a deer in 15 minutes, then processes and packs the meat on the spot. He offers culture tours visiting taro farms and fishponds. He also has a snorkel and beach-cookout excursion, and, weather permitting, a North Shore boat ride

Pelipo Solatario at Moaula Falls

to a hundred waterfalls and a black-sand beach for a picnic. Tours are customized and can be any length from a half day to four or five days.

Lawrence Aki *(Molokai Ranch Cultural Hike, tel 808/553-9803 or 800/274-9303, $$$$$)* knows the trails of West Molokai like he knows the lines on the palm of his hand. With an orator's sense of timing, he tells the story of Iaamaomao, the chief who keeps all the wild winds of the world in a calabash and releases them at will. He relates legends and history as he guides hikers down the tawny hillsides of Molokai Ranch, through fields of wildflowers, stopping at archaeological sites and conjuring Hawaii's gods and kings from thin air. He knows which stones are holy, which woods are poison, and how to chart the year by the shadows of the rising and setting sun.

Bill Kapuni *(tel 808/553-9867, $$$$$)* specializes in snorkel and dive adventures, although he can arrange just about any outdoor experience. He knows almost everyone on the island and knows their expertises. Bill is president of the Molokai Voyaging Canoe Society and an expert on early Polynesian boatbuilding and navigation. While you're out on the water, he shares his stories of the epic Polynesian voyages of discovery in the Pacific (see pp. 24–26).

Alex Puaa *(Molokai Off-Road Tours, tel 808/553-3369, $$$$$)* takes people into the wild Molokai outback and into forest preserves. His all-day Molokai Highlights tour includes the best of the old fishponds, a visit to the Kalaupapa Lookout, and the coffee and macadamia nut plantations. ∎

Top: Hiking guide Pelipo Solatorio was born and raised in Halawa Valley. Bottom left: Walter Naki explains taro growing on one of his cultural tours. Bottom right: Lawrence Aki points out archeological sites on his history walk.

Kamakou Preserve

Pepeopae Trail
209 E2
Nature Conservancy of Hawaii
923 Nuuanu Ave.,
Honolulu, HI 96817
808/537-4508;
808/553-5236
(Molokai)

THIS 2,774-ACRE PRESERVE WAS ESTABLISHED TO PROTECT the best forests on Molokai. Its terrain ranges from gulch bottoms to summit rain forest, with the crowning glory being the montane bog, Pepeopae, at the top of the mountain. Within the preserve are at least 250 kinds of plants. Of these, 219 live exclusively in Hawaii. The unique environment shelters rare and endangered birds such as the *olomao* (Molokai thrush), and the *kakawahie* (Molokai creeper), whose sole remaining habitat on the planet is the Kamakou Preserve.

A hiker sets up his tripod in the native cloud forest at Kamakou Preserve.

The preserve is managed by the Nature Conservancy of Hawaii, a local affiliate of the Nature Conservancy, a national nonprofit organization formed to protect the best of America's natural lands. They conduct organized tours of

the preserve, or you can hike the **Pepeopae Trail** on your own. You'll really appreciate what you see if you go with the Conservancy.

To reach the start, you'll need a four-wheel-drive vehicle. You hike on a boardwalk surrounded by tree ferns and ohia trees. Birds trill in the trees, and lush, spongy mosses drip at the wayside. The change from rain forest to bog is abrupt. The forest does not diminish, it simply stops, as if on command. Before you is a vast, orderly garden of miniatures, ohia trees 4 inches tall with glorious scarlet blossoms as big as the plant, mounds of grasses, and mosses shading from russet to silver. Tended only by the winds and rains, mist, and sunshine, wild Pepeopae looks as if lovingly nurtured by a bonsai gardener. From the viewing platform here, the rest of Molokai lies below.

There are two interesting stops on the Forest Reserve Road leading to Kamakou. The **Sandalwood Pit** is a ship-shaped depression in the earth. In the days of the sandalwood trade, Hawaiians would toss the cut timber into the hull-size pit. When it was full, they hauled the fragrant cargo down the mountainside to vessels bound for China.

Waikolu Valley Lookout overhangs a notch in the mountains where waterfalls plunge into unseen green depths and the ocean laps at the lips of the valley. ■

Moomomi Dunes

THE MOOMOMI DUNES RISE ALONG THE NORTHWEST coast of the island, in view of the Kalaupapa Lighthouse. The 920-acre preserve, managed by the Nature Conservancy of Hawaii, is the best remaining area of native strand vegetation in the state.

The appeal here is the utter isolation and feeling of freedom. Moomomi is windswept, salt-sprayed, and uncompromised. There's a rocky ledge offshore, so the ocean arrives in great plumes.

Clinging tenaciously to this wild landscape are tiny, low-to-the-ground plants. The silvery green *hinahina (Heliotropium anamalum)* colonizes the dunes, almost hiding its fragrant, tiny white blossoms. The leaves of the pale silver *enaena (Gnaphalium sandwicensium)* feel as soft as the coat of a baby seal. The vine *Pau-o-Hiiaka* is said to have appeared first at Moomomi, to cover the goddess Hiiaka and protect her from the sun as she slept.

The people of Pelekunu (see p. 217) used to come out of their rainy valley to dry fish here, living in the shelter caves lining the beach.

Important archaeological sites at the dunes have revealed bones of a flightless ibis, a four-foot goose *(moa nalu)* that laid eggs the size of coconuts, a long-legged owl, and an oceanic eagle, all long extinct. The area is still visited by native shorebirds, the *hunakai* (sander-ling) and *kolea* (golden plover). Endangered Hawaiian monk seals haul themselves out of the ocean for sunbaths, and green sea turtles steal ashore at night to hide their eggs in the dunes.

There's a gold-sand beach here, but the wind often drives the sand about in the hot air. Bring drinking water, a hat, and sunscreen to go exploring. The Nature Conservancy of Hawaii offers monthly hikes. Jeep trails crisscross the terrain; it's about a 20-minute walk from the parking area to the beach. ∎

Wind scours the lonely stretch of beach at Moomomi Dunes.

Moomomi Dunes
- 208 C3
- Hawaii 480, 3 miles past Hoolehua town

Western Molokai

YOU COULD PAINT THE WESTERN END OF MOLOKAI IN shades of umber, russet, sage, and heather. Its geography is gentle, dramatic only in the sweep of undulating hills ending in ocean.

Molokai Ranch
🅰 208 B2
Maunaloa
🅰 208 B2

**Papohaku
Beach Park**
🅰 208 B2
✉ Kaluakoi Rd.

**Visitors staying
at Molokai Ranch
get to participate
in ranch activities,
which includes
rodeo games.**

The **Molokai Ranch** dominates the scene. Cattle drives, roundups, and rodeos raise clouds of red dust against the intense blue skies. These days much of the ranch action is staged for tourists, who can saddle up and play *paniolo* (cowboy, see pp. 160–161). The ranch has developed three campsites where you can stay in "tentalows" or Mongolian-style yurts. It may be wilderness, with deer nibbling beneath your windows, but you won't be roughing it (see p. 257). To control aggressive plants colonizing pastureland, the ranch in 1974 imported African browsers such as giraffes, zebras, kudus, and elands.

Molokai's sole real resort, **Kaluakoi,** with its 18-hole golf course, is a manicured enclave in the wilderness.

The only town out this way, **Maunaloa,** was, until recently, a sleepy little plantation village forgotten by time. Its only attraction was the **Big Wind Kite Factory** *(tel 808/552-2364)* where you could get free kite-flying lessons. Big Wind's old daffodil-yellow building is about the only thing that hasn't changed in Maunaloa, and you can still learn to fly a kite. However, most of the beautiful kites—hula dancers, geckoes, big red hibiscus—end up as decorator items. Today Maunaloa has a triplex movie theater, a Kentucky Fried Chicken, a luxe lodge, and new homes going for half a million or more.

Five miles northwest of Maunaloa, the wide, white sands of **Papohaku Beach** run for 3 miles beside the turquoise ocean, then mound into dunes. Strong rip currents and rogue surf make this a magnificent beach to see, but treacherous for swimming. Every May, the island's biggest festival, **Ka Hula Piko,** is held at the beach park. According to Molokai tradition, the hula was born on the summit of nearby **Mauna Kaana,** where Laka, who came to be regarded as the goddess of the dance, had the first *hula halau* (hula school, see pp. 168–169). ■

Visitors come to the rugged little island of Lanai for what it *doesn't* have—traffic, fast food chains, malls, cities. What it has are two luxury resorts, two championship golf courses—and plenty of privacy.

Lanai

Stone marker at the Garden of the Gods

Lanai

LANAI IS SHAPED LIKE A CRUSTY OYSTER, BUT FOR THE FEW WHO HAVE discovered its pleasures, Lanai is a pearl. Once the world's largest pineapple plantation, it is now a retreat for the rich and famous, and those who want to try the lifestyle for a while.

Least known of the major Hawaiian Islands, Lanai was formed by a single volcano, giving it a configuration unusual in the archipelago. The single mountain is eroded into deep, red gorges that end in cliffs at the sea or taper into lonely beaches. The only way to get around on your own is to rent a four-wheel-drive vehicle. There are few paved roads.

The volcano's caldera is the broad, fertile Palawai Basin, which was once the island's pineapple basket. The fog and mists now look ghostly hovering over empty fields.

Lanai is 17 miles long and 13 miles wide, 89,000 acres of serenity unmatched in Hawaii. There are 47 miles of coastline, scalloped into coves interrupted by 2,000-foot cliffs.

Considered to be the abode of demons, Lanai was uninhabited until the 15th century when Kaululaau, rebellious son of a Maui king, was banished to the island. With cunning and daring, the young man vanquished the evil spirits and made Lanai safe for habitation.

At least for a while. In 1778, a Big Island chief, Kalaniopuu, raided the island and killed almost everyone. In the party was a warrior named Kamehameha, who would one day rule the Islands, and return to Lanai to go fishing.

Two attempts were made to establish utopia on Lanai, once by the Mormon Church and the other by Walter Murray Gibson (see pp. 32–33), who arrived in 1861. Both failed.

Others established short-lived sugar and ranching operations. In 1922, James Dole (see p. 31) planted the island's first pineapple, and for the next 65 years the fruit was king, producing about 250 million pineapples a year. Dole built the island's only town, Lanai City, to house his workers. In the morning, the plantation whistle woke everyone up. The ten-room Hotel Lanai in Lanai City was the only place for visitors to stay.

In 1985, Los Angeles entrepreneur David H. Murdock purchased 98 percent of Lanai as part of the assets of a missionary-founded company. Murdock shut down the plantation and built two luxury hotels, forever changing the character of the island and the lives of the approximately 3,000 people who live there. ■

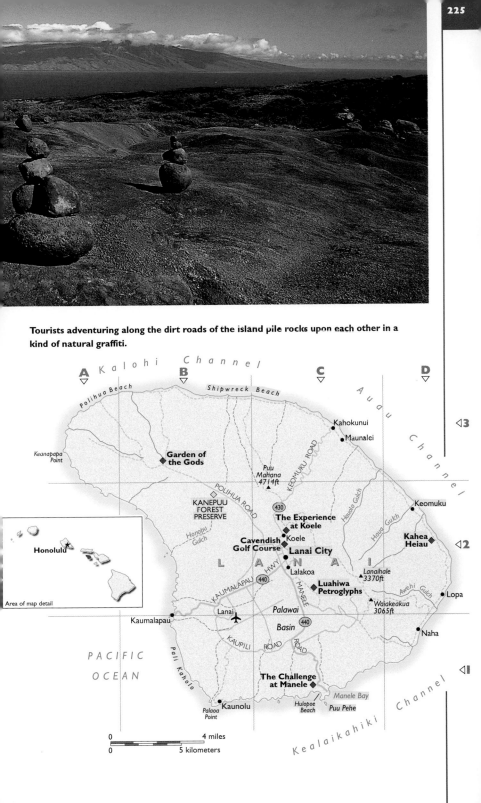

Tourists adventuring along the dirt roads of the island pile rocks upon each other in a kind of natural graffiti.

Map labels:

A B C D

Kalohi   Channel

Auau Channel

Polihua Beach

Shipwreck Beach

Keanapapa Point

Garden of the Gods

Puu Mahana 471ft

Kahokunui

Maunalei

3

KANEPUU FOREST PRESERVE

POLIHUA ROAD

KEOMUKU ROAD

Keomuku

Honolulu

Area of map detail

Honopu Gulch

Cavendish Golf Course

The Experience at Koele

Koele

Lanai City

Hauola Gulch

Hauo Gulch

Kahea Heiau

2

L A N A I

Lalakoa

Luahiwa Petroglyphs

Lanaihale 3370ft

Awehi Gulch

Lopa

KAUMALAPAU HWY

440

MANELE

ROAD

Lanai

Palawai

Basin

440

Waiakeakua 3065ft

Kaumalapau

Pali Kaholo

KAUPILI   ROAD

Naha

PACIFIC

OCEAN

The Challenge at Manele

1

Manele Bay

Palaoa Point

Kaunolu

Hulopoe Beach

Puu Pehe

Kealaikahiki   Channel

0   4 miles
0   5 kilometers

A lone hiker ponders the legend of love gone bad at Puu Pehe, Sweetheart Rock.

Lanai *makai*

TO SEE LANAI *MAKAI* (ALONG THE OCEAN), YOU HAVE TO visit the beaches in separate assaults, as there is no road that encircles the island. Hulopoe Beach and adjacent Manele Bay, in the south, form a state marine life conservation district. Snorkeling is excellent, and spinner dolphins often come to play, interacting with swimmers at Hulopoe, the island's most popular beach. Most Lanai children learn to swim in the tidal pools of the lava apron on the left of the lovely sandy beach. To get there, go to the end of Manele Road (Hawaii 440), 8 miles south of Lanai City.

Hulopoe Beach
📷 225 C1

Kaunolu
📷 225 B1

Shipwreck Beach
📷 225 B3

Manele, an ancient spatter cone, separates Hulopoe from the boat harbor. The red dirt cliffs fall sharply into a churning teal-blue sea. Offshore is a dramatic sea stack called **Puu Pehe** or, more popularly, Sweetheart Rock. It takes its name from the legend of a beautiful Maui girl kidnapped by a young Lanai warrior who hid her on the rock. The girl drowned during a storm and the broken-hearted warrior threw himself from the cliff.

From the top of the cone, easily reached by a trail, there are good views of the coast and Puu Pehe. Don't go near the edge, however,

as the loosely packed cinders often slide away. **Manele Bay,** sheltered by cliffs, is a haven for visiting yachts, pleasure boats, and fishing craft. A cattle-loading chute from ranching days is cemented into the cliff outside the breakwater. Ruins of an ancient fishing village are hidden in the thickets.

To really get a feel for what life might have been like in these fishing villages, visit **Kaunolu,** a national historic landmark. It's reached via Manele Road (Hawaii 440), 4.5 miles south of Lanai City to Kaupili Road and then a dirt track; signs mark the way. The site

contains house foundations, remnants of trails, and the sacred remains of Halulu Heiau, an ancient temple. On the eastern end of the site is a 62-foot cliff called Kahekili's Jump where warriors would test their courage by leaping out far enough over the sea to clear a treacherous ledge at the foot of the cliff. A timid leap ended in certain death.

Abandoned in the 19th century, some village platforms and walls are well preserved, and there's a fishing shrine. This was a favorite fishing retreat of Kamehameha the Great—the *aku* (skipjack tuna) still run plentifully in offshore waters. To the right is the tallest sea cliff on Lanai, Pali Kaholo, rising 1,000 feet.

The island's most notorious strand of sand is 8-mile-long **Shipwreck Beach**—take Keomuku Road (Hawaii 44) to its end at Kahokunui (8 miles northeast of Lanai City). The wild windswept place has earned its name. The earliest recorded shipwrecks were in the 1820s when an American and a British ship went aground, and over the years the reef

has trapped hundreds of other boats. The rusting hull of a World War II ship is still lashed by waves. Look for rocks painted white, marking the way to a famous collection of petroglyphs (see p. 158).

If you continue south from here, along the dirt road, you'll pass isolated coves you can have all to yourself, with Maui looming almost close enough to touch. The ghost town of **Keomuku** is also along the route. Abandoned when the sugar plantation failed, it once had a population of 2,000. The weathered old wooden church, Ka Lanakila o Ka Malamalama, built in 1903, rests beneath the coconut trees. A little farther along, you'll see the *heiau* (temple) that caused the village to become a ghost town: When plantation managers used stones from Kahea Heiau to build a sugarcane railway, the sweet water of the district turned salty within 24 hours, and most of the contract laborers died from a mysterious fever. The shoreline road runs a total of 15 miles to the old village of Naha, where you have to turn around and come back. ■

The reef at Shipwreck Beach is littered with grounded vessels, such as this World War II ship.

Golfing in Hawaii

You could play two different courses a day for a month and never repeat yourself, as there are more than 75 golf courses rolling across the green hills of Hawaii. They range from short and easy to long and tough, and are among the most beautiful anywhere. Special hazards include lava fields, ancient ruins, crashing surf, distracting scenery, and the sight of offshore leaping whales. Special equipment needed: a camera.

Lanai has three golf courses. The nine-hole public **Cavendish Golf Course** was built in 1947 for plantation workers. No reservations are needed. The island's first resort course, **The Experience at Koele** *(tel 808/565-4653)*, opened in 1991. Its 390-yard eighth hole that drops 250 feet to a wooded gorge became instantly famous. The other championship course, **The Challenge at Manele** *(tel 808/565-2222)*, was designed by Jack Nicklaus to live up to its name, but with sets of five tees players of all levels can have a satisfying game.

On Maui, the three 18-hole courses at **Kapalua Resort** *(300 Kapalua Dr., tel 808/669-8044)* are trendsetters. All championship venues, they comply with stringent environmental standards and are designated Certified Audubon Cooperative Sanctuaries, the only ones in Hawaii. They have the largest staff of PGA (Professional Golfers' Association) pros in the state. A brand-new golf academy opened in 2000, and they have a caddy program for junior golfers, with access to scholarships.

Other excellent courses on Maui are at **Kaanapali** *(tel 808/661-3691)*, **Wailea** *(tel 808/879-2966)*, and **Makena** *(tel 808/879-3344)* resorts.

The Big Island's top courses are at **Mauna Kea** *(Kohala Coast, tel 808/882-5400)*, **Mauna Lani** *(Kohala Coast, tel 808/885-6655)*, **Hapuna** *(Kohala Coast, tel 808/880-3000)*, and **Waikoloa** *(68-1792 Melia St., Waikoloa, tel 808/883-9621)*. The most photographed hole is Mauna Kea's 210-yard third, over a surf-dashed cove.

Kauai has some of the least expensive championship courses set amid some of the most extravagant scenery. The **Princeville** courses *(Princeville Resort, tel 808/826-3580 or 800/826-4400)* are renowned for these virtues. The nine-hole **Kukuiolono** *(Kalaheo, tel 808/332-9151)* course is a bargain. You can take your time on this quiet mature course, which was opened in 1928.

On Oahu, notable greens are the 27 holes of the **Hawaii Prince Golf Club** *(92-1200 Fort Weaver Rd., Ewa Beach, tel 808/944-4567)*, designed by Arnold Palmer and Ed Seay, and opened in 1992. The **Ko Olina Golf Club** *(92-1220 Aliinui Dr., Kapolei, tel 808/676-5309)* has earned the reputation of having "the toughest hole" on the LPGA (Ladies' Professional Golf Association) tour—the 18th. Ted Robinson designed this top course with his signature water features. ■

Above: Davis Love III hits up on the first hole during the first round of the PGA Grand Slam of Golf, Poipu Bay Resort Course, Kauai, in November 1999. Right: The winner of the tournament, Tiger Woods, poses with his trophy.

Lanai *mauka*

MAUKA MEANS "UPLAND." LANAI'S ONE AND ONLY TOWN, optimistically called Lanai City, sits at a cool elevation of 1,600 feet amid stands of tall Cook Island pine trees. Small, vintage 1920s plantation homes, with exuberant gardens, line the quiet streets and lanes. Almost everyone on the island lives here. The fun of this town is just walking around admiring the charming houses.

Lookouts on the Munro Trail peer into steep ridges and deep gulches.

Petroglyphs are found in abundance in the hills and brush on Lanai. The **Luahiwa** field covers 3 acres. The earliest rock etchings here are about 500 years old; in the 1870s, students from Maui added horses and surfers to the earlier stick figures of men and dogs—and gave the dogs leashes. Look for a group of black boulders and great big century plants off Manele Road, then cut across the old dirt pineapple tracks. Late afternoon is best for photography.

About a half-hour drive from Lanai City is the **Garden of the Gods,** a strange, raw landscape of weird, oddly placed volcanic boulders. Just after dawn and just before sunset, the earthy colors glow and almost vibrate.

On the way there is a self-guided nature trail into **Kanepuu Preserve.** It takes about 15 minutes to reach all eight stations and read the informative signage. Once a month, the Nature Conservancy *(tel 808/565-7430)* conducts guided hikes into this lowland forest, the only known one of its kind left in the archipelago. It owes its existence to George C. Munro, Lanai Ranch manager, who in 1918 erected fences around it to protect a grove of *lama* (native persimmon) and *olopua* (native olive). Munro, a knowledgeable naturalist, is also responsible for planting the Norfolk and Cook Island pines that have become icons of Lanai.

On a clear day, you can see five Hawaiian Islands from the 3,370-foot summit of **Lanaihale.** You'll need a four-wheel-drive to get there, and don't attempt it unless the weather is clear, for the 5-mile dirt track to the top is rutted and prone to washout. Most people consider the views of deep brooding gorges, misty forests, and all the other islands to be worth it. ■

Of the 132 Hawaiian isles and islets, most are uninhabited today. Some have become wildlife sanctuaries, others were military targets, one is privately owned, another is in its birth throes. There are just a few you can visit.

More Hawaiian isles

The endangered Hawaiian monk seal

More Hawaiian isles

NIIHAU LIES IN A TIME WARP, 17 MILES OFF THE WEST COAST OF KAUAI across the Kaulakahi Channel. Called The Forbidden Island, it has no electricity, no paved roads, no privately owned vehicles, no crime, and only one town, Puuwai. The 250 inhabitants are largely native Hawaiians who still speak their own language and live pretty much a traditional Hawaiian lifestyle in a close-knit community, adhering to a deeply felt spirituality.

The island is owned by the Robinson family, descendants of Eliza McHutcheson Sinclair, who bought it in 1864 from Kamehameha V for $10,000 in gold. Ranching is the main occupation on this 6-mile-by-18-mile island, but its most famous product is the shell lei. The small lustrous *pupu* (shells) are gathered only on this island and fashioned into exquisite jewelry commanding prices that can run into thousands of dollars.

The only way to visit Niihau is by helicopter tour, which may be doubling as the "poi bird," bringing in 400 pounds of the staple *(Niihau Helicopters, Hanapepe, Kauai, tel 808/335-3500)*. You will land at Keanahaki Beach, a remote corner of the island, nowhere near Puuwai. Islanders occasionally come to offer their shell lei for sale, but most of the time you will meet no one. One interesting thing you will see is a place along the shore where fresh water actually weeps from rock.

KAHOOLAWE

The island of Kahoolawe has an interesting past. By A.D. 1250 the island was inhabited, and by 1600 the temple at Hakioawa was built. The island served briefly as a penal colony for Catholics punished by an 1829 order of Queen

Kure
Atoll

Midway Islands

4 ▷

Pearl and
Hermes Atoll

△
A

Lisianski
Island

△
B

Laysan
Island

Maro
Reef

Gardner
Pinnacles

3 ▷

△
C

French
Frigate
Shoals

△
D

The small island of Lehua lies just off the private island of Niihau in the background.

Divers explore the ocean floor to learn about volcanism and the formation of the Islands.

Loihi

A fire burns 3,775 feet deep in the ocean, as a new Hawaiian Island is being born 18 miles southeast of the Big Island's Kau Coast. Named Loihi ("long"), the active volcano has two large craters, which rise 500 feet above its summit plateau. The base of the mountain lies 14,000 feet below sea level. Estimates for the time it will take Loihi to rise above the waves range from 100 to 10,000 years. Aided by mini-submarines, scientists are able to observe the formation of an island. They say Loihi could grow taller than Mauna Kea. ■

Kaahumanu, a convert to Protestantism, for practicing their faith. The island was reborn as a ranch in 1858. By 1925, the U.S. Army Air Corp was using Kahoolawe for military exercises. After the 1941 attack on Pearl Harbor, the U.S. Navy took control of the island, beginning the decades-long assault on it for target practice. Protests began in 1969. On May 7, 1994, to the sound of chants, drums, and conch-shell horns, the federal government returned Kahoolawe to Hawaii, with promises to clear the military ordinances and replant the largely denuded land. John Waihee, governor at that time, said Hawaii was "whole again." The island cannot be visited. ■

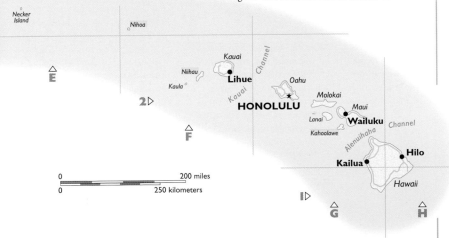

Hawaiian Islands & Midway Atoll NWR

Nihoa
🏕 233 F3

Laysan
🏕 232 C3

French Frigate Shoals
🏕 232 D3

Midway Islands
🏕 232 A4

Midway Phoenix Corporation

✉ 100 Phoenix Air Dr. SW, Cartersville, Ga 30120

☎ 888/Midway-1; 770/387-1327 (fax)

THE NORTHWESTERN HAWAIIAN ISLANDS THAT ANCHOR these Pacific paradises are mere dots in the vast blue ocean, yet they provide a vital habitat for endangered Hawaiian monk seals, green sea turtles, and more than 14 million seabirds of 18 species. Sooty terns are the most common bird that frequent this pristine, uninhabited niche, followed by albatrosses, shearwaters, petrels, tropicbirds, boobies, and noddies. Some extremely rare finches have found their last refuge on Earth on Nihoa and Laysan Islands, while Midway Atoll is said to have the world's largest population of "gooney birds."

One of the most curious creatures here is the frigatebird, which flies continuously at sea, yet has a hard time fishing because its feathers do not repel water like those of other seabirds. Its strategy is to frighten boobies and shearwaters into sur-

A swimmer and a Hawaiian monk seal are curious about each other at Midway Islands.

rendering their food. Hawaiians call the frigatebird *iwa*, thief. Another interesting critter, Hawaiian monk seals rear their pups at French Frigate Shoals, sharing the coves with green sea turtles. The turtles roam several hundred miles in search of food.

President Theodore Roosevelt established the **Hawaiian Islands National Wildlife Refuge** in

1909. The chain of islands, reefs, and atolls extends some 800 miles northwest of the main Hawaiian Islands, reaching to the Midway Islands and covering 1,766 acres of land above water, and 610,148 acres below. The remote tiny islands that comprise this refuge include Nihoa, Necker, French Frigate Shoals, Gardner Pinnacles, Maro Reef, Laysan, Lisianski, and Pearl and Hermes Reef. It is prohibited to enter lagoon waters or land on the islands of this refuge, to protect the nesting birds and monk seals.

You can, however, visit the **Midway Atoll National Wildlife Refuge**—if you have the means. Its pristine lagoons and long white-sand beaches provide a wonderfully relaxing retreat for naturalists, photographers, and escapists in general. The problem is, you have to figure out how to get here on your own. There is currently no scheduled air or boat service (although the harbor and airstrip are operational). Access is by private plane or boat only. There are no open accommodations, restaurants, or shops. All food and provisions must be brought in.

A bill before Congress hopes to transfer management of the Midway Islands to the National Park Service, honoring the islands' significance to American victory as the scene of the turning point in World War II. ■

Travelwise

Shaved ice is a favorite local treat.

TRAVELWISE INFORMATION

PLANNING YOUR TRIP

WHEN TO GO

Hotel occupancy and rates are highest mid-Dec.–March. Summer is busy when school is out. The last week of April, a Japanese national vacation, is the most crowded in Waikiki. Off season is mid-April–mid-June, and again Sept.–mid-Dec. The climate is ideal, and the rates tend to be lower.

CLIMATE

Hawaii has two seasons, summer and winter. Winter is wetter. Average winter daytime temperature is 78°F. Average summer daytime temperature is 85°F but cooled by gentle trade winds. Warmest months are Aug. and Sept. Evening temperatures drop about ten degrees, although winter nights can hover in the low sixties.

MAIN EVENTS

Contact the Hawaii Visitors and Convention Bureau (see p. 240), or the telephone numbers listed for further information.

JANUARY

Hula Bowl, Kahului, Maui, third or fourth Sat. The annual college all-star football game is played at War Memorial Stadium. Tel 808/871-4141.
Opening of State Legislature, Honolulu, Oahu, third Wed. The annual session opens at the state capitol with ceremonies, lei, music, hula, and speeches.
Lunar New Year, Honolulu, Oahu, day of the second new moon after the winter solstice (mid- to late Jan.). It opens the five-week Narcissus Festival of Chinese cultural events, mainly in Chinatown. Tel 808/953-3181.
Molokai Makahiki, Molokai, last Sat. An island-wide celebration of Hawaiian arts, crafts, games, and food. Tel 800/800-6367 or 808/553-3876.

FEBRUARY

Mauna Kea Ski Meet, Big Island, first weekend. Men's and women's slalom.
Pro Bowl, Honolulu, Oahu, first Sun. after Super Bowl. National Football League all-stars battle it out at Aloha Stadium. Tel 808/486-9300.
Buffalo's Big Board Classic, Makaha Beach, Oahu, first two weeks. Surfers compete on traditional long boards. Paddlers surf their outrigger canoes. Tel 808/951-7877.
Waimea Town Celebration, Waimea, Kauai, third weekend. Multiethnic entertainment and food, rodeo and sports meets. Tel 808/338-9957.

MARCH

Cherry Blossom Festival, all islands. Japanese cultural demonstrations over 11 weeks: flower arrangement, martial arts, food presentation, and tea ceremony. Tel 808/949-2255.
Polo season opens, Mokuleia, Oahu, first or second weekend. Bring a picnic and enjoy Sun. at the seaside field.
Prince Kuhio Festival, Lihue, Kauai, weekend closest to March 26. Tel 808/245-3971.

APRIL

Easter Sunrise Service, Honolulu, Oahu. At Punchbowl Cemetery.
Kapalua Celebration of the Arts, Kapalua, Maui. Weekend of free art classes and Hawaiian cultural events at the Ritz Carlton. Tel 808/669-6200.
Merrie Monarch Festival, Hilo, Big Island, week after Easter. The most prestigious hula event in the Islands. Tel 808/935-9168.

MAY

Lei Day, all Islands, May 1. Everyone wears a lei. Lei-making contests, and school pageants, with lei day courts and multi-cultural dancing.
Molokai Ka Hula Piko, Papohaku Beach Park, Molokai, third Sat. Outdoor hula

celebration with arts, crafts, and food booths. Tel. 800/800-6367 or 808/553-3876.
Kahikolu, Honolulu, Oahu, last Monday. This down-home, very friendly Memorial Day event honors Maiki Aiu, the mother of the Hawaiian Renaissance, and draws top local entertainers and hula groups. Tel 808/377-1247.

JUNE

King Kamehameha Celebration, all Islands, weekend closest to June 11. Parades, floral floats, street parties, and cultural events. King's statue in Honolulu is draped in massive lei.
Taste of Honolulu, Honolulu, Oahu, end June. Restaurants participate in this annual Easter Seals fundraiser on the grounds of the Civic Center. Events include tastings from top chefs, wine tastings, cooking demos, and a market. Tel 808/536-1015.
Puuhonua O Honaunau Festival, Big Island, last weekend. Pageantry, games, entertainment, traditional fishing, and crafts in the National Historical Park. Tel 808/328-2288.
Hawaii State Farm Fair, Honolulu, Oahu, late June/early July. Carnival rides, games, food, entertainment, and agricultural events. Tel 808/848-2074.

JULY

Makawao Rodeo, Makawao, Maui, July 4. Parade and rodeo. Tel 808/572-2076.
Parker Ranch Rodeo, Waimea, Big Island, July 4. Cowboys strut their stuff. Tel 808/885-7311.
Prince Lot Hula Festival, Moanalua Gardens, Oahu, second Sat. Prettiest of the many hula events. Tel 808/839-5334.
Queen Liliuokalani Keiki Hula Competition, Honolulu, Oahu, late July. No expense spared in outfitting children for this hula competition. Tel 808/521-6905.

AUGUST

Hawaii State Farm Fair, Aloha Stadium, Honolulu, Oahu.

Early Aug. Rides, local food, local farm produce including flowers, entertainment. Tel 808/531-3531.

Koloa Plantation Days, Koloa, Kauai, last week. Week-long festival recalling plantation days. Look for a parade, sports, and a variety of cultural events.

Hawaiian International Billfish Tournament, Kailua-Kona, Big Island, timing based on new moon. For ten days an armada of boats search the Pacific for record marlin. Tel 808/329-6155.

SEPTEMBER
Aloha Festivals, all Islands. Parades, street parties, major cultural events.

OCTOBER
Maui County Fair, Kahului, Maui. Carnival rides, a parade, entertainment, and exhibits.

Eo E Emalani I Alakai, Kokee, Kauai, second Sat. Re-enactment of Queen Emma's visit to Alakai Swamp, plus hula and nature events. Tel 808/335-9975.

Halloween, Lahaina, Maui, Oct. 31. Annual spook spoof with costume contests and a bawdy street party. Tel 808/667-9175.

Ironman Triathlon World Championship, Kailua-Kona, Big Island. The small town erupts for this big swim-bike-run challenge with more than a thousand competitors. Tel 808/329-0063.

NOVEMBER
Kona Coffee Festival, Kailua-Kona, Big Island, early Nov. Farm tours, parade, pageantry, coffee tasting, recipe contest. Tel 808/326-7820.

Hawaii International Film Festival, Oahu, second week; various Neighbor Islands, third week. Draws top films focused on cross-cultural themes. Tel 808/528-3456.

Mission Houses Museum Christmas Fair, Honolulu, Oahu, end Nov. Hawaiian crafters sell local arts and Christmas decorations. Tel 808/531-0481.

DECEMBER
Honolulu Marathon, Oahu, early Dec. Runners race from Aloha Tower along the eastern shore and back to Kapiolani Park, Waikiki. Tel 808/734-7200.

Honolulu City Lights, Oahu. Downtown becomes a fantasia of lights, trees, and displays.

Christmas, all Islands. Most hotels are lavishly decorated, have special lobby displays. Santa often arrives by outrigger canoe.

WHAT TO TAKE

You should be able to buy anything you need in Hawaii, but prices are about 18 percent higher than on the U.S. mainland. Pharmacies offer a wide range of drugs, medical supplies, and toiletries, but bring any pre-scription drugs you might need. A second pair of glasses or contact lenses is a good idea. You will need sunscreen and a hat. Dress is casual, but top-end restaurants request what they call "dressy resort wear." Take a light waterproof jacket and a sweater in winter or if you are staying in the mountains. Most sports equipment can be rented. Lastly, don't forget the essentials: passport (if coming from outside the U.S.), driver's license, ATM cards or traveler's checks, and documentation for medical insurance.

INSURANCE

Take out adequate coverage for medical treatment, and baggage and money loss. Emergency treatment can be expensive.

PASSPORTS

Non-U.S. citizens tend to forget Hawaii is a state of the U.S. Visitors from most foreign countries need a valid passport with a U.S. tourist visa. Canadian citizens need only proof of residence. U.S. Customs, tel 808/522-8060; U.S. Immigration, tel 808/532-3721.

WHAT NOT TO BRING

You cannot bring any fresh fruits or vegetables to Hawaii even if you are coming from the U.S. mainland and do not have to go through Customs. You will be asked to sign a declaration form and warned that fees for non-compliance are high. Also, because there is no rabies in Hawaii, there is a strict animal quarantine law requiring all animals to be held for four months at the state quarantine station on Oahu. Under a carefully regulated program of inoculations prior to arrival in the Islands, your animal may qualify for a 30-day quarantine. Snakes are strictly forbidden. Hawaii Department of Agriculture, tel 808/973-9560. Animal Quarantine Station, tel 808/483-7171.

FURTHER READING

Hawaii by James Michener, Random House, 1959, is a novel encompassing much of Hawaii's history.

Hawaiian Mythology by Martha Beckwith, University of Hawaii Press, 1970, a collection of important Hawaiian mythology.

Holy Man, Father Damien of Molokai by Gavan Daws, University of Hawaii Press, 1973, a biography of the priest who worked among the lepers.

Hula Is Life by Rita Ariyoshi, Maiki Aiu Building Corporation, 1998, is the most important book about hula to be published.

I Myself Have Seen It by Susanna Moore, National Geographic, 2003, an esteemed novelist recounts her idyllic Hawaii childhood in the '50s.

Journal of a Residence in the Sandwich Islands, University of Hawaii Press, 1970, the diary of an early missionary.

Maui on My Mind by Rita Ariyoshi, Mutual Publishing, 1985, is a lavishly illustrated portrait of Maui.

Plants and Flowers of Hawaii by S.H. Sohmer and R. Gustafson, University of Hawaii Press, 1987, photographs and text about the unique flora of the islands. *Shoal of Time* by Gavan Daws, University of Hawaii Press, 1968, is the best history of Hawaii.

HOW TO GET TO HAWAII

AIRLINES

All major U.S. and many international airlines service Honolulu International Airport. Overseas flights also fly direct to Kona and Hilo airports on the Big Island; Kahului, Maui; and Lihue, Kauai.
Useful numbers:
Aloha Airlines, tel 800/367-5250 or 808/484-1111
American Airlines, tel 800/433-7300 or 808/833-7600
Continental Airlines, tel 800/231-0856 or 808/523-0000
Delta Airlines, tel 800/221-1212
Hawaiian Airlines, tel 800/367-5320 or 808/838-1555
Japan Airlines, tel 808/521-1441
Northwest Airlines, tel 800/225-2525
Qantas, tel 800/227-4500
United Airlines, tel 800/225-5825

AIRPORTS

Honolulu International Airport is the gateway to Hawaii and the Pacific. There is an overseas terminal, an inter-island terminal, and a commuter airline terminal. They are connected by the Wiki-Wiki Bus, a free shuttle. The Wiki-Wiki Bus takes you from your arrival gate to baggage claim if your flight has landed on the reef runway, built out into the ocean.

Renting a car
Rental car agencies have vans to collect you at the airport to take you to their lot.
Taxis are right outside the exit doorways. Fare to Waikiki is about $25.
An airport shuttle operates 24 hours a day between the airport and Waikiki hotels and condominiums. No reservation is necessary. You can board with two pieces of luggage and a carry-on at no extra charge. Bicycles and surfboards are not permitted. Fare is $8, tips appreciated, particularly if the attendant helps you with your bag. Call 808/539-9400, ext. 5. The Bus Nos. 19 and 20 run from the airport to Waikiki from 4:50 a.m. weekdays (5:25 a.m. weekends) to 11:45 p.m. weekdays (11:25 p.m. weekends). You may board only with a carry-on or small suitcase that will fit under your seat. Fare, $1.50, exact change only.

Lei greeting
Unless you are being met by a friend or a tour company representative, you will not receive a traditional floral greeting. However, you can arrange for one from Greeters of Hawaii (tel 800/366-8559, $20–$30, depending on the lei).

GETTING AROUND

BY AIR

The only way to travel from island to island is by plane. The major inter-island carriers are Hawaiian Airlines, Aloha Airlines, and Aloha's subsidiary, Island Air. Aloha and Hawaiian operate a full schedule of jet flights daily, and offer a variety of discounts for multiple flights. Island Air flies turboprop aircraft and services the Islands' smaller airports. Oahu is the only Island with a public transportation system: TheBus, tel 808/848-5555 or visit the web site geared to specific destinations (www.thebus.org). Taxi service is available at the airports. Many hotels provide airport transfers.

Aloha Airlines
From the U.S. mainland, tel 800/367-5250
Oahu, tel 808/484-1111
Maui, tel 808/244-9071
Big Island, tel 808/935-5771
Kauai, tel 808/245-3691
Molokai, tel 800/652-6541
Lanai, tel 800/652-6541

Hawaiian Airlines
From the U.S. mainland, tel 800/367-5320.
From Oahu, tel 808/838-1555
All reservations are made on Oahu. From other Islands, tel 800/882-8810.

BY CAR

Roads in Hawaii are well maintained and well marked. Freeways are part of the U.S. interstate network even though they connect with no other state. There are no toll roads. Rural roads are sometimes little more than one lane or have one-lane bridges. Although highways are numbered, Islanders will usually direct you by the name of the road. Directions are rarely given by the points of the compass. You will be directed *mauka* (toward the uplands) or *makai* (toward the sea). It's difficult to get lost. Places of major tourist or historical interest are marked with the distinctive Hawaii Visitors and Convention Bureau sign featuring a warrior in a red cape.

RENTING A CAR
All major rental-car agencies operate in Hawaii. Rates are among the most reasonable in the country. Airlines and hotels often have fly-drive or room-and-car deals. Inquire when making reservations. It is best to reserve beforehand, as car companies are sometimes sold out, particularly on holiday weekends, when Islanders travel. To rent a car you must be 25 years of age and have a valid driver's license and credit card. There are rental car desks at airports and many hotels.

MOTORING REGULATIONS
All passengers must wear a seatbelt. Children aged four and under must ride in a carseat. These are available by

reservation from the car rental agencies at an additional charge. Pedestrians always have the right of way, even if they are not in a crosswalk.

Speed limits: highways, 55 m.p.h. city streets, 25 m.p.h.

Traffic lights: Most places don't have them. In the larger cities and towns, the green light can get lost in exuberant foliage so be especially alert.

You may turn right on a red light from the right lane providing you come to a full and complete stop, except if there is a sign specifically forbidding such a maneuver.

Drivers in Hawaii are generally courteous in the extreme. It is considered rude to block intersections or not allow a merging car to get in front of you. It is customary to wave a thank-you for traffic courtesies. All distances on signposts are shown in miles.

Gasoline is sold by the gallon. One U.S. gallon equals 3.8 liters. 1.2 U.S. gallons equals 1 Imperial gallon.

BREAKDOWN
Contact your rental car agency. Accidents see p. 241

PARKING
Street parking is available, however check signs for tow-away times, which are usually during rush hour and strictly enforced. Parking in Waikiki and downtown Honolulu can be very expensive. Restaurants will usually validate. Some hotels on all islands charge guests a per diem for parking. Inquire when reserving your accommodations.

TRANSPORTATION IN WAIKIKI & HONOLULU

Taxis do not cruise for fares. Usually they must be called by telephone. Charley's (tel 808/531-1333) and Sida (tel 808/836-0011) are the two biggest taxi companies. Your hotel bell desk or concierge will call a cab for you. There are

extra charges for luggage. You are not allowed on city buses with luggage. TheBus routes traverse the island. You can make a circle of the island on one fare if you do not leave the bus. It's the cheapest circum-island tour.

PRACTICAL ADVICE

COMMUNICATIONS

POST OFFICES
As a state, Hawaii uses the U.S. postal service and the same rates apply as on the U.S. mainland. All first-class mail leaves Hawaii by air. Airport Post Office, 3600 Aolele Street, tel 800/275-8777; Waikiki Post Office, 330 Saratoga Road, tel 800/275-8777. Most hotels will take care of your mail for you.

TELEPHONES
The area code for all Hawaii is 808. The international country code is 1. Underwater fiber-optic cables connect Hawaii to Asia and the U.S. with excellent service and quality. Most long-distance calls can be dialed directly from any phone; however, hotels often attach high charges to outgoing in-room calls. To dial inter-island, dial 1 plus 808 plus number; for the continental U.S. or Canada, dial 1 plus area code, plus the number. For international calls dial 011, followed by the country code, city code, and the phone number. Directory assistance for the same island is 1 plus 411; inter-island is 1 plus 808/555-1212; Mainland is 1 plus area code plus 555-1212.

ELECTRICITY

is standard U.S. 110–120 volts, 60 cycles AC. Large hotels have voltage and plug converters, and often provide hair dryers and irons.

ETIQUETTE & LOCAL CUSTOMS

Aloha is said as hello or goodbye. Thank you is *mahalo*. People usually greet each other with a hug and a kiss. If you are given a lei, it will be slipped over your head and about your shoulders with part of the lei hanging in back. It will usually be bestowed with a kiss. You will see people waving a closed fist with the pinky and thumb extended. This is the "shaka," and means everything's "cool." When visiting someone's home or a hula school it is the custom to leave your shoes outside the door. It is a mark of affectionate respect to call an older person "auntie," or "uncle." Do not pat a child on the head as the head is sacred. Friday is "Aloha Friday," and the wearing of colorful Hawaiian clothing is encouraged. Many restaurants set the table with chopsticks. Most will provide forks upon request. When visiting rural towns, be discreet when taking photographs. At sacred sites, such as temple ruins, do not climb on stone walls or platforms. Also, leave no offerings, as you do not know what might give offense.

HOLIDAYS

U. S. holidays are generally observed. All government offices are closed New Year's Day, January 1; Martin Luther King, Jr. Day, third Monday in January; Presidents' Day, third Monday in February; Memorial Day, last Monday in May; Fourth of July; Labor Day, first Monday of September; Discoverers' Day (honoring both Christopher Columbus and the Polynesian discoverers of Hawaii), second Monday in October; Veterans' Day, November 11; Thanksgiving, fourth Thursday in November; and Christmas, December 25. Hawaii holidays, when state and county offices are closed, are often celebrated with great enthusiasm. Kuhio Day, March

PRACTICAL ADVICE

26, honors Prince Jonah Kuhio Kalanianaole, Hawaii's first delegate to the U.S. Congress; Kamehameha Day, June 11, celebrates the life of the warrior king who united the Hawaiian Islands, and Admissions Day, the third Friday in August, marks the admittance of Hawaii as the 50th state of the U. S., August 21, 1959.

MEDIA

NEWSPAPERS

There are two English-language newspapers with statewide circulation, the morning *Honolulu Advertiser* and the afternoon *Honolulu Star Bulletin*. The *Hawaii-Hochi* is published on Oahu in English-Japanese. Neighbor Island newspapers are the *Hawaii Tribune Herald* and *West Hawaii Today* on the Big Island, the *Maui News* on Maui, and the *Kauai Times* and *Garden Island* on Kauai. The Catholic diocese of Honolulu publishes the *Hawaii Catholic Herald*. There are a wide variety of free tourist publications with maps, discount coupons, and good information available at airports, hotel lobbies, and street kiosks.

TV CHANNELS

Hawaii receives a broad range of American network and cable channels. There are ethnic stations and Hawaii Public Broadcasting Station (PBS). Channel numbers vary from island to island. Most hotels offer cable TV viewing.

RADIO

The most popular morning drive-time show features Frank B. Shaner and Brickwood Galluteria on KINE (105 FM). They take you on a romp of lively banter, serial skits, and good Hawaiian music, along with news, weather, and traffic updates. KINE offers Hawaiian music throughout the day. Hawaiian mixed with rock and reggae, sometimes called "Jawaiian" pops up on KCCN AM 1420. For contemporary

hits spliced with surf reports, it's KIKI/HOT 1 on 94 FM; KQMQ AM 690 or FM 93.1; 97.5 The Edge; or 97.5 KPOI. Public radio stations on Oahu are KIFO AM 1380 for news, KIPO FM 89.3 for news, jazz, international, and classical; KHPR FM 88.1, classical, news, discussion. Maui's public radio is KKUA FM 90.7.

MONEY MATTERS

The currency is the U.S. dollar. Some stores in Waikiki and major Oahu malls accept Japanese yen. Currency can be exchanged in most banks. There are currency services at Honolulu International Airport. No other airports in Hawaii have currency services. In Waikiki you may exchange currency at banks and at larger hotels, if you are a guest. Traveler's checks in U.S. denominations are widely accepted, but you must have a picture identification, such as driver's license.
Most major shopping malls and banks have ATMs for bank cards and international credit cards. They are typically accessible 24 hours a day.
Credit cards are widely used. Visa and MasterCard are the most common.

OPENING TIMES

Office hours are generally 8 a.m. to 4 p.m.
Banks: 8 a.m. to 3 p.m.
Post Office: 8 a.m. to 4:30 p.m.
Stores: 9:30 a.m. to 9 p.m.
Grocery stores: many 24 hours
Gas stations: 7 a.m. to 6 p.m.
Museums: 9 a.m. to 3 p.m. See individual listings.

SENIOR CITIZENS

Public transportation, many attractions, and most movie theaters have senior citizen discounts. Ask about senior discounts when booking your hotel, not at the time of paying the bill.

TIME DIFFERENCES

Hawaii is east of the International Dateline at Hawaiian Standard Time and never uses daylight-saving time. It uses the 12-hour, not the 24-hour, clock. Hawaii is:
—two hours behind Pacific Standard Time (PST);
—four hours behind Central Standard Time (CST);
—five hours behind Eastern Standard Time (EST);
—ten hours behind GMT.
During daylight-saving time on the mainland, Hawaii is three hours behind PST, six hours behind EST, and so on.
For the correct local time, tel 808/983-3211.

TIPPING

Tipping is expected in Hawaii. In fact, many people rely on tips for survival. Tip airport porters $1 per bag; the same for hotel bellhops. Tip taxi drivers 15 percent of the fare, more if they handle baggage. Tip valet parkers $2 above any parking fee. Tip 15 to 20 percent in a fine restaurant. Tip room maids $1 to $2 per night. Tip hairdressers and barbers 15 to 20 percent. Tipping doormen, theater ushers, and gas station attendants is not expected.

TOILETS

Stores and restaurants are required to have restrooms available to customers, including wheelchair clients. In addition, most malls and beach parks have restrooms. Usually picture signs designate men or women. Hawaiian is widely used: *kane* (men), *wahine* (women).

TOURIST OFFICES

Hawaii Visitors and Convention Bureau Offices:
2270 Kalakaua Ave., Suite 801
Honolulu, Hawaii 96815
Tel 808/923-1811
Tel 800/GO-HAWAII

1260 Hornby St., Suite 104
Vancouver, British Columbia
V6Z 1W2, Canada
Tel 604/669-6691

c/o American Venture Marketing
Herderstrasse 6–8
Neu-Isenburg, Germany 63263
Tel 49-6102-722410

P. O. Box 208
Sunbury, Middlesex TW16 5RJ
United Kingdom
Tel 020/8941-4009

TRAVELERS WITH DISABILITIES

The Aloha State is accessible.
Most hotels are equipped with
wheelchair-configured rooms;
most intersections have ramped
curbs. The Hawaii Center for
Independent Living (414 Kauwili
Street, Suite 102, Honolulu, HI
96817; tel 808/522-5400) will
provide you with further
information. For $15 they have a
book, Aloha Guide to Accessibility.
Check their website at
www.hawaii.gov/health/cpd.
E-MAIL: cpdppp@aloha.net.
A limited number of hand-
controlled rental cars are
available from Avis (tel 800/331-
1212) and Hertz (tel 800/654-
3131). Handicapped parking
placards from other states are
recognized. A recent court
decision has ruled that seeing-
eye dogs can now enter Hawaii
without the usual quarantine
requirements. Documentation
must be presented that the
dog has been vaccinated against
rabies and that it is a trained
seeing-eye dog. For further
information contact the Animal
Quarantine Station, tel 808/483-
7171 or www.hawaii.gov. For
further information on planning
your trip from start to finish,
check your Internet browser
for www.access-able.com.

EMERGENCIES

Call 911 to summon police,
report a fire, or call an
ambulance. Because of liability

concerns in a litigious society, it
is best to summon police to the
scene of a traffic accident.
Most hotels have a physician
on call.

CONSULATES

Australia, tel 808/524-5050
Japan, tel 808/543-3111
New Zealand, tel 808/547-5117
UK citizens should refer to
their consulate in Los Angeles,
tel 310/477-3322, or, in an
emergency, to the Australian
consulate.
For others, consult the local
telephone directory.

LOST PROPERTY

If you think you have lost
something in a taxi, store, or
restaurant, notify the establishment. TheBus Lost and Found,
tel 808/848-4444. Report stolen
property to police (tel 911).
Keep a copy of the police report
for your insurance claim. Report
lost passports to your nearest
consulate or embassy. Lost
credit cards should be reported
immediately to police and to the
credit card company.
American Express, tel 800/528-
4800
Diners Club, tel 800/234-6377
MasterCard, tel 800/826-2181
Visa, tel 800/336-8472

HEALTH AND SAFETY

For serious injuries, tel 911.
Hawaii has one of the lowest
crime rates in the U.S., but crime
exists, particularly in Waikiki and
in the parking lots of tourist
attractions. Be as cautious and
prudent as you would be
anywhere. Never leave valuables
in your car, even for a minute
while you take a photograph.
Water safety When surf is up,
do not walk close to the water's
edge, whether on a beach or
rocky ledge. Rogue waves
commonly sweep people out
to sea. Obey all signs warning
of surf conditions and riptides.

Do not swim in the ocean at
sunrise, sunset, night, or when
the water is murky: These are
the times sharks may come
close to shore. They are also
attracted by blood. Do not dive
into streams, mountain pools, or
the ocean: Hidden rocks may be
just below the surface. Many
streams on Oahu are
contaminated with leptospirosis.
Never drink the water in
freshwater streams and pools.
Land safety There are no
poisonous snakes or insects
whose bite is fatal. When hiking,
stay on marked trails as volcanic
soil can be unstable. Never hike
alone. Always take water. Notify
someone of your plans and
when you expect to return.
Bring a cell phone, if you have
one. If you get lost, stay put until
help arrives. Obey all posted trail
safety rules, and never embark
on a trail that is closed.
Tanning Remember you are
close to the equator, and the
sun's rays are stronger. A fair-
skinned person can burn in ten
minutes without sunscreen.
Dermatologists advise applying
sunscreen as soon as you
shower in the morning. Reapply
every two hours and after
swimming. Also wear a hat and
sunglasses. Many people get
sunburned while snorkeling.
Smoking It is against the law to
smoke in public buildings, such as
airports, retail stores, theaters,
banks, government offices, and
hospitals. Most hotels have
nonsmoking rooms, in fact, many
smaller hotels prohibit smoking
completely. Restaurants offer
nonsmoking seating.

HOTELS & RESTAURANTS

Excellent resorts, hotels, vacation condominiums, and bed-and-breakfast stays can be found all over Hawaii. Many of the world's leading hotel chains have Hawaii properties. Dining opportunities are multiethnic, varied in setting, and unusually good in overall quality of cuisine. Most restaurants are largely smoke-free but will have smoking sections.

HOTELS

Most establishments have designated nonsmoking rooms. If a property has a good restaurant, the restaurant symbol will be indicated in the listing even though the restaurant may not be reviewed separately. All hotels provide parking (many charge a per diem), and have air-conditioning unless otherwise noted. All swimming pools are outdoors.

Keep in mind that all beaches in Hawaii are public, so if you choose less expensive off-beach accommodations, you can plunk down on the sand right in front of the poshest hotel.

Major credit cards are accepted at hotels, except where noted.

A sales and room tax of 11.41 percent will be added to your bill. When reserving, ask about possible room and car packages, family plans, or special interest packages such as golf or honeymoon deals.

Packages

Airlines often package flights with rooms and cars. Try:
American Airlines (tel 800/321-2121, www.im.aa.com);
Continental (tel 800/634-5555, www.coolvacations.com);
Delta (tel 800/872-7786, www.leisureweb.com);
United (tel 800/328-6877, www.unitedvacations.com).

Two packagers with excellent records for securing well-priced hotels and custom tours designed to suit your interests are:
American Express (tel 800/AXP-6898, www.americanexpress.com/travel);
Pleasant Hawaiian Holidays (tel 800/448-3333, www.2hawaii.com).

Bed & Breakfasts

B&Bs provide a wonderful opportunity to meet local people, and stay in a real neighborhood rather than a resort enclave. The following agencies have multi-island listings:
Bed & Breakfast Hawaii (P.O. Box 449, Kapaa, HI 96746; tel 800/733-1632; fax 808/822-2723);
Hawaii's Best Bed & Breakfast (P.O. Box 563 Kamuela, HI 96743; tel 800/262-9912; fax 808/885-0559; www.bestbnb.com).

Multi-island hotel chains

Aston (tel 800/92-ASTON, fax 808/922-8785, www.astonhotels.com) has a reputation for comfort and style in a broad range of prices. They count a number of lovely holiday condominiums in their portfolio. Package deals are a specialty.
Marc Resorts Hawaii (tel 800/535-0085, fax 800/633-5085, www.marcresorts.com) specializes in distinctive affordable accommodations and discounted packages on every island but Lanai.
Outrigger (tel 800/OUTRIGGER, fax 800/622-4852, www.outrigger.com) can be counted on for good rates and, as a regular customer said, "the kind of rooms I'd be happy to book my mother into." Outrigger is adding upscale properties to their chain so be sure and specify budget expectations.
Prince Hotels (tel 800/321-6248, fax 808/946-0811), with prime properties on Oahu, Maui, and the Big Island, are noted for quiet luxury and fine dining.
Sheraton (tel 800/325-3535, www.sheratonhawaii.com) has hotels on Oahu, Kauai, and Maui.

PRICES

HOTELS

An indication of the cost of a double room without breakfast is given by $ signs.

$$$$$	Over $280
$$$$	$200–$280
$$$	$120–$200
$$	$80–$120
$	Under $80

RESTAURANTS

An indication of the cost of a three-course dinner without drinks is given by $ signs.

$$$$$	Over $80
$$$$	$50–$80
$$$	$35–$50
$$	$20–$35
$	Under $20

ORGANIZATION & ABBREVIATIONS

All sites are listed first by price, then in alphabetical order, with hotels preceding restaurants.

The abbreviations used are:
L = lunch   D = dinner

AE = American Express; DC = Diner's Club; MC = MasterCard; V = Visa

OAHU

HONOLULU

SOMETHING SPECIAL

🏨 KAHALA MANDARIN 🍴 ORIENTAL, HAWAII

Quiet elegance in Oahu's most exclusive neighborhood, Kahala, five minutes from Waikiki. Dolphin lagoon, canopy beds. Two excellent restaurants, indoor-outdoor Plumeria Beach Café and Hoku's for fine dining.
$$$$$
5000 KAHALA AVE., HONOLULU 96816
TEL 800/367-2525, 808/739-8888
FAX 808/739-8800
www.mandarinoriental.com
🛏 364 🅿 🇻

⊞ MANOA VALLEY INN
$$
2001 VANCOUVER DR.
HONOLULU 96822
TEL 800/535-0085 OR
808/947-6019
FAX 800/633-5085
www.manoavalleyinn.com
Tucked amid the big trees
and gracious old houses of
Manoa, this inn, once a private
residence, is on the National
Register of Historic Places. Each
room has its own period decor.
Includes continental breakfast.
⬧ 8 units (3 with shared
bath)

🍴 CHEF MAVRO
French/Hawaii Regional Cuisine
Famed French chef George
Mavrothalassitis pairs fine
wines with courses in three prix-
fixe menus, changed monthly. One
of Chef Mavro's classics: *onaga*
(snapper) baked in Hawaiian alae
salt crust with a delicate sauce and
ogo (a sea vegetable), paired with
Marcel Deiss Pinot Blanc Alsace
1997. A la carte menu also.
$$$$
1969 S. KING ST.
TEL 808/944-4714
⬧ 68 🅿 valet 🕐 Closed L
⬥ All major cards

🍴 ALAN WONG'S RESTAURANT
$$$
1857 S. KING ST.
TEL 808/949-2526
Hawaii Regional Cuisine
Master chef Alan Wong
proves no fat doesn't mean
no flavor. Dishes are so
perfectly prepared, infused
with herbs and spices, you
won't miss the salt or
pepper shakers. Try grilled
lamb chops with coconut
macadamia nut crust or
pan-roasted salmon in
soy balsamic sauce with
Japanese eggplant.
⬧ 100 🕐 Closed L
🅿 Valet
⬥ All major cards

🍴 SAM CHOY'S DIAMOND HEAD RESTAURANT
$$$
449 KAPAHULU AVE.
TEL 808/732-8645
Hawaii Regional Cuisine
"Never trust a skinny chef," is
Choy's motto, and "never exit
a skinny customer" may be his
goal. Mammoth dinners are a
trademark—entrées come
with soup and salad.
Amazingly, the quality is there,
too. Creative choices:
wontons stuffed with Brie,
duck with Kau orange sauce.
Brunch served on Sunday.
⬧ 180 🅿 Valet
🕐 Closed L ⬥ AE, MC, V

🍴 L'URAKU
$$$
1341 KAPIOLANI BLVD.
TEL 808/955-0552
Euro-Japanese Cuisine
The chef trained in the
traditional imperial court
cuisine of Japan. He combines
this with Hawaii's tropical
bounty and European culinary
techniques. Try beautifully
presented almond crusted
snapper. Bright, modern decor.
⬧ 90 🅿 ⬥ AE, MC, V

🍴 DON HO'S ISLAND GRILL
$$
1 ALOHA TOWER DR.,
SUITE 193
TEL 808/528-0807
Local food
It's so tropical tacky it's great.
Food is retro-Polynesian:
coconut-crusted shrimp, Maui
onion rings with mango
ketchup, teriyaki beef kabobs.
Also look for fresh fish, steak,
pizza, local dishes such as tofu
with ginger sauce. Best of all is
the Hawaiian music. Stars and
hula dancers drop in—and
often the old smoothie, Don
Ho himself.
⬧ 200 indoors, 50 outdoors
🅿 ⬥ All major cards

🍴 INDIGO
$$
1121 NUUANU AVE.

TEL 808/521-2900
www.indigo-hawaii.com
Eurasian
Make a meal of appetizers
such as lemongrass chicken
with peanut sauce or wontons
filled with goat cheese, sweet
peppers, and sun-dried
tomatoes with a fruit sauce.
Try for an outside table in a
Balinese-style garden.
⬧ 87 indoors, plus 55 in
private room, 85 outdoors
🅿 Valet 🕐 Closed L
Sat.–Mon., D Sun.–Mon.
⬥ DC, MC, V

🍴 LEGEND SEAFOOD RESTAURANT
$$
CHINESE CULTURAL PLAZA
100 N. BERETANIA ST.
TEL 808/532-1868
Chinese
At lunch, carts laden with
steaming bamboo baskets of
dim sum dumplings cruise
among the white-linen
dressed tables. Try taro puffs
or vegetable dumplings.
Dinner specializes in Chinese
seafood dishes. Breakfast
served on Sunday.
⬧ 190 🅿 ⬥ All major
cards

🍴 PALOMINO
$$
66 QUEEN ST.
TEL 808/528-2400
Mediterranean
A lively "happening" place
featuring pastas, gourmet
pizza, spit-roasted meats,
risotto, beef tenderloin,
focaccia with garlic spreads, all
perfectly prepared. Finish with
crème brûlée.
⬧ 300 🅿 ⬥ All major
cards

🍴 WILLOWS
$$
901 HAUSTEN ST.
TEL 808/952-9200
Hawaii Regional Cuisine
People wept when the
Willows closed a few years
ago. Now it's back and better
than ever with thatched
pavilions clustered around a

HOTELS & RESTAURANTS

pond and tropical gardens. The buffet format has everything from *laulau* to macadamia nut cream pie. In between are stir-fry dishes, seafood, salads, Korean beef. Fine dining in a separate room at a higher price.

🔲 350 🅿 All major cards

WAIKIKI

SOMETHING SPECIAL

🏨 HALEKULANI 🍴

Elegant, thoroughly modern hotel built around a beautifully restored gracious core, which now serves as the restaurant wing for acclaimed Orchids (see p. 245) and La Mer (see this page). This is the prestige address in Waikiki. Go to Honolulu Symphony, Bishop Museum and Iolani Palace, Contemporary Museum, and Honolulu Academy of Arts for free.

$$$$$
2199 KALIA RD.
HONOLULU 96815
TEL 800/367-2343 OR
808/923-2311
FAX 808/926-8004
www.halekulani.com
ℹ️ 456 🏊 🍸

SOMETHING SPECIAL

🏨 ROYAL HAWAIIAN 🍴 HOTEL

The "Pink Palace" opened in 1927 and has hosted a long list of celebrities. All rooms look as if they could be in a tropical home, but the nicest are in the Historic Wing with its period furnishings. Beachside restaurants, Mai Tai Bar, luau.

$$$$$
2259 KALAKAUA AVE.
HONOLULU 96815
TEL 800/325-3535 OR
808/923-7311
FAX 808/931-7098
www.royalhawaiian.com
ℹ️ 526 units
🏊

🏨 HILTON HAWAIIAN 🍴 VILLAGE

$$$$
2005 KALIA RD.
HONOLULU 96815
TEL 800/HILTONS OR
808/949-4321
FAX 808/947-7898
www.hawaiianvillage.hilton.com

Three towers on 20 acres of landscaping with waterfalls and exotic wildlife. Shopping complex with fast food. Six restaurants including romantic fine dining at Bali by the Sea and opulent Golden Dragon Chinese restaurants (see p. 245). "Superpool" is 10,000 square feet.

ℹ️ 3,000 🏊 3 🍸

🏨 HYATT REGENCY 🍴 WAIKIKI

$$$$
2424 KALAKAUA AVE.
HONOLULU 96815
TEL 808/923-1234
FAX 808/923-7839
www.hyattwaikiki.com

Twin towers rise 40 stories each in the heart of Waikiki, across the street from the beach with ocean views. Rooms are spacious and recently refurbished. Four restaurants (see p. 245) and five cocktail lounges make for a busy entry ambience.

ℹ️ 1,230 units
🏊 🍸

🏨 SHERATON MOANA 🍴 SURFRIDER

$$$$
2365 KALAKAUA AVE.
HONOLULU 96815
TEL 800/325-3535 OR
808/921-4640
FAX 808/923-0308
www.moanasurfrider.com

Oldest hotel in Waikiki is in mint condition and on the National Register of Historic Places. Victorian splendor amid the new high rises. Ask for a room in the old section where the wallpaper is floral and the armoires huge. Restaurant on the beach.

ℹ️ 793 units 🏊

🏨 ILIMA 🍴 $$$

445 NOHONANI ST.
HONOLULU 96815
TEL 808/367-5172 OR
808/923-1877
www.ilima.com

Tasteful rooms are large with kitchenette, bed, and sleep-sofa. Staff is friendly and helpful. Walk to beach.

ℹ️ 99 units 🅿 limited 🏊 🍸

🏨 NEW OTANI KAIMANA 🍴 BEACH HOTEL $$$

2863 KALAKAUA AVE.
HONOLULU 96815
TEL 800/356-8264 OR
808/923-1555
FAX 808/922-9404
www.kaimana.com

On an uncrowded stretch of sand at the foot of Diamond Head on the quiet end of Waikiki. Slip into a crisp cotton robe and enjoy Japanese tea service. Hau Tree Lanai (see p. 245) is one of the few beachside restaurants in Waikiki.

ℹ️ 124 units 🍸

🏨 ROYAL GARDEN 🍴 AT WAIKIKI $$$

440 OLOHANA ST.
HONOLULU 96815
TEL 800/367-5666 OR
808/943-0202
FAX 808/945-7407
www.royalgardens.com

A gem for the money, with impressive, marble lobby and romantic, stylish rooms. Continental breakfast included. Notable Japanese restaurant, Shizu. Walk to beach.

ℹ️ 205 units 🏊 🍸

SOMETHING SPECIAL

🍴 LA MER
French

Elegant, expensive, and epicurean. Hawaii's only 5-diamond restaurant. Look for *kumu* (goatfish) in a rosemary-salt crust. Desserts? Don't even make a

HOTELS & RESTAURANTS

choice—get the symphony, which has samplings of four desserts. A la carte and masterfully orchestrated prix-fixe dinners. Jacket or long-sleeved, collared shirt required.

$$$$$
HALEKULANI HOTEL
2199 KALIA RD.
TEL 808/923-2311
⚑ 100 🅿 🕐 Closed L
🕲 All major cards

SOMETHING SPECIAL

🍴 BALI BY THE SEA
Continental/Hawaii Regional
Romance, ocean views, and superb cuisine are hard to find in one place, but Bali does it with panache. Rack of lamb crusted with macadamia nuts is always perfectly done. Duck comes glazed with currants and litchi. Desserts caused the American pastry chef to be decorated by the French government.

$$$$
HILTON HAWAIIAN VILLAGE
2005 KALIA RD.
TEL 808/941-2254
⚑ 130 🅿 🕐 Closed L
🕲 All major cards

🍴 ORCHIDS
$$$$
HALEKULANI HOTEL
2199 KALIA RD.
TEL 808/923-2311
Contemporary Seafood Cuisine
Festive seaside dining with views of Diamond Head and banks of orchids. Mustard-herb crusted rack of lamb is an excellent choice.
⚑ 97 indoors, 88 outdoors
🅿 🕲 All major cards

🍴 PRINCE COURT
$$$$
HAWAII PRINCE HOTEL
100 HOLOMOANA ST.
TEL 808/956-1111
Hawaii Regional Cuisine
It's hard to find a seat on weekends when locals come for the sumptuous buffets. Sunday brunch is a legend. Look for the most delicate dim sum, among 50 dishes.

Or order from the gourmet seasonal menu. Big windows look out on Ala Wai Harbor.
⚑ 180 🅿
🕲 All major cards

SOMETHING SPECIAL

🍴 GOLDEN DRAGON
Chinese
An opulent ebony and scarlet Asian setting open to sea breezes. Specialty: Imperial Beggar's Chicken—comes with mallet to break the clay pot. Have your fortune read by the tea lady.
$$$
HILTON HAWAIIAN VILLAGE
2005 KALIA RD.
TEL 808/946-5336
⚑ 136 indoors, 54 outdoors
🅿 🕐 Closed L & all Mon.
🕲 All major cards

🍴 HAU TREE LANAI
$$$
NEW OTANI KAIMANA BEACH HOTEL
2863 KALAKAUA AVE.
TEL 808/921-7066
Hawaii Regional Cuisine
From breakfast onward, this beachside terrace is a winner. Begin with eggs Benedict, scones, poi pancakes, and Belgian waffles. A sunset supper is ultra-romantic with torches. Opakapaka (pink snapper) steamed with Chinese vegetables in a ginger cilantro glaze is a good choice.
⚑ 165 outdoors 🅿
🕲 All major cards

🍴 HY'S STEAK HOUSE
$$$
2440 KUHIO AVE.
TEL 808/922-5555
American
Ever wonder where the beef Wellington and chateaubriand went? Hy's has them. Also waiters in tuxes, and showy flames. Relax.
⚑ 220 🅿 valet
🕐 Closed L
🕲 All major cards

🍴 KACHO
$$$
WAIKIKI PARC HOTEL
2233 HELUMOA RD.
TEL 808/924-3535
Japanese
Kaiseki, the court cuisine of imperial Japan, is served in exquisite presentations that might include chilled crab in a slightly sweet sauce, or a basket of shrimp, pumpkin, and green bean tempura. Steak is a good choice, served with a clear dipping sauce composed of soy, musk lime, chili, radish, and plum. Beautiful traditional Japanese breakfast.
⚑ 28 plus 14 at sushi bar
🅿 🕲 All major cards

🍴 ROY'S
$$$
6600 KALANIANAOLE HWY.
TEL 808/396-7697
Hawaii Regional Cuisine
Twenty minutes from Waikiki in Hawaii Kai. Roy's has become a foodie shrine, but lacks all reverence. The place is full of clatter and chatter. The menu changes nightly but you can count on the famous crab cakes and at least half a dozen freshest seafood entrées—maybe blackened ahi (tuna) with a light piquant soy-mustard sauce.
⚑ 200 indoors, 50 outdoors
🅿 🕐 Closed L 🕲 All major cards

🍴 CIAO MEIN
$$
HYATT REGENCY WAIKIKI
2424 KALAKAUA AVE.
TEL 808/923-2426
Chinese/Italian
Considering that Marco Polo brought proto-spaghetti home from China, the marriage of these two great cuisines is a natural. You can have wok-seared Szechwan eggplant and roast duck cannelloni in one evening. Meals are served family style so the varied tastes are spread around.
⚑ 200 🅿 🕐 Closed L
🕲 All major cards

🆂 Air-conditioning 🅿 Outdoor swimming pool 🎽 Health club 🕲 Credit cards   **KEY**

HOTELS & RESTAURANTS

DUKE'S CANOE CLUB
$$
OUTRIGGER WAIKIKI
2335 KALAKAUA AVE.
TEL 808/922-2268
American
On the beach, thatched umbrellas, Hawaiian music, drop-dead sunsets, steaks, great ribs, seafood, and well-stocked salad bar, including a made-for-you Caesar stand. What more can you want of Waikiki? Breakfast is served. Memorabilia of surfer legend and Olympic swim champ Duke Kahanamoku abound.
🏠 350 indoors, 150 outdoors 🅿 at Outrigger East 💳 All major cards

KEO'S WAIKIKI
$$
AMBASSADOR HOTEL
2028 KUHIO AVE.
TEL 808/951-9355
Thai
Keo's introduced Thai food to Hawaii, among banks of orchids, small starry lights, and Siam art treasures. Indulge in Evil Jungle Prince sauced with coconut and basil, delectable curries, eggplant with peanut sauce. Exceptional desserts—pumpkin filled with light custard. Breakfast too.
🏠 260 🅿 💳 All major cards

KYO-YA
$$
2057 KALAKAUA AVE.
TEL 808/947-3911
Japanese
It's the most beautiful Japanese restaurant in the state. Delicate Kyoto-style cuisine is served in porcelain and lacquer dishes. Try lightest tempura or tender *misoyaki* butterfish.
🏠 76, 170 upstairs (Tatami-style seating) 🅿
🕐 Closed L Sun. 💳 All major cards

PARC CAFÉ
$$
WAIKIKI PARC HOTEL
2233 HELUMOA RD.

TEL 808/931-6643
Themed Gourmet Buffets
These are no ordinary buffets—the food is actually gourmet and prepared around a theme, such as Hawaiian buffet including *laulau*, and taro au gratin. The array of side dishes and salads makes it hard to get to the prime ribs. Classic coconut cake is the star of the dessert station.
🏠 130 🅿 💳 All major cards

WINDWARD OAHU

SCHRADER'S WINDWARD MARINE RESORT
$-$$$$$
47-039 LIHIKAI DR.
KANEOHE 96744
TEL 808/239-5711 OR
800/735-5711
FAX 808/239-6658
www.hawaiiscene.com/schrader
It's a stretch to call this rural motel a resort. Situated on beautiful Kaneohe Bay, close to water sports. Price depends on size of cottage and proximity to the water.
🛏 20 units, full kitchens or kitchenettes 🍽

PAT'S KAILUA BEACH PROPERTIES
$
204 S. KALAHEO AVE.
KAILUA 96734
TEL 808/261-1653
FAX 808/261-0893
www.patskailua.com
Agency has fully furnished home rentals and B&B stays on and near Oahu's most beautiful beach, Kailua Beach.
🛏 39 units

BUZZ'S STEAK HOUSE
$$
413 KAWAILOA RD.
KAILUA 96734
TEL 808/261-4661
American
Rickety, casual place across from Kailua Beach. President Clinton dined here, and they're proud enough to have

PRICES

HOTELS
An indication of the cost of a double room without breakfast is given by $ signs.
$$$$$ Over $280
$$$$ $200–$280
$$$ $120–$200
$$ $80–$120
$ Under $80

RESTAURANTS
An indication of the cost of a three-course dinner without drinks is given by $ signs.
$$$$$ Over $80
$$$$ $50–$80
$$$ $35–$50
$$ $20–$35
$ Under $20

a plaque marking the table. Steaks, seafood, salad bar.
🏠 120 🅿 💳 No credit cards

PUNALUU RESTAURANT
$
53-146 KAMEHAMEHA HWY.
PUNALUU 96730
TEL 808/237-8474
American/Local food
Fresh-caught local fish impeccably cooked is a highlight. The bar is big on, surprise, herbal teas and kava. Good vegetarian dishes. Hawaiian plate with *laulau* on weekends, along with Hawaiian music.
🏠 100 indoors, 30 outdoors
🕐 Closed L, D Sun. 💳 DC, MC, V

NORTH SHORE

TURTLE BAY RESORTS
$$$$$
57-091 KAMEHAMEHA HWY.
KAHUKU 96731
TEL 800/203-3650 OR
808/293-8811
FAX 808/293-1286
www.turtlebayresorts.com
A recreational resort offering golf, tennis, horseback riding, water sports, and a children's

program. Safest swimming beach on the North Shore on one side of the peninsula; raging surf on the other in winter.

(i) 443 units 🏋

⊓ JAMESON'S BY THE SEA
$–$$$
62-540 KAMEHAMEHA HWY.
HALEIWA
TEL 808/637-4336
American
Beer is a specialty at this seaview place—from Ireland's Guinness stout to a non-alcoholic German beer. Dine on soups, burgers, appetizers such as Thai summer rolls or salmon pâté, and entrées including mango-grilled shrimp. The Fudge Works counter tempts with chocolate coconut macadamia fudge.

⬚ 80 indoors, 55 outdoors
🅿 🕐 Closed upstairs L & Mon.–Tues. D 🗠 All major cards

⊓ CHOLOS HOME STYLE MEXICAN II
$
NORTH SHORE MARKETPLACE
66-250 KAMEHAMEHA HWY.
HALEIWA
TEL 808/637-3059
Mexican Cuisine
They make their own salsa, the music is loud, tacky Mexican artifacts abound, the cooking is authentic, and the food is good and cheap. The fish taco plate uses fresh local seafood, and the vegetarian dishes such as spinach quesadilla are memorable. Seating is indoors and out—if you can get a seat. Surfers love the place. Breakfast, lunch, and dinner.

⬚ 52 indoors, 22 outdoors
🗠 No credit cards

WAIANAE COAST

⊞ JW MARRIOTT IHILANI
⊓ RESORT & SPA AT KO OLINA
$$$$$
92-1001 OLANI ST.
KAPOLEI 96707
TEL 800/626-4446 OR

808/679-0079
FAX: 808/679-0080
www.ihilani.com
Set in the manicured Ko Olina Resort, with sandy coves for swimming, Ihilani is like being on a neighbor island, but with Waikiki only 35 minutes away. Rooms are luxurious, with large lanai. The spa is state-of-the-pamper with thalassic and hydro therapies plus some unique Hawaiian treatments.

(i) 387 units 🌊 🏋

MAUI

WEST MAUI

⊞ HYATT REGENCY
⊓ MAUI
$$$$$
200 NOHEA KAI DR.
LAHAINA 96761
TEL 800/223-1234 OR
808/661-1234
FAX 808/667-4498
www.maui.hyatt.com
A fantasy beach resort built in the 1980s in 40 acres with gardens, waterfalls, and pool. The restaurants are known for ambience as well as food.

(i) 806 units 🌊 🏋

SOMETHING SPECIAL

⊞ RITZ-CARLTON
⊓ KAPALUA
Quiet good taste and tropical style permeate every aspect of this elegant hotel. The food is noteworthy (see p. 248), the beach is one of the best on Maui, and the hotel is committed to sharing the Hawaiian culture in a variety of programs. Three championship golf courses rise into the hills behind.
$$$$$
ONE RITZ-CARLTON DR.
KAPALUA 96761
TEL 800/262-8440 OR
808/669-6200
FAX 808/669-1566
www.ritzcarlton.com
(i) 548 units
🌊 🏋

⊞ THE WESTIN MAUI
⊓ $$$$$
2365 KAANAPALI PKWY.
LAHAINA 96761
TEL 800/WESTIN-1 OR
808/667-2525
FAX 808/661-5764
www.westinmaui.com
Two 11-story towers preside over an aquatic fantasyland. The beachside swimming pool is scalloped in heated pools, and accented with a high water slide, waterfalls, and swim-up grottoes.

(i) 761 units 🌊 🏋

⊞ NAPILI KAI BEACH
⊓ RESORT
$$$$
5900 LOWER HONOAPIILANI RD.
LAHAINA 96761
TEL 800/367-5030 OR
808/669-6271
FAX 808/669-5740
www.napilikai.com
Traditional, charming low-rise units on 10 acres of lawn tucked in a cove on a beach. Rooms have shoji screens, lanai, cool colors, and rattan furniture. Attracts a loyal following.

(i) 163 units 🅢 Some 🏋

⊞ THE WHALER ON
KAANAPALI BEACH
$$$$
2481 KAANAPALI PKWY.
LAHAINA 96761
TEL 800/367-7052 OR
808/661-4861
FAX 808/661-8315
People return to this well-run holiday condo year after year. Only a third of the units are available for vacation stays. All have kitchens.

(i) 360 units 🌊 🏋

⊞ KAANAPALI
⊓ BEACH HOTEL
$$$
2525 KAANAPALI PKWY.
LAHAINA 96761-1987
TEL 800/262-8450 OR
808/661-0011
FAX 808/667-5978
www.kaanapalibeachhotel.com
Aloha spirit abounds at this

older hotel set among lawns and gardens. Super-friendly staff give lessons in Hawaiian crafts. Rooms sport wicker and rattan furnishings. Rates are lower than the neighbors'.
🛈 430 units ☒

🏨 KAPALUA VILLAS
$$$
500 OFFICE RD.
KAPALUA 96751
TEL 800/545-0018 OR
808/669-8088
FAX 808/669-5234
www.kapaluavillas.com
A less expensive way to stay at exclusive Kapalua Resort. Units are individually decorated. Access to all resort features, shuttle to beach. 2-night minimum.
🛈 266 units ☒ 🈺

SOMETHING SPECIAL

🍴 BAY CLUB
American
On a lava promontory with surf lapping almost at the napery, there's not a more romantic restaurant on the island. Entrées are old faithful Caesar salad tossed tableside, steaks, rack of lamb, duck. Excellent luncheon salads.
$$$
KAPALUA BAY HOTEL
ONE KAPALUA DR.
KAPALUA
TEL 808/669-5656
🔢 130 indoors, 54 outdoors
🅿 ⊗ All major cards

🍴 GERARD'S
$$$
PLANTATION INN
174 LAHAINALUNA RD.
LAHAINA
TEL 808/661-8939
French Cuisine
This is Lahaina's special occasion restaurant, very French in cuisine, formality of service, wine list, and ambience—including Edith Piaf singing softly, passionately in the sound system. Try the perfectly done rack of lamb and finish with pineapple tarte

tatin with ginger ice cream. Dine amid pink linen on the veranda, in the garden, or indoors.
🔢 50 indoors, 50 outdoors
🕐 Closed L ⊗ All major cards

SOMETHING SPECIAL

🍴 HULA GRILL
Hawaii Regional Cuisine
Celebrated chef and regional cuisine pioneer Peter Merriman offers fine dining, practically in the sand. Look for freshest grilled seafood with creative sauces and salsas, ribs steamed in banana leaves or crab/macadamia nut wontons. Finish with a giant ice cream sandwich: lush vanilla between two chocolate-mac nut brownies. Outdoor barefoot area has a lighter menu of burgers and pizza. And what would a place called Hula Grill be without hula? Dancing nightly.
$$$
WHALER'S VILLAGE SHOPPING COMPLEX
2435 KAANAPALI PKWY.
TEL 808/667-6636
🔢 200 indoors, 120 outdoors 🅿 ⊗ All major cards

🍴 THE BANYAN TREE
$$
ONE RITZ-CARLTON DR.
TEL 808/669-1566
Pacific Regional Cuisine
The indoor/outdoor restaurant has a Mediterranean feel, but the menu is definitely Pacific. Try the signature lemon-grass soup and seared *ahi* (tuna).
🔢 63 ⊗ All major cards

🍴 SANSEI RESTAURANT & SUSHI BAR
$$
KAPALUA SHOPS
115 BAY DR.
KAPALUA 96761
TEL 808/669-6286
Hawaii Regional/Japanese
A brilliant blend of cuisines results in delectables such as

shrimp cake in ginger-lime chili butter with cilantro pesto, or a sea vegetable ravioli. People drive from all over Maui for this one. Deep discounts for food ordered before 6 p.m. Late service and entertainment Thursday and Friday, with discounts after 10 p.m.
🔢 120 🅿 🕐 Closed L
⊗ All major cards

🍴 BEACH HOUSE
$
RITZ-CARLTON KAPALUA HOTEL
ONE RITZ-CARLTON DR.
TEL 808/669-6200
American
A great little find, all outdoors on a breezy lanai over the beach. Traditional Caesar salad, a plate with baby back ribs and grilled mahimahi, or Maui onion rings with buttermilk dressing.
🔢 50 🅿 🕐 Closed D
⊗ All major cards

CENTRAL MAUI

🍴 A SAIGON CAFÉ
$$
1792 MAIN ST.
WAILUKU
TEL 808/243-9560
Vietnamese
An excellent place to explore this interesting cuisine, definitely influenced by French. Cooked-at-your-table vegetarian dishes, clay-pot chicken, fresh fish seasoned with lemongrass, ginger, and garlic, and *pho*, the classic Vietnamese soup with a mound of fresh basil.
🔢 65 🅿 ⊗ MC V

🍴 RESTAURANT MATSU
$
161 ALAMAHA ST.
KAHULUI 96732
TEL 808/871-0822
Japanese/Local food
Islanders drive from far points for this low-key eatery with its daily specials, outstanding sushi, steaming noodle dishes, and fresh fish.

⚅ 32 🅿 🕒 Closed Sat.–Sun. D, Sun. L ⚉ No credit cards

EAST MAUI

🏨 FAIRMONT KEA LANI
🍽 MAUI
$$$$$
4100 WAILEA ALANUI
WAILEA 96753
TEL 800/659-4100 OR
808/875-4100
FAX 808/875-2250
www.fairmont.com
Like a Moorish apparition, stark white against blue sky. Decor in this resort may be the most consistently beautiful in the Islands, in tone-on-tone whites and creams. Luxury marble baths. Fine restaurants.
🛈 450 units ⚉ 🟡

🏨 FOUR SEASONS
🍽 RESORT WAILEA
$$$$$
3900 WAILEA ALANUI
WAILEA 96753
TEL 800/334-MAUI OR
808/874-8000
FAX 808/874-2244
www.fourseasons.com
Expect the usual Four Seasons spacious rooms and deluxe marble baths. Almost all have ocean views. Furnishings look like refined Europe married to the tropics. Service is efficient, yet relaxed. Less expected: the warm Hawaiian hospitality and reliably dramatic sunsets. Restaurants are noteworthy (see Spago, p. 250).
🛈 380 units ⚉ 🟡

(see Spago, p. 250).

SOMETHING SPECIAL

🏨 GRAND WAILEA
🍽 RESORT HOTEL & SPA
A rare combination of luxe and looney fun. A $30-million art collection decorates a fantasy playground of aquatic antics—waterfalls, slides, a river pool, water elevator, restaurant in a man-made tide pool, a floating wedding chapel. Toss in Hawaii's grandest spa, fine dining, and a nightclub with laser lights. Children have

their own program—even theater. Rooms are spacious.
$$$$$
3850 WAILEA ALANUI
WAILEA 96753
TEL 800/888-6100 OR
808/875-1234
FAX 808/874-2442
www.grandwailea.com
🛈 780 units ⚉ 🟡

🏨 HOTEL HANA MAUI
🍽 $$$$$
5301 HANA HWY.,
HANA 96713
TEL 800/321-4262 OR
808/248-8211
FAX 808/248-7202
On the edge of a 7,000-acre ranch, the units are charming, older cottages nestled in gardens or newer Sea Ranch Cottages overlooking the ocean. Horseback riding along coast. Picnic lunches. Shuttle to a fine black-sand beach. Pleasant restaurant.
🛈 66 units ⚉ 🟡

🏨 WESTIN MAUI PRINCE,
🍽 MAKENA RESORT
$$$$
5400 MAKENA ALANUI
MAKENA 96753-9986
TEL 800/321-6284 OR
808/874-1111
FAX 808/879-8763
www.princeresortshawaii.com
An incredible setting on the edge of the Maui wilderness. Modern, breezy rooms. Central atrium has a serene Japanese garden and waterfall flowing past exotic flowers. This beach resort is relaxation therapy. Restaurants Hakone (see this page) and Prince Court (see p. 250) are exceptional .
🛈 310 units 🅿 ⚉ 🟡

🏨 SILVER CLOUD
RANCH—UPCOUNTRY
$$$
1373 THOMPSON RD.,
KULA 96790
TEL 800/532-1111 OR
808/878-6101
FAX 808/878-2132
www.silvercloudranch.com
Former working cattle spread

has rooms in the main house, units with kitchenettes in the former bunkhouse, and a garden cottage. Full breakfast. Views are spectacular.
🛈 12 units ⚉ None

SOMETHING SPECIAL

🍽 HAKONE
Japanese
The sushi bar is very popular. Try the "volcano" erupting in red and orange roe. Also exquisitely presented Japanese fare. Sunday sushi buffet, Monday full buffet. *Kaiseki* dinner with 24-hr. notice.
$$$
MAUI PRINCE HOTEL
5400 MAKENA ALANUI
MAKENA RESORT 96753
TEL 808/874-1111
⚅ 98 plus 10 at sushi bar 🅿 ⚉ All major cards

🍽 JOE'S BAR & GRILL
$$$
WAILEA TENNIS CLUB
131 WAILEA IKE PLACE
WAILEA
TEL 808/875-7767
American
Fresh fish or lamb chops are given a gourmet tweak. Signature dish: meatloaf and garlic mashed potatoes.
⚅ 100 🅿 🕒 Closed L ⚉ All major cards

🍽 NICK'S FISH MARKET
MAUI
$$$
KEA LANI HOTEL
4100 WAILEA ALANUI
TEL 808/879-7224
American
Dine under the stars on exquisite seafood, live Maine lobster, steak, or pasta.
⚅ 100 indoors, 75 outdoors: 🅿 🕒 Closed L ⚉ All major cards

🍽 PRINCE COURT
$$$
MAUI PRINCE HOTEL
5400 MAKENA ALANUI
MAKENA RESORT
TEL 808/874-1111

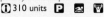

HOTELS & RESTAURANTS

Hawaii Regional Cuisine
A true epicurean experience.
Try medallions of venison and
poha berry compote. Sunday
brunch is served.
🍴 120 📶 🕐 Closed D
Tues.–Wed. & L
🚫 All major cards.

🍴 SPAGO
$$$
FOUR SEASONS HOTEL
3900 WAILEA ALANUI DR.
TEL 808/879-2999
Pacific Rim Cuisine
Try roasted rack of lamb with
ravioli and fennel sauce.
Sophisticated and relaxed,
with original art on the walls.
🍴 56 indoors, 79 outdoors
📶 🕐 Closed L 🚫 All
major cards

SOMETHING SPECIAL
🍴 HALIIMAILE GENERAL STORE
Hawaii Regional Cuisine
Haute cuisine in the canefields.
Modern furnishings, original
art in an old plantation store. Start
with sashimi Napoleon, move on
to Szechwan barbecued salmon, or
a green salad topped with oranges.
$$
900 HALIIMAILE RD.
HALIIMAILE 96768
TEL 808/572-2666
🍴 150 📶 🚫 All major cards

🍴 STELLA BLUES CAFÉ
$$
LONGS CENTER
1215 S. KIHEI RD.
KIHEI
TEL 808/974-3779
American Cuisine
Everything's made from scratch
at breakfast, lunch, and dinner,
starting with banana maca-
damia nut pancakes. Salads,
such as chicken curry, use Maui
greens. The baby back ribs
at dinner are simmered in
mango-plum sauce. The turkey
for sandwiches is roasted in
Stella's oven.
🛏 50 indoors, 32 outdoors
🚫 D, MC, V

BIG ISLAND

KONA-KOHALA COAST

🏨 HAPUNA BEACH 🍴 PRINCE HOTEL
$$$$$
62-100 KAUNAOA DR.
KOHALA COAST 96743
TEL 800/882-6060 OR
808/880-1111
FAX 808/880-3112
www.hiltonwaikoloavillage.com
Vibrant atmosphere, with live
music in the lobby and around
the pool. Pale, modern rooms.
Emphasis on activities.
Outstanding cuisine (see
p. 252, Hakone).
🛏 350 units 🏊 🎾

🏨 HILTON WAIKOLOA 🍴 VILLAGE
$$$$
425 WAIKOLOA BEACH DR.
WAIKOLOA 96738
TEL 800/HILTONS OR
808/886-1234
FAX 808/886-2900
www.hiltonwaikoloavillage.com
Fantasy oceanside resort. Go
to your room by boat or
mini-bullet train. Swim with
dolphins. Rooms in three
towers. Pool with waterfalls,
slides, grottoes. River pool.
(See p. 251, Donatoni's.)
🛏 1240 units 🏊 🎾

SOMETHING SPECIAL
🏨 KONA VILLAGE RESORT
Thatched-roof bungalows with
first-class amenities along the
shore and around lagoons. Rates
include all meals, the Friday luau,
airport transfers, and most
activities. It's like staying in an old
Hawaiian village, in comfort.
$$$$$
QUEEN KAAHUMANU HWY.
KAUPULEHU 96740
TEL 800/367-5290 OR
808/325-5555
FAX 808/325-5124
www.konavillage.com
🛏 125 units 🚫 Non 🏊 🎾

🏨 MAUNA KEA BEACH 🍴 HOTEL
$$$$$
62-100 MAUNA KEA BEACH DR.
KOHALA COAST 96743
TEL 800/882-6060 OR
808/882-7222
FAX 808/880-3112
www.maunakeabeachhotel.com
The grande dame of the luxe-
on-lava hotels. Art treasures
are scattered everywhere.
Some families have been
coming here for two and
three generations. Superb
swimming beach, fine restau-
rants (see Batik, p. 251),
championship golf.
🛏 310 units 🏊 🎾

🏨 MAUNA LANI BAY 🍴 HOTEL & BUNGALOWS
$$$$$
68-1400 MAUNA LANI DR.,
KOHALA COAST, HI 96743
TEL 800/367-2323 OR
808/885-6622
FAX 808/885-1484
www.maunalani.com
Rooms are tropical modern.
Hotel is tucked in a quiet
sandy cove and built around a
network of ancient fishponds.
Outstanding cuisine is a
hallmark. Four ultra-luxe
bungalows at mega-rates offer
utmost privacy.
🛏 350 units 🏊 🎾

🏨 KANALOA AT KONA 🍴 $$$$
78-261 MANUKAI ST.
KAILUA-KONA 96740
TEL 800/688-7444 OR
808/322-9625
FAX 808/322-3818
www.outrigger.com
Spacious, elegant apartments
with koa cabinetry, bathroom
spas, located on Keauhou Bay,
6 miles from Kailua-Kona.
Good restaurant (see p. 252).
🛏 166 units (87 rentals)
🚫 None 🏊

🏨 MAUNA LANI POINT
$$$$
68-1050 MAUNA LANI PT. DR.
KOHALA COAST 96743
TEL 800/642-6284 OR
808/885-5022

PRICES

HOTELS

An indication of the cost of a double room without breakfast is given by $ signs.

$$$$$	Over $280
$$$$	$200–$280
$$$	$120–$200
$$	$80–$120
$	Under $80

RESTAURANTS

An indication of the cost of a three-course dinner without drinks is given by $ signs.

$$$$$	Over $80
$$$$	$50–$80
$$$	$35–$50
$$	$20–$35
$	Under $20

FAX 808/661-1025
www.classicresorts.com
Live in secluded luxury with access to all the amenities of Mauna Lani Resort. Dream kitchen, spacious master bath, designer furnishings, large lanai with spectacular views of the Kona coast.
🛏 116 units (56 rentals) ☑

🏨 WAIKOLOA BEACH
🍴 MARRIOTT–
OUTRIGGER RESORT
$$$$

69-275 WAIKOLOA BEACH DR.
WAIKOLOA 96738-5711
TEL 800/922-5533 OR
808/886-6789
FAX 808/886-7852
www.waikoloabeachmarriott.com
This beachfront hotel boasts \sandstone flooring, off-white tones, and a commitment to keeping it Hawaiian in ambience. Rooms are pale taupe and teal with bamboo accents. Fantasy pool, full Rainforest Spa.
🛏 545 units ☑ 🎽

🏨 KING KAMEHAMEHA'S
🍴 KONA BEACH HOTEL
$$$

75-5660 PALANI RD.
KAILUA-KONA 96740
TEL 800/367-2111 OR

808/329-2911
FAX 808/329-4602
Right in Kailua-Kona town, on the water. Walk to important historical sites, dozens of shops and restaurants. Rooms are nothing fancy but are reliable and clean.
🛏 458 units ☑

🏨 OHANA KEAHOU
🍴 BEACH RESORT
$$

78-6740 ALII DR.
KAILUA-KONA 96740
TEL 877/532-8468 OR
808/322-3441
FAX 808/322-3117
On a site once reserved for royalty, it has tide pools, petroglyphs, and reproduced royal cottage with pond. Next to beautiful black-sand beach. Rooms have rattan furnishings, and are well maintained.
🛏 311 units ☑ 🎽

🍴 BATIK
$$$$

MAUNA KEA BEACH HOTEL
62-100 MAUNA KEA BEACH DR.
TEL 808/882-5810
Continental/Hawaii Regional
Nuances of Asian opulence set the tone; subtle aromas of roasted spices pique the appetite. Rewards are nan bread baked in a tandoori oven, favorite Batik curry, plus new Pacific curries. Less exotic: beef Wellington in phyllo pastry or an excellent rack of lamb. Finish with famous Grand Marnier soufflé.
🛏 125 🅿 🕐 Closed D Tues. & Sat., & all L ☒ All major cards

SOMETHING SPECIAL

🍴 CANOE HOUSE

Hawaii Regional Cuisine

When the setting is as magnificent as this, with stars overhead and the ocean only feet away, it's rare to find cuisine to match, but Canoe House does it. Freshest seafood from local waters are cooked in a variety of ways. Baby back ribs come with a guava

hoisin sauce. For dessert, dare a ling hi mui mousse.
$$$$
MAUNA LANI BAY HOTEL
68-1400 MAUNA LANI DR.
TEL 808/885-6622
🛏 184 indoors, 66 outdoors
🅿 🕐 Closed L ☒ All major cards

🍴 COAST GRILLE
$$$

HAPUNA PRINCE HOTEL
62-100 KAUNAOA DR.
TEL 808/880-1111
American/Hawaii Regional
A lively open-air place specializing in freshest seafood and trendy culinary styles. Try *moi*, the fish raised in aquaculture ponds, cold-water lobster, or oysters from the oyster bar. Taro chips come from Waipio Valley. Ginger crème brûlée is the perfect finish.
🛏 140 indoors, 100 outdoors 🅿 🕐 Closed L ☒ All major cards

SOMETHING SPECIAL

🍴 DONATONI'S

Italian

Cruise from the hotel lobby to the restaurant by yacht. Dine on a terrace with trade winds wafting through the garden, and enjoy Italian fare—fusilli with artichokes and pancetta. You couldn't want a more romantic place.
$$$
HILTON WAIKOLOA VILLAGE
425 WAIKOLOA BEACH DR.
TEL 808/886-1234
🛏 176 indoors, 18 outdoors
🅿 🕐 Closed L ☒ All major cards

🍴 HAKONE STEAK
HOUSE AND SUSHI
BAR
$$$

HAPUNA PRINCE HOTEL
62-100 KAUNAOA DR.
TEL 808/880-1111
Japanese
If you've ever wanted to try fine Japanese cuisine but

couldn't figure it out, this is the place. The buffet is beautifully presented and each dish is tagged with an explanation. Choose from sushi, tempura, noodles, fish, sukiyaki, tender beef—and a very non-Japanese enticement of pies and cakes.

🍴 140 🅿 🕐 Closed D Thurs.–Fri., & L 🚫 All major cards

🍴 HUGGO'S
$$$
75-5828 KAHAKAI RD.
KAILUA-KONA 96740
TEL 808/329-1493
American
Surf 'n' turf with a bit of class, right on the water with manta rays gliding by. This is deservedly one of the most popular places in town. Big vulgar cocktails, live music, smashing sunsets.

🍴 130 indoors, 75 outdoors 🅿 🚫 All major cards

SOMETHING SPECIAL

🍴 THE TERRACE
Buffet
Sunday brunch (the only meal served) is an extravaganza of excellent food. Tables upon tables of fresh fruit, wonderful pastries and breads, prime rib, shrimp tempura, dazzling salads, pasta, Belgian waffles, eggs Benedict, and more. Eat outdoors overlooking the ocean.
$$$
MAUNA KEA BEACH HOTEL
62-100 MAUNA KEA BEACH DR.
TEL 808/882-7222
🍴 160 outdoors 🅿
🚫 All major cards

🍴 BAMBOO
$$
HWY. 270
HAWI
TEL 808/889-5555
Hawaii Regional Cuisine
The old Takata Store is dressed up in tropical mufti with wicker and bamboo. Try imu-pig quesadilla, fresh local seafood. Many dishes have a

Thai touch with coconut and lemongrass seasoning. Sunday brunch is served.

🍴 80 🅿 🕐 Closed D Sun.–Mon. 🚫 MC, V

🍴 EDWARD'S
$$
KANALOA AT KONA
78-261 MANUKAI ST.
KEAUHOU 96740
TEL 808/324-1434
Mediterranean
Open air over the ocean is the setting. Fish, poultry, and meat dishes may carry the sauces of Provence with garlic and tomatoes, or of Morocco with lemon, mint, and raisins. The niçoise salad is topped with seared fresh *ahi* (tuna). Breakfast is served.

🍴 60 outdoors 🅿 🚫 All major cards

🍴 OODLES OF NOODLES
$$
CROSSROADS SHOPPING CENTER
75-1027 HENRY ST.
KAILUA-KONA 96740
TEL 808/329-9222
Mixed
Global noodles—pasta to soba and mein. Design your own dish or choose Ahi Napoleon that looks like a little pagoda. Caesar salad is Asian spiced and comes in a lumpia basket. Opt for fettuccine with grilled chicken, roasted corn, and cilantro.

🍴 54 indoors, 27 outdoors 🅿 🚫 All major cards

🍴 THE COFFEE SHACK
$
HWY. 11
1 MILE S. OF CAPTAIN COOK
TEL 808/328-9555
American
This pink and white restaurant looks over old lava flows to the ocean. Sandwiches of fresh fish, or Reubens (grilled sandwiches) with tons of sauerkraut are enormous affairs on your choice of good bread. They grow their own coffee. Breakfast is served.

🍴 50 outdoors 🅿

🕐 Closed L Sun. & D 🚫 V, MC, D

🍴 SIBU CAFÉ
$
BANYAN COURT
75-5695 ALII DR.
KAILUA-KONA 96740
TEL 808/329-1112
Indonesian
Asian curries are accented with homemade condiments. There are good vegetarian dishes and a variety of flame-grilled satays (Asian kabobs). Decor is Balinese.

🍴 20 indoors, 21 outdoors 🅿 🚫 No credit cards

🍴 TESHIMA'S
$
HWY. 11
HONALO (15 MINUTES S. OF KAILUA-KONA)
TEL 808/322-9140
Japanese-American
This family-owned restaurant is a local favorite for the Japanese food developed on local plantations. Complete dinners, such as teriyaki steak, come with soup and *tsukemono* (pickled vegetables). Japanese breakfast is a specialty.

🍴 75 🅿 🚫 No credit cards

WAIMEA

🏨 AAAH, THE VIEWS
$
66-1773 ALANEO
KAMUELA 96743
TEL 808/885-3455
FAX 808/885-4031
www.beingsintouch.com
A sweet cottage beside a brook in an old-fashioned garden has stunning views from the slopes of Mauna Kea out to the distant ocean. You can also see Mauna Loa and Hualalai volcanoes.

🛏 3 🅂 None 🚫 No credit cards

🍴 EDELWEISS
$$
64-1299 KAWAIHAE RD.
KAMUELA 96743
TEL 808/885-6800

Continental
At this wildly popular country restaurant, a wide range of daily specials augment a menu that's been wowing locals and visitors for more than a decade. Many dishes are Austrian or German in origin, such as Wiener schnitzel and Black Forest chicken.
🍴 75 🅿 🕐 Closed Sun.–Mon. 💳 MC, V

SOMETHING SPECIAL

🍴 MERRIMAN'S
Hawaii Regional Cuisine
A shrine for foodies. Pioneering chef Peter Merriman, a master with fresh local ingredients, hires farmers to grow what he wants. Lamb comes from nearby Kahua Ranch. Try it roasted with plum sauce and a papaya-mint relish.
$$
65-1227 OPELU RD.
(ON HWY. 19)
KAMUELA 96743
TEL 808/885-6822
🍴 130 🅿 🕐 Closed L Sat.–Sun. 💳 All major cards

🍴 PANIOLO COUNTRY INN
$$
65-1214 LINDSEY RD.
KAMUELA
TEL 808/885-4377
American/Local food
Guys with big boots and belt buckles mosey in for the great chow. Breakfast stars a mean Loko-Moko—local favorite of hamburger patty on rice topped with fried egg and gravy. The hollandaise on the eggs Benedict is exquisite. Order the Belgian waffle with Waimea strawberries.
🍴 75 🅿 💳 All major cards

EAST HAWAII

🏨 HILO HAWAIIAN
🍴 HOTEL
$$$
71 BANYAN DR.
HILO 96720
TEL 800/367-5004 OR

808/935-9361
FAX 808/961-9642
www.castleresorts.com
This older hotel, in the leafy bowers of Banyan Drive and on Hilo Bay, is nicely maintained. Rattan furniture against quiet backgrounds. Plantings are mature and views splendid.
🛏 286 units (with refrigerator) 🏊

🏨 KILAUEA LODGE
🍴 $$$
OLD VOLCANO RD.
VOLCANO VILLAGE 96785
TEL 808/967-7366
FAX 808/967-7367
www.kilauealodge.com
A cozy inn just outside of Hawaii Volcanoes National Park, with a noteworthy restaurant (see this page). Rates include breakfast. Fireplaces, books, lush gardens.
🛏 14 units with central heating 🚭 None

🏨 SHIPMAN HOUSE BED & BREAKFAST INN
$$$
131 KAIULANI ST.
HILO 96720
TEL 800/627-8447 OR
808/934-8002
FAX 808/934-8002
www.hilo-hawaii.com
Queen Liliuokalani came to tea at this century-old Victorian manse with witch's hat turrets. Set amid lush gardens, the beautifully maintained house is on the national and state registers of historic places. Rooms have vintage furnishings and mini-refrigerators. Rates include breakfast.
🛏 5 units 🚭 None

🏨 VOLCANO HOUSE
🍴 $$
CRATER RIM DR.
HAWAII VOLCANOES NATIONAL PARK 96718
TEL 808/967-7321
People have dined here, with good views over the Kilauea caldera, while watching a volcanic eruption. Nicely furnished rooms have rocking chairs. Gets the tour bus crowd

at lunch, but you couldn't want a better location for exploring Hawaii Volcanoes National Park.
🛏 42 units 🚭 None

🍴 HARRINGTON'S
$$
135 KALANIANAOLE ST.
HILO 96720
TEL 808/961-4966
American
Before the calorie and cholesterol police spoiled a lot of dining fun, Americans enjoyed dishes such as scallops sautéed with mushrooms and Brie in a Chardonnay cream sauce, chicken Marsala, and generous steaks. They're hiding out here in a cozy restaurant on beautiful Reed's Bay.
🍴 112 🅿 🕐 Closed L Sat. 💳 MC, V

🍴 KILAUEA LODGE RESTAURANT
$$
OLD VOLCANO RD.
VOLCANO VILLAGE
TEL 808/967-7366
Continental
Cozy up around the fireplace in the cool uplands just outside Hawaii Volcanoes National Park. All meals come with wonderful soups, salads, and a loaf of homemade bread. Specials might be leg of antelope flambé, hasenpfeffer, or a vegetarian dish.
🍴 70 🅿 🕐 Closed L 💳 AE, MC, V

🍴 KEN'S HOUSE OF PANCAKES
$
1730 KAMEHAMEHA AVE.
HILO
TEL 808/935-8711
American
When all else fails, there's always Ken's, with reliably good burgers, hash, liver with bacon and onion, fish, and, of course, pancakes. Try kalua pig on a hoagie bun. Order lemon coconut custard pie whole or by the slice. Open 24 hours.
🍴 180 🅿 💳 All major cards

🅒 Air-conditioning 🏊 Outdoor swimming pool 🏋 Health club 💳 Credit cards | **KEY**

HOTELS & RESTAURANTS

SOMETHING SPECIAL

🍴 NAALEHU COFFEE SHOP

American/Local food

In a century-old building in a blink-and-you-miss-it town, you'll find a spotless place with fresh flowers on every table and simple food impeccably prepared. House specialty: the most delectable fried fish imaginable served with homemade pickled beets, fresh pineapple, and truly good macaroni salad. Mexican food served Thursday. If you drive to South Point, carry on a few miles farther for a truly good meal. Breakfast is served.

$
95-1148 NAALEHU SPUR RD.
NAALEHU 96772
TEL 808/929-7238
🔲 50 🅿 🚫 No credit cards

🍴 NORI'S SAIMIN & SNACKS

$
688 KINOOLE ST.
HILO 96720
TEL 808/935-9133
Local food
Mountains of tasty food without fuss or fancy decor is what you get. Specialty is *saimin*, the unique local noodle soup. Add barbecued meat sticks to the order.
🔲 100 🅿 🚫 MC, V

KAUAI

LIHUE & ENVIRONS

🏨 KAUAI MARRIOTT 🍴 RESORT & BEACH CLUB

$$$$$
3610 RICE ST.
KALAPAKI BEACH
LIHUE 96766
TEL 800/220-2925 OR
808/245-5050
FAX 808/246-2993
www.marriott.com/marriott /lihhi
Everything comes on a grand scale—enormous swimming pool, network of lagoons and waterways, extravagant gardens, marble, statuary, columns. All this on lovely Kalapaki Beach in view of dramatic Nawiliwili Harbor. restaurants (see this page).
ℹ️ 356 units, 232 villas 🏖 🏊

🏨 RADISSON KAUAI 🍴 BEACH

$$$$
4331 KAUAI BEACH DR.
LIHUE 96766
TEL 888/805-3843 OR
808/245-1955
FAX 303/369-9403
www.radissonkauai.com
Low-rise with big aspirations. Waterfalls, caves, tiki torches, fantasy pool, even a night club. Rooms in wicker and pastels. Beach is breathtaking, but unsafe for swimming.
ℹ️ 341 units 🏖

SOMETHING SPECIAL

🍴 GAYLORD'S

Continental, Hawaii Regional

This is Kauai's special occasion place. Locals come in droves for the ribs and the homemade desserts such as authentic Linzer torte and Kilohana mud pie with mocha ice cream, and more. Also find pastas, salads, seafood, all served on the lanai of a gracious sugar plantation manager's mansion. Sunday brunch.

$$$
KILOHANA SQUARE
3-2087 KAUMUALII HWY.
PUHI 96766
TEL 808/245-9593
🔲 143 outdoors 🅿
🚫 All major cards

🍴 BARBECUE INN

$$
2982 KRESS ST.
LIHUE
TEL 808/245-2921
Japanese/Pacific Rim Cuisine
Popular family-owned place serves complete Japanese dinners, turkey dinner, catch of the day, good salads, and burgers. Complete dinners often combine local ethnic specialties.
🔲 96 🕐 Closed Sun.
🚫 MC, V

🍴 CAFÉ PORTOFINO

$$
PACIFIC OCEAN PLAZA
3501 RICE ST.
LIHUE
TEL 808/245-2121
Italian
Fine cuisine is served with views of Nawiliwili Harbor and dramatic mountain silhouettes. They make their own *gelati*.
🔲 50 indoors, 50 outdoors
🅿 🕐 Closed L Sat.–Sun.
🚫 All major cards

🍴 DUKE'S CANOE CLUB

$$
KAUAI MARRIOTT & BEACH CLUB
3610 RICE ST.
NAWILIWILI
TEL 808/246-9599
American
Great views, a lot of atmosphere, and nightly live Hawaiian music come with reliably good prime rib, seafood, and noteworthy salad bar.
🔲 250 indoors, 190 outdoors
🅿 🚫 All major cards

🍴 HAMURA'S SAIMIN STAND

$
2596 KRESS ST.
LIHUE
TEL 808/245-3271
Local food
Pull up at a tangerine Formica counter for internationally acclaimed *saimin,* Hawaii's ubiquitous noodle soup. Add barbecued teriyaki meat sticks and a slab of pie. A great experience.
🔲 50 🅿 🚫 No credit cards

POIPU/KOLOA

SOMETHING SPECIAL

🏨 HYATT REGENCY 🍴 KAUAI RESORT & SPA

Gracious and relaxed is the mood of this elegant hostelry on 50 acres fronting golden

Shipwreck Beach. Fine dining, a 25,000-square-foot spa, and spacious rooms with marble baths.
$$$$$
1571 POIPU RD.
KOLOA 96756
TEL 800/55-HYATT OR
808/742-1234
FAX 808/240-6598
www.kauai-hyatt.com
📶 602 units 🌊 🏋

🏨 SHERATON KAUAI 🍴 RESORT
$$$$$
2440 HOONANI RD.
POIPU BEACH 96756
TEL 800/782-9488 OR
808/742-1661
FAX 808/742-9777
www.sheraton-hawaii.com
Completely rebuilt in 1997, this hotel is better than ever with lily ponds, gardens, and a prime spot on sunny Poipu Beach. It has more Hawaiian atmosphere than before, an excellent children's program, and a spa overlooking the ocean. Restaurants have sensational sunset views.
📶 414 units 🌊 🏋

🏨 GLORIA'S SPOUTING HORN BED AND BREAKFAST
$$$$
4464 LAWAI BEACH RD.
KOLOA 96756
TEL & FAX 808/742-6995
www.gloriasbedandbreakfast.com
It's expensive and there are only three units. Ah, but they're in a secluded cove with big lanais and Japanese *ofuro* tubs. The breakfast is outstanding with linen, crystal, and English china. Also included: spectacular sunsets with open bar and hors d'oeuvres. There's an oceanside swimming pool and lots of privacy.
📶 3 units 🚫 No credit cards

🏨 KIAHUNA 🍴 PLANTATION
$$$$
2253B POIPU RD.

POIPU 96756-9534
TEL 800/688-7444 OR
808/742-6411
FAX 808/742-1698
www.outrigger.com
Lush gardens and a broad expanse of lawn right on prime Poipu Beach. Completely rebuilt in 1994, after Hurricane Iniki, units are fresh and appealing, with kitchens. A notable garden surrounds the vintage plantation manager's home that serves as the lobby and restaurant (see this page).
📶 200 units 🚫 None 🌊

🏨 PRINCE KUHIO
$
5061 LAWAI BEACH RD.
KOLOA 96756
TEL 800/767-4707 OR
808/245-4711
FAX 808/245-8115
www.prosserrealty.net
The best buy on Kauai's south shore. Not luxe, but pleasant, and recently renovated. You get kitchens, ocean views, garden pool, Beach House restaurant. Across the street from a fine surfing beach, and adjacent to a great snorkeling cove and swimming beach.
📶 72 units (11 rentals)
🚫 None 🌊

🍴 ROY'S POIPU BAR & GRILL
$$$
POIPU SHOPPING VILLAGE
2360 KIAHUNA PLANTATION DR.
POIPU 96756
TEL 808/742-5000
Hawaii Regional Cuisine
Another restaurant by famous chef Roy Yamaguchi. Like the others, it's hip, loud, and has a cutting-edge daily menu that is a fusion of East and West. Pray for crab cakes.
🍴 220 indoors 🅿 🚫 All major cards

🍴 BRENNECKE'S BEACH BROILER
$$
2100 HOONE RD.
POIPU

TEL 808/742-7588
American
Casual, breezy atmosphere in full view of Poipu Beach is perfect for this surf 'n' turf eatery that lately steps out with good vegetarian offerings.
🍴 100 indoors 🅿 🚫 All major cards

🍴 PLANTATION GARDEN RESTAURANT & BAR
$$
KIAHUNA PLANTATION
2253 POIPU RD.
POIPU
TEL 808/742-2216
Hawaiian Regional Cuisine
Set in a historic home surrounded by a celebrated garden, they scarcely need good food. In fact, they serve very good Hawaiian fare. Seafood is freshest, herbs grown inches away.
🍴 60 indoors, 124 outdoors 🅿 🕐 Closed L 🚫 All major cards

COCONUT COAST

🏨 ALOHA BEACH 🍴 RESORT
$$$
3-5920 KUHIO HWY.
KAPAA 96746
TEL 888/823-5111 OR
808/823-6000
FAX 808/823-6666
www.abr.com
In 1998 this beachfront resort was totally remodeled, repositioned as a family-friendly place where children 19 and under stay free.
📶 216 units 🌊 🏋

🏨 HOTEL CORAL REEF
$$
4-1516 KUHIO HWY.
KAPAA 96746
TEL 800/843-4659 OR
808/822-4481
FAX 808/822-7705
www.hotelcoralreef.com
Cheap and cheerful on the beach, walk to shopping. Continental breakfast included.
📶 24 units 🚫 None 🚫 MC, V

🍴 THE BULL SHED
$$
4-796 KUHIO HWY.
WAIPOULI 96746
TEL 808/822-3791
American
Sage local carnivores make quiet pilgrimages to this oceanside dining room for macho-sized meals of steaks, chops, and ribs. Toss some pasta and seafood to the timid, or send them to the salad bar.
🔢 150 🅿 🕐 Closed L
🔷 All major cards

🍴 MEMA
$$
WAILUA SHOPPING PLAZA
4-361 KUHIO HWY.
WAILUA
TEL 808/823-0899
Thai
Look for lemongrass soup, a wild variety of coconut-milk-based curries, vegetables with spicy peanut sauce.
🔢 60 🅿 🕐 Closed L
Sat.–Sun. 🔷 All major cards

🍴 WAILUA MARINA RESTAURANT
$$
5971 KUHIO HWY.
WAILUA
TEL 808/822-4311
American
Obviously designed for big riverboat crowds, this manages to be a truly nice restaurant by virtue of its setting beside the hauntingly beautiful Wailua River, and its satisfying menu, which ranges from signature stuffed pork chops to fresh seafood and teriyaki steak. Courtesy transport for Wailua area.
🔢 125 indoors, 175 outdoors 🅿 🕐 Closed Mon. 🔷 AE, MC, V

🍴 CAFFE COCO
$
4-369 KUHIO HWY.
WAILUA
TEL 808/822-7990
Local Cuisine
A funky little place lost among fruit trees has earned a big reputation for fresh tropical juices, fish wraps, salads, and vegetarian dishes. A good bet: The Pacific Rim platter with seared *ahi* (tuna) with mango sweet-sour sauce, tofu pot stickers, and noodle salad with peanut dressing. Dinner reservations required.
🔢 20 indoors, 60 outdoors
🅿 🕐 Open L Tues.–Fri., D Tues.–Sun.
🔷 MC, V

PRINCEVILLE-HANALEI AREA

SOMETHING SPECIAL

🏨 PRINCEVILLE RESORT 🍴 KAUAI
Step into the lobby and look out at a grand vista of Hanalei Bay, and magnificent mountains streaming with waterfalls. Serene swimming pool, fine restaurants (see Cafe Hanalei and La Cascata, this page), outstanding rooms with handsome appointments, views even from the bathroom shower. Two top-notch golf courses.
$$$$$
5520 KA HAKU RD.
PRINCEVILLE 96722
TEL 800/826-4400 OR
808/826-9644
FAX 808/826-1166
www.princeville.com
ℹ️ 252 units 🏊 🏷️

🏨 HANALEI BAY RESORT 🍴 & SUITES
$$$$
5380 HONOIKI RD.
PRINCEVILLE 96722
TEL 800/827-4427 OR
808/826-6522
FAX 808/826-6680
www.hanaleibaykauai.com
The landscaping is bright with flowers and leads the eye to the bay and mountains. Nicely furnished units are large with kitchens. Enjoy the romantic restaurant Bali Hai (see p. 257).
ℹ️ 187 units 🏊

PRICES

HOTELS
An indication of the cost of a double room without breakfast is given by $ signs.
$$$$$ Over $280
$$$$ $200–$280
$$$ $120–$200
$$ $80–$120
$ Under $80

RESTAURANTS
An indication of the cost of a three-course dinner without drinks is given by $ signs.
$$$$$ Over $80
$$$$ $50–$80
$$$ $35–$50
$$ $20–$35
$ Under $20

SOMETHING SPECIAL

🍴 CAFÉ HANALEI
American/Continental
There is not a finer view on earth. Breakfast buffet with omelet and crepe stand. Lunch ranges from soup to salads and sandwiches, while dinner features a good bouillabaisse, fresh seafood, and a seafood buffet Friday eves.
$$$
PRINCEVILLE HOTEL
5520 KA HAKU RD.
PRINCEVILLE
TEL 808/826-2760
🔢 110 indoors, 70 outdoors
🅿 🔷 All major cards

🍴 LA CASCATA
$$$
PRINCEVILLE HOTEL
5520 KA HAKU RD.
PRINCEVILLE
TEL 808/826-2761
Mediterranean
It feels like a Tuscan villa with Hawaiian vistas. Pastas, fresh seafood, tiramisu. Sauces are light. Try fire-roasted rack of lamb on porcini polenta with caramelized onions.
🔢 125 indoors 🅿
🕐 Closed L 🔷 All major cards

H O T E L S   &   R E S T A U R A N T S

SOMETHING SPECIAL

🍴 BALI HAI
Pacific Rim Cuisine

Start with a big slushy tropical drink at adjacent Happy Talk Bar and marvel at the South Pacific setting and grand views of Hanalei Bay. Finish with a flaming dessert. In between, *ono* (wahoo) seared and served over crab cakes with papaya-ginger beurre blanc.

$$

HANALEI BAY RESORT & SUITES
5380 HONOIKI RD.
PRINCEVILLE
TEL 808/826-6522
🛏 77 indoors, 45 outdoors
Ⓟ 🅰 All major cards

🍴 POSTCARDS CAFÉ
$$

5-5075-A KUHIO HWY.
HANALEI 96714
TEL 808/826-1191
Healthy
Best breakfasts on the island, but no bacon. It's a vegan's nirvana—with seafood for the backsliders. Vacationing Hollywood stars flock here. Look for taro fritters and prawns, veggie curries and organic smoothies.
🛏 39 indoors, 21 outdoors
Ⓟ 🅰 All major cards

🍴 ZELO'S BEACH HOUSE
$$

5-5156 KUHIO HWY.
HANALEI
TEL 808/826-9700
Mixed
More microbrewed beer on the menu than food. Casual, happy, always packed. Flagrant tropical decor. Get tacos, burgers, fish, salads, chef's specials such as crusted *ahi*.
🛏 90 indoors, 32 outdoors
Ⓟ 🅰 MC, V

WEST KAUAI

🏨 WAIMEA PLANTATION
🍴 COTTAGES
$$$$

9400 KAUMUALII HWY.
WAIMEA 96796

TEL 800/922-4632 OR
808/338-1625
FAX 808/338-2338
www.waimea-plantation.com
Plantation cottages with updated facilities and period furniture set beside the sea.
ⓘ 50 units 🅢 None 🏊

MOLOKAI

KAUNAKAKAI & EAST END

🏨 MOLOKAI SHORES
$$$

KAMEHAMEHA HWY.
KAUNAKAKAI 96748-1037
TEL 800/535-0085 OR
808/553-5954
FAX 808/553-3241
www.marcresorts.com
One- and two-room suites set beside the sea in lavish gardens. All have kitchenettes and ocean views.
ⓘ 100 units 🅢 None 🏊

🏨 PUU O HOKU RANCH
$$$

KAMEHAMEHA V HWY.
KAUNAKAKAI 96748
TEL 808/558-8109
FAX 808/558-8100
www.puuohoku.com
Extravagant scenery on a 14,000-acre ranch in the middle of glorious nowhere. Basic wicker furnishings, kitchens. Serenity is here.
ⓘ 17 units (6 in cottages, 11 in lodge) 🅢 None 🅰 No credit cards

🍴 MOLOKAI PIZZA CAFÉ
$$

KAHUA CENTER, OLD WHARF RD.
TEL 808/553-3288
Italian/Local Cuisine
Pizza, pasta, and submarine sandwiches are the staples in this casual, friendly gathering spot. Also daily themed menus such as Hawaiian, Mexican, prime rib.
🛏 60 indoors, 12 outdoors
🅰 No credit cards

🍴 KANEMITSU BAKERY & RESTAURANT
$

79 ALA MALAMA ST.
KAUNAKAKAI
TEL 808/553-5855
Local food
The smell of fresh bread is the lure to this unpretentious diner. Burgers, fried chicken, sandwiches all come on the famous Molokai bread. Buy loaves for munching later. Good place to order a picnic lunch. Breakfast is served.
🛏 75 🕐 Closed D, & L Tues. 🅰 No credit cards

🍴 OVIEDO'S
$

145 ALA MALAMA
KAUNAKAKAI
TEL 808/553-5014
Filipino
Home-cooked Filipino specialties in a warm friendly atmosphere. Adobo (stews) are a specialty. Look for chicken with green papaya.
🛏 12 🕐 Closes 5:30 p.m. Mon.–Fri., 4 p.m. Sat.–Sun. 🅰 No credit cards

WEST END

🏨 LODGE AT MOLOKAI
🍴 RANCH
$$$$

MAUNALOA HWY.
MAUNALOA 96770
TEL 877-PANIOLO
TEL 877-726-4656
FAX 808/534-1606
www.molokai-ranch.com
New lodge in old plantation style graces rural Maunaloa town. Individually decorated suites.
ⓘ 22 units 🅢 None 🏊 🎽

SOMETHING SPECIAL

🏨 SHERATON MOLOKAI LODGE AND BEACH VILLAGE

Comfy canvas bungalows, all with private open-to-the-skies baths at a beachside site on sprawling Molokai Ranch. Rooms are also available at the elegant little Lodge at

Molokai Ranch in Maunaloa town (see above). Maunaloa Room Restaurant at the lodge (see this page).

$$$$
100 MAUNA LOA HWY.
MAUNALOA 96770
TEL 888/488-3535 OR
808/552-2741
FAX 808/552-2773
www.starwood.com/hawaii
[i] 40 bungalows, 22 lodge rooms   All major cards

PANIOLO HALE RESORT CONDOMINIUMS
$$$
LIO PL.
MAUNALOA 96770-0190
TEL 800/367-2984 OR
808/552-2731
FAX 808/552-2288
www.lava.net/paniolo
Simply furnished studios to 2-room condos with kitchens. Most have ocean views. Two-night minimum.
[i] 77 units (16 rentals)
None

MAUNALOA ROOM
$$$
MOLOKAI RANCH LODGE
MAUNALOA
TEL 808/660-2725
Hawaii Regional
"Sexy food?" Well. yes. Executive Chef Martina Hilldorfer says, "I like my cuisine to be a little sexy, a little off the grid—fun." Try her Mai Tai mahi mahi with rum syrup, pineapple chutney and sesame rice, or Molten Lava, a cake runny with chocolate.
43 indoors, 38 outdoors
  All major cards

LANAI

THE LODGE AT KOELE
$$$$$
1 KEAMOKU DR.
LANAI CITY 96763
800/321-4666 OR
808/565-7300
FAX 808/565-4561

www.lanai-resorts.com
This baronial lodge in the cool uplands of Lanai City just misses being stuffy. English manor furnishings, fireplaces in the Great Hall, wicker chairs on the porch. Known for its fine dining (see below) and visiting artists program. Courtesy shuttle to airport and beach hotel.
[i] 102 units   None

SOMETHING SPECIAL

MANELE BAY HOTEL
Elegant, relaxed, and breezy, overlooking Hulopoe Beach, the best on the Island for swimming and snorkeling. Dining is exceptional (see Ihilani and Hulopoe Court, right).
$$$$$
1 MANELE RD.
LANAI CITY 96763
TEL 800/321-4666 OR
808/565-7700
FAX 808/565-2483
www.lanai-resorts.com
[i] 249 units

HOTEL LANAI
$$$
828 LANAI AVE.
LANAI CITY 96763
TEL 800/795-7211 OR
808/565-7211
FAX 808/565-6450
E-MAIL: h-lanai@aloha.net
Graciously decorated in whites and pastels, this was once Lanai City's only hotel. The front porch is still the local gathering place for impromptu music and "talk story." Restaurant.
[i] 11 units   None

SOMETHING SPECIAL

FORMAL DINING ROOM
American
Eat Lanai game such as venison loin rolled in cracked black pepper with sweet potatoes and pineapple cider sauce. This

restaurant is a consistent award winner. Jackets required (available from concierge).
$$$$
THE LODGE AT KOELE
TEL 808/565-4580
51   P   Closed L
  All major cards

IHILANI
$$$$
MANELE BAY HOTEL
TEL 808/565-2290
Mediterranean
Open to sea breezes yet plush and romantic. Daily menu might feature steamed lobster with risotto of portobello and shiitake mushrooms and lobster mint sauce.
55 indoors, 70 outdoors
P   Closed L   All major cards

HULOPOE COURT
$$$
MANELE BAY HOTEL
TEL 808/565-7700
Hawaii Regional Cuisine
Stunning murals. Try guava-glazed chicken breast with purple sweet potatoes, or charcoaled pork chop with roasted pineapples and chili sauce. Breakfast is served.
90 indoors, 85 outdoors
Closed L   All major cards

BLUE GINGER CAFÉ
$
409 SEVENTH ST.
LANAI CITY
TEL 808/565-6363
American
It's plain and homey, the food reliable. Burgers, omelets, a few Filipino specialties, and *saimin*. Breakfast is served.
35 indoors, 16 outdoors
No credit cards

SHOPPING IN HAWAII

You'll find an intriguing mix of European designer shops, Asian specialty stores, American chains, and a new wave of stores devoted to "made in Hawaii" goods, ranging from creamy coconut-based soaps scented with Hawaiian flora to fine art. Farmers' markets and craft fairs provide excellent shopping opportunities. Check local newspapers to see what's going on. Macy's department store is a reliable source for needs, whims, and gifts.

HOURS

Hours vary widely by population density. Some supermarkets are open 24 hours. Most open at 7 a.m. and close at 9 p.m. Department stores and other retail outlets open between 9 and 10 a.m., and close at 9 p.m. Smaller stores in smaller towns close anywhere between 5 and 7 p.m. Most are open on Sunday.

PAYMENT AND RETURNS

Most stores, including supermarkets, accept credit cards. Few will accept an out-of-state personal check. If you have a complaint about a purchase, return it as soon as possible with the receipt. In case of serious dispute, contact the state Consumer Resource Center, Tel 808/587-3222.

WHAT TO BUY

The most popular souvenir is a box of chocolate-covered macadamia nuts. Following the coffee-craze, Kona coffee is hot. Check the label to see just how much Kona is in the blend; better yet, buy pure—expensive but worth it. Other good food bets are jams and jellies from tropical fruit, fresh pineapple, teas, such as *mamake*, from Hawaiian plants, syrups, cookies, and taro chips. Good places to shop for these taste treats are supermarkets, Long's Drugs throughout the Islands, and ABC stores in resort towns. Look for bowls and art objects carved from Hawaiian woods such as koa, and milo, also mango and Norfolk Island pine. Graphically strong Hawaiian quilts in spreads, pillows, and wall hangings blend with contemporary furnishings. Cheaper imitations are being sewn in developing nations. Ask about origins, or buy a kit and sew your own. Locally designed fashion goes way beyond aloha shirts and matching muumuu, although you will probably succumb and end up wearing a garden to dinner. Tropical flowers may be shipped around the globe. Hawaiian music CDs and tapes can warm a winter day back home. Good buys from Asia include jade, porcelain, interesting cooking utensils, vintage kimono, and obi (belts), which make good table runners.

The following is a list of the most interesting and characteristic shops, arranged by island.

OAHU

Ala Moana Center 1450 Ala Moana Blvd., five minutes from Waikiki, has 200 shops including department stores such as Sears, J.C. Penney, and Neiman-Marcus. **Shirokiya** (tel 808/973-9111) is fun, often featuring a demo of some esoteric culinary gizmo. The edible gift department has beautifully packaged teas. **Products of Hawaii Too** (tel 808/949-6866) specializes in Hawaii-made gifts. **Iida's** (tel 808/973-0320) has Japanese lanterns, umbrellas, teapots, chopsticks tucked everywhere and hanging from the ceiling.

Aloha Flea Market 99-500 Salt Lake Blvd. Halawa, tel 808/486-6704. More than a thousand vendors peddle everything from cheap T-shirts and extra luggage to carry home your treasures, to fashion, art, watches, and maybe an antique find. Go early, wear a hat. It's outdoors in the Aloha Stadium parking lot.

Aloha Tower Marketplace is a breezy, gaggle of shops and restaurants beside busy Honolulu Harbor. Star of the group is **Martin & MacArthur** (tel 808/524-6066), long famous for handcrafted koa furniture and now expanded to include top-of-the-line clothing and gifts.

Haleiwa Boutiques, art galleries, and surf shops. For fashionably outrage-ous clothing and accessories, best bets are **Silver Moon Emporium** (66-250 Kamehameha Hwy., tel 808/637-7710), and **Oogenesis** (66-249 Kamehameha Hwy., tel 808/637-4580).

Hilo Hattie's 700 N. Nimitz Hwy., Honolulu, tel 808/537-2926. Still has touristy neon muumuu, but also quality aloha wear and souvenirs such as Kona coffee (free samples) and tropical jewelry. Free shuttles operate from Waikiki. Also has neighboring island locations.

Hula Supply Center 2346 S. King St., Honolulu, tel 808/941-5379. Hula dancers come for their feathered gourd rattles and costume accessories. Find everything from cellophane skirts to shell jewelry. Great sarongs, woven lauhala bags, Hawaiian print backpacks, artistic T-shirts, and lots of fun kitsch.

Kapahulu Ave., Waikiki is a string of interesting shops and restaurants in unpromising storefronts. **Bailey's Antique Clothing and Thrift Shop** (517 Kapahulu Ave., tel 808/734-7628) is a hodge-podge of vintage "silky" aloha shirts with coconut buttons, smart reproductions of perennial favorites, and Hawaiian kitsch. At **Na Lima Mili Hulu Noeau** (762 Kapahulu Ave., tel 808/732-0865) buy prize feather lei or drop in for an inexpensive lei lesson. **Kilohana Square** (1016 Kapahulu Ave.) is a little group of shops, primarily quality Asian and European antiques, grouped around a picturesque courtyard.

SHOPPING

The Little Hawaiian Craft

Shop Royal Hawaiian Shopping Center, 2233 Kalakaua Ave., tel 808/926-2662. The best place in Waikiki for quality Hawaiian gifts. Feather hatbands, Niihau shell lei, dried botanical collages, reproductions from the Bishop Museum's Hawaiiana collection.

Waikele Shopping Plaza 94-790 Lumiaina St., Waikele, tel. 808/680-9598. A 64-acre discount mall with everything from locally designed surf wear to a Saks Fifth Avenue outlet. It's 20 miles from Waikiki. TheBus 48 goes, or call Da Shopping Shuttle (tel 808/853-2338).

Victoria Ward Center This ever expanding center, at Ward Ave. and Auahi St. across from Ala Moana Beach Park, is a complex of two shopping centers, the 65-unit Ward Warehouse, and 30-unit Ward Center, plus a 16-movie megaplex, and various strip mall shops and restaurants. Shops range from chains to great local specialty stores. At **Native Books and Beautiful Things** (Ward Warehouse, tel 808/596-8885) look for reasonably priced petroglyph art by Lynn Cook, one-of-a-kind koa and milo lamps and bowls, lauhala placemats. **Honolulu Chocolate Co.** (Ward Center, tel 808/591-2997) carries locally made expensive gourmet candies. The **Mamo Howell** boutique (Ward Warehouse, tel 808/591-2002) carries the latest from this popular local designer's line of quality Hawaiian wear for men, women, and children.

MAUI

Banyan Tree Craft Fair is a presentation of the Lahaina Arts Society, the 2nd and 4th weekends of every month beneath the historic banyan tree behind Lahaina Courthouse on Wharf St., tel 808/661-0111. On alternate weekends the emphasis is on Hawaiian crafts

at the **He Ui Cultural Arts Festivals** (tel 808/667-9194). **Coast Gallery Wailea** 3750 Wailea Alanui Dr., Wailea Shopping Village, tel 808/879-2301. Quality paintings, sculptures, prints, and jewelry by both international and Maui artists.

Front Street, Lahaina has respectable boutiques in old grog shops. **Lahaina Scrimshaw** (845A Front St., tel 808/661-8820) carries both collectors' pieces and contemporary scrimshaw. **SGT Leisure** (855B Front St., tel 808/667-0661) puts a bright happy spin on T-shirts and casual resort wear. **Lahaina Body & Bath** (713 Front St., tel 808/661-1076) and sister shop **Lei Spa Maui** (505 Front St., tel 808/661-1178) concentrate on Maui-made soaps, masks, lotions, potions, candles, and perfume.

Haimoff & Haimoff Creations in Gold 130 Bay Dr., Kapalua Resort, tel 808/669-5213. Imaginative, original design jewelry at good prices.

Honolua Store 502 Office Rd., Kapalua Resort, tel. 808/669-6128. Gentrified old country store with snacks, some resort clothing, and a take-out food counter. Picnic tables outside.

Makawao, Upcountry, draws shoppers from Honolulu who come for the off-beat chic and the arts. **Maui Hands** (3620 Baldwin Ave., Makawao, tel. 808/572-5194), housed in an old theater, presents Maui art and collectibles. For hip fashion, head into **Hurricane** (3639 Baldwin Ave., tel 808/572-5076). For an educated selection of children's gifts, it's **Maui Child Toys and Books** (3643 Baldwin Ave., tel 808/572-2765).

Mandalay Imports Four Seasons Resort, Wailea, tel 808/874-5111. Thai silks, Asian treasures, and ethnic jewelry. **Maui Crafts Guild** 43 Hana Hwy., Paia, tel 808/579-9697. On

the cutting edge of Maui crafts. The selection is interesting and reasonably priced for the quality.

Maui Swap Meet Hwy. 350 and S. Puunene Ave., Kahului, tel 808/877-3100. Down-home Maui fun. Every Saturday from 8 a.m. until noon, about a hundred vendors peddle protea, veggies, antiques, arts, and crafts.

Totally Hawaiian Gift Gallery Lahaina Cannery Mall, 1221 Honoapiilani Hwy., tel 808/667-2558. Locally made or inspired gift items include dolls in muumuus, sculptures from native woods, tropical perfumes and soaps, and rolls of Hawaiian-print paper to wrap your gifts.

BIG ISLAND

Blue Ginger Mamalahoa Hwy., Kainaliu, tel 808/322-3898. You can't miss this eclectic shop (it's bright blue) with its original jewelry, Asian imports, local crafts, and unusual clothing.

Cook's Discoveries Cook's Corner, 64-1066 Mamalahoa Hwy., Waimea, tel 808/885-3633. Hawaiian quilts, sculptures in native woods, Hawaiian wear, distinctive pareau (beach wraps), Hawaiiana collectibles.

Hilo Farmers' Market Kamehameha Ave. & Mamo St., Hilo. Wed. & Sat. from 6 a.m. to 3 p.m. If you want the really good stuff, like Waimea strawberries, get there early. Other winners: pure home-extracted coconut oil (great for the hair), kapa, lauhala, homemade children's clothing.

Holualoa town Exceptional shops and galleries along its main street, Mamalahoa Hwy. Stop for free Kona coffee at the Star Visitor Center (Mamalahoa Hwy., tel 808/322-2128). **Studio 7** (76-5920 Mamalahoa Hwy., tel 808/324-1335) shows the work of respected Island artists, including gallery owners Setsuko and Hiroki Morinoue. More fine art at **Holualoa Gallery** (76-5921 Mamalahoa Hwy., tel 808/322-8484). Of particular note: the raku pottery. Traditional Hawaiian lauhala weaving at **Kimura Lauhala Shop** (77-996 Hualalae Rd., Hwy. 182, tel 808/324-0053).

Hula Heaven Kona Inn Shopping Village, Kailua-Kona, tel 808/329-7885. Browser's heaven. Wander among vintage aloha shirts, dashboard hula dolls, vintage ukulele, old fabric prints.

King's Shops Waikoloa Resort, 250 Waikoloa Beach Dr., Kohala Coast. On the edge of the lava field. **Kubuku Sarong Shop** (tel 808/886-8581) is a bright space of children's comfy cottons. **Jourabachi** (tel 808/886-1172) is the glamour shop with lots of style and sequins. Sales are great.

Sig Zane Designs 122 Kamehameha Ave., Hilo, tel 808/935-7077. A very personal collection of art, aloha wear, and linens deeply rooted in the Hawaiian culture.

Volcano Art Center Hawaii Volcanoes National Park, tel 808/967-7565. In the old Volcano House Inn. Fine island art, much of it centered on a volcano theme. Look for ceramics, tiles, finest lauhala, paintings, prints.

KAUAI

Hanapepe town has great treasures in its rickety stores. At **Kauai Fine Arts**, (3905 Hanapepe Rd., tel 808/335-3778) you can leaf through Victorian-era botanical prints, antique maps and prints of old Hawaii, kapa art, and some contemporary art. **Kilohana Plantation** 3-2087 Kaumualii Hwy., Puhi. Delightful shops crammed into every room of a former plantation manager's home. Niihau shell lei turn up in the cloak room at **Hawaiian Collection Room. Sea**

Reflections (tel 808/245-5210) is awash in shells and precious jewelry from the ocean. Look for rarest coral, the white bamboo. **Kong Lung**, Kilauea Rd., Kilauea, tel 808/ 828-1822, housed in a historic old plantation store, draws faithful shoppers from other islands who come for the home furnishings, aloha wear, stationery, and just to look at the table settings.

Ola's 5-5016 Kuhio Hwy., Hanalei, tel 808/826-6937. Owned by an artist who paints, and makes, furniture—big imaginative pieces. They also carry the work of other fine artists in a variety of mediums including daring blown, hand-painted glass, innovative jewelry, and home furnishings.

Yellowfish Trading Company Hanalei Center, 5-5161 Kuhio Hwy., tel 808/826-1227. Has a reputation among collectors and Hollywood stars such as Robert Redford and Demi Moore for the depth of its kitsch and breadth of its vintage aloha shirt racks.

MOLOKAI

The Big Wind Kite Factory 120 Maunaloa Hwy., Maunaloa, tel 808/552-2364, is just that. They make and sell glorious kites too beautiful to be risked, that end up on walls as art. They've also got the latest aerodynamic kites, inexpensive paper kites, and colorful windsocks. You can tour the small factory and watch them stitch up flying hula girls, geckos, and fish.

Coffees of Hawaii Plantation Store Kualapuu, tel 808/567-9023, focuses on Molokai-made products from Muleskinner coffee to coconut jewelry. They also carry items from around the islands, usually at lower prices than the point of origin. **Molokai Fish and Dive** 61 Ala Malama, Kaunakakai, tel 808/553-5926, is like taking a course in Philosophy 101. Just read the

profound T-shirts and have a good laugh. This really is a sporting goods store, too, as its name implies.

The Outfitter Maunaloa Hwy., Maunaloa, tel 808/552-2741, is where you go to get geared up for a wide range of sports. Find biking shorts, Molokai Ranch logo wear, and a good selection of Hawaiian music.

Plantation Gallery 120 Maunaloa Hwy., Maunaloa, tel 808/552-2364. A jumble of Hawaiian handicrafts and whimsical imports from Bali and points East.

LANAI

Akamai Trading & Gifts 408 8th Ave., Lanai City, tel 808/565-6587. Sells, among its life necessities such as film and bagels, beautifully crafted bowls carved from the pine trees that are the island's icons, and other reasonably priced souvenirs.

Gifts with Aloha 363 7th St., Lanai City, tel 808/565-6589. An odd mix of aloha wear, jewelry, hanging art, candles, Lanai jams and jellies, fine art, and children's wear.

Heart of Lanai 363 7th Ave., Lanai City, tel. 808-565-6678. Local arts and crafts including Hawaiian quilts and jewelry.

Lanai Art Studio 339 7th Ave., Lanai City, tel. 808/565-7503. Grew out of the Lanai Art Program, which began when the island switched gears from being the world's biggest pineapple plantation to becoming one of the most exclusive resort isles anywhere. Island artists, trained by visiting multimedia masters, show their wares—watercolors, ceramics, jewelry. Some local artists in the program have contributed to the art collection of the two resort hotels, the Lodge at Koele and the Manele Bay Hotel.

ENTERTAINMENT & ACTIVITIES

ENTERTAINMENT & ACTIVITIES IN HAWAII

Much of the fun of Hawaii is found in outdoor activities. Every Island offers excellent land and ocean options. Some, such as golf, have been covered in the main chapters. Here are the best contacts for walking, horseback riding, boating, diving, sports lessons. You'll also find sunset bars and after-dark entertainment.

OAHU

AFTER DARK

LUAU
Paradise Cove luau, tel 808/842-5911. Buses bring thousands to a remote beach for a well-done mass luau, with entertainment, games, pageantry.
Royal Hawaiian luau, Royal Hawaiian Hotel, 2259 Kalakaua Ave., tel 808/923-7311, Mon. & Thurs. Upscale luau on the seaside lawn beneath pink lanterns.

SHOWS
Atrium Court, Aloha Tower Marketplace, tel 808/528-5700. Free changing programs of nightly entertainment from Hawaiian to jazz. Tues., Wed., Thurs.
Don Ho, Waikiki Beachcomber Hotel, 2300 Kalakaua Ave., tel 808/922-4646, the king of Hawaiian entertainment, performs Sun., Tues., & Thurs.
Legends in Concert, Royal Hawaiian Shopping Center, tel 808/971-1400. Las Vegas glitz and impersonations of stars such as Elvis and Marilyn.
Magic of Polynesia, Waikiki Beachcomber Hotel, 2300 Kalakaua Ave., tel 808/539-9460. A dramatic extravaganza of illusion and dance starring magician John Hirokawa.

SUNSET
Alii Kai **Catamaran,** Pier 5, Aloha Tower, tel 808/539-9400. Polynesian-style catamaran sets sail with up to a thousand passengers for a well-organized sunset cruise, including an appetizing buffet and lively Hawaiian revue.
Banyan Veranda, Sheraton Moana Surfrider Hotel, 2365 Kalakaua Ave., tel 808/922-3111. Enjoy top-notch Hawaiian entertainment beneath the banyan tree on the ocean terrace of this Victorian grande dame.
House Without A Key, Halekulani Hotel, tel 808/923-2311. Hula and music beneath a century-old tree.
Mai Tai Bar, Royal Hawaiian Hotel, 2259 Kalakaua Ave., tel 808/923-7311.
Waikiki Beach Marriott Resort, Moana Terrace Café and Bar, 2552 Kalakaua Ave., Waikiki, tel 808/922-6611. A different lineup of top Hawaiian entertainers including beloved singer Genoa Keawe, and slack key artists Martin Pahinui, George Kuo, and Aaron Mahi perform nightly in this outdoor space overlooking the ocean. This is a place to encounter authentic Hawaiian music.

ACTIVITIES

HIKING
Hawaii Department of Land and Natural Resources, 1151 Punchbowl St., Room 130, Honolulu 96813, tel 808/587-0300. Trail maps available at small cost. Also camping permits.
Hawaiian Trail and Mountain Club, P.O. Box 2238, Honolulu 96804 www.geocities.com/yosemite/trails/3660. Send $1.25 and a legal-sized self-addressed envelope for hike schedule and information on hiking and camping in Hawaii.
Sierra Club, P.O. Box 2577, Honolulu 96803, tel 808/538-6616. Regularly scheduled hikes at varied skill levels.

KAYAKING
Twogood Kayaks Hawaii, 345 Hahani St., Kailua, 96734, tel 808/262-5656. Paddle a kayak out to offshore islands.

SAILING
Tradewind Charters, 796 Kalanipuu St., Honolulu 96825, tel 808/973-0311, www.tradewindcharter.com. Private sunset, moonlight, daytime sails; also lessons, whale watching, and deep-sea fishing.

SCUBA DIVING
Captain Bruce's Scuba Charters, on the pier, Waianae Boat Harbor, tel 808/373-3590, www.captainbruce.com. Experienced divers explore west Oahu waters. Also certification.

SURFING LESSONS
Aloha Beach Service (next to Sheraton Moana Surfrider) 2365 Kalakaua Ave., tel 808/922-3111 ext. 2341. Even grandmothers can be standing, riding the waves in one lesson.

WINDSURFING
Naish Hawaii, 155-A Hamakua Dr., Kailua 96734, tel 808/262-6068. World champion Robbie Naish and family run the operation. Lessons, rentals, sales, complete tours.

MAUI

AFTER DARK

LUAU
Maui Marriott luau, 100 Nohea Kai Dr., Kaanapali Beach, tel 808/661-5828. Nightly luau except Mon. Was featured on NBC's *Today.*
Old Lahaina luau, 1251 Front St., tel 808/667-1998. Nightly.

SHOWS
Ulalena, Maui Myth and Magic Theater, 878 Front St., Lahaina, tel 808/661-9913. A multi-million-dollar musical about Maui's legends and history. Tues. through Sat.
Warren & Annabelle's, 900

Front St., Lahaina, tel 808/667-6244. Magician and ghost pianist in intimate theater.

SUNSET
Scotch Mist Charters, Lahaina Harbor, tel 808/661-0386. Champagne sail aboard a 25-passenger sloop. **America II Sunset Sail,** Lahaina Harbor, tel 808/667-2195. Two-hour reasonably priced cruise on 1987 America's Cup contender.

ACTIVITIES

BICYCLING
Activity Warehouse, 758 Front St., Lahaina, tel 800/923-4004 or 808/661-1970. Cruisers and mountain bikes for rent. To check on maps and Maui bikeways, click on www.bikehawaii.com.

BOATING
Makena Kayak Trips, Makena, tel 808/879-8426. Explore reefs and remote coves on Maui's wild eastern shore. **South Pacific Kayaks,** Rainbow Mall, 2439 S. Kihei Rd., Kihei 96753, tel 800/776-2326 or 808/875-4848, www.mauikayak.com. Tours, rentals, lessons, snorkeling. **Trilogy Excursions,** Lahaina Harbor, tel 800/874-2666 or 808/661-4743, www.sailtrilogy.com. Catamaran picnic sails to Molokini or Lanai.

HIKING
Ekahi Tours, 532 Keolani Pl., Kahului, tel 808/877-9775. A resident of Kahakuloa Valley will share his home in one of the last functioning ahupuaa (ancient land management system). **Hawaii State Department of Land and Natural Resources,** 54 S. High St., Rm. 101, Wailuku 96793, tel 808/984-8109. For trail information and camping permits. **Hike Maui,** tel 808/879-5270, www.hikemaui.com. Expert guide Ken Schmitt plans several hikes a day from easy to strenuous. **Kapalua Nature Society,** tel

800/KAPALUA or 808/669-0244. Easy hikes in small groups. **Ritz Carlton Kapalua Eco-Tours,** tel 808/669-6200. Hikes into pristine nature areas with picnic lunch and swimming possibilities.

HORSEBACK RIDING
Adventure on Horseback, tel 808/242-7445, www.mauihorse whisperer.com. This is the horseback ride for horse lovers. It begins with breakfast and goes on for six hours with ocean panoramas, into a rain forest, and waterfall swimming. Breakfast and lunch are included. There's also a half- or full-day seminar available on horse whispering, the language of the horse.

SCUBA DIVING & SNORKELING
Ed Robinson's Diving Adventures, Kihei, tel 800/635-1273 or 808/879-3584, www.mauiscuba.com. Dive with an acclaimed underwater photographer. **Maui Dive Shop,** Cannery Mall, Lahaina, tel 808/661-5388. Charters and instruction arranged from several locations around the Island.

WHALE WATCHING
Pacific Whale Foundation, 101 N. Kihei Rd., Kihei, tel 800/WHALE11 or 808/879-8811. Dec.–May. Motor and sail vessels, and a sea kayak.

WINDSURFING
Maui Windsurfing Company, 520 Keolani Pl., Kahului, tel 800/872-0999 or 808/877-4816. Rentals, lessons for beginners to advanced.

BIG ISLAND

AFTER DARK

LUAU
Kona Village luau, Queen Kaahumanu Hwy., Kaupulehu, tel 808/325-5555. There are many good luau on the Big Isle, but this is the best. Fri. only.

ACTIVITIES

BOATING
Fair Wind Snorkeling and Diving Adventures, tel 800/677-9461 or 808/322-2788, www.fair-wind.com. Two cruises daily aboard a 60-foot catamaran cruise the Kona Coast to Kealakekua Bay for snorkeling. **Hahalua Lele,** Orchid Beach Club, 1 North Kaniku Dr., Mauna Lani Resort, 808/887-7320. Sail aboard Casey Cho's Polynesian-style sailing canoe to remote coves for snorkeling and good Hawaiian stories.

FISHING
Kona Charters Skippers Association, 74-857 Iwalani Pl., Kailua-Kona 96740, tel 800/762-7546, www.konabiggamefishing.com. Will arrange deep sea charters.

HIKING
Hawaii Department of Parks and Recreation, 25 Aupuni St., Hilo 96720, tel 808/961-8311. **Hawaii Forest and Trail,** 74-5035B Queen Kaahumanu Hwy., Kailua-Kona 96740, tel 800/464-1993 or 808/331-8505, www.hawaii-forest.com. Rob Pacheco has organized hikes and a variety of outdoor adventures, including birding. **Hawaiian Walkways,** tel 800/457-7759 or 808/775-0372, www.hawaiianwalkways.com. Owner/guide Hugh Montgomery knows less-traveled trails. **State Division of Forestry and Wild Life,** 19 E. Kawili St., Hilo 96720, tel 808/974-4221. Hiking information about various state-owned lands. Maps available.

HORSEBACK RIDING
King's Trail Rides, 808/323-2388, www.konacowboy.com. Two hours riding and two hours of snorkeling make the day for four people. Trip goes to monument marking the site where Captain Cook was killed in a battle with the Hawaiians. Gear and lunch included.

ENTERTAINMENT & ACTIVITIES

KAYAKING
Kohala Mountain Kayak Cruise, Sakamoto Building, P.O. Box 660, Kapaau 96755, tel 808/889-6922, www.kohala.net/kayak. Offers a most unusual adventure, discovering an old plantation irrigation system, through pristine forest, and under waterfalls.

SCUBA DIVING & SNORKELING
Fair Wind, 78–7130 Kaleiopapa St., Kailua-Kona 96740, tel 800/677-9461 or 808/322-2788, www.fair-wind.com. Family-owned and operated catamaran and Zodiac cruises along Kona Coast.
Nautilus Dive Center, 382 Kamehameha Ave., Hilo, tel 808/935-6939. Advanced divers only. Dive where molten lava enters the ocean.
Red Sail Sports, Hilton Waikoloa Village, 425 Waikoloa Beach Dr., Waikoloa, tel 808/886-2876. Action headquarters for diving excursions and rentals. They also have bicycle gear and tours.

WHALE WATCHING
Captain Dan McSweeney's Year-Round Whale Watching Adventures, P.O. Box 139, Holualoa 96725, tel 888/942-5376 or 808/322-0028, www.ilovewhales.com. Guaranteed you'll see a whale or sail again for free.

KAUAI

AFTER DARK

LUAU
Smith's Tropical Paradise, 174 Wailua Rd., Kapaa, tel 808/821-6895. Mon., Wed., & Fri.

ACTIVITIES

BOATING
Captain Andy's Sailing Adventures, P.O. Box 87, Eleele 96705, tel 800/535-0830 or 808/335-6833.

Sunset cruise, snorkel trip, Na Pali Coast tour.
Captain Zodiac Raft Expeditions, P.O. Box 876, Eleele 96705, tel 800/535-0830 or 808/335-6833, www.planet hawaii.com/zodiac. Na Pali Coast adventures.
Kayak Kauai, 5070-A Kuhio Hwy., Hanalei, tel 800/437-3507 or 808/826-9844. Rentals and river trips.
Outfitters Kauai, 2827-A Poipu Rd., Poipu 96756, tel 808/742-9667. Novice kayak river trips and advanced Na Pali excursions.
Smith's Motor Boat Service, 174 Wailua Rd., tel 808/821-6892. Motor cruise to Fern Grotto at reasonable price.

HELICOPTER TOURS
Island Helicopters, tel 800/829-5999 or 808/245-8588, www.islandhelicopters.com. Hour-long island overview includes Waimea Canyon, Na Pali Cliffs.
Ohana Helicopter Tours, 3416 Rice St., Lihue, tel 800/222-6989 or 808/245-3996, www.ohana-helicopters.com. Two different island tours to choose from.

HIKING
Hawaii State Department of Land and Natural Resources, Box 167, Lihue 96766, tel 808/274-3444. Contact them for trail maps and camping permits.
Kauai Nature Tours, P.O. Box 549, Koloa, HI 96756, tel 888-233-8365 or 808/742-8305, www.kauainaturetours.com. Educational hikes to Sleeping Giant, Na Pali coast, Waimea Canyon, and more.

HORSEBACK RIDING
CJM Country Stables, end of Poipu Rd., Poipu, 1.6 miles east of Hyatt Regency Hotel, tel 808/742-6096. Variety of rides including breakfast-beach ride.

SURFING
Margo Oberg Surfing School, Nukumoi Surf Shop,

2100 Hoone Rd., Poipu, tel 808/742-8019. Champion surfer even teaches children.

MOLOKAI

ACTIVITIES

BOATING
Fun Hogs Hawaii, meet at Slip 11, Kaunakakai Wharf, tel 808/567-6789. Fish, dive, snorkel, bike, kayak.
Nature Conservancy, Box 220, Kaualapuu 96757, tel 808/553-5236. Hikes to Moomomi Dunes and Kamakou Preserve.

HORSEBACK RIDING
Molokai Horse and Wagon Ride, Box 1528, Kaunakakai, tel 808/558-8380. Take a horse-drawn wagon through mango groves to Iliiliopae Heiau.
Molokai Ranch, Maunaloa, tel 808/522-2741. Trail rides and round-ups.

LANAI

AFTER DARK

Lodge at Koele, Lanai City, tel 808/565-7300. Invited literati, artists, master chefs, musicians, cinema greats, and other creatives share talent and talk in an on-going, free program.

ACTIVITIES

BOATING
Trilogy Excursions, 180 Lahainaluna Rd., Lahaina, Maui, tel 800/TRI-COON, www.maui.net/~trilogy. Dive-snorkel aboard a trimaran. Excursions operate from Maui.

HORSEBACK RIDING
The Stables At Koele, Lanai City, tel 808/565-4424.

ILLUSTRATIONS CREDITS

Abbreviations for terms appearing below: (t) top; (b) bottom; (l) left; (r) right.

Cover: (l), Images Colour Library. (middle), Pictures Colour Library. (r), Powerstock/Zefa. Spine: Powerstock/ Zefa. Back cover: Photo Resource Hawaii, Inc. Illustration by Maltings Partnership. 1, Christina Beauchamp/ Photo Resource Hawaii, Inc. 2/3, Hawaiian Images. 4, Val Kim/Photo Resource Hawaii, Inc. 9, Richard A. Cooke/Corbis UK Ltd. 11, Pacific Stock/Bruce Coleman. 12/13, Stock Photos Hawaii. 14, Richard A. Cooke/ Corbis UK Ltd. 15, Ann Cecil/Stock Photos Hawaii. 16/17, George Stein-metz/National Geographic Society. 18/19, Ron Dahlquist. 21, Douglas Peebles Photography. 25, Hawaiian Images. 28/29, Herb Kane/Hawaiian Paradise Trading Company, Ltd. 30, Ann Cecil/Stock Photos Hawaii. 31, Ariyoshi Ink. 32, Bettmann/Corbis UK Ltd. 34/35, Bettmann/Corbis UK Ltd. 37, Tony Novak-Clifford/Maui Arts and Cultural Center. 39, Ann Cecil/Stock Photos Hawaii. 41, Ann Cecil/Stock Photos Hawaii. 42(l), Honolulu Academy of Arts. Gift of Mrs. C. Montague Cooke, Jr., Mr. Charles M. Cooke III and Mrs. Heaton Wrenn in memory of Dr. C. Montague Cooke, Jr., January 16, 1951 (1066.1). 42(r), Honolulu Academy of Arts. Gift of Mrs. C. Montague Cooke, Jr., Mr. Charles M. Cooke III and Mrs. Heaton Wrenn in memory of Dr. C. Montague Cooke, Jr., January 16, 1951 (1066.1). 43, David Muench/ Corbis UK Ltd. 45, Robert Holmes/ Corbis UK Ltd. 46, Marc Schechter/ Photo Resource Hawaii, Inc. 48/49, Ariyoshi Ink. 50/51, AA Photo Library/ Kirk Lee Aeder. 51, Douglas Peebles/ Corbis UK Ltd. 52, Mark Gibson/Cor-bis UK Ltd. 53, AA Photo Library/Rob-ert Holmes. 55, Phil Schermeister/ Corbis UK Ltd. 56/57, John S. Calla-han/Photo Resource Hawaii, Inc. 59, Douglas Peebles Photography. 60, Photo Resource Hawaii, Inc. 61, Dylan Dawson/Photo Resource Hawaii, Inc. 62, John S. Callahan/ Photo Resource Hawaii, Inc. 64/65, Fitz Prenzel/Bruce Coleman. 65(t), Ann Cecil/Stock Photos Hawaii. 65(b), AA Photo Library/Rob-ert Holmes. 66, Catherine Karnow/ Corbis UK Ltd. 67, AA Photo Library/ Robert Holmes. 68, Richard Cummins/ Corbis UK Ltd. 69, D.R. & T.L. Schrichte/Stock Photos Hawaii. 70/71, Douglas Peebles Photography. 71, Franco Salmoiraghi/Photo Resource Hawaii, Inc. 72, Photobank Photo-library. 73, Chris Johns/ National

Geographic Society. 74, Robert Holmes/Corbis UK Ltd. 75, Honolulu Academy of Arts Purchase, 1927 (2400). 76(t), Franco Salmoiraghi/ Photo Resource Hawaii, Inc. 76(b), Ariyoshi Ink. 77, Douglas Peebles Photography. 78. Douglas Peebles Photography. 79(tl), Tony Cheng/ Associated Press. 79(tr), Ann Cecil/Stock Photos Hawaii. 79(b), Richard A. Cooke/Corbis UK Ltd. 80, Wolfgang Kaehler/Corbis UK Ltd. 81, Ann Cecil/Stock Photos Hawaii. 82, Ariyoshi Ink. 83, D.R. & T. L Schrichte/Stock Photos Hawaii. 84, Robert Harding Picture Library. 86/87, Phil Schermeister/Corbis UK Ltd. 87(t), Nik Wheeler/Corbis UK Ltd. 87(b), Bettmann/Corbis UK Ltd. 88, Chris Johns/National Geographic Society. 89, Al Yelman/Stock Photos Hawaii. 90, Dylan Dawson/Photo Resource Hawaii, Inc. 91, Dylan Dawson/Photo Resource Hawaii, Inc. 93(t), Ron Dahlquist. 93(b), Ted Streshinsky/Corbis UK Ltd. 94/95, John S. Callahan/Photo Resource Hawaii, Inc. 96/97, John S. Callahan/ Photo Resource Hawaii, Inc. 97, D.R. & T. L. Schrichte/Photo Resource Hawaii, Inc. 98/99, Stock Photos Hawaii. 100, Ariyoshi Ink. 101, D.R. Schrichte/Stock Photos Hawaii. 102/103, Richard Cummins/Corbis UK Ltd. 103, Catherine Karnow/ Corbis UK Ltd. 104/105, Catherine Karnow/Corbis UK Ltd. 105, Ann Cecil/Stock Photos Hawaii. 106/107, Macduff Everton/ Corbis UK Ltd. 107, Rick Doyle/Corbis UK Ltd. 109, Rick Doyle/Corbis UK Ltd. 110, Ariyoshi Ink. 111, Ann Cecil/ Stock Photos Hawaii. 112, Ann Cecil/ Stock Photos Hawaii. 113, Douglas Peebles Photography. 114/115, D.R. & T. L. Schrichte/Stock Photos Hawaii. 115(t), Catherine Karnow/Corbis UK Ltd. 115(b), Michael S. Yamashita/ Corbis UK Ltd. 116, Ann Cecil/Stock Photos Hawaii. 117, Ariyoshi Ink. 119, Phil Schermeister/Corbis UK Ltd. 120, Ron Dahlquist. 121, Sharon Dahlquist. 122/123, Hawaiian Images. 123, Photobank, Inc/Larry Dunmire. 124, Robert Holmes/Corbis UK Ltd. 126, Larry Dunmire. 127, Pacific Stock/ Bruce Coleman. 128, Dave G. Houser/ Corbis UK Ltd. 129, David Olsen/Stock Photos Hawaii. 130, Tami Dawson/ Photo Resource Hawaii, Inc. 131, Phil Schermeister/ Corbis UK Ltd. 132, Ron Dahlquist. 133, Douglas Peebles Photo-graphy. 134, Douglas Peebles Photo-graphy. 135, Douglas Peebles Photo-graphy. 136, Ron Dahlquist. 136/137, Ron Dahlquist. 138/139, Ron Dahl-quist. 139, Ron Dahlquist. 140, Ron Dahlquist. 141(t), Ron Dahlquist. 141(b), Douglas Peebles Photography. 143, David Muench/Corbis UK Ltd. 145, G. Brad

Lewis/ Gettyone/Stone. 147, Ann Cecil/ Stock Photos Hawaii. 148, Ann Cecil/ Stock Photos Hawaii. 149, Hawaiian Images. 150, Douglas Peebles Photo-graphy. 151, Hawaiian Images. 152/153, Macduff Everton/Corbis UK Ltd. 153, Hawaiian Images. 154, Dave G. Houser/Corbis UK Ltd. 155, Douglas Peebles Photo-graphy. 156, Douglas Peebles Photography. 157, Franco Salmo-iraghi/Photo Resource Hawaii, Inc. 158, Dave G. Houser/ Corbis UK Ltd. 159, Franco Salmoiraghi/Photo Resource Hawaii, Inc. 161, Richard A. Cooke/Corbis UK Ltd. 162, Ann Cecil/Stock Photos Hawaii. 163, Doug-las Peebles Photography. 164, Tami Dawson/ Photo Resource Hawaii, Inc. 165, Douglas Peebles Photography. 166, Douglas Peebles/Corbis UK Ltd. 166/167, David Olsen/Stock Photos Hawaii. 168, Richard A. Cooke/ Corbis UK Ltd. 169(t), Douglas Peebles Photography. 169(b), David Alan Har-vey/National Geographic Society. 171, Douglas Peebles Photography. 172, Ariyoshi Ink. 173, Franco Salmo-iraghi/Photo Resource Hawaii, Inc. 175(t), Marc Schechter/ Photo Resource Hawaii, Inc. 175(bl), George Theofanis/Stock Photos Hawaii. 175(br), AA Photo Library/ Robert Holmes. 176, Ariyoshi Ink. 177, Jack Jeffrey/Photo Resource Hawaii, Inc. 178/179, Michael T. Sedam/Corbis UK Ltd. 179, Ron Dahlquist. 180, Douglas Peebles. 181, G Brad Lewis/Photo Resource Hawaii, Inc. 182, Pacific Stock/Bruce Coleman. 183, AA Photo Library/ Kirk Lee Aeder. 186, Ron Dahlquist. 187, Ann Cecil/Stock Photos Hawaii. 188, Ann Cecil/Stock Photos Hawaii. 189, Douglas Peebles Photography. 190, Ann Cecil/Stock Photos Hawaii. 191, Ann Cecil/Stock Photos Hawaii. 192(t), Ann Cecil/Stock Photos Hawaii. 192(b), Ronald Grant Archive. 193, Ann Cecil/Stock Photos Hawaii. 194, Douglas Peebles Photography. 195, Ann Cecil/Stock Photos Hawaii. 196, Ann Cecil/Stock Photos Hawaii. 197, Ariyoshi Ink. 198, Douglas Peebles Photography. 198/199, Douglas Peebles Photography. 200, Ann Cecil/Stock Photos Hawaii. 201, Ann Cecil/Stock Photos Hawaii. 202/203, Douglas Peebles Photography. 203, G Brad Lewis/Photo Resource Hawaii, Inc. 204, Paul A. Souders/Corbis UK Ltd. 204/205, David Boynton/Photo Re-source Hawaii, Inc. 207, AA Photo Library/Kirk Lee Aeder. 209, Ariyoshi Ink. 210/211, Richard A. Cooke/ Corbis UK Ltd. 212, Brett Uprichard/ Stock Photos Hawaii. 213(t), Robert Holmes/Corbis UK Ltd. 213(b), Hawaii State Archives. 215(t), John de Mello/Stock Photos Hawaii. 215(b), Ariyoshi Ink. 216, Douglas Peebles

Photography. 217, Douglas Peebles Photography. 218, Ariyoshi Ink. 219(t), Ariyoshi Ink. 219(bl), Ariyoshi Ink. 219(br), Ariyoshi Ink. 220, Douglas Peebles Photography. 221, G Brad Lewis/Photo Resource Hawaii, Inc. 222, Pacific Stock/Bruce Coleman. 223, AA Photo Library/ Kirk Lee Aeder. 224/225, AA Photo Library/Kirk Lee Aeder. 226, Ron Dahlquist. 226/227, Douglas Peebles Photography. 228/229, Mark J. Terrill/ Associated Press. 229, Mark J. Terrill/ Associated Press. 230, Ron Dahlquist. 231, Pacific Stock/Bruce Coleman. 232, Tami Dawson/Photo Resource Hawaii, Inc. 233, Roger Ressmeyer/ Corbis UK Ltd. 234, Jonathan Blair/ Corbis UK Ltd. 235, Catherine Karnow/Corbis UK Ltd.

The world's largest nonprofit scientific and educational organization, the National Geographic Society was founded in 1888 "for the increase and diffusion of geographic knowledge." Since then it has supported scientific exploration and spread information to its more than nine million members worldwide.

The National Geographic Society educates and inspires millions every day through magazines, books, television programs, videos, maps and atlases, research grants, the National Geography Bee, teacher workshops, and innovative classroom materials.

The Society is supported through membership dues, charitable gifts, and income from the sale of its educational products. Members receive NATIONAL GEOGRAPHIC magazine— the Society's official journal—discounts on Society products, and other benefits.

For more information about the National Geographic Society, its educational programs, publications, or how to support its work, call 1-800-NGS-LINE (647-5463), or write to: National Geographic Society, 1145 17th Street, N.W., Washington, D.C. 20036 U.S.A.

Printed in Italy.

Published by the National Geographic Society
John M. Fahey, Jr., *President and Chief Executive Officer*
Gilbert M. Grosvenor, *Chairman of the Board*
Nina D. Hoffman, *Executive Vice President,*
  President, Books and School Publishing
Kevin Mulroy, *Vice President and Editor-in-Chief*
Marianne Koszorus, *Design Director*
Charles Kogod, *Director of Photography*
Elizabeth L. Newhouse, *Director of Travel Publishing*
Barbara A. Noe, *Senior Editor and Series Editor*
Cinda Rose, *Art Director*
Caroline Hickey, *Senior Researcher*
Carl Mehler, *Director of Maps*
Joseph F. Ochlak, *Map Coordinator*
Lise Sajewski, James M. Ariyoshi, *Editorial Consultants*
R. Gary Colbert, *Production Director*
Richard S. Wain, *Production Project Manager*

Edited and designed by AA Publishing (a trading name of Automobile Association Developments Limited, whose registered office is Norfolk House, Priestley Road, Basingstoke, Hampshire, England RG24 9NY. Registered number: 1878835).
Rachel Alder, *Project Manager*
David Austin, *Senior Art Editor*
Betty Sheldrick, *Senior Editor*
Bob Johnson, *Designer*
Inna Nogeste, *Senior Cartographic Editor*
Richard Firth, *Production Director*
Steve Gilchrist, *Prepress Production Controller*
Cartography by AA Cartographic Production
Picture Research by Zooid Pictures Ltd.
Drive maps drawn by Chris Orr Associates, Southampton, England
Cutaway illustrations drawn by Maltings Partnership, Derby, England

Revised 2003

Copyright © 2000, 2003 National Geographic Society. All rights reserved. No part of this book may be reproduced or transmitted in any form or by any means, electronic or mechanical, including photocopying, without permission in writing from the National Geographic Society, 1145 17th Street N.W., Washington, D.C. 20036-4688.

Library of Congress Cataloging-in-Publication Data
Ariyoshi, Rita.
  The National Geographic traveler. Hawaii / Rita Ariyoshi.
    p. cm.
  ISBN 0-7922-7944-1
  1. Hawaii--Guidebooks. I. Title: Hawaii. II. Title.

  DU622 .A69 2000
  919.6904'42--dc21
                                            00-055420

Printed and bound by Mondadori Printing, Verona, Italy.
Color separations by Leo Reprographic Ltd., Hong Kong.
Cover separations by L.C. Repro, Aldermaston, U.K.

Visit the Society's Web site at http://www.nationalgeographic.com

The information in this book has been carefully checked and to the best of our knowledge is accurate. However, details are subject to change, and the National Geographic Society cannot be responsible for such changes, or for errors or omissions. Assessments of sites, hotels, and restaurants are based on the author's subjective opinions, which do not necessarily reflect the publisher's opinion. The publisher cannot be responsible for any consequences arising from the use of this book.

NATIONAL GEOGRAPHIC
TRAVELER

A Century of Travel Expertise in Every Guide

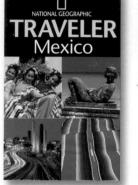
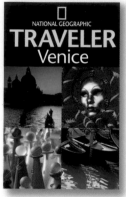

- **Amsterdam** ISBN: 0-7922-7900-X
- **Arizona** ISBN: 0-7922-7899-2
- **Australia** ISBN: 0-7922-7431-8
- **Barcelona** ISBN: 0-7922-7902-6
- **Boston & Environs** ISBN: 0-7922-7926-3
- **California** ISBN: 0-7922-7564-0
- **Canada** ISBN: 0-7922-7427-X
- **The Caribbean** ISBN: 0-7922-7434-2
- **China** ISBN: 0-7922-7921-2
- **Costa Rica** ISBN: 0-7922-7946-8
- **Cuba** ISBN: 0-7922-6931-4
- **Egypt** ISBN: 0-7922-7896-8
- **Florence & Tuscany** ISBN: 0-7922-7924-7
- **Florida** ISBN: 0-7922-7432-6
- **France** ISBN: 0-7922-7426-1
- **Great Britain** ISBN: 0-7922-7425-3
- **Greece** ISBN: 0-7922-7923-9
- **Hawaii** ISBN: 0-7922-7944-1
- **Hong Kong** ISBN: 0-7922-7901-8

- **India** ISBN: 0-7922-7898-4
- **Italy** ISBN: 0-7922-7562-4
- **Japan** ISBN: 0-7922-7563-2
- **London** ISBN: 0-7922-7428-8
- **Los Angeles** ISBN: 0-7922-7947-6
- **Mexico** ISBN: 0-7922-7897-6
- **Miami and the Keys** ISBN: 0-7922-7433-4
- **New Orleans** ISBN: 0-7922-7948-4
- **New York** ISBN: 0-7922-7430-X
- **Paris** ISBN: 0-7922-7429-6
- **Rome** ISBN: 0-7922-7566-7
- **San Diego** ISBN: 0-7922-6933-0
- **San Francisco** ISBN: 0-7922-7565-9
- **Spain** ISBN: 0-7922-7922-0
- **Sydney** ISBN: 0-7922-7435-0
- **Thailand** ISBN: 0-7922-7943-3
- **Venice** ISBN: 0-7922-7917-4
- **Washington, D.C.** ISBN: 0-7922-7903-4

AVAILABLE WHEREVER BOOKS ARE SOLD